HISTORY OF THE

1ST BATTALION 14TH PUNJAB REGIMENT
SHERDIL-KI-PALTAN

(LATE XIX PUNJABIS)

The Naval & Military Press Ltd

Published by
The Naval & Military Press Ltd
5 Riverside, Brambleside, Bellbrook
Industrial Estate, Uckfield, East Sussex,
TN22 1QQ England

Tel: +44 (0) 1825 749494
Fax: +44 (0) 1825 765701
www.naval-military-press.com
www.military-genealogy.com

In reprinting in facsimile from the original, any imperfections are inevitably reproduced and the quality may fall short of modern type and cartographic standards.

PREFACE.

In 1870 Lieutenant-Colonel G. H. Thompson compiled the hitherto-unrecorded history of Her Majesty's 19th Punjab Regiment of Native Infantry into a Digest of its Services since 1857. It was brief, unillustrated and without background for the events narrated. Ever since then The Digest has been continued in the same modest form, and similarly in manuscript.

In an era full of vivid history and transformed by education and nationalization the need for a more comprehensive and published History has been marked. This modest book therefore expands The Digest, continues it up to recent times and adds a measure of contemporary military history.

By the compiler this volume is dedicated to "The Sherdils" as some tribute to all that the Battalion has stood for, has imparted, has accomplished and has suffered.

The book may also encourage steps towards the production of a fuller and better second volume. Hitherto the store of material has not been kept stocked. Side by side with the formal writing up of the Adjutant's Diary, Quarterly Summary and Digest of Services let there be collected those more intimate records of regimental and social events, character portraits, notable anecdotes, photographs, sketches and caricatures where the future author may find the humour, colour and human interest which are lacking in the present essay.

December 1946.   G. PIGOT

NOTE.

As the time has passed when serving officers and men can be expected to be familiar with the pre-1923 titles of regiments other than their own, those units have in most places been described by the names they bore immediately before the Second World War. The only post-war change which need be mentioned is that the 10th (Training) Battalion has become The Regimental Centre, a return to the title of 1866.

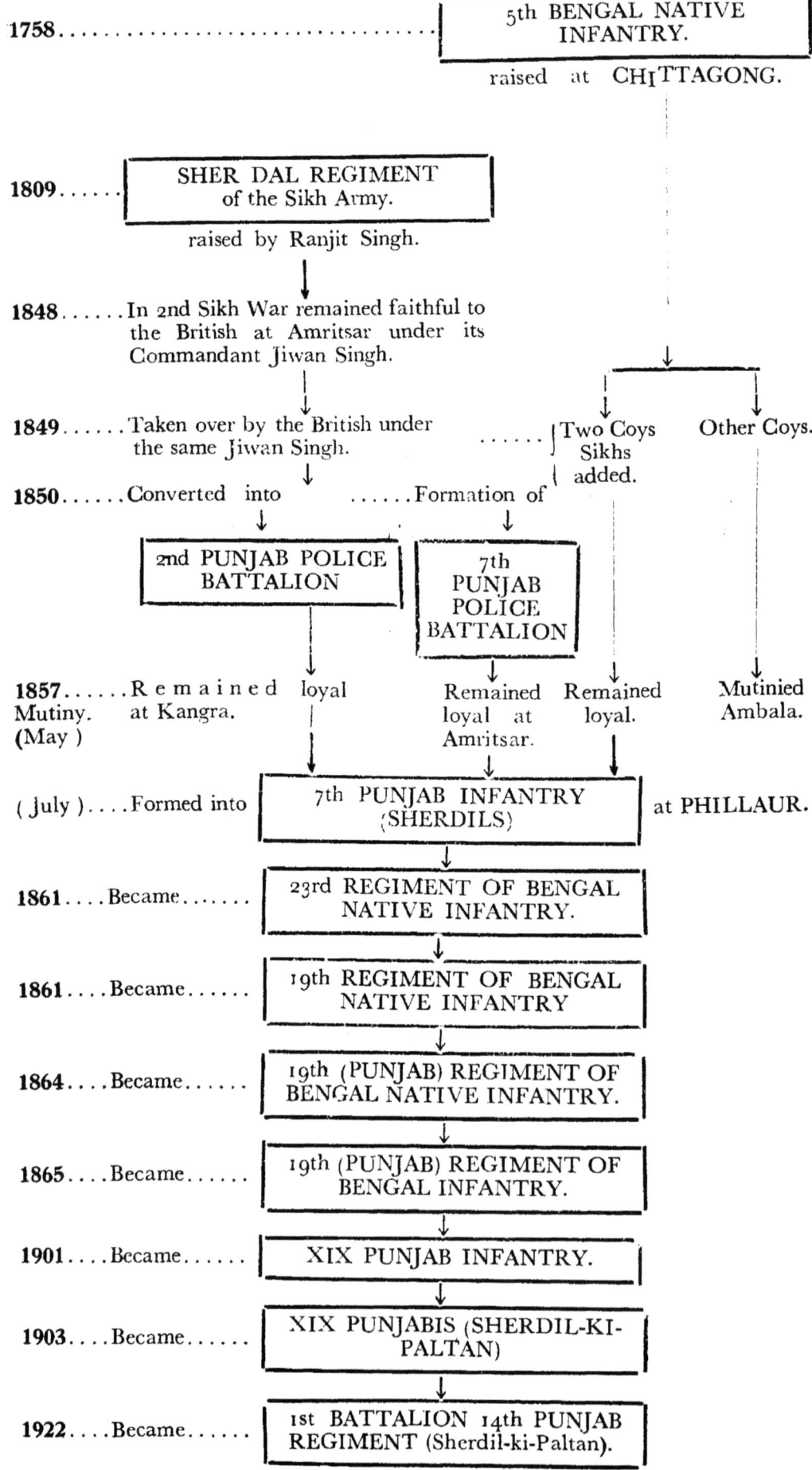

FRONTISPIECE

THE ORIGINS OF
The 1st Battalion 14th Punjab Regiment.
(SHERDIL-KI-PALTAN)

1758 .... 5th BENGAL NATIVE INFANTRY.
raised at CHITTAGONG.

1809 ...... SHER DAL REGIMENT of the Sikh Army.
raised by Ranjit Singh.

1848 ...... In 2nd Sikh War remained faithful to the British at Amritsar under its Commandant Jiwan Singh.

1849 ...... Taken over by the British under the same Jiwan Singh. ...... Two Coys Sikhs added. | Other Coys.

1850 ...... Converted into ...... Formation of

2nd PUNJAB POLICE BATTALION | 7th PUNJAB POLICE BATTALION

1857 ...... Remained loyal at Kangra. | Remained loyal at Amritsar. | Remained loyal. | Mutinied Ambala.
Mutiny.
(May)

(July) .... Formed into 7th PUNJAB INFANTRY (SHERDILS) at PHILLAUR.

1861 .... Became .... 23rd REGIMENT OF BENGAL NATIVE INFANTRY.

1861 .... Became ...... 19th REGIMENT OF BENGAL NATIVE INFANTRY

1864 .... Became ...... 19th (PUNJAB) REGIMENT OF BENGAL NATIVE INFANTRY.

1865 .... Became ...... 19th (PUNJAB) REGIMENT OF BENGAL INFANTRY.

1901 .... Became ...... XIX PUNJAB INFANTRY.

1903 .... Became ...... XIX PUNJABIS (SHERDIL-KI-PALTAN)

1922 .... Became ...... 1st BATTALION 14th PUNJAB REGIMENT (Sherdil-ki-Paltan).

CONTENTS

		Page.
FRONTISPIECE.	The origins of the Regiment	i
PREFACE.	Preface	ii

CHAPTER.

I.	The origins of the Regiment	1
II.	The Indian Mutiny up to the raising of the Regiment.	8
III.	The Regiment in the Indian Mutiny, 1857-59	24
IV.	1859-65. JULLUNDUR—MEERUT—GWALIOR—AGRA—ALIGARH	44
V.	THE BHUTAN WAR, 1865-66	49
VI.	1866-78. ALIGARH—PESHAWAR—TALAGANG—MULTAN	55
VII.	THE SECOND AFGHAN WAR, 1873-80	59
VIII.	1880-91. SIALKOT—FEROZEPORE—LAHORE—RAWALPINDI—SECOND BLACK MOUNTAIN and MIRANZAI campaigns	72
IX.	1891-1904. ZHOB—DERAJAT—MULTAN—SIALKOT—MALAKAND—KOHAT—KURRAM—MULTAN—FEROZEPORE	82
X.	TIBET, 1904	89
XI.	1904-14. JULLUNDUR—MOHMAND operations—DERA ISMAIL KHAN—MALAKAND—QUETTA.	94
XII.	FIRST WORLD WAR, 1914-17—QUETTA—EAST PERSIA	100

Page.

XIII. FIRST WORLD WAR, 1918—PERSIA—
TRANSCASPIA to the actions of KAAKHA ... 111

XIV. FIRST WORLD WAR, 1918-19—TRANSCASPIA.—
The actions of DUSHAK and ANNENKOVO ... 125

XV. 1919-23. KARACHI—PESHAWAR—KHYBER—
PALESTINE ... 145

XVI. 1923-34. SAUGOR—MANZAI—AURANGABAD—
KHYBER ... 156

XVII. 1935-39. JHELUM—MOHMAND operations—
WAZIRISTAN operations—BANNU ... 168

XVIII. WORLD WAR II, 1939-45—BANNU—LAHORE—
SECUNDERABAD—MALAYA ... 181

XIX. WORLD WAR II, 1939-45—MALAYA, 1941 ... 192

XX. WORLD WAR II, 1939-45—MALAYA, 1941-42 ... 209

APPENDICES.

Appendix

    A. Colonels, Commandants and Adjutants ... 226

    B. The Colours ... 230

    C. Medals ... 232

    D. Standing Orders 1940 ... 233

    E. Stations ... 339

MAPS.

Maps
1. INDIA, 1910.

2. EASTERN PUNJAB, 1851.

3. UNITED PROVINCES, 1857.

4. The BHUTAN War, 1864-66.

5. SECOND AFGHAN WAR, 1878-80.

6. NORTH-WEST FRONTIER.

7. TIBET; '03-'04.

8. PERSIA and TURKESTAN.

9. SEISTAN and SARHAD.

10. TRANSCASPIA.

11. MALAYA.

SKETCHES

Sketch.

A. Actions at TRIMMU GHAT, 1857.

B. The Ridge before DELHI, 1857.

C. Battles of RATANPURWA and BUTWAL, 1859.

D. Attack on BALA PASS, 1865.

E. The Affair of KHUSHK-I-NAKHUD, 1879.

F. Battle of AHMED KHEL, 1879.

G. The Affair of ARZU, 1880.

H. BLACK MOUNTAIN Campaign, 1891.

J. Second MIRANZAI Expedition, 1891.

K. KAAKHA Position, 1918.

L. Attack on DUSHAK, 1918.

M. Action at ANNENKOVO, 1919.

N. MOHMAND Operations, 1935.

O. WAZIRISTAN Operations, 1937-38.

P. KEDAH (MALAYA), 1941.

Q. Action at CHANGLUN, 1941.

R. JITRA Position, 1941.

S. PERAK, 1941.

T. KAMPAR to KUALA LUMPUR, 1942.

U. Battle of KAMPAR, 1942.

V. Action of RANTAU PANJANG, 1942.

W. BATU PAHAT to SINGAPORE, 1942.

X. JOHORE STRAIT, 1942.

Y. SINGAPORE, 1942.

CHAPTER I

THE ORIGINS OF THE REGIMENT

(Maps 1 and 2 and Frontispiece)

The 1st Battalion 14th Punjab Regiment had its official origin in 1857 at the beginning of the Indian Mutiny. It was raised as the 7th Regiment of Punjab Infantry. Its antecedents, however, extend considerably further back through the undermentioned units from which the Regiment was formed. The 5th Native Infantry, whose Sikhs were incorporated, had been raised in the Bengal Army nearly a century previously. The 2nd and 7th Punjab Police Battalions and the Gurdaspur Foot Levy had been formed in the Punjab after the Second Sikh War. The 2nd Punjab Police Battalion itself was a conversion of a regiment famous in the Sikh Army—the "Sher Dal ki Paltan", whose designation has survived as "Sherdil". A few words no this earlier history will therefore be relevant. *"Frontispiece"*

The 5th Bengal Native Infantry

The 5th Bengal Native Infantry was raised at CHITTAGONG in September 1758 as the 4th Regiment of the Bengal Army. A little later its number was changed to 2nd; and in 1796 when there was a grouping of infantry into two-battalion regiments it became the 1st Battalion 2nd Bengal Native Infantry Regiment. When this grouping process was reversed in 1824 the Battalion was renumbered as the 5th Regiment. Its campaigns included the 1st Afghan War, during which it formed part of the ill-fated garrison of KABUL under Major-General Elphinstone and was decimated in the tragic withdrawal to JELALABAD. *"Frontispiece" "Map 1."*

At the end of the 2nd Sikh War the East India Company proceeded with the policy formed after the first campaign of offering military service to the Sikhs, who had proved such brave and stubborn opponents. The Commandants of regular regiments were ordered to enlist each 200 Sikhs. Thus Sikhs come into the 5th Bengal Native Infantry in about 1849, although the Regiment was not then in the Punjab and had not taken part in the Sikh War. These Sikhs alone remained faithful in 1857 when, as will be related, the rest of this Regiment succumbed to the wave of mutiny.

The Sher Dal Regiment

"Frontispiece"

The early Sikh troops, the "Dal Khalsa" or "Army of God", were for the most part irregular cavalry. Infantry, except in the case of the fanatical Akalis, was then considered an inferior service; it was represented mainly by the Dogra-Rajput militia of the Jammu chiefs, and had little organization or permanence. But after 1807 Sikh infantry came rapidly to the fore as Maharaja Ranjit Singh introduced a standing army of regular cavalry regiments, batteries and battalions, organized and trained to that discipline and precision which he had observed to underlie the British victories over the Mahrattas. At first this European discipline was most unpopular, and it was only by liberal pay and personal leadership that the Maharaja carried through his reorganization. By the time of his death the regular army, the "Khas Fauj", comprised 4,000 cavalry, 19 batteries and over 29,000 infantry in 31 battalions. This strength was greatly increased in later years, and almost doubled by the end of the 1st Sikh War.

The Sher Dal Regiment is thought to have been raised in about 1809. It took part in the Sikh attempt to wrest Kashmir from the Afghans in 1814 and was engaged in the second campaign there five years later. It is known to have been recalled from Kashmir to join Avitabile's command at AMRITSAR in 1845, and as its pay rolls were not maintained in the Punjab before that year it is to be presumed that the Regiment was stationed in Kashmir throughout the long interval. During the first campaign against the British the Sher Dal Regiment was guarding the Golden Temple at AMRITSAR. It remained there, loyal to the British, during the second war of 1848; and for this it was rewarded by being taken into the service of the Punjab Administration.

A Sikh battalion was organized on the European model into 8 companies each of approximately 100 sepoys. There was an honorary Colonel, a Commandant, an Adjutant, a Major, an Accountant and a Clerk. Companies were commanded by Subadars who were each assisted by 2 Jemadars, a Serjeant (junior to a Naik) and a Quartermaster N. C. O. who had the French title of Fourrier. Each of the four sections in a company was under a Havildar. Each company also included a Drum-Major and a Drummer. Regimental followers comprised 3 hour-gong strikers, 4 colour-bearers, 8 tent-pitchers, 18 camel-drivers and 6 spademen basides mistries, cooks and water-carriers. Monthly pay varied as follows in different battalions:—Commandant Rs. 150 to 60, Subadar 30 to 20, Jemadar 22 to 15, Havildar 15 to 13, Naik 12 to 10, Serjeant 12 to 8, Sepoy Rs. 8-8-0 to 7-0-0.

Enlistment was voluntary. In the early day the ranks of

infantry were largely filled by Muhammadans from Agra and Oudh, Pathans, Gurkhas and Dogras from Kashmir. But by 1818 Punjabis formed a majority, and after the death of the broadminded Ranjit Singh Sikhs largely excluded the other classes. The Gurkhas wore green jackets and shakos. Other infantry adopted the red jacket of the Company's army, but with black instead of white crossbelts and with a pagri instead of cap or shako. All ranks were eventually equipped with the muzzle-loading Brunswick; previously only havildars had borne muskets, while the men carried pikes and swords.

Fighting organization developed in 1838 from the battalion, with two horsed guns attached, into brigades of 4 battalions, a battery, a squadron of cavalry and a company of Sappers and Miners. Training was directed by French, Italian and even American officers —Ventura, Allard, Court, Avitabile—and by a corps of assistant instructors who were ex-soldiers or deserters from the Bengal Native Army.

Following the custom of calling regiments after contemporary commandants, the "Sher Dal" was often known as "Jiwan Singh ki paltan". This Jiwan Singh was a remarkable man. Of him the Punjab Board of Administration recorded: "He is the only Sikh officer in the Punjab who not only remained faithful to his trust but by his ability and address managed to keep his regiment faithful also." As a youth he soldiered under Kharak Singh and was wounded in Kashmir. Later on he distinguished himself on the Waziristan border and was then made Adjutant of the Sher Dal Regiment. For his services with them in the second Kashmir campaign he was appointed Commandant; and when the Regiment was taken over by the English in 1849 he was confirmed in command. He met a tragic death in the same year at the hands of one of two drunken British soldiers in AMRITSAR City when urging them to return to barracks. Three of his brothers were officers in the same regiment, and transferred with their companies on the formation of the 7th Punjab Regiment. One son remained in the 2nd Punjab Police Battalion, and rose to the rank of Inspector. A great-grandson, Hardev Singh, has served in the present Sher Dal Paltan, the 1st Battalion 14th Punjab Regiment.

The 2nd (Sherdil) and 7th Punjab Police Battalions.

In 1846, at the end of the 1st Sikh War which had resulted in the annexation by the English of the Cis-Sutlej States and an extension of the East India Company's sphere of influence to the rest of the Punjab, it wa found expedient to raise a "Frontier Brigade" of local troops—the 1st, 2nd, 3rd and 4th Regiments

"Frontispiece"

of Sikh Infantry and the Corps of Guides, which now form the five battalions of the Frontier Force Regiment. The further extension of responsibility which came with the conclusion of the 2nd Sikh War and the annexation of the whole Punjab led, in 1849, to the formation of the "Punjab Irregular Force"—six locally enlisted regiments who are now the battalions of the Frontier Force Rifles. After the Mutiny these two forces were combined with five regiments of Punjab Cavalry and three light batteries into the Punjab Frontier Force. It is interesting to note that at first only ten Sikhs per company were permitted to be enlisted in these new regiments.

In 1850 the "Board of Administration for the affairs of the Punjab" considered the future of the four infantry regiments of the Sikh army which had remained faithful to the English during the 2nd Sikh War—the "Sher Dal" under Jiwan Singh, the "Suraj Mookee", the "Kattar Mookee" and "Subhan Khan's." It was decided to utilize them as military police units, and the approval of the Governor General to this course was expressed as follows :—"The pledge which was given to General Courtland's three regiments and to Jiwan Singh's regiment must of course in good faith be redeemed. His Lordship concurs in the reasoning by which you arrive at the conclusion that it will be better to employ these men as military police than to apportion them among the new irregular regiments." At that time there was need of six such police corps. It was explained:—"Of the six Police Battalions four have long been organized, having simply been transferred from the Maharaja in 1849. The fifth has been raised at RAWALPINDI. The sixth was intended to be formed in BANNU from the remains of the Levies temporarily entertained there".

Thus the Sher Dal Regiment at AMRITSAR became the 2nd Punjaub Police Battalion under the supervision of Lieutenant J.W. Younghusband, afterwards Inspector-General of Police. The Sikh name was retained as a secondary title, but in British usage soon became corrupted first into "Shere Dill" and finally into "Sherdil". Jiwan Singh was followed as Commandant by Attar Singh in 1855. From 1824 Attar Singh had had a notable career in the Sikh regiment of Hari Singh, taking part in the original capture of both PESHAWAR and BANNU. After the 1st Sikh War he entered British Service under Edwardes, and during the 2nd campaign loyally distinguished himself at the siege of MULTAN. The Adjutant was Doola Singh.

"Frontispiece"   The 7th Punjaub Police Battalion was formed at AMRITSAR in 1850 by Captain R. Lawrence, with Dewa Singh as Commandant. Enlisted in the Sikh Army in 1808, Dewa Singh had since 1818 commanded the famous regiment of his name. In that command he had campaigned at DERA ISMAIL KHAN in 1821, at PESHAWAR in 1837, in KULU in 1840, and during both Sikh Wars. It is likely that he gathered many of his old comrades to form the nucleus of the British police unit. It is said of this battalion in the Police Administration Report of 1852-53:—"A splendid body of young lads, sons of the best yeomen of the Manjha. In power and sinew they are not equal to Lieutenant Younghusband's men, but a few years will supply this quality also. They average 5 feet $8\frac{3}{4}$ inches in height and are as fine a body of Indian youth as could well be brought together". The Adjutant was Gomez Allard, an Indian Christian who took service under Maharajah Ranjit Singh in 1823 and came into British service with Subhan Khan's Regiment, of which he had been Adjutant.

The Punjab Police Battalions were distinguished from the ordinary detective police, whom they were designed to aid, by their stricter discipline, their military organization and their arms. Besides forming a reserve to the civil power they garrisoned frontier forts and provided guards, escorts, etc. There is evidence that during numerous tribal expeditions which followed the extension of British rule to the Pathan foothills these police battalions frequently co-operated with the Punjab Irregular Force and were sometimes included in the punitive columns.

This corps of military police was initially organized by Major Neville Chamberlain, who later rose to distinction in command of the Irregular Force and during the Mutiny became Adjutant-General to the forces before DELHI. He was styled Commandant of the Corps and was assisted by four supervising Captains. Each battalion contained 800 sepoys, mostly Sikhs and Punjabi Musalmans but some Dogras. The men were armed with percussion muskets and bayonets, the officers and N.C.O.s with pistols. Fifty camels were kept for transport. There was a Native Commandant with a monthly salary of 200 rupees, and an Adjutant with pay at 100 rupees. On the model of the Punjaub Irregular Force battalions there were only 8 companies, each under one subadar and one jemadar on a monthly pay of 50 rupees and 30 rupees respectively. Havildars received 12 rupees and naicks 10, which was 2 rupees more than under the Sikhs. Sepoys were given 7 rupees. The monthly pay list of a police battalion totalled 8,238 rupees.

The uniform of the 7th Punjaub Police Battalion was blue according to the general rule. That of the 2nd Battalion, however, was red as it had been decided that "the four Durbar regiments might keep their red clothing to avoid a slight to them and to maintain their espirit-de-corps". The Sikh standards were taken over from these regiments on their reconstitution, but it is not known whether Colours were actually issued instead. Such action was approved, but Neville Chamberlain wrote—"If no great desire be manifest for Colours it would be better not to issue any."

It is probable that these police battalions, or at least those in the more important locations, were modernized in certain directions within a few years of their formation. For instance, the opening of the Mutiny found the 2nd (Sherdil) Battalion supervised by Captain Younghusband with at least one other British officer to assist him. And had Lieutenant Stafford of the 4th Bengal Native Infantry not been appointed to command the 7th Punjab Infantry when it was formed in July 1857 he would, from the 13th of that month, have been "lent to the Foregin Department for duty with the 2nd Police Battalion". By 1857 that battalion had acquired a band and chosen "The British Grenadiers" as its regimental march.

Prior to 1857 the police battalions were administered in 4 divisions each under a Captain with headquarters at LAHORE, JHELUM, MULTAN and in the Derajat. After conversion at AMRITSAR the 2nd Battalion was stationed at BANNU, but shortly before the outbreak of the Mutiny was transferred to the KANGRA VALLEY. The 7th Battalion remained where it had been formed, at AMRITSAR.

During the Mutiny the police battalions proved their worth and loyalty, even in the more difficult of their duties : *e.g.*— the holding of frontier forts, the guarding of bridges and fords and the provision of protective parties. Some insight into such duties is given by the accounts in the next chapter of the doings of the 2nd Punjab Police Battalion at KANGRA and near GURDASPUR.

One of the two GURDASPUR Companies accompanied Brigadier-General John Nicholson's Moveable Column to the siege of DELHI. From this company were found his personal orderlies, and by them he was carried out of action when stricken down during the final assault on the city.

Another achievement of the police battalions was to provide personnel for the raising of additional military regiments in the Punjab. As one of his earliest acts the Chief Commissioner ordered each police battalion, as well as every regiment of the Punjab Irregular Force, to enlist an extra four companies. These augmentations were completed in the 2nd and 7th Police Battalions by mid-July of 1857, and from then the 7th Punjab Infantry was then ordered to be formed.

After the Mutiny the continuance of military police battalions in the Punjab was reconsidered. They were found unduly expensive and no longer expedient. The 2nd and 7th Battalions were therefore disbanded along with the rest from 1st July 1861.

The Gurdaspur Foot Levy.

On 1st January 1846 the British authorities formed ten Levies of a thousand men each to provide garrison duty at various places in rear of the troops engaged in the 1st Sikh War. These were disbanded three months later on the signing of the peace treaty. But at the beginning of the second campaign in 1848 the idea was revived and the Gurdaspur Levy was one of those then formed. An official return dated 1st October 1857 shows its strength as 306 of all ranks.

The Gurdaspur Foot Levy comprised locally enlisted Sikhs and Punjabi Musalmans. During the Mutiny the corps stood firm and was engaged in supplementing the local military police, particularly in controlling the fords and ferries across the River BEAS. In 1857 a detachment of the 2nd Punjab Police Battalion was at GURDASPUR, and when that unit threw off its extra companies to help from the 7th Punjab Infantry at PHILLAUR a number of transfers took place from the Gurdaspur Foot Levy to complete the required strength.

CHAPTER II

THE INDIAN MUTINY UP TO THE RAISING OF THE REGIMENT.

(Maps 1 and 2. Sketch 'A')

The Causes.

In narrating the formation of the 7th Punjab Infantry in the first year of the Mutiny it is desirable to summarize the causes and early course of the upheaval which while half destroying the Bengal Army finally established the military reputation of the Punjab.

Several causes may be mentioned as leading directly to the outbreak. First there was the loosening by ever-increasing centralization of the links of mutual regard between the sepoy and his European officer. Little by little the regimental officer had been deprived by higher authority of his independence of action until even the exercise of his judgement was denied to him. It was no longer in his power to be the friend of his men; for his every act, whether concerning promotion, reward or punishment, must be submitted for approval—to the despair of the faithful sepoy and the secret joy of the ill-disposed.

Secondly, a spirit of discontent among Hindustani sepoys and mistrust of their rulers existed as a legacy from the 1st Afghan War of 1838-42, a campaign which had brought the sepoys untold suffering in a foreign country, had interfered with their religious observances and had produced the disillusionment of defeat. The regulation of 1856 whereby all future enlistment in the Army was to be for general service only heightened their suspicion.

Another cause was that with the annexation of Oude in 1856 the many thousands of sepoys recruited in that province lost the special legal privilege which they had previously enjoyed. A further grievance was that the special allowance paid to units who took part in the conquest of the Punjab in 1845-49 had not been continued to those who carried out the subsequent garrison duties.

Finally, a widespread though baseless belief had arisen tha

Government had secret designs against the sepoys' caste and religion. Many minor circumstances had combined to lend colour to this idea when, in 1857, it came to be bruited about that the cartridges of the new Enfield Rifle which was about to be issued had been defiled by a fat of pigs and oxen. This unfortunate rumour, appealing as it did to the most sensitive feelings of the high-caste Bengal sepoy, served as the breath which fanned the smouldering embers of discontent into the lurid flames of mutiny and murder.

Taking advantage of the discontent among all ranks and screening behind the more impassioned religious alarm of the Hindu sepoys was a Muhammadan conspiracy to restore Moghul rule at DELHI. Clever, designing men formed centres of seditious influence, and by playing on both religious fears and national hopes moved the minds of the mass towards revolt. There would seem to have been but a single general movement, yet several plots and numerous centres of action each with its local object. Thus in Oude and in the North West Provinces the goal of the mutineers was DELHI; in the Punjab their object was to seize the forts and arsenals; in the Peshawar Valley it was to invoke the co-operation of the frontier tribesmen. Uniform procedure and organized discipline were however discernible in almost every successful outbreak; the officers were shot down; the treasury was seized; and then the rebels instead of falling to pillage and dividing the spoil, marched away to their appointed rendezvous with recognized leaders in command and treasure intact.

The first mutinies.

In March 1857 Native Infantry of the Bengal Army broke into open mutiny near CALCUTTA and were disbanded, together with seven companies of the 34th Native Infantry adjacent. "Map 1."

On 10th May the main outbreak occurred at MEERUT. The mutinous 3rd Light Cavalry, 11th Native Infantry and 20th Native Infantry marched the same night to DELHI. There they were joined by the three native infantry regiments of the cantonment, and DELHI City was soon in rebel hands. The gallant defence and heroic blowing up of the DELHI Magazine was the only incident in shining contrast with the surrounding darkness of treachery and massacre.

The 5th Bengal Native Infantry at AMBALA.

On the same day there was an abortive outbreak at AMBALA; and this, as it concerns the 5th Bengal Native Infantry, will be described in some detail. AMBALA at this date was a large and important military station. Its garrison was there to protect the vast "Map 2."

area of Cis-Sutlej States from Sikh encroachment and to act in support of the outpost stations of LUDHIANA and FEROZEPORE. The troops present were two troops Royal Horse Artillery, 9th Lancers, 5th Bengal Native Infantry and 60th Bengal Native Infantry. The two British battalions were absent in the hills at KASAULI and DAGSHAI. There was also in AMBALA a Musketry School which included parties from many Indian units of this part of India and where the new Enfield rifles were in use. In the second half of March there had been disaffection at the School when rumours had reached the various detachments that they would be outcast in their regiments should they use the new cartridge. The official handling of this situation had been clumsy and unsympathetic; the use of the cartridge had been enforced. Subsequently incendiarism had broken out in the Cantonment. At the end of March it was revealed by a Sikh sepoy of the 5th Bengal Infantry how the series of mysterious fires was the work of sepoys and that the three Indian units had planned a rising; but no official action was taken of this and the situation was allowed to deteriorate.

The plot for Sunday 10th May aimed at attacking the British cavalry and artillery while unarmed at Divine Service. On that day the newly-built garrison church in the space between the Native Cavalry and Native Infantry lines was due to be used for the first time. At the last moment, however, it was found to be unready, and consequently the Service was counter-ordered to be held at the old church in the British Troops Lines. The disloyal Indian units stood to arms according to their plan, and the 5th Bengal Native Infantry even threatened their officers; but they were perplexed and deterred from action by the protected location of the church parade, and were eventually persuaded to dismiss.

In the face of this open disaffection the civil authorities acted with vigour in employing Sikh police to protect the Treasury and Civil Lines; and in summoning military assistance from the Maharajahs of Patiala and Jind. But the Army authorities continued to lack energy and decision. The Commander-in-Chief, although informed in SIMLA on the 11th, did not concentrate the British battalions in AMBALA until 15th May. And in dealing with the mutinous Bengal regiments first weak conciliation was tried, then the half-measure of splitting them up. Two companies of the 5th with a squadron of the cavalry were sent to JAGADHRI on the SAHARANPUR road. Another two companies were despatched to RUPAR on the SUTLEJ, but had to be withdrawn on showing further disaffection.

The final crisis in the history of the 5th Bengal Native Infantry occurred at AMBALA on 28th May. On the preceding evening the siege train which had been summoned from PHILLAUR for the recapture of DELHI arrived under escort by the Nusseree Gurkha Battalion. The Gurkhas had already been suspect at SIMLA, so when men of the 5th Native Infantry were found urging them to revolt action was at last taken against the Bengal sepoys. Major Maitland paraded his Regiment and, under the cover of two British companies, secured the surrender of their arms.

In July, as we shall see, the two Sikh companies of the 5th who had remained loyal were given back their arms and sent to PHILLAUR to help form the 7th Punjab Infantry. The Hindustani sepoys of the 5th remained in AMBALA for over a year, disarmed and disgruntled yet pacified by the presence of 200 men of British regiments. In August 1858 they were disbanded and marched in daily parties of 20 back to their homes in Oude.

The revolt in Hindustan.

The revolt, begun as described in Bengal and at MEERUT, spread rapidly during the summer months of 1857. Indian units mutinied at BENARES, AZAMGARH, ALLAHABAD, FYZABAD, CAWNPORE, LUCKNOW, SITAPUR, FATEHGARH, ALIGARH, MORADABAD, SHAHJANPUR, NOWGONG and JHANSI. Many of these mutineers flocked to the siege of CAWNPORE, where the Europeans were massacred after their capitulation on 27th June, and to the siege of LUCKNOW which lasted until 25th September. The rebel troops of MHOW, NEEMUCH, NASIRABAD, ERINPURA and KOTAH, and those of the Punjab, moved on DELHI. Even in the early days of temptation there were, however, many exceptional cases of loyalty in the Bengal Army. The 1st Battalion The Sikh Regiment, then the newly-raised "Regiment of Ferozepore" saved the fort at ALLAHABAD. SAUGOR was defended by the 1st Battalion The Rajput Regiment among others. The most important loyal force at this time was that engaging the rebels at DELHI. It consisted, as we shall see, of the troops sent by the Commander-in-Chief for AMBALA, the remaining garrison of MEERUT and an increasing stream of reinforcements and munitions from all parts of the Punjab. Other principal forces in these early days were that under Brigadier-General Havelock, which after regaining CAWNPORE endeavoured to relieve LUCKNOW, and a reinforcing column from CALCUTTA under General Outram.

"Map 1."

The Punjab.

At the time of the outbreak of the Mutiny there were in the Punjab and what is now the North West Frontier Province only 12 large British units—one cavalry regiment at AMBALA, one

"Map 2."

infantry battalion each at KASAULI, DAGSHAI, SABATHU, JULLUNDUR, SIALKOT, FEROZEPORE, LAHORE Cantonment, RAWALPINDI, NOWSHERA and two at PESHAWAR. Together with the Artillery these totalled some 10,500 men. The Bengal Army Indian units comprised 6 cavalry regiments, 26 infantry battalions and some artillery, in all about 36,000 men. The Punjab Irregular troops, 8 cavalry and 11 infantry regiments had a strength of 13,500 men, mostly Sikhs and Punjabi Musalmans. There were also the 7 military police battalions of similar class composition.

The Punjab Administration was electrified by the first telegraphic news of the happenings at DELHI—"The sepoys have come from MEERUT and are burning everything". "A general massacre of all Christian population has taken place there (KARNAL) and at DELHI". The weak and dilatory example of the military authorities at AMBALA was not followed elsewhere in the province under the energetic leadership of its Commissioner, Sir John Lawrence. It is true that some mutinies in Bengal units did occur, but as many more were forestalled by the firm action at once taken.

At LAHORE a plot was discovered for overpowering the British troops in the Fort on 15th May while the Indian units in the Cantonment rose. It was decisively checkmated by a clever and dramatic disarming of the troops implicated, a cavalry regiment and three infantry battalions.

A simultaneous massacre of Christians and assumption of power by the mutineers was planned to take place at AMRITSAR, FEROZEPORE, JULLUNDUR AND PHILLAUR. Here the magazine and vital SUTLEJ bridge-of-boats were to be seized by the 3rd Bengal Native Infantry. Detachments of British troops with artillery were despatched immediately from LAHORE and JULLUNDUR, and by forced marches succeeded in forestalling rebel action at AMRITSAR and PHILLAUR. The aresenal fort at FEROZEPORE was made secure, but the disarming of the Indian garrison there was only partially successful and one mutinous regiment got away. At JULLUNDUR, owing to the help that was sent from there to outposts, a defensive attitude had to be adopted, and the two battalions of Native Infantry were able to march to join the rebels at DELHI.

The 2nd Punjab Police Battalion at KANGRA.

Ever since 1809 KANGRA FORT had been held by the Sikhs as "the key to the hills", and on the annexation of the Jullundur Doab in 1846 it became a British outpost.

The news about DELHI was sent from LAHORE on 12th May and reached KANGRA on the 15th. The FORT was held by a half company of native artillery and half the 4th Bengal Native Infantry, a regiment the more suspect for having mutinied some years previously. Close by in the city was stationed the 2nd Punjab Police Battalion (Sherdil-ki-Paltan) under Attar Singh, who was Jiwan Singh's successor, and Captain Younghusband. The latter was at once instructed by the Commissioner to seize the FORT. Just after dawn on 16th May the Battalion marched into the FORT with the Commanding Officer at their head and the band playing "The British Grenadiers". They at once occupied the inner citadel and took over the gate and magazine guards.

The Peshawar Valley.

The military and political situation in PESHAWAR was particularly unfavourable when on 11th May the alarming news from DELHI and LAHORE became known. There was hardly one of the encircling Pathan tribes that was not then under blockade for hostile behaviour. Could these tribes but combine offensively they would have little difficulty in sweeping the British from the PESHAWAR VALLEY. Every tribesman watched to see whether revolt within the Cantonment would provide the opportunity for his intervention, perhaps an opening to still wider profit from plundering east of the INDUS. Fortunately there were men of decision in control at PESHAWAR, Lieutenant-Colonel John Nicholson as Deputy Commissioner, Brigadier Cotton and General Reed in command of the troops, and Lieutenant-Colonel Neville Chamberlain with the Punjaub Irregular Force. It is remarkable that in their anxiety over the local situation they did not neglect the needs of the rest of the Punjab but to this end organized a Moveable Column which might operate wherever most required. It was this force which later made the recapture of DELHI possible, and with it the 7th Punjab Infantry first saw active service. From PESHAWAR warnings were at once sent to all stations. Some of the Irregular Force units of Sikhs, Punjabi Musalmans and Pathans whose antipathy to the Poorbeah sepoy could be relied on were brought in from frontier outposts, and other troops were redistributed so as to isolate the more suspect of the Bengal regiments. From MARDAN the Guides were despatched independently towards DELHI, and marched the 580 miles in 27 days of May and June. Three Bengal infantry regiments were disarmed at PESHAWAR, one at ABAZAI and two at MULTAN. One which mutinied and fled from MARDAN was later destroyed, partly by Mohmand tribesmen and partly by loyal troops. The cavalry regiment and Bengal Infantry who sacked SIALKOT were, as we shall see, later intercepted by the Moveable Column. The mutinous regiments of

"Map 6"

JHELUM, JULLUNDUR, LUDHIANA managed to get away to DELHI.

Recruiting in the Punjab.

In pursuit of his objects of recapturing DELHI while safeguarding the rest of the Punjab Sir John Lawrence took the bold course of extensive local recruitment. He relied unerringly on the admiration of the Sikhs for the British battalions who had outmatched them in the recent campaigns. He counted on the natural dislike of Punjabi Musalman for the Poorbeah, and on the attraction for the Pathan of the very name of DELHI. The touchstone of his success was the firm action taken at LAHORE and PESHAWAR. Extensive additions were made to irregular horse and foot. The proscribed sections of Pathans even paid fines in their eagerness to enlist along with the rest. Units of the former Sikh Army were revived. Each of the seven police battalions was ordered to enlist and train an extra four companies so that they might contribute to newly-raised units. Between June and September of 1857 Hodson's Horse, one battalion of Gurkhas, two of Mazhbi-Sikh Pioneers and sixteen of Punjab Infantry were formed and equipped.

The Punjab Moveable Column.

"Map 1."   Drawing its original units from places as distant as DERA GHAZI KHAN, BANNU, ABBOTTABAD and MURREE, the Moveable Column marched through the Punjab towards DELHI. A week was spent in disarming and punishing mutineers at LAHORE. At JULLUNDUR Brigadier-General John Nicholson took over command from Nevile Chamberlain. As the column marched into PHILLAUR on 25th June its two Native Infantry Corps, by then strongly suspect, were dramatically disarmed under the guns of the fort by the only British battalion of the force.

When the Column marched on from PHILLAUR on 28th June it was not towards DELHI, as all hoped, but to AMRITSAR. There it would be well placed to deal with the fresh disaffection of which Brigadier General Nicholson was now forewarned and which soon came to a head at JHELUM and SIALKOT. News of revolt in the former station was received at AMRITSAR on 7th July and induced Nicholson to disarm the Bengal battalion there.

"Map 2."   AMRITSAR was also the headquarters of the 7th Punjab Police Battalion, now busy training its extra recruits and preparing the detachment for the 7th Punjab Infantry.

The action at TRIMMU GHAT, 12th and 16th July 1857

Having learnt on 10th July of the happenings at SIALKOT, Brigadier-General Nicholson decided to disarm his only cavalry, the other half of the rebel 9th Light Cavalry, and to intercept the mutineers before they could reach GURDASPUR. As the operations which follow concern detachments of the 2nd Punjab Police Battalion from KANGRA they will be described in some detail. By mounting the Oxfordshire and Buckinghamshire Light Infantry on 200 ekkas and the detachments of the 3rd and 6th Battalions Frontier Force Rifles on horses of the disarmed cavalry, the Column was able to cover the 44 miles to GURDASPUR in a single march which ended at 6 p.m. on 11th July. At this place there were already located the newly-formed Irregular Sikh Cavalry (now Sam Browne's), two companies of the Sherdils (2nd Punjab Police Battalion) and the Gurdaspur Foot Levy.

Taking one Sherdil company with them the Column moved on next morning and shortly after noon made contact with the enemy at TRIMMU GHAT. Here an island divided the RAVI into two channels, the westerly shallow and normally fordable without difficulty, the easterly deep except where some sandbanks provided a passage. The SIALKOT mutineers had already crossed and taken up a position about a mile east of the river, the 46th Bengal Native Infantry with one flank resting on a sarai and the other on a small village and clump of trees. The rebel wing of the 9th cavalry was posted on the flanks, and there was one 12-pounder gun. In front of this position ran a deep waterchannel, bridged only at the crossing of the GURDASPUR Road.

"Sketch A."

Brigadier-General Nicholson's plan was to advance to close range and then bring overwhelming fire to bear from his 9 guns and accurate Enfield rifles. The Column therefore approached with the Irregular Cavalry screening the batteries in front, a company of the Oxfordshire and Buckinghamshire Light Infantry on each flank and the remainder of the Column in rear. The crossing of the bridge involved a temporary division of the force, and hardly had the guns got over than the enemy cavalry charged them. This critical situation was just saved by the resistance of the escort companies, and after the guns had opened fire infantry, police and artillery closed to about 300 yards range. The mutineers, though fighting bravely and charging recklessly, could not for long withstand the devastating fire now poured into them. Abandoning 120 dead, 200 wounded and all baggage, but withdrawing their gun, they retreated onto the island with the intention of recrossing the RAVI. But overnight the river had risen considerably with the melting of Himalayan snows, and the further channel was now unfordable. Entrapped, the mutineers prepared for a desperate resistance at the north end of the island where they emplaced their gun and fortified the little village of MIADI. Leaving the companies of Frontier Force Rifles and 2nd Police Battalion to contain them there, Brigadier-General Nicholson withdrew the rest of his much exhausted force to GURDASPUR.

For the next three days this watch on the enemy was maintained, and it is recorded that certain of the rebels who attempted to regain the east bank were either drowned or "captured by the Police". Another company of Sherdils was brought up from GURDASPUR for river bank duty, and on the evening of the 13th the Column returned and camped. During the next two days boats were collected from distant ferries and other arrangements made for a decisive attack on the 400 mutineers who now remained.

Early on 16th July the guns were advanced to the bank opposite the enemy position and a heavy bombardment opened. Meanwhile from a point $1\frac{1}{2}$ miles downstream out of sight of the enemy, the Oxfordshire and Buckinghamshire Light Infantry and the original Sherdil company under Captain Adams, Deputy Commissioner of Gurdaspur, were ferried across to the south end of the island. From there the final advance on the village was carried out through deep sand, Brigadier-General Nicholson leading. First enemy piquets were driven in, then their redoubt was assaulted with the bayonet and their gun taken. Only a very few rebels managed to escape. Almost all of those not killed or wounded were driven into the river and drowned. The Column's casualties were only 3 officers and 6 men wounded.

The 2nd Punjab Police Battalion at KANGRA.

"Map 2."

The remainder of the 2nd Punjab Police Battalion was still at KANGRA where, as we have seen, they had taken over the FORT from the Wing of the 4th Bengal Native Infantry in May. The attitude of the latter regiment had been satisfactory in the meantime; but when news came of the SIALKOT disaster Major Reynell-Taylor, the Deputy Commissioner, feared that the other wing at NURPUR might easily be affected and ordered total disarming. On the evening of the 11th July, the Wing of the 4th Native Infantry paraded in front of the 2nd Punjab Police Battalion on the latter's parade ground at KANGRA and their arms were taken into custody without difficulty. The same night one company of Sherdils marched off to NURPUR 34 miles away to enforce the disarmament there, though in fact their intervention proved unnecessary as arms were given up on the order of the Commanding Officer.

After 16th July no Bengal regiment in the Punjab east of the INDUS retained its arms, and Nicholson's Moveable Column at GURDASPUR was free to resume its march on DELHI. It was also now possible to give effect to the orders for the formation of the 7th Punjab Infantry at PHILLAUR and its movement onwards to DELHI.

Formation of the 7th Punjab Infantry.

Preparations for the raising of the Regiment and the six others formed simultaneously had been made since early June. Both Punjab Police Battalions, the 2nd at KANGRA and GURDASPUR and the 7th at AMRITSAR, had been enlisting and training their 400 recruits and selecting the equivalent number of trained ranks for transfer.

A small draft of the Gurdaspur Foot Levy had also been earmarked, and the loyal Sikhs of the 5th Bengal Native Infantry at AMBALA had already been moved to PHILLAUR.

It was natural that the Chief Commissioner of the Punjab who at this time was denied all telegraphic communication with the Governor-General, should constitute any new corps as part of the Punjab Irregular Force already under his control. Thus it was decided to continue the series of six Punjab Infantry Regiment which dated back to the Frontier Brigade of 1849. During the Mutiny this affinity of the Regiment with early frontier troops was popularly recognized by the occasional designation of "7th Punjab Irregulars" and officially in the Bengal Army List as follows :—

"25 Regiments of Punjab Irregular Infantry Civil"

"Raised 18th May 1849".

"7th Infantry. Raised at PHILLAUR."

The arrangements for raising the Regiment were settled while those for forming the others of the series were still incomplete, and thus the senior number 7 was allotted. But actually, owing to the difficulties in the way of concentration at PHILLAUR and the need for hastening towards DELHI, the Regiment was not the first to be brought together and indeed one half of it did not meet the other until on 21st August at KARNAL. More quickly collected were the present 2nd Battalion 14th Punjab Regiment at NOWSHERA, the 3rd at MULTAN, the 4th at

PESHAWAR and the 10th at KOHAT. The remainder of the series, comprising the present 15th and 16th Punjab Regiments, were being raised at LAHORE, PESHAWAR, RAWALPINDI and FEROZEPORE.

The formal orders by the Chief Commissioner for the formation of the Regiment ran as follows:—

"The augmentation of four companies directed to each of the infantry corps and police battalions under the Chief Commissioner's orders having been nearly completed they will at once be drafted into new regiments, which are to be numbered, constituted and officered as follows:—

Number and designation.	At what station to be formed.	To be composed of four companies from	Officers.
7th Regiment, Punjab Infantry.	PHILLAUR directed towards DELHI.	2nd Police Battalion at KANGRA. 7th Police Battalion at AMRITSAR.	Commandant Lieutenant J. S. Stafford, 4th Native Infantry. 2nd-in-Command. Doing duty officer.
etc.,	etc.,	etc.,	etc.

The above regiments will, for the present, consist of eight companies each, which are to be recruited as rapidly as possible up to 100 sepoys per company. This will afford time for the officers to become acquainted with their men, and they will thereby be enabled to make better selections for the non-commissioned grades of two additional companies to be constituted hereafter, and each regiment will eventually consist of ten companies each of the strength noted in the margin.

1 subadar.	
1 jemadar.	The transfers to the new regiments will be paid up up to the day they are struck off their present corps and the usual transfer papers are to be furnished with them. They are to be marched to their several destinations without loss of time, and in all practicable cases under an European officer.
6 havildars.	
6 naicks.	
2 buglers.	
80 sepoys.	
2 bhisties.	
1 lascar.	
1 sweeper.	

Note. The existing 1st to 6th Punjab Infantry were now ordered to expand from eight companies to ten of the above strength.

To ensure the early efficiency of the new regiments, which is of the utmost importance, it is essentially necessary that the transfers to them should have a fair proportion of old and trained soldiers, and Commanding Officers are strictly enjoined to see that this order is strictly carried out. All classes and tribes to be fairly and proportionately represented in the transfer companies, and the fewer Hindoostanees the better. The following proportions are as far as possible to be observed :—

Seikhs from British territory	4 parts
Goorkhas, Hill races (Rajputs)	2 parts
Punjabee Mohammadans, not Pathans	4 parts

(Pathans were permitted to be enlisted in regiments forming at Peshawar).

These regiments will be armed with muskets which, with accoutrements, can be obtained on indent from the nearest magazines or from those of disarmed corps of the line. Light (half-mounting) clothing only will be prepared for the present. The colour to be drab (khakee) and the pattern in all respects the same as that in use with the infantry corps of the Punjab Irregular Force, a loose tunic and pantaloons.

For convenience the corps have been numbered 7 to 13 inclusive, but any appointments made up for them will not, for the present, bear any numerical designations. They are in all respects to be placed on the same footing with the infantry corps of the Punjab Irregular Force and Seikh Infantry, as regards pay and allowances, pensions, establishments, but for the present no carriage establishment will be maintained for them. On any move taking place carriage for the baggage of the men will be supplied at the public expense, according to the scale allowed for the above corps. A copy of the scale of the carriage will be allowed to Commanding Officers hereafter by the Staff Officer of the Punjab Irregular Force. Emergent indents for arms, accoutrements, ammunition, camp equipage, etc., to be forwarded to the office of the Military Secretary for countersignature.

The first muster rolls and pay abstracts of the new regiments are to be forwarded for countersignature to the office of the Military Secretary. Afterwards they will, in usual course, be transmitted to paymasters direct. Officers commanding corps from which transfers are made will report direct at an early date the Military Secretary for the Chief Commissioner's information what steps they may take for carrying out the foregoing arrangements, and all doubtful points (should there be any) should at once be referred for orders."

As these arrangements worked out in practice only 300 men were initially transferred from each of the two police battalions named. In the case of the Sherdils the great majority of these were sent from headquarters at KANGRA; but some undoubtedly must have been drawn from the two companies at GURDASPUR, and with the latter were included the transfers which had been arranged from the Gurdaspur Foot Levy. Both police battalions must have completed their quotas from the Sikhs of the 5th Native Infantry already at PHILLAUR. The transfers from GURDASPUR marched with the Punjab Moveable Column on 20th July, were joined by those from the 7th Punjab Police Battalion at AMRITSAR on the 22nd, and the whole arrived in PHILLAUR on the 26th. Lieutenant Godby joined en route at JANDIALA where his regiment, the 35th Native Infantry, was encamped after having been disarmed. An order by Brigadier-General John Nicholson dated 24th July appointed him "to command a wing of the 7th Sikh Police Battalion, attached to the Column". Lieutenant John Francis Stafford, the only other European officer initially posted to the Regiment, belonged to the 4th Bengal Native Infantry recently disarmed at KANGRA and was Garrison Staff officer there when he was appointed Commandant. He left KANGRA on 27th July with the transfer companies of the 2nd Police Battalion and, following the HOSHIARPORE route, would have arrived at PHILLAUR in time to assume full command but for mischance on the way. Unfortunate delay was caused by there being only one old ferry boat at DERA GOPIPUR for the difficult crossing of the River BEAS. When PHILLAUR was reached the remainder of the Regiment under Lieutenant Godby had already marched on 1st August with the Moveable Column. Thus the 7th Punjab Infantry never actually concentrated at its assembly station PHILLAUR. Yet the Regiment is officially regarded as having been formed there during the last week of July, and Lieutenant Stafford's date of appointment as Commandant was fixed as 1st August. The following Moveable Column Order by Brigadier-General Nicholson dated 5th August indicates that although the formation of the new regiment was recognized, there was at that date doubt as to its status and title :—

"Lieutenant Godby to be 2nd-in-command of the 2nd Sikh Police Battalion, and Assistant Surgeon J. Drake to be in medical charge of the Battalion". The companies from the 2nd Police Battalion brought with them and passed on to their new regiment the soubriquet of "Sherdil". And when the Police Battalion itself was disbanded in the years after the Mutiny its early Sikh title was adopted by the offspring regiment, namely "Sherdil-ki-Paltan".

The exact class composition at the beginning is not known; but some months later, when Pathans had been received among reinforcement drafts and the increase in companies had taken place, there were four companies of Jat Sikhs, four of Punjabi Musalmans and Pathans mixed, and two of Dogras. Each company was subdivided into four sections. That some British rank and file specialists were included is shown by the following extract from the Punjab Gazette of 22nd December 1857:—

"7th Regiment of Punjab Infantry. Havildar Maula Bux and Drummer George Franklin are transferred from the 20th Native Infantry."

The musket with which the Regiment was armed was the "Brunswick". So far only British regiments had been rearmed with the Enfield rifle. The accoutrements were of brown leather with pouches carrying 60 rounds.

In connection with the order that the Regiment would be dressed on the pattern of the Punjab Irregular Force it is interesting to note that the main difference from the Bengal Army was in the substitution of khaki for red jackets and of pagris for caps. British regiments had already begun to change from "lall koorte" into drab jackets, but the outbreak of the Mutiny found the Bengal Native Army still in red with blue kamarbands, white shorts (white Jodhpur trousers for Native Officers) and the Kilmarnock Cap. There must have been busy tranformation scenes at PHILLAUR as khaki blouses, pantaloons and pagris were adopted by the blue-clad policemen from AMRITSAR, the red-coated Sikhs from AMBALA and later by the main body of Sherdils from KANGRA who were unique among police units for wearing the red of the old Sikh Army.

Only two British officers were posted on the formation of the Regiment. Others from both Her Majesty's and the Bengal Native Army were added gradually. But during the greater part of the Mutiny period the regular establishment of European officers was confined to regimental headquarters as follows:—

- a Commandant, with pay of rank and additional pay at 230 rupees monthly;

- a 2nd-in-command, with consolidated pay of rupees 500;

- an Adjutant and Quartermaster, with pay of rank and additional pay at 170 rupees monthly;

- a Medical officer, with staff pay at 165 rupees monthly.

Any other British officers available were termed "Doing duty officers", and were employed in commanding important detachments and in supervising the work of companies under their subadars. Headquarters included a subadar-major and a native adjutant. The latter was usually a subadar.

At this point it will be relevant to summarize the changes that had occurred in the organization of the East India Company's Bengal Native Infantry. Up to 1786 a regiment was commanded by a British captain, assisted by 2 lieutenants, 2 ensigns, 3 British serjeants, 3 British drummers, 1 Native Commandant and 1 Native Adjutant. The whole totalled 20 native officers, 10 trumpeters, 30 drummers, 130 non-commissioned officers and 670 privates.

The next organization was :—

- 1 British Commandant.
- 1 British Adjutant.
- 1 British Assistant Surgeon.
- 1 Native doctor.
- 1 British Serjeant-Major.
- 1 British Quartermaster-Serjeant.
- 1 Drill havildar.
- 1 Drill naick.
- 1 British drum and fife major,

while each of the eight companies had :—

- 1 British subaltern.
- 1 British serjeant.
- 1 subadar.
- 1 jemadar.
- 4 havildars.
- 4 naicks.
- 1 drummer.
- 1 fifer.
- 68 privates.

In 1817, following the abolition of the native commandant and the native adjutant to be noticed above, the appointment of subadar-major was created. In 1818 colour-havildars were appointed.

In 1824 the British officer establishment was changed to 1 colonel, 1 lieutenant-colonel, 1 major, 5 captains, 10 lieutenants and 5 ensigns.

The recruiting of sepoys and their training were carried out by commanding officers for their own units as long as they were in the Punjab. During the two years of the Mutiny when the Regiment was east of the River JUMNA recruits were supplied from an Infantry Depot in the Punjab, probably at AMRITSAR. The limit for enrolment was for 3 years, after which service was terminable, except in war time, at 2 months' notice on either side.

PHILLAUR, the official birthplace of the Regiment, was at this time of great importance. The fort was originally built by Maharaja Ranjit Singh as an outpost commanding the bridge of boats over the River SUTLEJ and confronting the English at LUDHIANA. Now it formed the gateway to the Doab and, besides, included a 2nd class arsenal with 50 guns, 80,000 shot and shell, 5,000 muskets and nearly 3,000,000 rounds of small-arms ammunition. From here was sent out on 21st May the first siege train for the recapture of DELHI. From here too was supplemented the immense second train which left FEROZEPORE in August.

CHAPTER III.

THE REGIMENT IN THE INDIAN MUTINY, 1857—59.

(Maps 2 and 3, Sketches B and C)

The Delhi Field Force, 1857.

Although the Regiment served in it for only a few days it will not be out of place to recount the fortunes of the Delhi Field Force. It will be recollected that, after regrettable delay, the Commander-in-Chief's force marched from AMBALA on 18th May 1857. General Anson died en route at KARNAL, and General Bernard became Provincial Commander-in-Chief. On 5th June the force reached ALIPORE, 10 miles from DELHI, and was joined there two days later by the weak Meerut Brigade. The latter had been in contact with the Delhi mutineers on the east side of the River JUMNA since 27th May and had now concentrated via the ford at BAGHPAT. Next morning the combined force advanced to attack, supported by no more than 4 medium, 4 field and 16 light guns. The enemy held a strong position astride the road at BADLI-KI-SERAI, 6 miles from the city, and were much superior in artillery. After a critical check in the attack the enemy guns were charged and the whole position carried. Wisely General Bernard at once exploited this success. By evening his tired troops had swept through the gutted cantonment up to the SUBZIMANDI suburb and had secured the whole of the HINDU RAO Ridge overlooking the city, afterwards the famous DELHI RIDGE. The mutineers lost 13 guns and about 1,000 men. British losses were 53 killed and 100 wounded. No Indian unit was engaged on this date, but henceforth Punjab and Gurkha regiments together with Sikh artillerymen played a part in every operation. Arriving next day the Guides Infantry went straight into action at the end of their long march. The next reinforcements came on 22nd June, five British companies from AMBALA and 4th Battalion 12th Frontier Force Regiment. A little later came the 1st Battalion 13th Frontier Force Rifles from LUDHIANA.

"Sketch B."

It soon became clear that the force before DELHI had not the means to besiege the city, let along capture and hold it. Only on the north face was the place invested; elsewhere the mutineers in occupation had complete freedom of action. In every artillery engagement the rebels had the advantage in weight and number of guns, also in stocks of ammunition.

Indeed, after a time the medium artillery of the force had to rely on the collection of shot fired by the enemy. Out-numbering their opponents by thousands, and reinforced by contingents of mutineers from BAREILLY, JHANSI, NASIRABAD, ROHTAK and elsewhere in the Punjab, the rebels at once turned to the counter-siege and attack of the British force. Desperate and many were their assaults on the piquets which formed THE RIDGE position, on the flank at SUBZIMANDI and even against the rear so as to sever communication with the Punjab. Thus it was only with the greatest difficulty and heroism that the Delhi Field Force was able to maintain itself on THE RIDGE and in the Cantonment during the two months preceding the arrival of the Punjab Moveable Column. Sickness, particularly the scourge of cholera, was added to the hardships of wounds, heat and lack of rest. Just before succour came the force had 1,100 combatants in hospital, which left not more than 2,700 British and 1,800 Indian troops fit for duty.

Even in this brief narrative mention should be made of the feeling of isolation experienced by those in command before DELHI, and in only slightly less degree in the rest of the Punjab. The cutting of the telegraph wires by the rebels and the lack of news or help from CAWNPORE and LUCKNOW accentuated the gulf which seemed fixed between the Punjab and the rest of Hindustan in this most critical period of the Mutiny. Communication with the capital, CALCUTTA, only existed via MULTAN and BOMBAY. Confirmation of suspicions regarding the state of affairs "down country" soon brought the conviction that if rebel DELHI was to fall its capture must be achieved by troops within the Punjab. This isolation had the one advantage of committing decisions to the determined leaders on the spot instead of to those at the distant centre of government. Sir John Lawrence, staking all on the spell of DELHI and the maintenance of firmness, drained the rest of the Punjab for reinforcements and forbade either treaty or withdrawal. General Wilson, who commanded the Delhi Field Force after the death of General Bernard and the retirement of General Reed, wrote at the end of July—" It is my firm determination to hold my present position and to resist any attack to the last. The enemy are very numerous, and may possibly break through our intrenchments and overwhelm us, but the force will die at their post. Luckily the enemy have no head and no method, and we hear dissensions are breaking out among them. Reinforcements are coming up under Nicholson. If we can hold on until they arrive we shall be secure ".

The Punjab Moveable Column which marched from

PHILLAUR under Brigadier John Nicholson on 1st August 1857 comprised the following units:—

    200 of 20th Lancers (Mooltani Horse)

    17th Light Field battery (9-pounders)

    2nd Battalion The Oxfordshire and Buckinghamshire Light Infantry (from SIALKOT)

    Wing of the 2nd Battalion The Gloucestershire Regiment (from FEROZEPORE)

    Wing of the 3rd Battalion 10th Baluch Regiment (from MULTAN)

    Wing of the 7th Punjab Native Infantry under Lieutenant Godby, 2nd-in-command.

While halting on the 11th August the Column was joined by:—

    The 2nd Battalion 13th Frontier Force Rifles, and close behind followed:—

    The 4th Battalion 13th Frontier Force Rifles, Wing of the 1st Battalion The King's Regiment (relieved from JULLUNDUR and PHILLAUR).

Thus with the arrival of the Column on 14th August about 4,200 troops, including 1,300 British, were added to the weakened force before DELHI.

From this moment the tide turned. Preparations were resumed for an assault on the City after the arrival of the siege train from FEROZEPORE. The rebel sepoys while still investing the force on three sides were now less ready to face combat or bombardment, and dissensions were growing in their midst. Muhammad Bakht Khan, their commander, however, made a determined effort to intercept the essential siege train, using reinforcements he had received in 6,000 men with 16 guns. A Brigade under Brigadier Nicholson went out against them and won a decisive victory on 25th August at NAJAFGARH, 20 miles from DELHI.

Since the finale is so well known and in the meantime the 7th Punjab Infantry had left the Force, suffice it here to mention the barest facts of the dramatic events which followed. The siege train arrived on 4th September, and the bombardment was begun at once. The assault on DELHI was made on 14th September with three forward columns and one in reserve. The City was finally captured on the 20th after seven days of continuous fighting with heavy loss on both sides.

Lieutenant Stafford with the Sherdil wing of the Regiment arrived in PHILLAUR from KANGRA on about 3rd August and almost immediately set out for DELHI by forced marches. But before he could arrive there it was decided that the 7th Punjab Infantry should be sent to KARNAL. Ranghur villagers of that district had given trouble from the earliest days of the Mutiny, and during the march of the Delhi Field Force a regiment of Native Infantry had been left at KARNAL but had later mutinied. Punitive action had been taken from DELHI in mid-July; but now, a month later, the area KARNAL-PANIPAT-ROHTAK again needed attention, particularly during the transit of the vulnerable siege train. Accordingly a cavalry force was sent from DELHI to ROHTAK on 16th August, and on the same day Captain Stafford's wing, which was then within two marches of the City, was ordered back to KARNAL. The Delhi wing under Lieutenant Godby set out for the same place on 17th August, only five days after their arrival on THE RIDGE.

MEERUT DISTRICT. Action of THANA BHAWAN, 18th September 1857.

No sooner were the Regiment united at KARNAL, than they were transferred to the command of General Penny at MEERUT, in place of the 60th Rifles whom he sent to the Delhi Field Force. Immediately after arrival in MEERUT on 26th August the wing under Lieutenant Godby was detached with a punitive column to HAPUR east of Delhi; and at the beginning of September another company with a squadron of Nathan's Horse and one troop Royal Horse Artillery formed a force in the MUZAFFARNAGAR District. This company was commanded by Lieutenant J. W. H. Johnstone who was now posted from the 18th Infantry which had mutinied at BAREILLY in May. A sharp action took place at THANA BHAWAN 20 miles north-west of MUZAFFARNAGAR on 18th September when Lieutenant Johnstone was hit in the arm and his company suffered 9 killed and 5 wounded in an assault on the walls of the town. An official return of 15th September gave the rank and file strength of the Regiment as 799, only one short of establishment. A few days later a further 66 men arrived from the 2nd Punjab Police Battalion, and with them came Lieutenant J. C. P. Baillie a brother officer of Lieutenant Godby in the former 35th Native Infantry. Lieutenant Baillie was now appointed the first regular Adjutant. Hitherto in succession Lieutenant Godby and Lieutenant T. E. Vander Gucht from the 5th

Native Infantry had officiated as Adjutant in addition to their other duties. Subadar Sirbaz Khan was appointed Native Adjutant. Lieutenant Stafford was promoted Captain with effect from 11th August. About this time the Regiment carried out the expansion proposed in the original instructions for its formation. The executive "Punjab Order" ran:—"The newly raised regiments of Punjab Infantry having nearly obtained their full complement of men will now be organised into ten companies each of the following strength". Jemadars Luckha Singh and Urjoon Singh were promoted Subadars "for the augmentation."

DELHI District—Battle of NARNAUL, 16 November 1857.

While regimental headquarters and one wing remained at MEERUT, the other marched to DELHI on 16th October to do garrison duty there. At this time several punitive columns were operating in the District. One under Colonel Greathead went through BULANDSHAHR to AGRA and CAWNPORE. Another under Brigadier Showers was dealing with mutineers in the west towards BIKANER. A third under Lieutenant-Colonel Gerrard, which included Lieutenant Godby's wing, marched south-west on about 8th November. The Jodhpur Legion who since 1835 had comprised some artillery, three squadrons of cavalry and one local battalion had mutinied at ERINPURA in August and were now moving towards DELHI. The British column reached REWARI on 13th November, and on arrival at KANONDE two days later was joined by the present 2nd Battalion 16th Punjab Regiment which had just been formed. Continuing on 16th November, the column was approaching NARNAUL at 11 a.m. when news was obtained of the enemy about to attack. A local pensioner indicated the approximate position of the Legion's camp on the far side of a nala near the town and gave its strength as 2,500 cavalry, 5 mobile guns and 1,000 infantry. The Column's order of battle was as follows :—

    1st Brigade of Royal Horse Artillery.
    6th Dragoon Guards (now 3rd Carabiniers).
    Detachment of Guides Cavalry.
    Detachment of Guides Infantry.
    15th Lancers (Mooltani Horse).
    1st Bengal Fusiliers.
    Wing 7th Punjab Infantry.
    Detachment of Hariana Field Force comprising :—
        70 Punjab Mounted Police.
        90 Isa Khel Horse.
        90 Tiwana Horse.
        4 6-Pounder guns.
        500 of the 23rd Punjab Infantry.
        260 of the Patiala Infantry.

The opposing forces met outside the town. On the enemy opening with shot, grape and shrapnel from three guns the infantry of the Column was ordered to double out into line while the field guns replied and the cavalry and horse artillery took post on the flanks. When the enemy's bombardment slackened the British line advanced rapidly and the Dragoon Guards and Guides Cavalry charged from the right. The enemy met this assault without flinching, and hand-to-hand fighting ensued as the horsemen swept along the whole front and through the rebels' guns. Then came the frontal wave of the infantry, with the 1st Bengal Fusiliers leading and the 7th Punjab Infantry forming the second line. At their hands two guns were captured, while others further left fell to the Mooltani Horse on that flank. Reforming after the inevitable confusion of an assault the line pressed forward afresh against the rebel infantry, who disputed every foot of the ground back to their camp. When the camp came into view the 1st Bengal Fusiliers and 7th Punjab Infantry, supported by the horse artillery, charged across the nala and captured it together with the two guns in action there.

But the enemy fought back gamely. Before the British line could be reformed the mutineers' counter-attack recaptured both camp and guns, and it was not till later that two companies of Fusiliers with two of the 7th Punjabis and small parties of Guides Cavalry and Dragoons were able to restore the situation. Those rebels who still fought on now retreated with their last gun into a large serai at the edge of the town. The Guides Infantry climbed over the roofs of adjacent houses until they reached a point from which the interior of the serai was under their fire. The enemy then broke and fled in all directions, whereupon the Fusiliers and 7th Punjab Infantry rushed into the enclosure, killing all who remained there and capturing the gun. After NARNAUL and surroundings had been searched for fugitives these two units and the Guides Infantry bivouacked in the serai, while the remainder of the Column spent the night in the enemy's camp. Thereafter the Moveable Column returned to DELHI, having accomplished their task.

The enemy's casualties were estimated at 350, 300 corpses being actually counted. No specific mention of the enemy's cavalry is made in records, and it would appear that the report of their strength in that respect was greatly exaggerated.

British losses were Lieutenant-Colonel Gerrard and 7 other ranks killed, 5 officers and 71 other ranks wounded. The Regiment suffered only to the extent of one sepoy wounded.

Captain Caulfield who succeeded Lieutenant-Colonel Gerrard

on the battlefield particularly mentions in his despatch Lieutenant Godby commanding the 7th Punjab Infantry.

The reconquest of The Doab, 1857.

As the Regiment is now about to leave DELHI and come under the control of the Commander-in-Chief in India it will be appropriate to summarize further what had been happening outside the Punjab.

"Map 1." After its first relief by Generals Outram and Havelock LUCKNOW had again been invested by the rebels. But meanwhile a new force of three weak brigades was on the march from CALCUTTA under General Sir Colin Campbell, the new Commander-in-Chief in India. This force finally cleared the rebels from LUCKNOW between 14th and 23rd November, after suffering 123 killed and 429 wounded. The Commander-in-Chief then had to hurry back to help the CAWNPORE garrison. The troops there were now engaged with the Gwalior Contingent of mutineers, under Tantia Topi, who had cut their communications with LUCKNOW and forced them to abandon CAWNPORE for entrenchments outside the City. On his arrival Sir Colin Campbell heavily defeated this enemy force on 6th December.

On 9th December a moveable column under Lieutenant-Colonel T. Seaton, C. B., was detached from the Delhi Field Force to escort a large convoy of supplies of every sort to the Commander-in-Chief, and to deal with any rebels met *en route*. The column consisted of detachments from the 6th Dragoon Guards, 9th Lancers and Hodson's Irregular Horse, nine guns, 1st Bengal Fusiliers and the 7th Punjab Infantry. The Left Wing under Lieutenant Godby started from DELHI with the Column, while the remainder of the Regiment, less one company, marched from MEERUT on 7th December and joined at KHURJA.

On this date the following British Officers were serving with the Regiment:—

Captain Stafford.......Commandant.
Captain Sage .... Joined from the 11th Native Infantry on 14th October, and now remained with the company left for duty at MUZAFFARNAGAR.
Lieutenant Godby......2nd-in-Command.
    ,, Johnstone.
    ,, Campbell ... Joined at MEERUT on 8th October from the 8th Native Infantry.

Lieutenant Baillie ......Adjutant.
     ,, Lewis ......Joined on 1st December from the 20th Native Infantry.
Assistant Surgeon Drake was still in medical charge.

The action of GUNGIRI, 15th December 1857.

On arrival at ALIGARH the convoy was parked under the walls of the fort in charge of a wing of the 3rd Bengal European Regiment and a company of the 4th Battalion 13th Frontier Force Rifles who had been left there by Colonel Greathead's force. The Moveable Column then prepared to clear this part of the Gangetic Doab of the various enemy forces still at large. The first move was eastward to GUNGIRI where there were already a detachment of Afghan Horse, three companies of the 3rd Battalion 10th Baluch Regiment and two 6-pounder guns. Arriving there on 15th December the Column was settling into camp when a patrol of Hodson's Horse reported that a considerable body of mutineers was advancing to attack. The force stood to as follows:— "Map 3."

    One troop Royal Horse Artillery (six 9-pounders and two 6-pounders).
    One troop 6th Dragoon Guards (3rd Carabiniers).
    Detachment of 9th Lancers.
    Hodson Horse.
    One Section Field Artillery (18-pounders).
    One 8½-pounder howitzer.
    Two companies of Sappers.
    1st Bengal Fusiliers.
    One company of the 3rd Bengal Europeans.
    7th Punjab Infantry, less one company.

The cavalry and artillery advanced. The guns opened on the enemy as soon as they came in sight, and the cavalry charged them. The mutineers were completely routed by the horse, and the infantry were not employed. Two enemy guns were captured and a third was later abandoned as the mutineers fled into the fields, throwing away their arms or defending themselves desperately until killed. British losses were 13 cavalrymen killed and 35 wounded. Those of the enemy included 200 killed.

The Action of PATIALI, 17th December 1857.

Following up this success at once the Column halted the same night at KASGANJ and the following day reached SAHAWAR. Early on 17th December they marched towards PATIALI in the expectation of encountering more rebels. On approaching the town Hodson's Horse which was acting as advanced guard came upon the hostile camp and the enemy forming up. The British force also deployed, and while waiting for the slow-moving guns to come up on the flanks were served out with grog and bread. The action began with an artillery duel, eleven guns on each side. The British infantry then advanced. But before they could get to close range the horse artillery with Hodson's Horse charged the enemy batteries, killed the gunners and started a general rout. The 7th Punjab Infantry were detailed to guard the gardens around the town, and the main body of cavalry was sent round to pursue fugitives in the plain beyond. A great many were found and cut down, or else were drowned in the jheels. The enemy lost 12 guns and 700 killed. Casualties in the Moveable Column were one sowar killed, three British and one Indian ranks wounded.

The Action of MAINPURI, 27th December 1857.

The Column now retraced their steps to ALIGARH, picked up the convoy and continued the march. But after passing through ETAH Lieutenant-Colonel Seaton heard that a rebel force under Raja Tej Singh was at MAINPURI somewhat south of his line of march. He therefore turned aside and attacked these insurgents on 27th December. Few details of this action are available. The enemy were found in position outside the cantonment, were at once attacked and completely routed with a loss of 250 killed. All of their six guns were captured. Raja Tej Singh and 16 horsemen alone escaped. Since leaving DELHI the Column had captured 22 guns and killed 1,400 insurgents.

Meanwhile the provision of transport had enabled the Commander-in-Chief at CAWNPORE to begin a drive north-westwards towards Lieutenant-Colonel Seaton's force, which now resumed its march with the addition of Probyn's Horse. Ahead of the Commander-in-Chief marched a column under Brigadier Walpole, which on 3rd January joined that under Lieutenant-Colonel Seaton at BEWAR and with it reached FATEHGARH three days later. The Commander-in-Chief's own force left CAWNPORE on 24th December and after rounding up rebels here and there, and gaining a decisive victory at the bridge of KALI NADI, reached FATEHGARH on 3rd January. The Doab had been reconquered and most of the remaining mutineers had been driven across the GANGES into Oudh.

The Ganges Cordon, 1858.

On the evening of 6th January 1858, the day of their

arrival, the Regiment were hurried on from FATEHGARH to establish a lines-of-communication post at SARAI MIRAN, 51 miles from CAWNPORE, and from there to keep watch on the adjacent GANGES fords. The first task which fell to the Regiment in January was covering the passage towards CAWNPORE of an important convoy under escort by Probyn's Horse. Thereafter until mid-March they were mainly employed in guarding the river crossings. Piquets under British officers watched about 30 miles of the GANGES and frustrated many attempts by rebel parties to break back from Oudh.

During the whole of January the Commander-in-Chief maintained his concentration at FATEHGARH, apparently inactive yet actually intent on deceiving the rebels into believing that he would cross into Rohilkand while he quietly assembled at CAWNPORE the siege-train necessary to achieving his real object, the final capture of LUCKNOW. When on 1st February the Commander-in-Chief marched for CAWNPORE he left behind in FATEHGARH a small force under Brigadier Seaton. To strengthen the 7th Punjab Infantry at SERAI MIRAN he dropped there one squadron Alexander's Horse, two guns and three companies of the 2nd battalion Prince of Wales' Volunteers, the whole under Lieutenant-Colonel Watson of the last named regiment. However, on 13th March this detachment, less two companies of the Regiment which stayed to garrison SARAI MIRAN, marched to join the FATEHGARH force. During the next few weeks the Regiment were employed in patrolling the river bank for some distance upstream of the town; and it is thought that during this period the earlier detachment, less Captain Sage, rejoined from MUZAFFARNAGAR. Captain Sage went to command The Fatehgarh Levy. The two companies at SARAI MIRAN were under Lieutenant Gordon, who had been posted from The Gloucestershire Regiment as 2nd-in-command *vice* Lieutenant Godby who now transferred to Probyn's Horse.

Meanwhile the Commander-in-Chief's force had arrived before LUCKNOW on 1st March, and in the following twenty days of hard-fought operations relieved General Outram's garrison at ALAM BAGH and cleared the whole city.

The Action of KHANKHUR, 7th April 1858.

Next month the Regiment took part in an interesting operation which involved a night march of over 20 miles, an attack and return to FATEHGARH, all within 25 hours. The order-of-battle shows 50 horsemen attached to the Regiment; and that this was a semi-permanent measure is evidenced by the mention on subsequent occasions of the term "Cavalry of 7th Punjab Infantry". The strength-state was 6 British Officers, 6 Native and 180 rank and file, which indicates that one wing of the Regiment remained behind in the fort and on outposts.

Three strong bodies of rebels had appeared between the RAMGANGA and GANGES upstream of FATEHGARH and were actually sending horsemen across into the Doab to plunder and collect revenue. Having insufficient cavalry to intercept these raiders Brigadier Seaton determined to upset the enemy's plans by attacking one of their concentrations, that at KHANKHUR near the KAMPIL ford. Crossing the bridge of boats at 10 p.m. on the 6th April the following force reached the enemy position at dawn after a circuitous march of 20 miles :—

Alexander's Horse.
4th Field Battery............ ...5 guns.
2nd Battalion The Prince of Wales' Volunteers.
7th Punjab "Irregular" Infantry.
Horsemen attached to 7th P. I.
Fatehgarh Organized Police Horsemen.

The enemy who were occupying the village and the groves to right and left of it advanced to meet the attack, and their infantry then lined a nala bank. The punitive force deployed, the British regiment leading in "line of loosened files", the 7th Punjab Infantry in their immediate support, the guns on the right and the majority of cavalry on the left. Rebel cavalry were threatening on both flanks until engaged by artillery. Their guns answered only feebly. There followed a fire duel between the opposing infantry, but when The Prince of Wales' Volunteers resumed their advance the mutineers began to retreat, at first in small parties and then *en masse* precipitately. Three small guns, some standards and a quantity of ammunition were captured. The cavalry pursued the enemy for the next hour while the infantry killed all found in the position. The rebels were estimated to have consisted of 800 horse and 1800 foot, of whom 250 were killed.

Brigadier Seaton's force rested in the groves until 3 p.m. when the return march was begun. Great heat and fatigue were experienced; but although enemy cavalry hovered on the flanks there was no actual interference with the column. The British casualties were :—

Killed—5 men (including one in the Regiment) and 4 followers :

Wounded—1 officer and 12 men, who included Lieutenant

Johnstone (his second wound) and 4 sepoys of the 7th Punjab Infantry.

At the end of April the Commander-in-Chief transferred his forces to Rohilkand, and himself led the main force from FATEHGARH towards BAREILLY. Two more columns crossed the GANGES higher up with the same objective. There were also minor operations in Oudh, but the complete pacification of that province was to be deferred until the end of the rainy season.

During April, May and June the Regiment remained on Ganges Cordon duty at FATEHGARH and in outposts. On 15th May Lieutenant J. H. Johnstone left to take up an extra-regimental appointment, and Lieutenant H. C. J. Jarrett, "supernumerary", was appointed to the establishment in his place. In June Assistant Surgeon Hood replaced Assistant-Surgeon Drake as medical officer.

Western Bihar. The Action of DEHAIGN, 14th July 1858.

At the end of June 1858 the 7th Punjab Regiment were ordered to join a field force which was being formed under Brigadier Berkley to reduce the several insurgent strongholds around SORAON in Western Bihar. Picking up the SARAI MIRAN companies *en route*, the Regiment reached ALLAHABAD on 9th July, crossed the GANGES next day and arrived in camp on 12th July.

On 14th July a force as below captured the nearby village and fort of DEHAIGN.

Half of 'E' troops R. H. A.

Detachment of Lahore Light Horse (60 sabres) Detachment of 6th Madras Light Cavalry (52 sabres).

Two guns : two mortars.

Detachment of 1st Battalion, Duke of Cornwall's Light Infantry (200 bayonets).

Detachment of 2nd Battalion, The Dorsetshire Regiment (80 bayonets).

Detachment of 1st Battalion (Ferozepore) The Sikh Regiment (70 bayonets).

7th Punjab Infantry (542 bayonets).

Lieutenant Gordon was in command of the Regiment as Captain Stafford was ill.

The rebels surrendered the village after only slight resistance and retired to the 'fort' which was completely hidden from view by trees and thick jungle. The 'fort' proved afterwards to be merely a small brick building in a rectangular enclosure which was surrounded by a low wall, a thick abbattis of thorns, and a ditch. Cavalry patrols advanced on a wide front to surround the stronghold, while the horse artillery moved to where they could engage any enemy attempting to break away. The attack was preceded by a bombardment from the field guns and mortars; but as observation was unobtainable the effect could not be judged. The 7th Punjab Infantry were then put in to take the place, the detachment of Dorsetshires being in support and the 24-pounder howitzer following with a company of the Duke of Cornwall's Light Infantry as escort. The Regiment dashed forward in two main parties led respectively by Lieutenant Gordon and by Captain Colls who was the Field Engineer with the force. The former party assaulted the gateway, while the latter, with Lieutenant Baillie as 2nd-in-Command, stormed the walls in flank. A smaller party under Lieutenant Lewis passed round to the rear in order to cut off retreat. The mutineers were overtaken just as they were entering the fort. About 150 were killed in the ditch and most of the remainder were cut down inside, or shot or sabred in the surrounding scrub to which they fled. In all about 500 were killed. The Regiment's casualties, over half of the total, were:—2 sepoys killed, 6 wounded. It is recorded that sepoy Assa Singh's wound necessitated the immediate amputation of a limb.

The Action of TIROUL, 16th July 1858.

The operation against the fort of TIROUL two days later was a more serious affair. The force was the same except that the Regiment had its attached cavalry, 28 strong. Captain Stafford was still too ill to command. Again there was an approach march of 7 miles, and again the adjacent village was scarcely defended. The fort, however, in which this time the enemy were already established, was found to be a formidable work. Roughly square, it had loopholed walls 7 feet thick at the top and rising 20 to 25 feet above the bottom of the surrounding ditch. There were 7 bastions with 3 guns in action. Outside the ditch all round was a breastwork with flanking-fire rifle pits, and in front of this was a double line of thick thorn abbattis. Impenetrable jungle surrounded the fort closely on three sides. On the fourth side, where was the only gateway, the trees were thinner but nevertheless an obstacle to observation.

The fort was bombarded from this side, and the high trajectory mortars and howitzers soon found the range of its interior. But while daylight lasted the thorn obstacle under the rebels fire ruled out the practicability of assault. After dark Captain Colls, who again was attached, led a small party of the Regiment right up to the abbattis and succeeded in setting it alight. But heavy fire from the walls and the flanks then compelled this party to withdraw after losing both the havildar and the naick; and the enemy were able to extinguish the fire before it had spread. Later in the night another attempt to burn the abbattis was organized by a party of the Duke of Cornwall's Light Infantry under the Brigade Major; but at the last moment it was found that the enemy had slipped away in the darkness. Five guns with 500 rounds were found abandoned. The fort was guarded by three companies of the Regiment while arrangements were made for its destruction. The Regiment incurred 6 out of the 8 casualties, namely 2 NCOs killed and 4 sepoys wounded. Brigadier Berkley writes in his despatch:— "I received every assistance from all officers engaged, and the Punjab Infantry, on whom, from necessity, after the artillery, the hard work fell, were most gallantly and ably commanded by Lieutenant Gordon".

The success of this action caused the rebels to abandon a similar stronghold at BAISPUR, and this too was duly destroyed by the force.

On 29th July 1858 the Regiment with their cavalry troop left the Saraon Field Force on transfer to another under Brigadier Kelly at AZAMGARH. This place is also in Western Bihar, but north of the GUMTI River. On the last day of its long hot-weather march via JAUNPUR the 7th Punjab Infantry received orders to press on past the camp at AZAMGARH in an attempt to intercept a large body of Oudh mutineers at the crossing of the TONRI River 18 miles further to the northwest. So great were the heat and fatigue of this forced march that the Regiment suffered 20 casualties from sunstroke. Actually the rebels crossed the river some hours before it was possible to arrive there. As these mutineers remained in the vicinity $1\frac{1}{2}$ companies under Lieutenants Lewis and Fitz G. Calogan were left at MAHARAJGANJ to keep them under observation, while on 18th August the rest of the Regiment returned to join Brigadier Kelly's force at AZAMGARH. Lieutenant Fitz G. Calogan had joined on 15th August from the 22nd Native Infantry. "Map 3."

From 21st August until the beginning of October 1858 this column moved about the District in pursuit of rebel parties, the Regiment being reduced by the detachment at MAHARAJGANJ.

The Winter campaign in Oudh, 1858-59.

At the end of September General Sir Colin Campbell, now Lord Clyde, was able to begin his long-prepared reconquest of Oudh, in which he had so far only recovered the capital and principal centres and where most of the remaining mutineers from Bihar, Rohilkand, and the Doab had now sought refuge. The campaign lasted until the end of the year. The broad plan was to sweep the mutineers northwards across the GOGRA River by the co-ordinated advance of some nine columns, and thereafter to force them further north over the RAPTI River into Nepal.

The column with which Colonel Kelly left AZAMGARH on 18th October for the invasion of Oudh was as follows:—

> 20th Lancers (Jat Lancers).
> J Battery, Royal Artillery.
> Company of Royal Engineers.
> Company of Punjab Sappers.
> 1st Battalion The Border Regiment.
> 7th Punjab Infantry, with cavalry.

The companies at MAHARAJGANJ were brought in so that the Regiment marched complete. The undermentioned officers were present:—

> Captain Stafford.. .. ..Commandant.
> Lieutenant Gordon.... . .. 2nd-in-Command.
> Lieutenant Campbell........ ... " Doing duty ".
> Lieutenant Baillie .. ..Adjutant.
> Lieutenant Lewis .. . ." Doing duty ".
> Lieutenant Fitz G. Calogan.. .. .." Doing duty ".
> Assistant-Surgeon Hood.

Shortly afterwards Lieutenant Campbell was permitted to return to his own regiment, the 6th Bengal Europeans.

On reaching BAHRAMPUR the column split into two. The smaller part proceeded direct to AKBARPUR whence it turned south to establish touch at DOSTPUR with General Sir Hope Grant's parallel advance on the west. The main part, in which the Regiment was included, marched up the right bank of the GOGRA, drove the enemy across the river out of TANDA and halted at AKBARPUR on 30th October.

"Map 3."

The 7th Punjab Infantry were now transferred to the most easterly column, that from GORAKHPUR under Brigadier Rowcroft. This was marching across the BASTI District to converge with

Sir Hope Grant's troops who crossed the GOGRA at FYZABAD on 25th November in pursuit of the enemy. After crossing the river to BASTI the Regiment were ordered to follow after the column. En route the right wing under Lieutenant Gordon were left at DOMARIAGANJ to guard the bridge of boats over the RAPTI. The remainder of the Regiment halted 25 miles further on at SIMRI. Here they were included, together with two guns and the 2nd Battalion The Black Watch, in a separate command under Colonel Smith whose object was to secure the east flank of main operation. After the united forces of General Sir Hope Grant and Brigadier Rowcroft had defeated the rebels under Nana's brother, Bala Rao, at TULSIPUR on 23rd December and again on 4th January 1859 at KUNDA KOT over the Nepalese frontier, Colonel Smith's Field Force took up the role of preventing the fugitives from breaking back into Oudh. To this end it was employed during January 1859 in marching along the frontier. During February the force was based on a camp at DEKHARI, with the Regiment in two wing outposts. The detachment from DOMARIAGANJ was brought into the CHILIA outpost. It is recorded that many attempts by the half-starved mutineers to regain their home territory during this period were defeated by the vigilance of the Sherdils.

The Nepalese Tarai. The battle of RATANPURWA, 25th March 1859.

On 17th March the 7th Punjab Infantry were ordered to rejoin Brigadier Kelly's force which, by permission of the Nepalese authorities, was about to enter the Tarai. The remaining mutineers were now bottled up in this jungle-covered territory between the frontier line and the lofty DUNDWA Range, and the intention now was to drive them into those mountains.

Sketch 'C'

After concentrating at KHAJURIA on the frontier north of GORAKHPUR the undermentioned force marched at 4 p.m. on 25th March to attack a large concentration of rebels that was reported to be at JHARAIYA —

> 20th Lancers (Jat Lancers) (464 sabres).
> 'J' Field Battery Royal Artillery (4 guns).
> 1st Battalion The Somersetshire Light Infantry (200 bayonets).
> 3rd Battalion The Frontier Force Regiment (766 bayonets).
> 7th Punjab Infantry (4 British, 15 Native officers, 573 bayonets).

A halt was made at BETHARI while the cavalry reconnoitred

for the enemy without success. A cautious advance was then made through the dense jungle with the 3rd Battalion Frontier Force Regiment leading in extended order. At JHARAIYA villagers reported that the mutineers had moved back to BUTWAL at the foot of the hills. Owing to a misunderstanding the British infantry had omitted to bring cooked rations with them, so were left at JHARAIYA to cook a meal when the advance was resumed in the afternoon. This resulted in their being absent from the action which followed, in spite of their utmost efforts to arrive in time.

About 4 p.m. when near RATANPURWA and 3 miles short of BUTWAL the cavalry reported enemy ahead and to the left, so the 7th Punjab Infantry (less two companies) was deployed behind the 3rd Battalion Frontier Force Regiment with the battery on the left and one squadron of cavalry on each flank. The baggage was kept well back escorted by two companies of the Regiment and a troop of the Lancers.

Contact was made half a mile further on. The enemy infantry, afterwards found to number about 4,000, were holding a strong position along a series of mango topes with their west flank on a ridge and the east on the edge of very thick jungle. Artillery and cavalry, the latter totalling 1,200, were observed on both flanks. The mutineers were known to be under the command of Bala Rao. Artillery fire soon drove the enemy infantry out of the mango clumps into the intervening irrigation channels where they were engaged by the fire of the 3rd Battalion Frontier Force Regiment. Simultaneously a threat arose on both flanks from the determined efforts of enemy horsemen to reach the column's baggage. Their attack on the right was stopped by the fire of two companies of the 7th Punjab Infantry under Lieutenant Gordon who formed to the right to meet it; and this check was turned to a rout by the dashing charge of a squadron of 20th Lancers. The enemy movement on the left was thrown back by the charge of another squadron, which then wheeled inwards and captured the gun on the ridge. The line of infantry and remaining cavalry then advanced and drove the enemy back to the edge of the jungle. There the mutineers made a last stand, and inflicted a number of casualties, before renewed bombardment and a final assault by the 3rd Battalion Frontier Force Regiment and 7th Punjab Infantry scattered them in flight.

It was now 6 p.m. and too late for pursuit through the dense thickets. Besides, the troops were exhausted after 14 hours of marching and fighting in intense heat. Accordingly the force bivouacked at RATANPURWA with cavalry patrols observing the remnants of the mutineers. Camp fires indicated that they had retreated high up into the hills. They lost their 6 guns with 15 cartloads of ammunition; and judging alone by the numbers found in the open their total of dead and wounded must have been high. Casualties in the Column were 36, including 1 naick and 5 sepoys wounded in the Regiment. The Commandant, Captain Stafford, was brought to notice in the despatch on this operation.

The battle of BUTWAL, 28th March 1859.

Brigadier Kelly's force spent the next two days at RATANPURWA reconnoitring the enemy's dispositions and assimilating the reinforcements which arrived on 27th March. That evening they moved nearer to the hills, beyond BUTWAL. On the 28th they successfully attacked the mutineers and terminated all opposition in this part of the Tarai. *Sketch 'C'.*

First there was a night advance for four miles to the foot of the range. *En route* an enemy cavalry piquet was surprised and destroyed. Two attacking columns were then formed: the right under Captain Stafford comprised his own 7th Punjab Infantty with one company of The Somersetshire Light Infantry attached: the left column was composed of the 3rd Battalion Frontier Force Regiment and another company of the Somersets. At dawn the remainder of the force, namely Lahore Light Horse, 20th Lancers, Pathan Horse, three companies of the Somersetshire Light Infantry and The Border Regiment (less three companies guarding the camp), established a cordon of piquets along the lower slopes to prevent the enemy above breaking into the plain. As soon as it was light the columns advanced by two sets of parallel spurs and soon came upon the foremost enemy crouching among the bushes and rocks. The Regiment advanced with the forward companies extended, two companies supporting them close behind and the remainder in reserve. In spite of the steep slopes, growing resistance and increasing heat, a steady pace was maintained and the rebel skirmishers were driven back onto the higher spurs. Here serious resistance were met by both columns, and at one time the Regiment was completely held up by fire until the enemy's position was made untenable by the cross fire of the attached British company which Captain Stafford had moved to a commanding feature on the open flank. Towards midday the crest of the range was stormed and the remaining mutineers driven into the valley behind. Between 300 and 400 are thought to have been killed on this day. 6 elephants, 25 camels add 300 horses were captured together with many weapons of all sorts. Bala Rao escaped, but Nawab Mirza Nadir of LUCKNOW surrendered with 50 of his retainers.

The Regiment had the undermentioned casualties among

the force total of 5 killed and 10 wounded:

Killed	Wounded
Havildar Sham Singh.	Lieutenant Baillie.
„ Towrabaz Singh.	Jemadar Ahmedjee.
Naick Jewn Singh.	Havildar Kimega.
Sepoy Jangi.	Sepoy Mahe Singh.
	„ Sahib Singh.
	„ Gunga Singh.
	„ Hazrao Shah.
	„ Shurufdeen.

Captain Stafford, Lieutenant Gordon and Lieutenant Baillie were mentioned in despatches. Subadar Esur Sing, Subadar Subaz Sing, Jemadar Ahmedjee and Jemadar Lalloo also received mentions and subsequently were awarded the Indian Order of Merit, 3rd Class.

After this action Brigadier Kelly's force was withdrawn from the Tarai and broken up. The Regiment returned whence it had come, to Colonel Smith's frontier force which was now in camp at TULSIPUR.

The Action of JARWA PASS, 20th May 1859.

"Map 3."

On 11th May 1859 the 7th Punjab Infantry were transferred to the force which Major-General Sir Hope Grant was assembling to attack Nana Sahib and Bala Rao in their final position in the JARWA PASS just over the Nepalese frontier north of TULSIPUR. By 20th May the force was within striking distance. An early advance was made on that day to the DUNDWA Range. There Sir Hope Grant left the rest of his force as a block to prevent the mutineers breaking back into Oudh and with only the 7th Punjab Infantry entered the narrow pass. The enemy made little resistance on the position they were holding and were soon in retirement. In the course of the day they were driven completely over the 2,000 foot pass and down into the DEOKHOR VALLEY on the north side where the remnants dispersed. The enemy lost their remaining 2 guns, about 50 killed and a considerable number of wounded, some of whom were captured. The Regiment bivouacked on the spot and next day, after the General had inspected the foremost positions gained, withdrew through the pass into Indian territory. Sir Hope Grant's force was then broken up. Further skirmishes occurred with small rebel bands in the Nepal jungles, in Bundelkand and in Central India; but the action at JARWA was the final clearing of Oudh and virtually the end of the Mutiny Campaign.

The 7th Punjab Infantry were now ordered to return to the Punjab, and after having been in tents and on continuous active service for two years marched into JULLUNDUR Cantonment in July 1859. The Regiment were welcomed by Sir John Lawrence in these words written to Captain Stafford:—
"The Lieutenant-Governor is glad to find that the 7th Punjab Infantry is now, or shortly will be, returning to the Punjab. Sir John Lawrence has viewed with the utmost satisfaction the exemplary conduct of all ranks in the Regiment since its first formation and departure from the Punjab in July 1857. The Regiment has been continuously in the field since that period and has not once troubled the Lieutenant-Governor with a request to be allowed to return, whatever anxiety they may have felt to be allowed to do so. This alone the Lieutenant-Governor considers to be most creditable to all ranks, as well as to yourself and your European Officers".

In common with the other units loyally engaged, all ranks of the Regiment were awarded The Mutiny Medal and six months extra batta.

CHAPTER IV.

1859—1865.

JULLUNDUR—MEERUT—GWALIOR—AGRA—ALIGARH

(Maps 1, 2 and 3.)

The 7th Punjab Infantry remained peacefully at JULLUNDUR for two years. It was not involved in any of the external campaigns of that period, i.e., against the Kabul Khel Wazirs in December 1859, against the Mahsuds in the following year, in China in 1860, or in the Sikkim Expedition of 1860-61. The time was, however, one of administrative activity, as might be expected after the hectic events and hurried developments of the Indian Mutiny.

From 1st November 1858 Queen Victoria had assumed the direct Government of India, and the East India Company practically ceased to exist. It was decided that the Company's European troops should form part of the Imperial Army. Next year, in 1861, the reorganization of Indian units was undertaken by the New Commander-in-Chief, General Sir Hugh Rose. All cavalry regiments except three became silladar; Indian artillery was almost entirely abolished; in addition to those old units which had been disbanded for disloyalty many new corps were broken up. Among these were the Punjab Infantry numbered 10 to 14. The system of three Presidency Armies was continued. The Punjab Frontier Force was borne on the rolls of the Bengal Army, but remained under the control of the Punjab Government.

From 3rd May 1861 the Regiment was redesignated the "23rd Regiment of Bengal Native Infantry". On 29th October, however, a renumbering was ordered so as to exclude Gurkha units, and under this the Regiment became the "19th (Punjab) Regiment of Native Infantry" in the Bengal Army. Simultaneously strengths were reduced. While other Bengal corps retained ten companies each reduced to 70, Punjab Infantry reverted to an organization of eight companies, each of 1 subadar, 1 jemadar, 5 havildars, 5 naiks, 2 drummers and 75 privates. The "non-effective native staff" comprised the subadar-major, drill havildar, drill naik, 8 colour havildars, 8 pay havildars, drum-major, fife-major and 2 "native doctors "—a total regimental strength of 735.

The brass band which had been formed during the operations in Oudh was now officially recognized as from 1st November 1858. An Officers' Mess had always existed, since the Regiment had passed its first two years under canvas. But it is interesting to note that in the old Bengal Army officers' messes were only instituted in the year before the Mutiny.

The establishment of Britsh officers in infantry regiments was reduced to six. The staff pay allowed in addition to pay of rank was as follows :—

Commandant Rs. 600 per mensem: Senior Wing Commandant Rs. 270 plus 80 for the repair of arms in the four companies: Junior Wing Commandant Rs. 230 plus the same allowance: Adjutant Rs. 100 plus 50 for office upkeep: Quartermaster Rs. 150 plus an allowance for tent repair. The sixth was the medical officer. This number of officers proved insufficient even in peace time, and first (in 1863) one "doing duty officer", and then (in 1865) another, were introduced.

Hitherto all Indian Service officers had been on the strength of the various regiments, and the consequent anomalies and inequalities in promotion had been greatly accentuated by expansion during the Mutiny. Now three Presidency Staff Corps were created, on the general lists of which all officers were to be borne and receive promotion according to vacancies in the Corps establishment. Recruitment to the Corps was from British Service officers of at least 3 years service and qualified in Urdu. The tenure of regimental command and staff appointments was fixed at 5 years.

In 1864 the class composition of the 19th Punjab Native Infantry was redefined as "Punjab" Musalmans and Trans-Sutlej Sikhs in nearly equal proportions, with a few Dogras. The only change apparent from the composition of 1857 was some increase in Musalmans and the elimination of the few Gurkhas from among the Dogras. The minimum height standard for recruits was fixed at 5 feet 3 inches, and the age limits at 20-35 years. In the same year Good Conduct Pay was introduced at rupees one and two per mensem after six and ten years' service respectively. In these days the pay of Indian Officers was not uniform in each rank. Thus, two subadars each received rupees 100 per mensem, two 80 and four 67; the four senior jemadars were paid 35 and the remainder 30.

Full dress uniform of red with blue facings was now adopted by the Regiment. The lace worn by officers was white. The khaki service uniform which Punjab regiments had always worn was introduced universally in 1860. In that year also came the grant to Indian ranks of furlough, i. e., long hot-weather leave with free travel. But this was limited to 10% of the strength each year.

A welcome reform was the increase of the summary powers of Commanding Officers so as to avoid resource to all but the highest form of Courts Martial. "The Commander-in-Chief trusts that the extensive powers now conveyed to Commanding Officers will be temperately and judiciously exercised to the advancement of the discipline and character of the Native Army." It should be noted that at this date corporal punishment was still allowed. As early as 1827 it had been abolished, except when accompanied by dismissal for the more serious crimes; but in 1845, following mutinies in the Bengal Army, it had been re-introduced.

There were many changes in officers after the Mutiny. From April 1859 Captain Stafford was promoted Brevet Major for his services in the campaign. Lieutenant Gordon left India with his British unit, The Gloucestershire Regiment. Lieutenant Baillie became Senior Wing Commander in his place. Lieutenant Baillie also acted as "Station Interpreter" at JULLUNDUR, and officiated for a while as the "Major of Brigade". Lieutenant A. Copland, a brother officer of Major Stafford in the old 41st Native Infantry, came to the Regiment in 1859 and was appointed Adjutant. Lieutenant Vander Gucht went to the Home Department at CALCUTTA and was replaced by Lieutenant S.C. Mctieve from the 24th Punjab Infantry (the present 4th Battalion). Lieutenant H.A. Lewes left after three years with the Regiment, and Lieutenant Campbell who had been attached from the 6th Europeans resigned his appointment. Assistant Surgeon C. Prentis took the place of Assistant Surgeon Hood who had served with the Regiment during the greater part of the Mutiny. Subadar Sirbaz Khan was appointed Subadar-Major from 1st June 1861, and Subadar Subaz Singh, I.O.M., became Native Adjutant in his stead. Jemadar Ahmadjee, I.O.M. of BUTWAL fame, was promoted Subadar on the death of Esur Singh, I.O.M.

British officers came and went on leave. A contemporary order on this subject is of interest. "The Commander-in-Chief requests that officers in command of divisions and brigades exercise some moderation in the grant of privilege leave. In a few instances it has recently occurred that regiments have been rendered inefficient by the abuse of the privilege. Officers have been allowed to leave their corps when beyond all doubt their applications would have been refused at Headquarters had a reference been made. Another abuse has also crept in. It sometimes happens that when general leave for an officer is impossible owing to the paucity of officers with his regiment he obtains privilege leave, makes a very long journey, and at the expiry of the two months asks for general leave of absence on the grounds of the distance he has to travel, the expense to which he has been put, and the inability under which he labours to return to his regiment within the limit prescribed by his original leave of absence. The Commander-in-Chief desires that it may be fairly understood he will not in future yield to such solicitations, and officers overstaying their privilege leave will have to submit to the penalties of such irregularity".

Another order shows that officers were expected to wear uniform at all times in public : "It has been brought to the notice of the Commander-in-Chief that, owing to the long protracted field service in which the Army has been engaged during the last two years, a great laxity has come to be a habit amongst the officers of the Army as regards dress, uniform, etc. Officers in command of divisions, brigades and regiments will therefore be good enough to insist on officers appearing dressed in uniform in places of public resort, according to orders applicable to the season, the sword being worn on all occasions with uniform. This rule is not to interfere with the dress of officers when they may be engaged in sport, or during their morning rides when off duty".

On 19th May 1861, a few days after its first change of designation, the Regiment marched out of JULLUNDUR and on 14th June arrived at MEERUT to take the place of disbanded 13th Punjab Infantry. As MEERUT was one of the cantonments where great damage had been done to buildings by the mutineers of 1857, it may be remarked that under the "Hutting Regulations" now introduced units were expected to build and repair their own accommodation from a special allowance for that purpose. Living quarters were to be constructed as separate huts, one for each infatry section and arranged in the "lines" which have ever since given that name to Indian troops' barracks. Guardrooms, magazines, bells-of-arms and hospitals continued to be built by Government.

"Map 2."

Just before the move of the Regiment Lieutenant Baillie left to take up an appointment after nearly 4 years of distinguished duty. He was replaced as second-in-command temporarily by Captain A. B. Fenwick, and from 1st August 1862 by Captain J. Ruggles, from the old 41st Native Infantry. Captain Ruggles, who was promoted Major in June of 1865, was destined to become the first Colonel of the Regiment.

On 15th October 1862 the 19th Punjab Infantry was relieved at MEERUT and marched to GWALIOR. From AGRA the Regiment acted as escort to the Commander-in-Chief, and with him reached MORAR, the cantonment of GWALIOR, on 24th November. Five days later there was a parade inspection by General Sir Hugh Rose who reported as follows : "The Commander-in-Chief was extremely pleased with the efficiency and military appearance of the Corps. His Excellency is much pleased by the care bestowed by Major Stafford on the instruction and interior economy of this Regiment, as shown by their general conduct when forming his escort and their performance on parade".

On 15th September 1863 the 19th Punjab Infantry were relieved at GWALIOR and marched to ALIGARH. Except for an advanced party, however, the Regiment were detained for the cold weather at AGRA and did not reach their destination until 7th April 1864. Then followed a quiet year in ALIGARH, while in Bhutan there developed the crisis which was shortly to take the Regiment there. A company detachment was found at FATEHGARH, where the 7th Punjab Native Infantry had been on service exactly six years before.

In February 1863 Lieutenant J. E. Waller and W. H. Meiklejohn had joined from the general list of the Staff Corps. Early in 1864 there came Lieutenant C. H. Bergman from the disbanded 60th Native Infantry, and Lieutenant W. A. Garden from the 39th.

CHAPTER V

THE BHUTAN WAR, 1865–66

(Maps 1 and 4. Sketch D).

In February 1865 the Regiment was ordered to take part in the Bhutan Campaign which then entered its second phase. Before narrating what ensued a short account of the country, its people and the origins of the war will be given.

The independent country of Bhutan extends for 220 miles along the Himalaya mountains. To the south lies Assam and the protected state of Cooch Behar; to the north is Tibet. The inhabitants of Bhutan and Tibet are both Mongolians, and are racially identical. Tibet is locally known as Bot; and Bhutan is a corruption of Botistan, "the country of the Tibetans". Indeed the Bhutiahs—as the hillmen are called—are supposed to be the descendants of a Tibetan military expedition which remained in the country and acquired independence. The spiritual ruler of Bhutan is the Dharma Rajah, while as temporal head there is a Deb Rajah who exercises some measure of control through the governors (Penlows) of Provinces and the governors (Jungpens) of Forts. In 1864 the virtual ruler of the country was the Penlow of Tongsoo.

"Map 4."

With the exception of a strip of low ground from 10 to 20 miles wide adjoining India, the country is entirely mountainous. Communication with the interior of Bhutan is through a number of mountain passes called Dooars, which name has come to be applied also to the frontier plain.

For many years past the Bhutiahs had marauded the people across their southern border, raiding especially into Assam. Yet the military resources of the country were unsignificant. But for a few hundred men distributed among the stockaded forts which guarded the Dooar passes there was no organized force, no semblance of an army. Weapons consisted of matchlocks, bows, catapults, heavy swords and large knives. Some fighting men wore chain armour or iron helmets, and carried circular leather shields. In their personal bearing, however, the Bhutiahs established in this campaign a reputation for individual courage which before had been underestimated.

By assuming control of Assam the British Government incurred the legacy of its relations with Bhutan. The arrangements undertaken for the rule of certain frontier Dooars, the execution of financial settlements and the frequent incursions by Bhutiahs were constant sources of dispute during the next 60 years. Early in 1864 a Mission was sent to settle outstanding differences with the Deb and Dharma Rajahs. The Mission was inhospitably treated and with difficulty reached the capital, after becoming separated from the greater part of its escort. At POONAKHA its members were insulted and kept in virtual detention. The leader, Mr. Eden, was threatened and eventually compelled to sign an impudent treaty. As a result of this outrage the British Government decided to annex the Dooar passes and the plains between DEWANGIRI and DHALIMKOT.

Accordingly in December 1864 four columns entered Bhutan. The Right Column secured DEWANGIRI, left a garrison there and withdrew. The Right Centre Column occupied BISSENGIRI without opposition. The Left Centre Column captured first BUXA FORT and then the BALA PASS. The Left Column from JALPAIGURI took DHALIMKOT after some resistance, and finally CHAMURCHI.

The Bhutiahs had not calculated on the British putting their threats into effect and were unable to offer any organized opposition at the time. Nevertheless the Penlow of TONGSOO devised surprisingly rapid and effective arrangements for rallying the best of the fighting men, obtaining help from Tibet and organizing a counter-offensive. At the end of January 1865 when the Field Force was about to disperse and leave the Bengal Police Battalion in charge the Bhutiahs launched concerted attacks on all the main posts. At DEWANGIRI five thousand Bhutiahs invested the garrison from commanding positions, and five days later compelled them to withdraw for lack of ammunition and water. Two guns had to be abandoned. The attacks on BISSENGIRI and CHAMURCHI were however repulsed, while the BALA PASS was successfully defended for a while. The disaster at DEWANGIRI was the prime factor in deciding the Government to extend the campaign.

Additional troops were at once ordered to join the Bhutan Field Force, namely two batteries, the 2nd Battalion The Border Regiment, the 19th (Punjab) Regiment of Bengal Native Infantry, the 10th Battalion 15th Punjab Regiment and the 2nd Battalion 16th Punjab Regiment. The augmented force was reorganized into two brigades.

The Regiment, including the detachment withdrawn from FATEHGARH, left ALIGARH by train on 17th February 1865. The following British officers accompanied:—

Major J. F. Stafford	Commandant.
Captain J. Ruggles	2nd-in-Command and Wing officer.
Lieutenant W. A. Garden	Wing officer.
Lieutenant A. Copland	Adjutant.
Lieutenant C. H. Bergman	Quartermaster.
Lieutenant J. E. Waller	"Doing duty officer".
Lieutenant J. H. Baldwin	"Doing duty officer".
Lieutenant W. H. Meiklejohn	"Doing duty officer".

Assistant-Surgeon J. Richardson joined *en route* on 12th March.

The Regiment detrained at COLGONG on 21st February, crossed the GANGES by ferry next day and marched to reach JALPAIGURI on 7th March. After crossing the TEESTA RIVER by pontoon bridge at PAHARPUR they continued through the low and unhealthy country of the Western Dooars, and then up the LAKHI DOOAR to join the Left Brigade in camp below the BALA PASS on 14th March. Already here were the 5th Mountain Battery (three Armstrong guns), the 6th Battery (2·8-inch mortars), one company of Sappers and Miners, a wing of the 10th Battalion 9th Jat Regiment and the 1st Battalion 16th Punjab Regiment. Brigadier-General Fraser-Tytler waited only for the arrival of the Sherdils before starting the offensive which he had planned.

The assault on the BALA PASS-15th March 1865.

The original attack on the pass by the Bhutiahs had taken place on 27th January. The detachment of the 10th Battalion 7th Rajput Regiment then garrisoning the summit resisted gallantly for eight days, while the enemy proceeded to build, and snipe from, their own stockaded post on higher ground. A counter-attack by the rest of the Rajputs on 4th February failed, whereupon the whole battalion was withdrawn from the pass. The enemy then occupied the British stockade, strengthened their own post and constructed two more.

"Sketch 'D'."

The plan for capturing this position was to deliver the main attack on the west flank, which the enemy might be expected to imagine was secured by the RIVER TORSA, while a frontal attack played a diverting role. Thus the first objective became a prominent wooded knoll on the long spur of BALA HILL which descended beyond the enemy's right flank to the river. Separating this knoll from the Bhutiahs main post on the summit of the hill was a saddle on which stood the original stockade of TAZIGONG. There were innumerable branch spurs of great steepness all thickly covered with bush. Below were gorges filled with streams now greatly swollen by rain.

The flank attack column under Brigadier-General Fraser-Tytler consisted of the 19th Punjab Native Infantry (600 rifles) and one company of the Jats accompanied by a section of Sappers and Miners, one section of 6-pounder guns and one of 5½-inch mortars. In order to deceive the enemy these troops marched some miles south in daylight and then, unseen, crossed to a position of assembly on the right bank of the river. Starting again at 7 p.m. the column moved to the village of SANTARABANI three miles upstream. This village had just previously been surrounded so as to ensure secrecy. Leaving SANTARABANI at midnight the column crept silently up the river bank for another eight miles, round the bend in the river close to the enemy's position and then west to a ford which had already been reconnoitred. The river was crossed at daylight, and the climb up the spur begun. The night had been dark, the river deep and the ascent from the left bank was both steep and rough. Thus it was not till 11 a.m. on 15th March that the Regiment was in position on the knoll, and the guns in action from as near as they could get. The frontal force had long been in contact with the enemy. They had crept forward at dawn to the foot of the pass and seized the two lower stockades which the enemy had omitted to hold during the night. The other two posts above were obviously defended. The higher, on the summit of BALA HILL, was a formidable work. It consisted of a large sangar with 20 foot long palisades backed with stone walls four feet thick and fitted with loopholes.

Both groups of artillery bombarded these posts for a few minutes and caused some damage. At about 11-15 a.m. the flank attack was launched down the slope of the knoll towards the saddle. One wing of the Regiment swarmed straight at TAZIGONG, the other with the company of Jats swept past it up BALA HILL. It was the finest rush, so said Brigadier-General Tytler, that he had ever seen; and it appeared to surprise the enemy. An entrance was quickly forced into TAZIGONG, and the defenders driven out, killed or captured. But the upper stockade had to be scaled, and this was achieved only with difficulty. Havildar Prem Singh of the Regiment was the first over the top, and was wounded. A short struggle within this post disposed of all the enemy and completed the capture of the pass.

Those Bhutiahs who escaped fled down the reverse slope and, except for a party who returned to bury their 44 dead, were no more seen. Casualties in the force were 3 NCOs and men of the Regiment killed with 10 wounded, the Brigade Major and 9 men of the Jats being also wounded. After the action the 19th Punjab Native Infantry were left to hold the position while the rest of the Column returned to camp.

During this attack and for some time afterwards the Regiment was commanded by Captain Ruggles, since Major Stafford had fallen ill on the line of march from the GANGES and was unable to leave camp. The good work of the Sherdils was officially commended as follows in a telegram which Sir Hugh Rose the Commander-in-Chief sent immediately on receiving Brigadier-General Fraser-Tytler's dispatch on the operation. "I thank you and your gallant troops, especially the 19th under Captain Ruggles, for their good and gallant service". Another telegram stated: "The Government of India desires to join in the commendation expressed by His Excellency the Commander-in-Chief at the gallant conduct of the officers and troops engaged in the recapture of the BALA PASS on the 15th March, especially of those officers mentioned in the margin of your letter. The Government of India will gladly confer the Order of Merit on Havildar Prem Singh, 19th Punjab Native Infantry, and on any other soldiers who may have distinguished themselves should His Excellency the Commander-in-Chief desire to recommend them for this distinction." Havildar Prem Singh died of his wounds before he could receive the decoration. Other awards were as follows:—

Indian Order of Merit, 2nd Class
Subadar Ahmedjee.
Indian Order of Merit, 3rd Class
Havildar Fazulla.
Naick Hira.
Sepoy Bhugwan Singh.
Sepoy Muhammad Akram.

Conclusion of the campaign.

Brigadier-General Fraser-Tytler's brigade, less the 19th Punjab Native Infantry, marched next to BUXA. On its arrival the enemy abandoned the posts which they had held since 26th January against the 1st/3rd Gurkha Rifles. At CHAMURCHI next day the Bhutiahs fled as soon as the artillery of the Brigade opened fire.

On the same day, 24th March, the Right Brigade from

KAMRIKATA captured the DARANGA PASS. On 2nd April they stormed DEWANGIRI with a loss to the enemy of 130 killed and 120 wounded. This concluded the fighting in Bhutan, but long delay occurred before peace was attained. In negotiations with the Bhutiahs the surrender of the two guns originally lost at DEWANGIRI was insisted on, and to this the Penlow of TONGSOO was slow to agree. In the meantime, for supply reasons, most of the troops were withdrawn into the Dooars, where they were much afflicted during the hot weather by cholera and malaria. On the other hand, the Regiment by remaining in the BALA PASS suffered from the uncertainty of supply, stormy weather and insufficient protection in bivouac. On 15th May the Sherdils withdrew from BALA HILL after destroying what remained of the enemy defences, and on 23rd reached JULPESH on the old frontier 12 miles east of JALPAIGURI.

At the end of the hot weather an advance into the interior of Bhutan was decided on in order to accelerate a settlement. The Regiment left JULPESH for BUXA on 26th October with the Left Brigade, and on 2nd November entered Bhutan proper. Major Stafford was once more in command. Lieutenant E. W. Smyth joined on 31st October and Lieutenant J. Finnis on 2nd December. From 3rd November the Brigade was halted at TABZIL on the route to POONAKHA while the troops improved the road for guns. Early in February 1866 the Right Brigade also advanced from DEWANGIRI until brought to a halt on the MONAS RIVER by transport difficulties. On 23rd February the Bhutiahs brought in the British guns, and after this the Field Force was quickly withdrawn to India.

The Regiment left TABZIL on 1st March, and following the same route as taken from ALIGARH returned to that station on 20 March 1866. All ranks who had taken part in the campaign were granted the India Medal with the Clasp for Bhutan. For his special war services Captain Ruggles was promoted to brevet-major, with seniority from 13th June 1865.

CHAPTER VI

1866-1878

ALIGARH—PESHAWAR—TALAGANG—MULTAN

(Maps 1 and 6).

These were exceptionally quiet years for the 19th Punjab Native Infantry in a period of numerous campaigns. Two battalions of the Bengal Army took part in the Abyssinian War of 1867-68, and two in the expedition to Malta of the latter year. 1868 also brought the first Black Mountain Campaign in which the present 2nd and 4th Battalions of the Regiment participated. The Lushai Expedition of 1871 involved the 3rd Battalion. Both the 2nd and 3rd Battalions were included in the operations of 1877-78 against the Afridis of the JOWAKI SALIENT.

The stay of the Regiment at ALIGARH and FATEHGARH was interrupted for the month of November 1867 by escort duty at AGRA, where the Governal-General held a Durbar. "Map 1."

The subsequent relief move to PESHAWAR, due to begin on 15th October 1868, was advanced so as to permit of the Regiment acting as reserve to the Hazara Field Force while passing through RAWALPINDI. Marching out of ALIGARH on 30th August they reached RAWALPINDI on 20th October. In fact, the brief Black Mountain campaign was by then already finished. The march was resumed on 7th November and PESHAWAR reached eight days later.

This was the Regiment's first appearance on the North-West Frontier of the Punjab, and it was not long before some active experience was gained. On 25th February 1869 a force set out from KOHAT to punish the Bizoti Orakzais of the KOHAT PASS. In order to divert the tribesmen's attention another force moved out from PESHAWAR and in this the 19th Punjab Native Infantry were included. After assembling previously at FORT MACKESON this column entered the PASS from that end on the day of the operation and co-operated with the KOHAT troops. No casualty was incurred, and on the following day the column returned to PESHAWAR. "Map 6."

During these two years on the Frontier the enlistment of Trans-Indus Pathans was begun and the strength of this class rose to 170. Simultaneously the Hindustanees, of whom 64 has been admitted in 1862 from the cadre of Lieutenant-Colonel Stafford's old regiment, were allowed to waste. Dogras too decreased owing to the difficulty of recruiting them from PESHAWAR and before many years this class lapsed from the Regiment until restored in 1921. It is interesting to note that although the Band and Drums were now over twelve years old a couple of European drummers were still included in the establishment.

While at PESHAWAR Lieutenant-Colonel Ruggles, then second-in-command, painted an interesting picture which now hangs in the Officers' Mess. It shows a Muhammadan havildar in the full dress of 1870. The scarlet tunic is split in Highland fashion immediately below the belt buckle and has brass buttons. Shoulder straps and facings at the cuffs and under the buttons are dark blue. Pantaloons are of the same colour. The dark blue lungi is worn with a red khula and a gold fringe. The waistbelt is white with a gilt buckle. Contrary to present practice the havildar's crimson sash is worn over the left shoulder.

"Map 1." The Regiment left PESHAWAR on relief on 23rd October 1871 and, marching via ATTOCK and CAMPBELLPORE, arrived at TALAGANG on 3rd November. In this since-abondoned cantonment of the Sind Sagar Doab the 19th Punjab Native Infantry passed the next four years. In the winters of 1872 the 1873 the Regiment went to camp training at HASSAN ABDAL and RAWALPINDI, respectively, and there gained experience in brigade manoeuvres which before long was to be put into practice in Afghanistan. During 1874 a wing detachment was provided in ATTOCK FORT.

These were years of considerable administrative change. The number of British officers was fixed at seven. The junior rank of ensign was abolished and that of sub-lieutenant substituted. The time scale for promotion was:—Lieutenant after 1 year, Captain after 12 years, Major after 20, Lieutenant-Colonel after 26 and Brevet-Colonel after 5 years as substantive Lieutenant-Colonel. The monthly pay of junior Subadars was raised to Rs. 80 and that of the two grades of Jemadar to Rs. 50 and Rs. 40. The retiring pensions of Indian ranks were:—Subadar-Major Rs. 25; Subadar Rs. 20: Jemadar Rs. 15: Havildar and Naik Rs. 7: Sepoys Rs. 4: and followers Rs. 3. The personal allowance for the Subadar-Major was instituted; at this date it was Rs. 25 monthly and was known as brevet pay. Good conduct pay of Re. 1, Rs. 2 and Rs. 3 was awarded to sepoys after 3, 9 and 15 years' service respectively. Men still served for as long as they were physically fit.

In full dress the Zouave tunic with slashed cuffs was introduced, and for a while puttees were substituted for white gaiters. In 1870 khaki drill was discarded for white as the hot weather uniform; but four years later khaki returned to favour. A sepoy received Rs. 4 yearly for the upkeep of his clothing.

In 1870 the Enfield rifle was issued in place of the percussion musket with which the Regiment had hitherto been armed. This was the rifle which had caused the controversy of the greased cartridges at the beginning of the Mutiny. Five years later, however, the Regiment was re-equipped with the Snider.

So far the Regiment had known but one Commandant. Lieutenant-Colonel Stafford was promoted from brevet to substantive rank in October 1868 and shortly afterwards fell ill. He was in England on long sick leave from 1870 to 1872. He spent the hot weather of 1874 in MURREE, SIMLA, and MUSSOORIE, but his health did not improve. Granted another two years' sick leave ex-India in 1875 he felt compelled to resign from 17th September of that year. He had served for 30 years, including 18 years as Commandant of the Regiment which he had raised. Lieutenant-Colonel Ruggles followed in command, but only for a year. He was promoted brevet-colonel in June of 1876 and retired in September with the honorary rank of Major-General. Besides serving with the Regiment in Bhutan, General Ruggles had taken part in the defence of LUCKNOW during the Mutiny and had fought in China. His medals are displayed in the Officers' Mess. Colonel E. B. Clay of the Staff Corps was then brought in as Commandant. He retired as an honorary Major-General on the last day of 1879, and was followed in command by Lieutenant-Colonel Copland.

Captain Bergman went home on a year's leave in 1871 and was again in England in 1875-76, this time on medical certificate. Major Copland took two years' leave to Europe in 1874. Sub-Lieutenant H. A. Sawyer joined in 1871 and almost immediately took over the Adjutancy vacated by Captain Bergman. Lieutenant D. E. Gouldsbury was the next arrival, in 1872. He at once became Quartermaster and two years later Adjutant. Lieutenant H. T. Faithful, who joined in December 1877, was Adjutant throughout the Afghan War described in the next chapter.

The names of the sixteen Indian Officers first appear in the Indian Army List of 1877. Boodh Singh who had become Subadar-Major during the Bhutan Campaign was invalided in May 1876. Urjoon Singh, who succeeded and was appointed to the Order of British India in the following year, served until the end of first phase of the Afghan War. Subadar Ahmedjee, I. O. M., and Subadar

Futteh Singh were invalided as a result of Bhutan. Jemadar Ameer Khan became the first Jemadar Adjutant in October 1876.

In the autumn of 1875 came a change of station to MULTAN. Headquarters and the right wing under Lieutenant-Colonel Ruggles marched out of TALAGANG on 1st November and arrived on 24th. Captain Waller, who in the absence of Major Copland and Captain Bergman acted as 2nd-in-Command, followed with the other wing in April 1876.

Colours were now authorised for the nineteen battalions of the Bengal Army which were raised during the Mutiny, and were presented to the Regiment at MULTAN in 1876. These Colours, which were replaced in 1908, are now preserved in the Officers' Mess. The King's Colour was a Union Jack with "XIX" in gold in the centre and the Imperial Crown above. The Regimental Colour was dark blue. In the inner top corner was a golden "XIX" encircled by a wreath and the words "REGIMENT, PUNJAB NATIVE INFANTRY". Five years later battle honours were to be added on a scroll below, viz. "AHMED KHEL" and "AFGHANISTAN 1878-80". That campaign was now impending.

On 1st January there occurred an event which has been annually commemorated ever since. Before 17,000 troops at the DELHI Assembly Her Majesty Queen Victoria was proclaimed Empress of India.

CHAPTER VII.

THE SECOND AFGHAN WAR, 1878-80.

(Map 5 : Sketches E, F, G.)

The treaty of peace concluded between the East India Company and the Amir of Afghanistan just before the Indian Mutiny was loyally kept until Dost Muhammad's death in 1863. During the period of civil strife which then ensued in Afghanistan Sher Ali Khan—the son who had established himself on the throne—became more and more embittered against the Government of India because of their policy of impartiality and non-interference across the border. His hostility eventually led him to a pro-Russian attitude; and when in 1878, after consistently refusing to receive a British envoy, he ostentatiously welcomed an ambassador from the country with which Great Britain's relations were then strained it was decided to present an ultimatum to the Amir and to prepare for a campaign against him.

One of these preparations was the raising of infantry establishments to 800 sepoys, i.e., by 200, thus making 912 Indian ranks in all. Another was the immediate reinforcement of the small garrison at QUETTA. Thus it came about that the 19th Punjab Native Infantry received orders for QUETTA on 24th September and marched from MULTAN 5 days later.

The following officers accompanied the Regiment :—

Colonel E. B. Clay	Commandant.
Major A. Copland	2nd-in-Command and Wing Commander.
Brevet Lieutenant-Colonel C. H. Bergman	Wing Commander.
Captain J. E. Waller	Quartermaster
Captain W. H. Browne	Wing Officer
Captain D. E. Gouldsbury	Wing Officer
Lieutenant W. S. Hewett	Wing Officer
Lieutenant H. T. Faithful	Adjutant
Lieutenant W. S. Marshall	Wing Officer
Surgeon J. Mullane	Medical Officer
Subadar-Major Urjoon Singh	O. B. I.

Subadars	Kehr Singh
	Zamin Shah
	Kazem
	Kapoorah
	Elahie Bakhsh
	Churn Singh
Jemadars	Nehal Singh
	Ameer Khan—Jemadar Adjutant
	Sham Singh
	Sher Ali
	Atta Muhd. Khan
	Muhd. Gool Khan
	Shah Beg
	Ursulla

Lieutenant A. J. Brander remained at MULTAN in command of the depot.

The march lay across the INDUS to DERA GHAZI KHAN, down the west bank of the river RAJANPUR, across the BUGTI HILS to SIBI and thence up the BOLAN PASS. QUETTA was reached on 4th November. The Regiment was followed along this route by a stream of troops and stores from the Bengal Army. Madras and Bombay Army contingents concentrated via the port of KARACHI and the railhead base of SUKKUR.

It should be explained that in those days the CHENAB River near MULTAN could only be crossed by ferry; there was no railway crossing of the INDUS at SUKKUR or elsewhere, and the west bank railway from KARACHI extended only to SIBI at the foot of the BOLAN PASS. In the north the railhead was at JHELUM. It should also be realized that the vaguely defined Afghan frontier was then approximately the same as India's present-day administrative border. The whole of the KHYBER PASS and the KURRAM VALLEY were Afghan. QUETTA was on the very frontier, the KHOJAK PASS as well as the PESHIN VALLEY and the SIBI District being in Afghanistan.

"Map 5." The plan of campaign devised by the Commander-in-Chief, Sir Fredrick Haines, and put into action immediately after the expiry of the ultimatum on 22nd November was as follows. The main army, Lieutenant-General Sir Sam Browne's Peshawar Valley Field Force which included the 2nd Battalion of the Regiment (20th Punjab Native Infantry), was to advance by the KHYBER PASS to the JELALABAD area. The Kurram Valley Field Force under Major-General F. S. Roberts and including the present 10th Battalion (21st Punjab Native Infantry) was to move over the PEIWAR KOTAL. Advancing from QUETTA the Kandahar Field Force under Lieutenant-General D. M. Stewart was to occupy Southern Afghanistan.

It may be of interest to mention some of the administrative arrangements made for Indian troops in this campaign. Their appalling sufferings in the 1st Afghan War had been taken to heart and many welfare improvements made; but much still remained to be desired. A greatcoat or poshteen was now provided, also balaclava cap, jersey, mittens, waterproof sheet and two pairs of socks, but one blanket was still considered sufficient for the rigours of the Afghan winter. Tentage was carried; but the scale, even in the hot weather, was 44 men to a double tent, and the only provision for followers was "condemned mattress covers". The ration, which was distributed through the regimental buniah, comprised ata, dhall, ghi and salt. Meat was issued only on payment. A firewood ration was sanctioned for KABUL, but elsewhere fuel had to be gathered or purchased. Medical arrangements in the field were entirely regimental. Doolies, dandies and camel kajawahs were provided for the sick at the scale of 5 per cent. of strength. 70 rounds of Snider rifle ammunition were carried on the man.

Southern Afghanistan—First campaign, 1878-79.

The Kandahar Field Force eventually increased to 12,864 all ranks and became the strongest in gun power; but when the Regiment reached QUETTA the garrison only numbered 1,808, and practically all of the requirements of an advanced base were lacking. The next month and a half were spent in organizing the 2nd Division, under Major-General Biddulph, in administrative arrangements and in reconnoitring as far as KUCHLAK which then marked the frontier. The Regiment was allotted to the 1st Brigade. Meanwhile the 1st (Quetta) Division was making its way up the BOLAN PASS.

"Map 5."

On 24th November 1878, two days after the declaration of war, the 2nd Division entered the PESHIN VALLEY. Headquarters and the Right Wing of the Regiment were included in a temporary formation under Colonel Clay which led this advance as far as HAIKALZAI. The remainder of the Division closed up on 27th November and began to improve the KHOJAK and GWAJHA PASS routes over the AMRAN Range. The wing 19th Punjab Native Infantry, however, was detailed to a force of all arms which now set out from the PESHIN VALLEY to reconnoitre the little-known CHOTIALI route to FORT MUNRO and DERA GHAZI KHAN. This force proceeded as far as LORALAI. On return headquarters and a wing of the Regiment were located successively at KHUSHDIL KHAN, GULISTAN and KILA ABDULLA. The other (left) wing had been left behind in QUETTA for garrison duty and did not proceed to Afghanistan during the first campaign.

The 2nd Division began its slow passage of the KHOJAK PASS on 21st December. The Regiment crossed on the last day of the year, marching from KILA ABDULLA to an intermediate camp at CHARAJAT and thence next day to CHAMAN. Before continuing the advance on 4th January the 1st Brigade was finally constituted under Brigadier-General Lacy with E Battery R.H.A., 19th Punjab Native Infantry (less wing) and 32nd Pioneers. Meanwhile the 1st Division had arrived from MULTAN under Lieutenant-General Stewart and, advancing as a left column by the GWAJHA PASS route, joined the other division at ABDUR RAHMAN on 6th January. On the day previous both columns had had a brush with Afghan horsemen; but thereafter resistance melted away and KANDAHAR was occupied on 9th January without opposition. The immediate objective of the Kandahar Field Force was thus gained with the loss of only 2 officers and 9 men wounded. But the corpses of nearly 12,000 camels marked the trail from CHAMAN.

The HELMAND District—The affair of KHUSHK-I-NAKHUD.

While the 1st Division visited KELAT-I-GHILZAI the 2nd, less the 2nd Brigade, left KANDAHAR on 16th January to survey the HELMAND District around GIRISHK and to tap its resources. Crossing the ARGHANDAB River to KAREZ-I-ATA and moving thence by two roads, the division arrived at GIRISHK on 29th January. There was no opposition *en route*, but considerable difficulty over supplies. Two days previously the Regiment had been dropped at GUMBAZ-I-SURKH on the ARGHANDAB and was engaged in foraging in this locality until the withdrawal on KANDAHAR began on 23rd February. During this movement the Regiment rejoined its brigade; but a small party under a havildar was detached to the 4th Battalion 10th Baluch Regiment (118 rifles), which with the Scinde Horse formed the rear guard of the Division.

"Sketch E." There had previously been rumours of hostile gatherings higher up the HELMAND, and Alizais had been thought to be threatening the flank of the main body on 25th February. On the next day when the rear guard was at KHUSHK-I-NAKHUD cavalry patrols reported large bodies of Afghans advancing on the camp from the hills to the north. Soon the enemy, who later were found to consist of 1,500 Alizai footmen and 50 horsemen, were seen advancing over the cultivation with flags flying. Colonel Malcolmson ordered the infantry to advance, engage the enemy with fire and entice them on to the open ground in front of the camp. The fire of the Baluchis and Punjabis had the effect, however, of making the Afghans move further west into the corps with the object of gaining the huts and walled gardens of SULTAN ALI KHAN on the left flank. Although a small party did succeed in this, the majority were stopped by a charge of the Scinde Horse, and after 10 minutes hand-to-hand fighting were put to flight. As dusk fell the troops were recalled from pursuit, and for greater security the camp was transferred to NURZAI Fort adjacent. But there was no further sign of the enemy, who left 200 dead. The only British casualties were in the Scinde Horse, 4 men killed, 1 officer and 23 men wounded.

The 2nd Division returned to KANDAHAR on 2nd March. As the attainment of the objects of the war was now in sight the Kandahar Field Force was reduced to a cavalry brigade and two infantry brigades, and the remaining troops at once began their march back to India. The Regiment left KANDAHAR on 7th April and crossed the KHOJAK PASS on the 13th. One company under Major Waller was left at the pass as an outpost, and the remainder reached QUETTA on 19th April.

Northern Afghanistan—First campaign, 1878-79.

After defeating the Afghans at ALI MUSJID the leading division of the Peshawar Valley Field Force occupied JELALABAD on 20th December 1878. There was no idea of occupying KABUL, and the further advance to GANDAMAK in April 1879 was merely to secure a healthier summer climate. The rear division on the KHYBER line-of-communication sustained frequent tribal attacks, and had to undertake punitive action against Zakka Khel Afridis, Mohmands and Shinwaris.

The Kurram Valley Field Force forced the passage of the PEIWAR KOTAL on 2nd December and advanced as far as the SHUTARGARDAN PASS. Later it withdrew to the KURRAM VALLEY and subdued the Afghan district of Khost.

This double threat to KABUL and the occupation of KANDAHAR made the Afghan Government change its attitude, and after the death of Amir Sher Ali Khan his son Yaqub Khan signed the peace of GANDAMAK on 26th May. By this the Indian Government secured their main object of representation at KABUL as well control of the hitherto Afghan districts of the KHYBER, KURRAM, PESHIN and SIBI. While a reduced force was to remain at KANDAHAR for the hot weather the Northern Force withdrew to India. In so doing it suffered greatly from burning heat and virulent cholera.

Quetta District.

"Map 5."   The Right Wing which had been left behind in Quetta under Major Copland did not remain long on mere garrison duties. On 18th February 1879 it left to join the Peshin Moveable Column at GULISTAN KAREZ and took part in punitive operations in that vicinity. On relief by the 2nd Battalion 12th Frontier Force Regiment this wing returned to QUETTA on 25th March 1879.

The reunited Regiment garrisoned QUETTA Fort during the hot weather of 1879. An incident worth recording was the attack by two Ghazis on an unarmed group of sepoys outside the Fort Gate on 10th April. Three men and a langri were killed before their assailants could be overpowered. The severe wave of cholera which had been ravaging the troops in Afghanistan reached QUETTA in June. The Regiment lost Subadar Gurdit Singh and several men, while the recruits had to be moved into camp at KATIR 12 miles away until the scourge had disappeared.

On 24th September a party of 260 under Brevet Lieutenant-Colonel Bergman left QUETTA via the HUNNU PASS into the LAKI VALLEY as escort to the Agent to the Governor-General. Sir Robert Sandeman joined the detachment at SANGAN and then proceeded to reconnoitre the route of the railway being constructed via HARNAI. On 3rd November the detachment moved to SIBI to escort Sir Richard Temple, the Governor of Bombay, who had come on a similar mission. Afterwards this party of the Regiment marched to TAL to construct a post there and reconnoitre the Marri country. Outposts were provided at CHOTIALI and between HARNAI and TAL. On relief on 5th February 1880 by the 2nd Battalion 5th Mahratta Light Infantry, the detachment returned to QUETTA, being forced by snow on the direct route to march via SIBI and the BOLAN PASS.

The second campaign—Northern Afghanistan.

After the Treaty of GANDAMAK a British Resident, Major Cavagnari, was installed at KABUL. But his presence was greatly resented by certain Afghans, and on 3rd September 1879 a Kabul mob which attacked the Residency massacred Major Cavagnari, his suite and the escort. This outrage brought on the second phase of the war.

On 24th September a strong Kabul Field Force under Major-General Roberts entered Afghanistan over the PEIWAR KOTAL. On the 6th October this force defeated the Afghans disputing the passage of the SANG-I-NAWISHTA defile near CHARASIA. KABUL was occupied six days later, and Amir Yaqub was deputed to India. The KHYBER PASS route up which brigades were now again moving was made the line-of-communication and the KURRAM route was closed for the winter. The next two months saw important vicissitudes at KABUL: a jehad declared by the mullahs: a counter-offensive undertaken by tribes against the British garrison: the abandonment of the city defences in the face of overwhelming hostile numbers: the investment of the British force from 15th to 23rd December in SHERPUR Cantonment outside the city: Major-General Robert's defeat of the besieging forces and the reoccupation of the city.

The second campaign—Southern Afghanistan.

In the south the second phase of the war began with the immediate re-concentration at KANDAHAR of the troops which had already started to leave the country. KELAT-I-GHILZAI was occupied at the end of October. It was further decided that a division of Bengal troops under Lieutenant-General Stewart should march to KABUL via GHAZNI. To this end the reserve brigades of the Bombay Army in the Bolan Pass were advanced to QUETTA so as to enable the 19th Punjab Native Infantry, 2nd Battalion 12th Frontier Force Regiment and Scinde Horse to proceed thence to KANDAHAR.

The Regiment was warned for service at the end of January 1880 and, after relief by the 1st Battalion 4th Bombay Grenadiers, left QUETTA on 19th February. Considerable difficulty was experienced from snow in the KHOJAK PASS, but KANDAHAR was reached on 4th March. The KHOJAK detachment under Brevet Lieutenant-Colonel Bergman followed 16 days later. When considering the composition of the Ghazni Field Force it was at first proposed to exclude the heavy battery at KANDAHAR and to return it to QUETTA with 19th Punjab Native Infantry as escort. Fortunately it was decided on reconsideration to include both units in the force.

Accordingly the 19th Punjab Native Infantry marched from KANDAHAR on 30th March. The Regiment was temporarily attached to Brigadier-General Palliser's Cavalry Brigade, which together with Force Headquarters at first formed the main body of the Ghazni Field Force. Colonel Clay had retired with the rank of Major-General on 1st January and Lieutenant-Colonel Copland was now Commandant. The few other changes in officers since the last campaign were that Captain Waller had been promoted, Captain Browne had left, Surgeon Major T.S. Veale was now in medical charge, Subadar Zamin Shah had become Subadar-Major and Gulab Singh, one of four new Indian Officers, was Jemadar Adjutant. The rifle strength of the Regiment at this date and during the two engagements which followed was only 470, but a draft arriving from QUETTA early in May raised the total to 9 British Officers and 643 Indian ranks.

The marching-out strength of the Ghazni Force was 7,193 fighting troops, 6,202 followers, 22 guns and 8,701 animals, of which 140 carried treasure. Two months' rations were taken. Forage for animals had previously been stocked along the route as far as SHAHJUI; but thereafter hostile Taraki country was entered where villages were deserted, supplies buried, and considerable difficulty in foraging was encountered.

At first the Force marched in three separate brigade-groups at one day's interval. But on 17th April the whole division concentrated at JAMRUD, the 17th stage, and next day marched to MUSHAKI as a single column 6 miles long.

The Battle of AHMED KHEL, 19th April 1880.

For some days previously large and increasing bodies of Tarakai and Sulieman Khel Ghilzais had been observed moving parallel to the force; but owing to their proclivity to disperse into the hills which bordered the route, and the vulnerability of the long transport column should a considerable part of the troops be detached for offensive action it was deemed wiser not to attack. Now, however, a serious encounter seemed imminent; and, in fact, on the 18th February spies brought information that the tribesmen would oppose the advance on the next day at the very spot where indeed they did.

At dawn on 19th April the Ghazni Field Force left MUSHAKI in the following order of march:—

Advanced guard.—(Brigadier-General Palliser).
        19th King George V's Own Lancers.
        "A" Battery, Royal Horse Artillery.
        19th Punjab Native Infantry.
Mainbody
        2nd Infantry Brigade (Brigadier-General Hughes)
        Sam Browne's Cavalry.
        "G" Battery, Royal Artillery.

Train
    6th Heavy Battery, Royal Artillery.
    4th and 10th Companies, Bengal Sappers and Miners
    Field Hospitals.
    Ordnance and Engineer Field Parks.
    Treasure.
    Supplies.
    Baggage.

Rear Guard
    1st Infantry Brigade (Brigadier-General BARKER).
    Prince Albert Victor's Own Cavalry.
    11th Mountain Battery, Royal Artillery.

The route followed the western edge of the valley and thus lay nearer to the GULKOH Range on that side than to the SHILGHAR Hills on the other. At 7 a.m. after covering 5 miles the advanced guard cavalry observed large bodies of tribesmen massed on the crest of a long incurving spur of the GUL KOH, over the foot of which the road passed by a low kotal to the deserted hamlet of AHMED KHEL just beyond. Lieutenant-General Stewart at once made his preliminary dispositions for attack. While the cavalry and artillery maintained their relative positions the 2nd Infantry Brigade were advanced level with them on the left; the 19th Punjab Native Infantry were transferred to this brigade but earmarked as general reserve; Brigadier-General Barker, whose brigade was only now leaving MUSHAKI, was ordered to reinforce the advanced guard cavalry with two squadrons P.A.V.O. Cavalry on the right where the ground was open, and to send up half his infantry.

"Sketch F."

The advance was resumed at 8 a.m. before these reinforcements had come up. When about 1,000 yards from the enemy the force was halted and the batteries, until then on the road, came into action. "A" and "G" Batteries took up positions right and left of the track, the heavy guns unlimbered on a knoll 1,500 yards further back and Force Headquarters occupied an intermediate hillock. The 2nd Infantry Brigade deployed in line of quarter-columns on the left with the 2nd Battalion East Lancashire, 2nd Battalion 12th Frontiers Force Regiment and 1st Battalion 3rd Gurkha Rifles from right to left. One squadron Sam Browne's Cavalry covered the right of "A" Battery. One company 19th Punjab Native Infantry under Lieutenant Marshall was sent forward between the two batteries. Sir Donald Stewart's personal escort, troop 19th K.G.O. Lancers, company 2nd Battalion King's Royal Rifle Corps and company 1st Battalion 15th Punjab Regiment, were used to fill a 400 yards gap between the East Lancashires and "G" Battery, while two squadrons 19th K.G.O. Lancers were on the extreme left.

Meanwhile a large party of the mass of tribesmen, including a considerable body of horsemen, moved down onto the lower slopes of the ridge with dhols beating and mullahs haranguing. And then suddenly, at about 9 a.m. when the guns had just opened fire but the infantry were not completely deployed, this swarm of men who proved to be 3,000 ghazis of the most desperate type charged down on the leading troops. Some were armed with matchlocks, others with pistols, and almost all carried tulwars and daggers. They came in three lines, covering the 600 yards which intervened at racing speed. The nature of the ground resulted in this assault first striking the flanks. On the left enemy horse and foot broke in among the two squadrons of 19th K. G. O. Lancers, forced them back to the Force Headquarters hillock and produced such confusion that one troop of Lancers while trying to rally to the right came smashing into the 19th Punjab Native Infantry in reserve nearby. Ammunition mules were stampeded among the Lieutenant-General and his staff as they were preparing to defend themselves against the enemy swordsmen only 20 yards away. The situation on this flank was, indeed, only restored by the cool promptitude of the 1st Battalion 3rd Gurkha Rifles who poured volley after volley into the fanatics as they surged past.

On the right flank the ghazis fought their way forward under fire to wthin 50 yards of the guns. When it had fired all its case shot the Royal Horse Artillery battery was withdrawn to a hill in rear, the field battery moved further left, and the protecting infantry, company 19th Punjab Native Infantry included, were forced to give some ground while fighting stubbornly. On the extreme right the situation soon became critical, since from their position and superior numbers the enemy were able to start encircling the flank. Accordingly the Commandant 19th Punjab Native Infantry was ordered to leave three companies in reserve and with the remainder to check the outflanking movement. This Lieutenant-Colonel Copland did by occupying a hill on the extreme right of the position whence he could both fire on the enemy and cover the Royal Horse Artillery guns now coming into action in their rear position. Against this little hill the tribesmen made a last assault. But in the face of fire from the Regiment and the battery this attack withered away. Simultaneously two squadrons of P. A. V. O. Cavalry which had arrived from the rear guard, together with the 19th K. G. O. Lancers who had been relieved from the other flank, carried out repeated charges which completed the rout on this wing.

Meanwhile the storm of ghazi footsoldiers had reached the left flank. All remaining reserves, viz., three companies 19th Punjab Native Infantry and two of Sappers and Miners, were thrown into the fight on the left of the Gurkhas. But here too breach-loader and bayonet eventually prevailed against pistol and sword, and the enemy attack was held. The ghazis first wavered and began to withdraw onto their supporters, who all the time had remained on the high ground. Then these too began to trickle away, and a general retreat set in. At this moment the remainder of the King's Royal Rifle Corps arrived from Brigadier-General Barker's brigade and formed up on the right of the East Lancashire. The P.A.V.O. Cavalry and Sam Browne's took up the pursuit on the right. But only very limited exploitation could be permitted for fear of other bodies of tribesmen attacking the long column of transport which stood almost unprotected on the road.

At 10 a. m. the 'cease fire' was sounded. The battle had lasted only an hour. The Force rested for two hours, while the wounded were tended and the dead buried, and then moving over the disputed kotal continued the march to NANI. In this battle the Force lost 17 men killed and 9 officers 115 men wounded out of a total of 4,651 engaged. The Regiment had 1 sepoy killed and 3 wounded. 1,000 enemy dead were counted on the ground, and the tribesmen's total losses were estimated at twice that figure. Both Lieutenant-Colonel Copland and Major Waller were 'mentioned' in the dispatch on this operation.

The Affair of ARZU, 23rd April 1880.

"Sketch G."

A halt was made at GHAZNI which was occupied without opposition on 21st April. Next evening large bodies of Afghans were reported to be holding the villages of ARZU and SHALEZ 5 miles south east of GHAZNI, and it was decided to attack them. At 3-30 a. m. on 23rd April one wing of the Regiment left camp to hold the citadel and guard the city gates while the 1st Infantry Brigade with six cavalry squadrons and two batteries marched to engage the enemy. The two villages lay half a mile apart and 800 yards beyond a low ridge, from which about 600 Afgnans could be seen to be in occupation. An artillery bombardment failed to dislodge them; it was apparent that the 7-pounder and 9-pounder shells had little effect against stout walls. Brigadier-General Palliser then tried to entice the enemy out towards the ridge by leaving that practically unoccupied and disposing his infantry on the right flank. At 8-30 a. m. when this plan had failed, he asked for reinforcements prior to assaulting the villages. Lieutenant-General Stewart first sent forward half of the East Lancashire and the Gurkhas; and then followed himself with the 19th K.G.O. Lancers, 'G' Battery and the remainder of the 2nd Infantry Brigade, which included the 19th Punjab Native Infantry less the city detachment and a camp piquet company.

Between 9 and 11 a.m. the 2nd Infantry Brigade deployed on the ridge with the 19th Punjab Native Infantry on the right. The artillery bombardment was renewed. A stir was now visible among the enemy in the villages; dhols were heard and men swarmed from the shelter of the walls; it seemed that the ghazi rush of AHMED KHEL was about to be repeated. But the guns now had the range exactly and their first few shells caused at least half of this mass to retreat, while the remainder halted. At 11-20 a.m. the Lieutenant-General ordered the infantry to advance, the Regiment against the north end of SHALEZ, the rest of the 2nd Infantry Brigade against ARZU and the 1st Infantry Brigade converging on SHALEZ from the south. After closing to 200 yards file-firing was opened, and before this terrible fusilade the greater part of the tribesmen broke cover and fled. As soon as both villages had been surrounded the cavalry took up the pursuit. By 12-30 p.m. all was over. The enemy's losses were about 400, Suliemen Khel and Andaris. British casualties were limited to one private and one sowar killed with 8 sowars wounded.

The LOGAR VALLEY.

"Map 5."

The Ghazni Field Force continued its march on 25th April, and three days later near SAIDABAD effected junction with a supporting column which had been sent out from KABUL. While Lieutenant-General Stewart then proceeded to assume supreme command at KABUL the Ghazni Force was ordered to occupy the LOGAR VALLEY to the South. The intervening range was to be traversed by two routes, the ZAMBURK PASS and the TANGI WARDAK through which breaks the LOGAR River. The Regiment made the passage by the latter route on 1st May in company with the Cavalry Brigade. After concentrating at BARAK-I-BARK on 3rd May the Force moved on down the valley to HISARAK. From 14th May it was redesignated the 3rd Division of the North Afghanistan Field Force, and continued in the LOGAR VALLEY under conditions of steadily increasing tribal hostility until 18th June 1880. The Division then marched to CHARASIA near KABUL, but a week later was forced by the supply situation to return to the fertile LOGAR VALLEY at ZERGHUNSHAHR. Throughout this period the Regiment was "unattached", i.e., was a divisional unit apart from any of the three brigades.

The end of the war.

On 22nd July 1880 Abdur Rahman Khan was established as Amir of Afghanistan, and all troops were to leave the country in October. But at the end of July there occurred the disaster to the Bombay Army at MAIWAND which led to the investment of troops in KANDAHAR by the army of Ayub Khan and to the despatch there on 9th August of the Kabul-Kandahar Force under Major-General Sir Frederick Roberts. The present 4th Battalion of the Regiment was one of the units which made that remarkable march of 321 miles in 22 days. Another force under Major-General Phayre advanced from QUETTA. With the combined forces Major-General Roberts won the battle of KANDAHAR on 1st September, and thus practically ended the war.

Meanwhile the withdrawal of troops from other parts of Afghanistan was proceeded with. The 3rd Division from the LOGAR VALLEY reached the CHARDEH PLAIN outside KABUL on 5th August, and was broken up. The 19th Punjab Native Infantry left KABUL for India on 10th August with a strength of 7 British officers and 607 Indian ranks. In conjunction with three troops Sam Browne's Cavalry the Regiment acted as escort to a convoy of sick, ordnance stores and telegraphic material. One day ahead moved another convoy, and one march behind came the last troops of the Kabul Field Force. Simultaneously the 14,000 troops on the KHYBER line-of-communication were withdrawn. The summer heat of the KABUL RIVER VALLEY was intense, but there was no tribal opposition. The Regiment reached JELALABAD on 18th August, LANDI KHANA on the 25th and HARI SINGH BURJ, the standing camp outside PESHAWAR, on the 28th. Three days later the Regiment marched on to KOHAT and thence via KHUSHALGARH to JHELUM. Entraining here the 19th Punjab Native Infantry arrived at SIALKOT on 25th September 1880, almost exactly two years after leaving MULTAN. During the period of the war the Regiment had lost 1 Indian officer and 125 other ranks killed or died of wounds or disease.

For their services in the campaign the 19th Punjab Native Infantry were authorized to bear the battle honours of "Afghanistan 1878-80" and "Ahmed Khel" on their Colours, and were granted the special war medal with clasp "Ahmed Khel". For the second phase of the campaign a further 6 months' batta was also allowed. Lieutenant-Colonel Copland was appointed a Companion of the Order of the Bath, and Major Waller was promoted to Brevet Lieutenant-Colonel. Subadar-Major Zamin Shah, who had replaced Urjoon Singh on 1st May 1879, was awarded the Order of British India, 2nd class.

CHAPTER VIII.

1880-91.

SIALKOT – FEROZPORE – LAHORE – RAWALPINDI SECOND BLACK MOUNTAIN AND MIRANZAI CAMPAIGNS.

(Maps 1, 6: Sketches H, J.)

The 19th Punjab Regiment of Bengal Native Infantry remained uneventfully at SIALKOT until the end of 1883. During these and subsequent years there were, however, several campaigns of note. The present 2nd and 10th Battalions of the Regiment were included in the Mahsud Expeditionary Force of 1861. In 1882 the 2nd Battalion was among the Indian Troops sent to Egypt. A second Indian Contingent formed part of the Suakin Expedition to Egypt in 1885, and the Third Burma War took place between that year and 1889.

The Afghan War led to many administrative changes. As a measure of economy eighteen Infantry Regiments were disbanded and battalion strength reduced to 832 combatant Indian ranks; in 1887, however, this strength was increased to 912. The number of British officers was raised from seven to eight—Commandant, Second-in-Command, Second Wing Commander, Adjutant, Quartermaster and three other Wing Officers apart from the Regimental Medical Officer. Promotion to Captain was given after eleven years instead of after twelve. The tenure of Regimental command, which hitherto had been unlimited, was fixed at seven years or up to the age of fiftytwo.

In 1883 the class composition of the 19th Punjab Infantry, last laid down in 1864, was redefined as follows:—

" Class Companies—
  Two of Punjabi Musalmans. (A and F).
  One of Independent Transborder Muhammadans (C Company, Afridis).
  One of Trans-Indus and Trans-Border Muhammadans exclusive of Afridis. (G Company, Yusafzais.)
  Four of Trans-Sutlej Sikhs ". (B, D, E and H.)

From 1866 infantry regiments were linked in threes for the purpose of reinforcing one another in time of war. Henceforward recruits were enrolled with a liability to transfer within this group, and the battalion stationed at the Regimental Centre was to undertake the supply and training of men for the other two units during a campaign. Linked with the 19th Punjab Native Infantry were the 22nd and 24th, the present 3rd and 4th Battalions of the Regiment. In 1888 the Regimental Centre of this group was fixed at MULTAN.

A reserve was now instituted for the Indian Army. The "active reserve" was confined to 100 sepoys per regiment of between 5 and 10 years' colour service. The "garrison reserve" consisted of an unlimited number of men with 21 years' colour or combined service. Neither class received further training.

In 1885 it was decided that since Indian troops now formed so large a part of the Army in India the prefix "Native" should be omitted from the designations of units. Thus from this year the Regiment was known as the 19th (Punjab) Regiment of Bengal Infantry.

There were minor changes in men's dress and equipment. The khaki uniform which had been re-introduced in 1874 was still splashed with colour. The safa, for instance, was a plain dark blue, and the putties worn with black boots were white. Narrow pantaloons were replaced by wide khaki knicker-bockers, and boots by country shoes. Later there was a return to boots, but these were brown. Paintings by Conroy in the Officers' Mess depict the dress of this period.

On 30th November 1883 the 19th Punjab Infantry left SIALKOT for FEROZEPORE on relief. The march was via LAHORE, where in the cantonment then called MEAN MEER the Regiment stayed from 8th December to 20th January while carrying out brigade training in company with the present 4th Battalion. FEROZEPORE was reached on 26th January 1884. A detachment of one company under a British Officer had been left behind at AMRITSAR, and this was relieved every few months during the next four years.

"Map 1."

As a sequel to the conclusion of peace the Amir of Afghanistan visited India in 1885. A Durbar was held at RAWALPINDI in his honour, and the 19th Punjab Infantry formed part of the troops concentrated for the occasion. Marching from FEROZEPORE on 9th March, the Regiment was joined by the AMRITSAR detachment at MEAN MEER and thence proceeded by train. The Durbar Camp lasted until 10th April; training manoeuvres were held as well as parades. While at RAWALPINDI the 19th were detailed to proceed to Egypt with other reinforcements for the Suakin Expedition; but this plan was dropped, and accordingly the Regiment returned to FEROZEPORE and AMRITSAR for the next two and a half years.

In 1886 Brevet-Colonel Copland, C.B., went on one year's leave pending retirement. Brevet-Colonel Bergman had gone the previous year on account of ill-health; so from 24th January 1887 Brevet-Colonel J. E. Waller became Commandant. Major J. G. Kelly was brought in as second-in-command from the present 3rd Battalion 16th Punjab Regiment.

In November 1887 the Regiment had a change of station to MEAN MEER, with a company at MULTAN. In April 1888 the AMRITSAR detachment rejoined. After two years in what was then one of the unhealthiest cantonments in India the 19th Punjab Infantry marched up to RAWALPINDI in October 1890. The march was continued almost at once to ATTOCK, where brigade manoeuvres were carried out during the last two months of the year.

Early in 1891 the Regiment was warned for the Hazara Field Force which was then being assembled for further punitive operations on the BLACK MOUNTAIN border. The undermentioned officers were present at this date:—

Brevet-Colonel J. E. Waller.	Commandant.
Lieutenant-Colonel J. G. Kelly.	Second-in-command. Wing Commander.
Major A. J. Brander.	Wing Commander.
Captain A. H. Wilmer.	Wing officer.
Lieutenant G. J. Fitz M. Soady.	Adjutant from 11-11-89.
Lieutenant E. Waller.	Joined 15-6-89. Quartermaster from 12-10-89.
Lieutenant A. Ward.	Attached from 21-3-90. Wing officer.
Lieutenant W. J. Windsor.	Attached from 7-3-90. Wing officer.
Surgeon-Major H. E. Drake-Brockman.	Medical officer.

Captain Gouldsbury, after sixteen years' service with the Regiment, had transferred to the Cantonment Magistrate's Department. Captain and Adjutant Faithful had just gone to the present 3rd Battalion 15th Punjab Regiment. Lieutenant G. A. Dale who had joined on 22-10-1889 was on a year's leave.

The following Indian officers were with the Regiment in the two campaigns of 1891:—

    Subadars—Sant Singh .. Subadar-Major from 1-8-89.
               Mir Aslam Khan.
               Ahmad.
               Ghulam Kadir.
               Punjab Singh.
               Kharak Singh.
               Lal Khan.
               Asa Singh.
    Jemadars—Mula Singh.
               Fateh Din.
               Hasham Ali.
               Sham Singh .. Indian Adjutant.
               Gopal Singh.
               Aman Khan.
               Behadur.
               Nand Singh.

The turn-over in Indian Officers since the Afghan War appears to have been rapid. Of those present in 1880 only Sant Singh and Ahmad now remained, and they had then been the most junior jemadars. The late Subadar-Major Zamin Shah had in 1884 obtained promotion to the first class of the Order of British India, and Subadar Kayem had been admitted to the second class just before going on pension in 1887.

The BLACK MOUNTAIN Expedition, 1891.

The BLACK MOUNTAIN is an extensive massif which fills an east bank bend of the River INDUS north of AMB. The crest of its southern part forms the boundary between the District of Hazara and the tribal territory of the Hassanzai and Akazai to the northwest. In October 1890 these tribesmen actively opposed the construction of roads up to the frontier ridge, thus violating the agreement made two years previously after the first campaign against them. Early in 1891, therefore, another Hazara Field Force was assembled with two brigades at DARBAND and a 3rd Brigade in reserve at RAWALPINDI. In the latter formation were included the 19th Punjab Infantry, together with the 1st Battalion King's Royal Rifle Corps and the 3rd Battalion 15th Punjab Regiment.

"Sketch H."

General Elles' two forward brigades advanced up the INDUS valley. Notwithstanding extremely wet weather they had by 25th March subdued all opposition on the western slopes of the MOUNTAIN and astride the SHAH NALA. On 26th March Brigadier-General Lockhart's reserve brigade started moving forward from RAWALPINDI. The 19th Punjab Infantry, a squadron of Probyn's Horse and a British Mountain battery were in the van; the other two battalions followed at intervals of a day's march. DARBAND was reached on the 29th. Next day the battery and the right wing of the Regiment under Lieutenant-Colonel Kelly went on to defend the pontoon bridge which had been built at KOTKAI. This wing, less a small detachment with the battery on the opposite side, held a bridgehead on the western bank. The rest of the Regiment and the cavalry went as far as TOWARA, where the whole brigade was concentrated by 31st March.

The campaign was virtually at an end by 7th April. On that date the detachment rejoined from KOTKAI, and the same evening the brigade left by forced marches to take part in the operations against the Orakzai tribes which had already started near KOHAT. The BLACK MOUNTAIN campaign was terminated in June, and except for a frontier covering force all troops were withdrawn. The 19th Punjab Infantry had had little excitement in these operations and had suffered no casualty; but at least they had the satisfaction of playing the leading part in the reserve brigade. A clasp "Hazara 1891" was awarded to all ranks of the Regiment for their services. It was to be worn with the newly-established "India Medal", a re-issue of the Second Burma War Medal of 1854.

The Second Miranzai Expedition, 1891.

"Map 6."

The Orakzais who inhabit the southern part of Tirah had become increasingly hostile since the Second Afghan War. In January 1891, therefore, the first Miranzai Expedition was sent into the KHANKI RIVER Valley under Brigadier-General Lockhart. There was little enemy opposition, and in February after frontier posts and roads had been begun on the SAMANA RANGE which marks the Miranzai frontier the force was broken up. But towards the end of March the Orakzais attacked the posts under construction at SANGAR and GULISTAN, and concentrated such strength that the weak protective troops had to be withdrawn from the SAMANA. A second Miranzai Field Force was assembled, the 2nd and 3rd Columns each of a Brigade group at DARBAND and the 1st at HANGU. Sir William Lockhart, summoned from Hazara, was again in command.

Marching via HARIPUR to entrain at HASSAN ABDAL, and taking to the road again at KHUSHALGARH, the 19th

Punjab Infantry reached KOHAT on 12th April. Continuing on the 15th the Regiment arrived next day at DARBAND and were there brigaded with the 2nd Derajat Mountain Battery, 6th Battalion 13th Frontier Force Rifles and 10th Battalion 15th Punjab Regiment to form the 3rd Column under Lieutenant-Colonel Brownlow.

The British officers were practically the same as those who had been in Hazara. While there Lieutenant R. C. Macpherson had joined, and Surgeon H.W.G. Macleod had assumed medical charge. Colonel Waller was detained at KOHAT to command the station, so the command of the Regiment devolved on Lieutenant-Colonel Kelly.

Reoccupation of the SAMANA RANGE, 1891.

Early on 17th April the expedition advanced to drive the enemy off tue SAMANA RANGE. The 1st Column from HANGU gained the hill feature called LAKKA without opposition, and thence worked along the crest of the range to DARBAND KOTAL. This kotal was also the objective of the 2nd Column which arrived there simultaneously and then moved on down the far slope to GWADA in the KHANKI VALLEY. "Sketch J."

The 3rd Column started northwards at 5-30 a.m. in support of the 2nd Column on its right. The 19th Punjab Infantry acted as advanced guard. On reaching the foot of the SAMANA the Column halted for some time until a heliograph report was received that the 1st Column was at LAKKA, and the 2nd could be seen getting onto its objective. Thereupon the 3rd Column turned about according to plan and marched rapidly towards PAT DARBAND with the village and post of SANGAR as its objective. The 10th Battalion 15th Punjab Regiment was now leading. Two companies of the Regiment under Captain Wilmer formed the rear guard. Beyond PAT DARBAND, which was reached at 11-30 a.m., the advance was lightly opposed. The battery went into action, and two companies of the 19th were sent out to assist the left flank of the advanced guard. It was very hot, and the troops suffered much from thirst. The newly-made road up the ravine was found to have been blocked by the tribesmen, and mule loads had to be manhandled at several points. Meanwhile Force Headquarters and the 1st Column had resumed their lateral movement along the ridge and, having cleared some enemy from the village of TSALLAI, were now closing in on SANGAR. Opposition faded away and the two columns reached this objective simultaneously at 4-30 p.m. The rearguard to the 3rd Column under Captain Wilmer, which had to bring in the transport of both forces, did not reach camp until nearly midnight. The night was spent in a combined bivouac, the two columns sharing the piquet and perimeter defences.

The attack on MASTAN, 18th April 1891.

Next morning, after returning almost all transport to DARBAND, the two columns continued the movement westwards. The object was to secure the MASTAN Plateau which is the dominating portion of the SAMANA RANGE. The advance was hotly opposed by enemy firing from the edge of the plateau near the village of SARTOP. Many of these tribesmen were armed with stolen Martini-Henris, the type of rifle then in use by British troops but not yet issued to Indian. With the 6th Battalion 13th Frontier Force Rifles leading, the 19th Punjab Infantry in the second line and two batteries supporting, the 3rd Column advanced straight on the village while the 1st moved round the flank via the south slopes. In this way the enemy position was carried by 8.30 a.m. After a halt for replenishing waterbottles from SARTOP spring the attack was resumed at 11 a.m. and the enemy driven out of MASTAN village. This success was exploited to the SARAGARHI villages further west before operations were stopped for the day. The 1st Column returned to SANGAR, while the 3rd bivouacked at MASTAN. A company from each of the 19th Punjab Infantry and 10th Battalion 15th Punjab Regiment remained behind at SARAGARHI for a while to cover the removal of the considerable supplies of atta which were found there. One blanket per man was brought up to MASTAN from SANGAR before nightfall and the troops enjoyed a quiet night.

The defence of MASTAN, 19th April 1891.

Next morning, however, when the 3rd Column made no movement the enemy became enterprising. At 8 a.m. on the 19th they started sniping the Water Piquet held by the 6th Battalion 13th Frontier Force Rifles, and an hour later attacked it. Day alarm stations as described below were at once taken up, except that the Derajat Battery which had been withdrawn to SANGAR overnight did not return until 11.30 a.m. South of the track to GULISTAN and facing west towards the SARAGARHI villages were two companies of the 10th Battalion 15th Punjab Regiment. North of this track facing west and north-west were three companies of the 19th Punjab Infantry. Two were under Captain Wilmer and Lieutenant Macpherson respectively, while the Commanding

Officer, Lieutenant-Colonel Kelly, assumed command of the third. The mountain battery was in support of this sector. Continuing the defences round to the east were two companies of the 6th Battalion 13th Frontier Force Rifles facing north on both sides of the Water Piquet and of the nala running up to the spring. Further east at what was the extreme right rear of the position were another two companies of the Regiment. The Yusafzai company under Major Brander, Subadar Ghulam Kadir and Jemadar Aman Khan held a rocky feature called Crag Piquet, while the Afridis, temporarily under Lieutenant Soady the Adjutant, were on a lower ridge to its left.

Having failed against the Water Piquet the enemy next assembled in greater force behind the villages of GHUZTANG and SARAGARHI and launched an attack on the camp which lasted till after dark. Pressure was particularly heavy against Crag Piquet, where broken ground allowed the tribesmen good cover and close approach. Early in the afternoon Jemadar Hasham Ali of the Yusafzai company was shot through the head and died. Late in the evening a Sikh company was put into the gap separating the 6th Battalion 13th Frontier Force Rifles from the Afridis and was at once hotly engaged. Sepoy Wazir Singh was shot through the head, while Lance Naik Jawand Singh and Sepoy Ram Singh were wounded. At dusk Lieutenant Ward brought up his Punjabi Musalman company to relieve the Afridis, and not long afterwards all day outposts withdrew to night positions. The evening situation was complicated by the approach of a baggage convoy from SANGAR and an attack on it near SARTOP. Two companies of the 10th Battalion 15th Punjab Regiment which were sent out to bring this convoy in did not complete their task until 9.30 p.m. The enemy followed up the withdrawal to night dispositions, and were now particularly active against the companies on the west. In the dark they came in very close to fire, and even hurled stones. At 9 p.m. shots were passing over the camp in all directions, and to judge by the shoutings of the tribesmen an assault seemed imminent. At 10-30 p.m., however, the enemy withdrew, and except for an unsuccessful attack on a south face piquet the rest of the night was uneventful. This day was the tenth anniversary of the battle of AHMED KHEL.

Just after day positions had been taken up again on 20th April enemy activity recommenced. Sniping against Crag and Water Piquets prevented any water being obtained until 10 a.m. and not before the remainder of the 10th Battalion 15th Punjab Regiment had been put into this sector. The 6th Battalion 13th Frontier Force Rifle was not present, having been sent out to SARTOP at dawn in order to facilitate the arrival of reinforcements from SANGAR.

The 1st Column arrived at 1 p.m. and one hour later the combined force began a counter-attack. The 1st Column advanced westwards over the plateau to its furthest limit, driving the tribesmen from village to village of the SARAGARHI group. Two hours were spent in destroying towers before the withdrawal at 5 p.m.

The 19th Punjab Infantry and 6th Battalion 13th Frontier Force Rifles of the 3rd Column were directed north. GHUZTANG was gained without casualty at 3.30 p.m., the enemy withdrawing into the KHANKI VALLEY at the last moment. The village was burnt and its tower blown up before the two battalions withdrew to MASTAN Camp. Tribal casualties on this day were estimated at 300 killed and wounded.

Subsequent operations.

On 21st April the 2nd Column, which had previously been withdrawn to SANGAR from the KHANKI VALLEY, passed through MASTAN under the force commander and reached GULISTAN at the western end of the plateau. Operating from there on the following four days this force attacked Aka Khel concentrations in the CHAGRU VALLEY and destroyed their villages.

The 3rd Column in MASTAN Camp continued action against Rabia Khel villages. On the afternoon of 21st April two companies 19th Punjab Infantry, with the same from the other two regiments and supported by the Derajat Battery, destroyed the five small villages of IBRAHIM KHEL. The destruction of the furthest of these villages was undertaken as a separate operation under Lieutenant-Colonel Kelly by one of his two companies. There was no opposition. On the following day an exactly similar force destroyed the three villages and four towers of BAZAI. There was slight opposition but no casualty was incurred.

On 23rd April two companies of the Regiment moved to GULISTAN to strengthen the defences of the Headquarters Camp during that night. They returned to MASTAN next day. The weather now turned from heat to rain and remained unsettled until the end of the campaign. At first there was no protection beyond individual waterproof sheets. Later some tents were forthcoming. On 28th April the 19th Punjab Infantry marched to SANGAR to garrison that camp along with a wing of the King's Royal Rifle Corps and the 3rd Mountain Battery during the absence of the 1st Column in the MISHTI and SHEKHAN country to the north. On their return to SANGAR on 4th May the Regiment and wing

King's Royal Rifle Corps accompanied Brigadier-General Lockhart back to MASTAN.

These two units remained at MASTAN when the rest of the 3rd Column, including Lieutenant Soady on loan to the 10th/15th, next moved to reinforce the 2nd Column at GULISTAN. There followed operations against the Mamuzai in the UPPER KHANKI VALLEY which lasted until 15th May. On the return of Force Headquarters and other units in addition to the rest of the 3rd Column, MASTAN Camp became overcrowded, and accordingly the Regiment moved into the new water point camp of SIRITANGI.

The Orakzais had submitted. Three main posts were to be established on the SAMANA, at MASTAN where now stands FORT LOCKHART, at DHAR near SANGAR and at GULISTAN. Pending their completion a force of two cavalry squadrons, a mountain battery and three Punjab infantry regiments was to remain in position. The break up of the remainder of the Miranzai Field Force was ordered on 6th June, on which date Colonel Waller rejoined from KOHAT. Two days later the Regiment marched from SIRITANGI to HANGU *en route* to KHUSHALGARH, and eventually reached RAWALPINDI on 13th June. The only battle casualties had been the four mentioned. For their services all ranks received the "Miranzai 1891" clasp.

CHAPTER IX.

1891—1904.

ZHOB—DERAJAT—MULTAN—SIALKOT—MALAKAND—KOHAT—KURRAM—MULTAN—FEROZEPORE.

(Maps 1, 6.)

The 19th (Punjab) Regiment of Bengal Infantry had spent less than three months in RAWALPINDI before going on the two expeditions of 1891. The Regiment had barely settled down again to cantonment life when they were again on the move. Starting on 4th November 1891 they marched for five weeks via KHUSHALGARH, KOHAT, BANNU, TANK and the GOMAL VALLEY to FORT SANDEMAN in ZHOB.

The next two years there were almost uneventful. Colonel J.E. Waller went on a year's furlough, leaving Major A. J. Brander in command. Lieutenant-Colonel J. G. Kelly had already transferred as Commandant to the present 4th Battalion of the Regiment (24th BI). The Indian Staff Corps, to which all British Officers belonged, had now been unified. The periods for qualifying for promotion to Captain and Major were reduced by two years in each case to 9 years and 18 respectively.

DERAJAT and MULTAN, 1893-96.

The 22nd BI (present 3rd Battalion) came in relief to FORT SANDEMAN, and on 9th December 1893 the Regiment marched off via DERA GHAZI KHAN to take their turn at the link group centre, MULTAN. Within a year, however, they were back again west of the RIVER INDUS for outpost duty in the Derajat. Lieutenant-Colonel A. J. Brander was now Commandant, Colonel J. E. Waller having retired in January 1894 with the honorary rank of Major-General.

"Map 6."

In 1894 the frontier between India and Afghanistan began to be demarcated along the Durand Line. This led to tribal opposition in WAZIRISTAN, to the despatch of the Regiment into DERAJAT, to the Mahsud Expedition of 1894-95 and eventually to the widespread frontier uprisings of 1897. The Delimitation Mission began work in October near the GOMAL RIVER. The escort force included the 20th BI (present 2nd Battalion). Mahsud hostility culminated in a desperate attack on the Mission's camp at WANA before light on 3rd November, and necessitated the Mahsud Expedition under Lieutenant-General Sir W. Lockhart. From 17th December the Wana, Jandola and Bannu Columns converged on KANIGURAM and MAKIN, overran Mahsud country in all directions, exacted retribution and secured submission by the middle of March 1895. One of the units of the Force was the present 4th Battalion 13th Frontier Force Rifles, stationed at DERA ISMAIL KHAN with outposts along the DERAJAT border, and it was to relieve them there that the Regiment moved at short notice on 9th November 1894. A depot was left at MULTAN. The move comprised the short rail journey to opposite DARYA KHAN, a boat crossing of the INDUS and the march up the west bank. On 13th December detachments were sent out from DERA ISMAIL KHAN to relieve the garrisons at TANK, JATTA, NILI KACH, KHAJURI KACH, MANJHI, DRABAND, GIRNI and ZAM. On 12th January 1895 yet another detachment took over JANDOLA from the 14th Sikhs. There were no incidents of note at these posts during the field operations, nor during the year which followed. The Regiment continued to garrison them up to 29th December 1896, when it again concentrated in MULTAN. Headquarters and the companies not in outposts had already moved there from DERA ISMAIL KHAN in March 1895. The detachment at NILI KACH was within the operational area and received the "Waziristan 1894-95" clasp to the India Medal.

Colonel Kelly of CHITRAL.

The Chitral Campaign of 1895 should be mentioned for its connection with Lieutenant-Colonel J. G. Kelly, who, leaving the Regiment in 1891, then found himself at BUNJI near GILGIT in command of the 32nd Pioneers.

After a series of murders and intrigues over the succession to the Mehtari of CHITRAL Umra Khan, chief of JANDOL, invaded the state. Aided and accepted by the Chitralis his forces besieged the small British garrisons in the forts at CHITRAL and MASTUJ, and overcame two parties between those places. The 1st (PESHAWAR) Division moved from NOWSHERA on 1st April. Lieutenant-Colonel Kelly, who was the senior officer in the CHITRAL-GILGIT area, was instructed to co-operate with this relieving column. He marched with half his Regiment and two mountain guns on 23rd March. After suffering great privations and twice defeating an immensely more numerous enemy in prepared positions this gallant force raised the seige of MASTUJ on 9th April, and of CHITRAL eleven days later. In one of the most remarkable marches in history they had in 21 days fought two actions besides covering 220 miles over mountainous country and through snow, without tents and practically without transport.

Colonel Kelly earned renown for his leadership in this relief of CHITRAL, was rewarded with the CB and a Brevet-Colonelcy, and was appointed an A.D.C. to H.M. the Queen.

The campaign, with the rest of which we are not concerned, resulted in the introduction of a new medal. This was called "The India Medal 1895" with the same ribbon as the previous General Service Medal.

Frontier Compaigns of 1897.

"Map 6." Although the Regiment took no part in them the whole of the Punjab frontier region was disturbed by the serious outbreaks which occurred in 1897 through increasing suspicion of British designs against tribal independence, and from the impulse of religious fanaticism. The blaze of revolt spread from north to south. The British garrison in MALAKAND was attacked and CHAKDARA FORT invested. The Mohmands raided into the PESHAWAR VALLEY. Control of the KHYBER PASS was completely lost. The SAMANA posts were besieged by Orakzais and Afridis.

The 24th Bengal Infantry (present 4th Battalion) took part in the spirited defence of MALAKAND; and after its relief they were included, along with the 22nd Bengal Infantry (now 3rd Battalion), in the Malakand Field Force which went on up the CHITRAL ROAD to subdue the Swatis and Bunerwals. Lieutenants McPherson and Churchill of the Regiment went with the 24th BI, and Lieutenant Duhan with the 35th Sikhs. The 2nd and 10th Battalions (then 20th and 21st BI) formed part of the Buner Field Force, which completed the defeat of the western tribes by January 1898. The 2nd Battalion from PESHAWAR had already in August been in action near SHABKADAR against Mohmand invaders. Next month with the Mohmand Field Force they penetrated the transborder country as far as NAHAKI.

In July of 1897 a Field Force had been sent to subdue the Madda Khel at the head of the TOCHI VALLEY in WAZIRISTAN; but it was not until October that troops could be freed from elsewhere for the invasion of TIRAH. The finale of this momentous year was the Bazar Valley Expedition against the Afridis in control of the KHYBER PASS.

SIALKOT

In the spring of 1897 it was decided to make MULTAN the regimental centre station of a group of Sikh Infantry regiments and to allot JHELUM to the 19th Bengal Infantry and its linked regiments. Accordingly the present 3rd Battalion 11th Sikh Regiment came to MULTAN in 1898, and the Regiment reached SIALKOT by train on 11th April.

Colonel Brander was again in command after a year's home leave. Lieutenant McPherson was back as Adjutant. Lieutenant C.W.G. Richardson, who had spent the previous year in Russia, was now Quartermaster. Major Wilmer was 2nd-in-Command. Next came Major E.T. Castrell, who was now brought into the Regiment. Other company commanders were McCarthy, Beames and Soady. Captain E. Waller was now with the Punjab Government, Lieutenants Dale and Windsor with the Burma Military Police. Lieutenants G.P. Evans and A. Young had joined. Lieutenants M. R. Pocock and H.C.D. Jarrett, shortly after posting, went for a while to the 22nd Bengal Infantry. The medical officer was Surgeon-Lieutenant A.H. Moorhead. The Indian officers were headed by Ghulam Kadir, who had been Subadar-Major since February 1893.

Some changes were now made in the men's hot-weather khaki dress. The pagri, hitherto khaki, became dark blue with a khaki fringe. Brown leather vertical shoulder braces were added to the 1897 leather belt and pouches. A khaki haversack and brown waterbottle were introduced. The men's winter uniform was now a scarlet jacket with white facings, blue pantaloons, black spats, blue pagri with red khula and two red bars on the gold fringe. This dress was just as first introduced after the Mutiny Campaign except that white spats had been changed to black in 1882. And although less and less used for service training it remained the same, except for a reversion to white spats, up to the Great War in 1914.

For service training British officers now adopted khaki dress and helmet, a brown leather belt with a flat gilt buckle, and outside brown leather slings for the plated sword scabbard. Formal dress continued to be a scarlet tunic with blue and gold facings, dark blue and red-piped overalls with black Butcher boots, white helmet with a blue and gold pagri.

MALAKAND 1898-99: SIALKOT, 1899-1900.

"Map 6."

In November 1898 the Regiment was involved in the aftermath of the recent frontier operations. The Guides Infantry were moved at short notice from MARDAN, and the Regiment went to relieve them there. The railway had by now been extended across the INDUS RIVER, but no branch line existed from NOWSHERA. After detraining there MARDAN was reached on 1st December. A depot was left behind at SIALKOT under Lieutenant Evans.

Twentyfive days later, however, the Regiment moved on up into the MALAKAND where their former Commandant, Colonel J. G. Kelly, C. B. E., A. D. C., was now commanding the Malakand Brigade. The right wing relieved a detachment of the 3rd Bombay Light Infantry at DARGAI FORT, while headquarters and the left wing replaced the same regiment at CHAKDARA.

Colonel Brander again went on a year's leave which was extended by six months. Captain Soady left on attachment to the Imperial Service Troops. Captain Richardson took long leave before joining the Staff College in 1900. He too went to the Indian contingent which had been sent to South Africa in 1899.

In March 1899 the Regiment was relieved so as to have a rest in a peace station before garrisoning CHITRAL. And so, after concentrating at KHAR and marching to NOWSHERA, the 19th Bengal Infantry returned to SIALKOT on 26th April.

KOHAT, 1900: KURRAM VALLEY, 1901.

"Map 6."

Plans, however, were changed, and the next move took the Regiment to the North-West Frontier. Detraining on 2nd July 1900 at KHUSHALGARH, they marched to KOHAT. As cholera was prevalent there the Regiment camped outside the cantonment from 6th to 27th July, but did not escape the scourge. There were 127 cases with 56 deaths.

Then followed six months of frontier garrison life without particular incident. Lieutenant-Colonel Wilmer was now Commandant, with Lieutenant Churchill as his Adjutant and Lieutenant P. Evans as Quartermaster. Lieutenant Duhan was at home on sick leave. 2nd Lieutenant J. Y. Tancred joined. The 20th B. I. and the linked 24th Bengal Infantry were now overseas in the China Expeditionary Force.

February 1901 found the Regiment marching in relief up the

KURRAM VALLEY. One wing was left at THAL and a small detachment at SADDA. Headquarters and the remainder were established at PARACHINAR on 12th February, and a peaceful year and a quarter ensued.

In April of 1895 the two Presidency Armies had been replaced by the Army Corps (later termed Commands) of Bengal, Madras and Bombay, each under a Lieutenant-General and the whole unified Army under a Commander-in-Chief. In consequence, from 13th September 1901 the Bengal connection was dropped from the Regiment's designation, which then became "XIX Punjab Infantry". It was about now too that Roman numerals, already embroidered on the Colours, came into common use with the regimental title.

It may here be noted that the Colours of the Regiment were no longer those originally presented in 1876. It is not known exactly when the old standards were replaced, but a painting in 1896 shows the Colours of that year. Both Colours differed in arrangement from the designs of the original pair. "PUNJAB INFANTRY" had replaced "PUNJAB NATIVE INFANTRY". And although at the time of the change the Regiment was still part of the Bengal Army, the word Bengal was again omitted in favour of the place of origin, the Punjab.

MULTAN and FEROZEPORE, 1902-04.

In the second half of June 1902 the XIX P. I. returned to KOHAT. This followed from a decision to entrust the KURRAM VALLEY to local levies. A further move by march and rail brought the Regiment on 6th August back to MULTAN, its former depot centre. Nothing of event happened until June of '03 when one wing went to FEROZEPORE. Headquarters and the other wing followed in March of the next year. This concentration was a preliminary to joining the operations in TIBET which are described in the next chapter.

These years were marked by much Army reorganization and innovation, following the appointment of Lord KITCHENER in '02 as Commander-in-Chief in India. The officers of the Indian Staff Corps were now known as Indian Army Officers. Burma was made an independent Command. Localized Contingents such as that of HYDERABAD were broken up. The Punjab Frontier Force was merged into the Military Districts of PESHAWAR, KOHAT and DERAJAT. Apart from these Districts there were nine divisions. As part of the renumbering of units of the Indian Army the Regiment was from 2nd October 1903 renamed "XIX

Punjabis", which title was to remain unchanged for nearly twenty years. About now the secondary title of the Regiment, altered by usage to "Sherdil-ki-Paltan", came to be used officially as such. Honorary Colonels were introduced for Indian Army regiments, and from 13th May '04 Major-General John RUGGLES, CB, was so appointed. The King's Indian Orderly Officers were instituted—six senior Sardars who attended on His Majesty as aides in England from April to August in their year's tour of duty. The XIX Punjabis were represented in the coronation contingent which went to England in 1902, and in the Durbar of next year at DELHI.

Lieutenant-Colonel Wilmer was in England throughout 1902. In April of '04 he had to take sick leave home from which he never returned. In his place as Commandant followed Major L. N. Herbert, who had come over from the linked 22nd Punjabis in 1901. Also brought into the Regiment for a while was the gunner Major W. Malleson whom we shall meet again in 1918. Captains Beames and Windsor rejoined for duty in '02. Captain Fitz M. Soady was with the 24th Punjabis. Captain Dale was with Grass Farms in the Punjab Command. Captain Richardson returned in 1902 from the South African War. Lieutenant P. Evans was still in Burma. Lieutenants Jarrett and Tancred were Adjutant and Quartermaster respectively. New arrivals were subalterns B. W. E. Dunsford and G. N. Thompson in '02, D. B. Ross in '03. Fateh Khan who was to be subadar-major during the first half of the Great War of 1914-18 was now the junior jemadar.

CHAPTER X.

TIBET, 1904.

(Map 7).

On 3rd June the XIX Punjabis were ordered to mobilize for service in Tibet, and during the following five months took an important if unspectacular part in the campaign already in progress there.

At intervals during the previous thirty years there had been difficulties over trade and over the Tibetan government's unwillingness to recognise British supremacy in the intervening state of Sikkim. In 1888 British troops had had to be sent to eject a Tibetan force from that territory, and these troops were maintained on the frontier up till 1895.

In 1903 the Government of India decided to send a political mission into Tibet under Major Younghusband with the object of settling outstanding disputes. The Mission, escorted by 200 officers and men of the 32rd Pioneers under Brigadier-General Macdonald, assembled at KHAMBA JONG in July 1903, but found that the Tibetans would not co-operate and indeed were determined to fight. It was therefore decided to try the effect of advancing the Mission to GYANTSE.

"Map 7.

The Tibetan Army at this time consisted of some 6,000 partially-trained regular troops normally distributed between the important towns of LHASA, SHIGATSE and GYANTSE. At their head were the Senior and Junior Ambans, Manchus appointed by PEKIN. Among the junior officers and men there was also a small number of Chinese, but the great majority were Tibetans. There were also about 60,000 levies, both horse and foot, who were entertained on a local basis whenever required. Only the regulars wore uniform—a grey or blue homespun coat and trousers with upturned felt hat, putties and soft leather boots. A few possessed iron helmets with chain body-mail and carried shields. Firearms were the rule, but varied from modern rifles to matchlocks of cumbrous length. Those not so equipped had the national long-bow, and all carried in addition the spear and heavy sword. The enemy also possessed a few "jingal" guns which, though very slow-firing and inaccurate, often outranged the British mountain artillery. The Tibetans proved to be brave and physically enduring but to lack the strength of discipline and any deep love of country. They were very poor rifle shots.

The Mission Escort was now increased to a force of 3,000 fighting men and 7,000 followers by the addition of 4 mountain guns, the Maxim gun section of the Royal Norfolk Regiment, the 8th Gurkha Rifles and two companies of Sappers and Miners. The intention to change to the CHUMBI Valley route between Bhutan and Sikkim was kept secret, so that the new force was able to occupy CHUMBI and PHARI JONG in mid-December while the main body of Tibetans were still watching KHAMBA JONG. The next step was made to TUNA. At the end of March 1904 when further administrative preparations were complete the force resumed their advance. A body of about 3,000 Tibetans who opposed them were severely handled first at GURU and then at LAMDANG GORGE. GYANTSE was occupied on 11th April. When the Mission had been installed with an escort of 2 guns and 6 companies in an adjacent village the remainder of the force withdrew to CHUMBI.

The second phase in this campaign—as in those of Bhutan and Afghanistan before—was brought about by enemy counter-offensive against an unduly weakened force of occupation. The Tibetans now announced that they would not negotiate at GYANTSE, and began to close in on that place. On 3rd May the 3,000 who were advancing from LHASA were defeated at the 1,600 foot KHARO LA Pass by a detachment from GYANTSE. On 5th May 1,600 enemy from SHIGATSE failed in an attack on the now tiny Mission garrison, but succeeded in reoccupying the Fort of GYANTSE and investing our troops. These events and other evidence of deliberate Tibetan hostility led to a decision that the relief of GYANTSE should be extended to the occupation of LHASA. For this further troops were required; and thus it came about that the XIX Punjabis together with 8 guns, one wing of the Royal Fusiliers and the 5th Battalion of the Regiment (40th Pathans) were ordered up from India. On the arrival of the first of these reinforcements the area about GYANTSE was cleared of enemy, and on the 6th July the Fort of GYANTSE was stormed. A week later the main force continued the advance against only slight opposition and on 3rd August entered LHASA.

Being the last of the reinforcing regiments to arrive, the XIX Punjabis were destined to serve on the Lines of Communication. Including 1 Jemadar and 20 other ranks of the 3rd Battalion 14th Punjab Regiment (22nd Punjabis) the Regiment entrained at FEROZEPORE on the evening of 29th June.

The following officers accompanied :—

Major L.N. Herbert	Commanding.
Major (afterwards General) S.H. Climo (24th Punjabis)	2nd-in-Command and 1st Double Company Commander.
Captain (afterwards General) E. Kirkpatrick (6th Royal Battalion, 13th Frontier Force Rifles)	2nd Double Company Commander.
Captain S.K.B. Rice (10th Battalion, The Sikh Regiment)	3rd Double Company Commander.
Captain F.T. Duhan	4th Double Company Commander.
Lieutenant H.C.D. Jarrett	Adjutant.
Lieutenant W.F.B. Edwards	(24th Punjabis).
Lieutenant R.F. Finlay	(5th Battalion, The Frontier Force Rifles).
Lieutenant B.W.E. Dimsford.	
Lieutenant D.B. Ross	Officiating Quartermaster.
Lieutenant G.N. Thompson.	
Lieutenant (afterwards General) C.N. Macmullen (2nd Royal Battalion, The Sikh Regiment).	
Lieutenant A.F. Pilkington	Medical Officer.

Captain Churchill and Lieutenant Tancred who were in England on a year's leave rejoined at the end of July, the former to take over the 3rd Double Company and the latter to be Quartermaster. Captain E. C. Barnes commanded the Depot at FEROZEPORE. Lieutenant-Colonel A. H. Wilmer, Commandant, was on sick leave in England throughout the campaign. Major (afterwards General) G. J. Fitz M. Soady had transferred to the 5th Battalion The Sikh Regiment as 2nd-in-Command on 18th April. Major W. Malleson was with Intelligence Bureau. Captain G. A. Dale was with the Grass Farms Department, Captain (afterwards General) C. W. G. Richardson was at Army Headquarters, and Captain G. Pennefather-Evans with the Burma Military Police.

Subadar-Major Ghulam Kadir, O. B. I., had just retired after 10 years in the appointment, and Ghulam Muhamad, the senior subadar, filled his position in Tibet. Jemadar Isar Singh was Native Adjutant.

The Regiment reached SILIGURI, the base, on 3rd July, and later continued by narrow gauge railway as far as GHUM where the march was begun. The first few stages lay up the hot and unhealthy valley of the TEESTA, the river which the Regiment had known just 39 years before. A cart road led to the advanced base at RANGPO. From there on the route, though being rapidly improved by the Pioneers and Sappers, was still a mere track. It struck up a wooded branch valley to the village of RONGLI, and in the next 15 miles climbed 10,000 feet up a spur of the Himalayas to the one-time British camp of GNATONG. Another 10 miles of steep zigzags brought the Regiment above the tree line to the knife edge pass of JALEP LA. From LANGRAM on the north slope of this pass the descent was continued to CHUMBI in the fertile valley of that name. Here, at the camp of NEW CHUMBI 1½ miles beyond the village and 9,780 feet high, the headquarters of the Regiment was established on 20th July.

The XIX Punjabis were entrusted with reopening the 125 miles of route between CHUMBI and GYANTSE, and in this task they were associated with small detachments from the three mounted Infantry Companies of the force. Altogether 10 intermediate convoy posts had to be established and fortified. Since supplies had to be delivered to GYANTSE as soon as possible the Regiment advanced at once. The first post was established at 11,200 feet amid the trees of LINGMO, the next on the icy plateau of DOTAK. A larger detachment was left at the important and extremely dirty Tibetan fort of PHARI JONG. The TANG LA pass for all its 15,200 feet of altitude was found wide and easy to cross. At TUNE the Regiment placed its most elevated detachment at a height of 14,950 feet. The next post was at DOCHEN beside the RHAM LAKE. Twelve miles beyond and lower was KALA on the lake of that name. The remaining detachments were among the villages and monasteries which onwards dotted the NYANG RIVER valley, —MANGTSA, KANGMAR and SAOGANG.

For 2½ months the XIX Punjabis operated in this desolate region protecting convoys, improving the track for the thousands of ekkas which had been carried over the passes, collecting grain and fuel and combating sickness. Even in these summer months the hardships from cold and wind were considerable. Night temperatures showed 10 to 21 degrees of frost. The floors of tents were dug down for warmth. The working parts of rifles and Maxim guns had to be left completely unoiled. Men as well as officers wore Balaclava caps, snow goggles, comforters, long-sleeved Poshteens, Gilgit boots and woollen underclothing. There were many cases of pneumonia : in fact, out of the 1,082 sick casualties in the force 607 were attributed to the rigour of the climate. The transport animals also—ponies, mules, bullocks and yaks—suffered severely from a variety of diseases. All but 40 of the 400 yaks succumbed.

During this period there was little enemy interference on the Line of Communication, since operations about GYANTSE and LHASA had driven the Tibetan forces north of the TSANGPO

RIVER.

On 23rd September after the Tibetan government had submitted the Mission and force retired from LHASA. From 10th October this withdrawal was continued from GYANTSE in several columns at day intervals, and with these the various detachments of the Regiment returned to NEW CHUMBI. The left wing of the 40th Pathans, which was remaining behind in Tibet, relieved our detachments at PHARI JONG and CHUMBI, and also garrisoned GYANTSE and GANGTOK. It was now the beginning of winter and even colder. The rearmost parties encountered a blizzard while crossing the TANG LA pass through 3 feet of snow. In sunshine many men who had lost their goggles were afflicted with snow blindness. During a night at PHARI JONG there were 27 degrees of frost and almost all tents were blown down. After a short rest the Regiment left CHUMBI on 21st October via the NATHU LA and GANGTOK and 10 days later marched into SILIGURI. JULLUNDUR was reached by train on 5th November, and a few days afterwards the Depot joined from FEROZEPORE. In Tibet 4 sepoys had died of disease, while Lieutenant Macmullen and 11 men had been invalided. Major Herbert was mentioned in despatches, and all ranks received the special medal for "Tibet 03-04". In 1905 a "GYANTSE" clasp to the medal was sanctioned, and war gratuities were paid out. These varied from Rs. 1,440 for a subedar to Rs. 144 for a sepoy. The Commanding Officer and other majors got Rs. 388, captains Rs. 288 and subalterns Rs. 144.

CHAPTER XI.

1904—1914.

JULLUNDUR—Mohmand Operations—DERA ISMAIL KHAN—MALAKAND—QUETTA.

(Maps 1 and 6.)

JULLUNDUR, 1904—08.

The XIX Punjabis spent the next four years in JULLUNDUR, with a double-company detachment at AMRITSAR. Lieutenant-Colonel Herbert became Commandant from April of '05 when he had already been officiating for twelve months. In all this much-beloved officer guided the destinies of the Regiment for eight years. In September '05 Major T.Y. Seddon was brought in as 2nd-in-Command from the 34th Sikh Pioneers. 2nd Lieutenants E.H. Pemberton and D.E. Knollys had joined towards the end of '04. Nihal Singh was now Subadar-Major. Jalal Khan had become Native Adjutant.

The Regimental Jubilee was celebrated in January 1908. At the opening Durbar the pensioners, who included 14 subadars, 3 jemadars and 96 other ranks, were presented to the Commandant. Among them were three Mutiny veterans. There followed a parade on which the pensioned Native officers first inspected their old Regiment in line, and then took the salute during its march past. The following two days were devoted to sports and dancing. The Regiment gave a dinner to all pensioners, and the Sardars dined with the officers in the Mess. Finally, on the 24th January new Colours were presented by Major-General J.A.H. Pollock, CB, commanding Jullundur Brigade.

These new Colours are those still borne by the 1st Battalion 14th Punjab Regiment. They differed from the old, which are now framed in the officers' mess, by having "PUNJABIS" on both standards, and mauve as the basis of the Regiment Colour instead of crimson.

Great progress was made in field training during these first years of Lord Kitchener's tenure as Commander-in-Chief. As part of the 3rd (Lahore) Division the Regiment went to the HOSHIARPUR Training Camp in December '04; to the RAWALPINDI manoeuvres in the following year; and back to HOSHIARPUR in 1906, the year during which the Lee-Enfield rifle was issued. In 1907 brigade training took place near JULLUNDUR itself.

Mohmand Operations, 1908.

In 1908 the Regiment was moved to the North-West Frontier to take part in operations against the Mohmands. In February there had been that most successful Bazar Valley Expedition whereby Major-General Sir James Willcocks of the 1st (Peshawar) Division had subdued the Zakka Khel and completely overrun their country in three weeks. Mohmands gathered from both sides of the Durand Line to support this Afridi tribe, and when they found that they were too late for that operation started hostilities on their own account. During March they started raiding into Peshawar District, and the military border posts at SHABKADAR, MATTA MUGHAL KHEL and ABAZAI had to be reinforced. Extra troops were moved into PESHAWAR, and the 1st, 2nd and 3rd Brigades of the Zakka Khel Field Force were remobilized ready for eventualities. During April the tribesmen sniped the Border posts and collected a lashkar of 10,000 men. They attacked the Royal Northumberland Fusiliers at MATTA and GARHI SADAR unsuccessfully on the night 23rd/24th April; and the counter-attack which the 1st Brigade carried out next morning put an end to fighting in that area.

"Map 6."

But large numbers of Mohmands, mainly from Afghanistan, were now threatening the western end of the KHYBER PASS and the 3rd (Reserve) Brigade had to be moved up to LANDI KOTAL from PESHAWAR. The XIX Punjabis received orders on 30th April to join this brigade. The rush of mobilization, even in those simple days, must have been considerable; for the Regiment left JULLUNDUR by train the very next day and reached PESHAWAR on 3rd May. However, the 3rd Brigade had already marched and the XIXth had to await its return. This brigade of Brigadier-General Ramsay's, which included three battalions of the present-day Regiment—the 21st Punjabis, 22nd Punjabis and 40th Pathans—particularly distinguished itself in the attack on 4th May which drove the Afghans back over the frontier at LANDI KHANA.

On return to PESHAWAR the 3rd Brigade was at once switched to the Mohmand border. It reached SUBHAN KHWAR camp near SHABKADAR on 11th May and took over the L. of C. forts and posts from the 1st Brigade. The 22nd Punjabis now transferred to the 2nd Brigade, and the XIXth took their place in the 3rd.

The third phase of the campaign which now began was the punishment of the Mohmand tribes. On 13th May the 1st and 2nd Brigades advanced on NAHAKHI across the border, while the same night the Regiment marched from PESHAWAR to SUBHAN KHWAR camp. During the next three weeks when one section of the tribe after another was overrun and subjugated the 3rd Brigade was employed on the Lines of Communication. The Sherdils had headquarters and six companies at SUBHAN KHWAR and SHABKADAR, with the remaining two at ABZAI FORT. There was much escorting of convoys, piqueting and patrolling, but nothing of moment occurred and not a single round was expended. One sepoy was killed accidentally. Jemadar Jalal Khan, who was attached to the 22nd Punjabis, was mentioned in despatches for gallantry. After welcoming the 22nd Punjabis back on 31st May the Regiment took its turn in the dispersal of the Force, and eventually reached JULLUNDUR on 5th June.

DERA ISMAIL KHAN, 1909-11.

"Map 6."

In December the XIX Punjabis ended their long stay in JULLUNDUR. The Brigade Commander's remarks on his final inspection indicate that they had earned a fine reputation there for efficiency, and had proved it in the short Mohmand operation. On 16th December the Regiment started off along the now well-known march route through FEROZEPORE and MULTAN. Crossing the RIVER INDUS for the fifth time in their history the "Sherdils" reached DERA ISMAIL KHAN on 27th January, 1909.

They remained there throughout that and the next two years. The Derajat was then remarkably peaceful, and little but intimate regimental matters are recorded. Lieutenants J. G. P. Drummond and N. M. Martin joined in 1910, Lieutenant P. Conder in 1911. 1911 was the year of King George V's coronation. Subadar Fateh Khan, OBI, represented the Indian Officers of the Regiment at the ceremony in LONDON, while to the Durbar in DELHI went Subadar-Majors Ghulam Kadar, OBI (retired), and Amar Singh, as well as Subadars Amir Khan and Jalal Khan. White gloves and gold sword slings in Review Order were a modification in officers' dress which was introduced at the end of the same year.

Other units in DERA ISMAIL KHAN were the 21st (Kohat) Mountain Battery, the present 5th Battalion The Sikh Regiment and the 40th Pathans who were later to be the 5th Battalion of the Regiment. All were good friends and there was a considerable amount of entertainment among the officers. The hot weathers even produced keenly-contested jerimundulum championships under finger bowls on after-dinner Mess tables; and most memorable of all such final bounts was that between "Sher Dil" representing the Regiment and "Kikar Singh" of the Sikhs. There was polo twice a week, and a continuous series of hockey matches.

Regiments in rotation provided a double-company detachment in JANDOLA FORT for three months at a time. Here within the South Waziristan hills realistic frontier training could be carried out. The garrison were sniped from time to time, now by Mahsuds now by Bhitannis. Occasionally a skirmish between the two tribes could be viewed from the walls of fort.

MALAKAND, 1912—14.

December 1911 saw the XIXth on the move again. Marching along the Waziristan foothills to BANNU and thence to KOHAT, PESHAWAR and NOWSHERA they reached MALAKAND FORT on 15th January 1912. Three months later Colonel L.N. Herbert went on pension and the Regiment lost one of its most outstanding Commandants. His long tenure had seen the transition from the old days and ways to the new; from the stereotyped in training to the flexible born of the Boer War and Lord Kitchener. The Maxim machine gun had added a third regimental weapon. In November, repeating what had been done thirteen years previously, headquarters and the left wing of the Regiment moved into CHAKDARA FORT, while the right went to garrison DARGAI. The two wings interchanged every four months, and thus the months passed uneventfully into and through 1913. Twice inspected by the General Officer Commanding, Peshawar Division, the XIXth earned words which show how they stood in general estimation on the eve of the First World War - "This is a good, sound, reliable and efficient Regiment in which an excellent spirit seems to prevail. The men are of good stamp, healthy and cheerful, and physically fit. Though isolated at CHAKDARA and DARGAI the Regiment has not lost smartness, while the field work is good intelligent. The Regiment is quite fit for active service."

"Map 1"

QUETTA, 1914.

Having concentrated at DARGAI and left there on 24th March 1914 the XIX Punjabis entrained at NOWSHERA and reached QUETTA on the last day of the month. After the isolation of the MALAKAND life in QUETTA was a delightful change for all ranks, and close contact and competition with so many units proved to be as stimulating as the climate. Intensive company and battalion training occupied the first three months; but then it became the Regiment's turn to find the company detachments for QUETTA's inner ring of outposts, HARNAI, MASTUNG and

"Map 8."

HIROK. The unfortunate effect of this was that when war came in August the XIXth were not concentrated, and thus were not conveniently available for field service.

On the eve of the First World War it will be as well to list the officers who were with the Regiment at the time of its arrival in QUETTA, and on whom its great expansion was to be founded.

Lieut.-Col.	T.Y. Seddon	Commandant.
Lieut.-Col.	G.A. Dale	Director of Farms, Northern Command.
Major	G.P. Evans	Offg 2nd-in-Command.
Major	G.R.D. Churchill.	
Major	F.T. Duhan	On leave.
Captain	H.C.D. Jarrett.	
Captain	E.C. Barnes.	
Captain	J.Y. Tancred	On leave.
Captain	D.B. Ross	Adjutant.
Captain	E.H. Pemberton.	
Captain	D.E. Knollys	On leave.
Captain	L.M. Heath	Adjutant from 3-4-14.
Lieutenant	R.W. Hornsby	Quartermaster.
Lieutenant	A.D. Bennett.	
Lieutenant	P. Conder.	
Lieutenant	J.G.P. Drummond.	
Captain	R.N. Chopra	Medical Officer.

Organization, 1914.

So sweeping were the changes in infantry organization after the World War that it is interesting to note the situation at its beginning. As in the majority of Indian infantry units, the establishment of the Regiment was 15 British officers including the Medical Officer, 16 Indian officers and 896 Indian other ranks. On mobilization the establishment was less—13 BOs, 17 IOs, 736 IORs; but out of the difference the Regiment had to form its own Depot, where the training of recruits was continued and regimental administration centred. Thus it was difficult to go on service at war establishment without receiving drafts from other regiments or completing with unsatisfactory reservists.

Service in the reserve was voluntary after three years' colour service. Reservists were trained for two months biennially by whichever of the 'linked' regiments was at the Regimental Centre, JHELUM. They were a motly collection. Only a few were young men; the majority were old with up to 21 years' total service ; many were white-bearded and quite unfit for active service overseas.

For inter-reinforcement in war the XIXth were linked with the 22nd and 24th Punjabis. There was a spirit of good comradeship between the three regiments, more especially between the British officers ; but there was no unifying title or 'link' *esprit-de-corps* to render less unpopular among the Indian other ranks their occasional transfer from one unit to another. Further, the usefulness of the 'link' arrangement was minimized by differences in the classes enlisted. The XIXth did not enlist Dogras as the 24th Punjabis did ; yet they took Afridis and certain other trans-border Pathans not to be found in the 22nd Punjabis. The system indeed soon broke down.

The Regiment was organized as a small headquarters, a machine gun section of two pack Maxims and eight companies armed with the new Short Magazine Lee-Enfield rifle (mark III) and bayonet. Each company was commanded by a subadar with a jemadar as second-in-command. There were four companies of Jat Sikhs, two of Punjabis Musalmans and two of Pathans. One of these was all-Afridi ; the other partly Muhammadzai and partly Yusufzai including transborder Dush Khel from Southern Dir. Each pair of companies, *e. g.*, one Sikh, one Muhammadan, formed a double-company commanded by a British officer who had one or two others as double-company officers to assist him. It was somewhat later in the war that Indian infantry adopted the British Army model of a Headquarter Wing, which included the machine gun sub-unit and administrative personnel and transport, together with four large companies each of four platoons commanded by subadars or jemadars.

CHAPTER XII.

FIRST WORLD WAR 1914-17—QUETTA—EAST PERSIA.

(Maps 8 & 9)

India at War.

The declaration of war against Germany on the 4th August 1914 caused intense enthusiasm in QUETTA, and excitement ran still higher when it became evident that troops from India were to be sent overseas at once. Before the end of August several QUETTA units had received orders to join one or other of the six expeditionary forces which India was despatching. The principal of these were:—

Two cavalry divisions .. ..⎫ to France as
The 3rd (Lahore) and 7th (Meerut) ⎬ the Indian
    Infantry Divisions .. ..⎭ Corps.

Five infantry brigades .. ..⎫ to Egypt.
Imperial Service Troops .. ..⎭

A mixed force .... to East Africa.

An infantry brigade ⎫ to the head of
    (later one division) ⎭ Persian Gulf.

Majors Duhan and Jarrett with Captains Barnes, Tancred and Knollys were fortunate in getting to France before the end of 1914. Major Duhan was killed in 1915 at YPRES. Captains Barnes and Tancred were wounded, and both returned to QUETTA before the end of that year.

The heavy casualties and sick wastage which soon occurred overseas, coupled with the general failure of the reservist organization, required large drafts to be sent out from the units destined to be left in India. As far as possible men were sent as complete companies under their own officers, or at least under their own Indian Officers, so that their interests did not suffer through absorption into a strange unit. The first draft from the Regiment, 70 N. C. Os. and men, embarked at KARACHI on 2nd November to join the 24th Punjabis in Mesopotamia. They subsequently endured the Siege of KUT. The next major despatch was on 5th January 1915, a specially formed double-company of Sikhs going under Major

G. P. Evans to the 15th Sikhs in France. Later in 1915 two more double-companies of young soldiers were ready for overseas. Of these No. 5 comprising 'L' Company of Punjab-Musalmans and 'M' Company of Pathans sailed for France on 13th October under Captain L. M. Heath to join the 59th Scinde Rifles.

In fact all battalions which did not have arduous security duties to perform—and there were frontier outbreaks from time to time—became training regiments. Every effort was made to enrol as many recruits as could be accommodated and to train them as rapidly as reasonably possible. Large recruiting parties were kept out in rotation. Pre-war standards of age, height and to some extent sub-class were relaxed. On the square were to be found immature youths side by side with bearded men. By August 1915 over 900 new recruits had been enrolled, a figure surpassed by only one unit in India. For his good work in recruiting Subadar-Major Fateh Khan was granted a Khillat of Rs. 300 and presented personally by the Viceroy in Durbar with a Sword of Honour. The training of recruits was still the particular responsibility of the Adjutant, and the XIXth were fortunate in having for the task of dealing with eight times the normal intake the highly trained Drill Staff which Captain D.B. Ross had perfected during recent years.

Mention should be made of the Indian Army Reserve of Officers. On the outbreak of war large numbers of Englishmen in civil employ in India and the Far East were granted commissions in the small reserve. They formed the main source of the new regimental officers, and made up for their lack of military training with their keenness and fondness for Indian troops. Eleven joined the Regiment during 1915. Many proceeded on field service to the chagrin of the regular officers.

The KACHA Detachment.

As already mentioned, the ill-luck of the XIX Punjabis to be on detachment duty around QUETTA at the outbreak of the war made it patent that the Regiment would not be included among those first despatched overseas. Rising hope again receded when the Regiment was ordered to provide the ROBAT detachment. ROBAT was 381 miles by route march beyond railhead at NUSHKI. The strength was a wing, and the normal tour of duty one year. Instituted in 1910 as a measure for combating the trade in small-arms and ammunition between the coast of the Persian Gulf and the tribes of the North West Frontier, this detachment at the junction of frontiers of Baluchistan, Persia and Afghanistan had become important for its political influence. How very important it was to become, how the detachment would grow into the Regiment itself, and

"Map 8."

the Regiment into a field force, none at this time could foresee; the officers merely regarded the commitment as a colossal piece of misfortune.

The detachment of two double-companies, with the machine gun section and that of the 12th Pioneers, left QUETTA on 17th March 1915. The Indian strength was 3 Indian Officers, 400 other ranks and 26 followers. The companies were Sikh (two), Punjabi-Musalman and Afridi. The British Officers were:

Lieutenant-Colonel G.A. Dale ...	in Command.
Major E.H. Pemberton. ...	Commanding one double-company and in charge of machine gun section.
Captain R.H. Hornsby ...	Double-company Commander and detachment staff officer.
Second Lieutenant G. Pigot ...	who had joined in QUETTA on 29th Jan. 1915 from the Unattached List.
Second Lieutenant C.R.K. Crossfield. ...	I.A.R.O.
Captain Yeates ...	12th Pioneers.
Major Overbeck-Wright, IMS. ...	Medical Officer.

"Map 8." After detraining at NUSHKI camel transport was collected and the long march began. The distance to KACHA, which was the actual location of the detachment some 42 miles short of ROBAT, was 355 miles. This was covered in 20 stages with rest-day halts at DALBANDIN, MERUI, NUSHKI CHAH and SAINDAK. There was at this date no road, merely a camel track following the Indo-Persian Telegraph line across 'dasht' and sand. In later years the importance of East Persia led to an extension of the NUSHKI railway by 138 miles to DALBANDIN, afterwards up to MIRJAWA and finally to DUZDAB on the Persian frontier. Later still there came into being a MT road linking QUETTA with MESHED along this route.

The great heat of the day caused much of the marching to be done at night. Carrying 6 months' supplies and rather more ammunition than usual, the detachment employed some 600 camels. In this utterly desert country water was non-existent except at the stage wells, and there was restricted. Camel grazing was pitifully scanty, and several scores of animals died on this march.

With the departure of the KACHA detachment the

number of trained soldiers at QUETTA headquarters was reduced to 200, and the enrolment and training of recruits became the sole pre-occupation. Captain L.M. Heath was the new Adjutant until he went on service to France and Mesopotamia. Lieutenant A.D. Bennett became Quartermaster. Until Captains Barnes and Tancred returned, the only other regular officers were Lieutenant-Colonel T.Y. Seddon, 2nd-Lieutenants G.E.F. Shute and S.H. Woolf. Drafts of 59 ranks for the 24th Punjabis and 69 for the 22nd Punjabis were sent to Mesopotamia in January 1916; and further parties left at the end of February for these linked regiments. The last draft to be sent overseas was 2 Indian officers and 98 other ranks to the 28th Punjabis in mid-October.

The Detachment becomes the Battalion.

The Detachment under Lieutenant-Colonel Dale became increasingly important, and more and more elements of Regimental headquarters were sent out to it. It was organised as a battalion from 1st February 1916. Command was finally transferred from 23rd November of that year, when Lieutenant-Colonel Seddon completed his tenure. Troops in QUETTA then became the Depot, and this was immediately moved to HYDERABAD (SIND). It had been hard, dull work in QUETTA, but its value did not pass unrecognized. On the occasion of his inspection in 1916, the Divisional Commander, Sir Malcolm Grover, remarked—"The general result in my opinion is highly satisfactory. The Battalion has already received special commendation from H.E. the Commander-in-Chief, and I wish to report in high terms on the excellent work that continues to be done by all ranks. The Battalion is already on Special Service (Field Service, Persia, from 1st February 1916) and is fit for any service."

On 12th January 1916 the 2nd Battalion XIX Punjabis was formed at the Depot, with Lieutenant-Colonel G.R.D. Churchill as Commandant.

Operations in EAST PERSIA.

Lieut.-Colonel Dale's detachment was not long at rest in KACHA. Its function was no longer merely to prevent commercial gun-running into Afghanistan. German intrigue in Afghanistan and among the Sarhad tribes of the Persian-Baluch frontier had been intensified since the outbreak of war and facilitated by the alliance of Turkey. Across Persia the road to Afghanistan lay open for arms, gold, agents and wireless sets. Germany had already established agents in KABUL; and although the Amir Habibullah himself was far-seeing enough to strive for peace with India, his brother Nasrulla was at the head of a pro-enemy faction. German and Turkish agents in Persia now made strenuous efforts to reach Afghanistan with persuasive evidence of German might. To bar their way it was decided to form a cordon, the Russians providing the necessary troops in the Khorasan Province of Persia and Great Britain continuing the line southwards. Thus within a month of its arrival the KACHA Detachment began to be reinforced and deployed. Some staff cars arrived from QUETTA and enabled long-distance reconnaissances to be made along the road to KIRMAN and to KHWASH (VASHT) in the Sarhad. In July 1915, leaving one company under Captain Hornsby and Lieutenant Pigot at KACHA, the detachment moved forward to ROBAT. Their next move, in August, was one of 90 miles to NASRATBAD the capital of Seistan province, and thence another 220 to BIRJAND. A little further north contact was made with the Russian Cossacks at the village of SEDEH, which was 700 miles from railhead at NUSHKI.

"Map 9"

In the month of July 1915 occurred the first case in the regimental history of collective desertion. In fairness to our Afridis it must be admitted that it was somewhat provoked by official distrust. Ever since November 1914 when Turkey entered the war against the Entente Powers it had been feared that the Trans-Frontier classes, over whose homes we had no control, might succumb to the propaganda of their mullahs and decline to bear arms against Caliphate. There had been only a few desertions from Cantonments; but Afridi recruiters more and more returned empty-handed or did not return at all. Then came reports of desertions to the Turks in Mesopotamia, and even to the Germans in France. Proud of our Afridis, who were always well-disciplined, smart and popular, it had seemed a matter for congratulation that they were out of harm's way at KACHA. The Afridi company were in good heart and shared the general enthusiasm of more active service when they started on the march to the north. Then Army Headquarters ordered them to be sent back from ROBAT to KACHA, and thence to QUETTA. It had been learnt that one of the alternatives which the Germans were offering to Pathan deserters was service in their Mission to Afghanistan, and that a few Afridis were already in German pay in Persia. If the danger of employing our Afridis in the Cordon could not be faced, the other risk of trusting them with their arms as they marched back was to be accepted, presumably in support of their honour and that of the Regiment. So decided Army Headquarters, contrary to Lieutenant-Colonel Dale's own recommendation. The reactions of Afridis to affront are, however, predictable only to those in touch with them. After returning from ROBAT to KACHA the Company was ordered to escort convoys to NUSHKI and thence proceed to QUETTA. The first party of thirty-nine under the colour havildar deserted near AMALAF during the third march. Abandoning the convoy, they set out for the HELMAND RIVER 65 miles to the north across the burning, waterless waste and salty sands of the GAUD-I-ZIRREH. "Map 9"

Doubtless they argued that they would be discharged ungenerously as a class on reaching QUETTA, and it would be better to desert now to their country with valuable weapons and ammunition. Tragedy overtook them. Chagai Camel Levies after long days of tracking came upon thirty-seven bodies and all the rifles and ammunition far out in the salt pan which is the old bed of the HELMAND. Their bodies were contorted and almost naked. Their hands were thrust into holes which they had dug in their vain quest for water. A mere few miles further lay the freshwater river, but only the havildar and the bugler had had the strength to stagger on till they reached it. Years later these two were recognized in their native Tirah. The second party were now disarmed. They marched back loyally with the next convoy. On their reaching QUETTA all Afridis were mustered out of the Regiment for the duration of the war.

As the Regiment spread north to establish the cordon reinforcements began to arrive. With the appearance of the 28th Light Cavalry (now 7th Light Cavalry) there began that long and close friendship which was to carry the two units in the van of a movement across Persia and almost up to the River OXUS in Russian Turkestan. The first two squadrons came on camels, but later all horses were brought out from QUETTA. Various squadrons or troops went to ROBAT (14 August), to NASRATABAD (21st August), to BIRJAND, to BANDAN and NEH on the road between the last two places and to far away KHWASH in the South. Then in September came the 6th Double-company under Captain A. D. Bennett and Lieutenant W.H. Chalmers, which comprised P company of Sikhs and Q of Punjabi Musalmans. They soon moved out from KACHA to DEHAN-I-BAGHI, a little telegraph station 90 miles west of ROBAT on the desert trade route from KIRMAN in Central Persia. Both German agents and raiding Baluch bands from the Sarhad were expected in that area. Lieutenant Pigot took a company from KACHA to NASRATBAD, and later on to BANDAN and NEH. Headquarters were now at BIRJAND. "Map 9"

SEISTAN.

A few words are due on Seistan, where during 1915 and

1916 there were always sub-units of the Regiment and through which at that time the south to north line of communication passed. It was an almost treeless though populous land of white 'pat' hemmed in by Afghanistan and the HELMAND on the east and by the vast Hamun, or lake delta of that river, on the west. There were water channels everywhere. The Hamun, covering between 2,000 and 1,500 square miles, filled up during the summer months and overflowed via the SHELAG RIVER into the GAUD-I-ZIRREH. At that season there was no dry road to BANDAN across the waist of the lakes. All troops and supplies had to be ferried for a mile or two in 'Tutins', which were boatshaped rafts made from the reeds. There were vast expanses of reeds through which the passage was made. The climate was one of extremes: sometimes up to 6 inches of snow in January: in summer fierce heat and stinging gadflies from which horses had to be protected by trousers. Above all Seistan was the home of the Bad-i-Sad-o-Bist-Roz, that 50-90 mile-an-hour wind which blows from the N. N. W. punctually and continuously from May to September over a width about 100 miles, and which is felt as far away as QUETTA. Under a clear sky it drives great clouds of gravel and dust, wears away rock, erodes the ground, banks up the water and makes movement difficult. It does, however, mitigate the heat and remove some of the flies. NASRATBAD itself, though the name means "the abode of victory", was an undistinguished collection of domed brick huts and a ruined fort. There was a small ill-kept Persian garrison, also a Russian consulate with Cossack guards. Only the British Consulate under Major Prideaux was inviting. The Seistani was a cheery, mud-larking agriculturist, utterly unwarlike and quite unreliable as a guide.

The East Persia Cordon Field Force.

From 1st February 1916 the Cordon troops were placed on field service and formed into the Seistan Field Force, which, a little later was redesignated the East Persia Cordon Field Force. Lieutenant-Colonel Dale continued to command both the Force and his unit until 14th May 1917 when he was made a Brigadier-General and command of the Battalion then devolved successively on Captain Drummond and Major Pemberton.

As the enemy increased their efforts, and as more troops became available, the Cordon was drawn tighter, many intercepting patrols were carried out and there were a few clashes.

Action of LERA DIK, 13th April, 1916.

"Map 9"

In April about half of Captain Bennett's double company with some 50 levies moved out east from DEHAN-I-BAGHI to intercept the return of an Ismailzai lashkar of 500 under Juma Khan, which had struck north from the Sarhad. At the same time a troop of the 28th Light Cavalry with some camel levies and a party of 30 of the Regiment under Subadar Mehdi Khan closed in from NASRATBAD.

On 13th April the 80 Sikhs and PMs suddenly met the lashkar in the LERA DIK plain north of GERAGHEH. An all-day fire fight ensued under a pitiless sun. The company were forced to fight in the open while the enemy retained the hill round which they had appeared. The Ismailzais captured the company's transport. At 1700 hours 400 of them made a sword charge. They were stopped at 100 yards and another fire fight lasted for an hour. Then a heavy sandstorm intervened and the enemy withdrew to the southeast. 2nd-Lieutenant W. H. Chalmers and 10 men had been killed, and there were 15 wounded. Captain Bennett was awarded the Military Cross for gallantry in command. The NASRATABAD column under Captain Wise, however, were well situated to intercept the Ismailzais next morning. They came on them when halted, scattered them to some hills where they were cleverly hemmed in by Subadar Mehdi Khan. They broke back into the plain again in order to reach other hills, but were caught in the open by the charging cavalry and finally routed. They left 50 dead and lost 2000 sheep with 50 camels.

In February 1916 2nd-Lieutenant Crossfield with his detachment at NEH had taken part in a predominantly cavalry success at DEH SALM 50 miles distant on the eastern edge of the LUT desert. Warned that an enemy party which included three Germans had just crossed that wilderness from KIRMAN, two troops 28th Light Cavalry set off at once from NEH, followed by the infantry. After a rapid march the cavalry surprised the enemy resting at the little oasis, drove them into waterless hills and pinned them there throughout the second day until the XIX Punjabis came up, having marched 70 miles in 48 hours. By night the party managed to slip out and escape to KIRMAN, except for one German Officer, WINKLEMAN, who was captured.

"Map 9"

In September 1916 when Lieutenant Pigot's detachment was at DEHAN-I-DAGHI an Afghan arms caravan of 26 camels was reported to be edging along the LUT desert to the north. The cavalry troop followed by 40 ranks of the Regiment at once set out to catch this party. Two days later they came upon them at the waterhole of SHORAB. Following a mounted charge in which Lieutenant Wahl of the 28th Light Cavalry who was in command was killed, the little force engaged the Afghans in difficult hills until dark and captured their caravan. The enemy dispersed during the night, losing 5 killed, 400 rifles and 60,000 rounds of ammunition.

This encounter was repeated in March 1917 under almost identical circumstances in the same locality of SHORAB. Captain Kreyer commanded the cavalry troop. Lieutenant Davies with his detachment of the Regiment joined up with the cavalry after marching 40 miles from DEHAN-I-BAGHI in 15 hours. A combined attack scattered the gunrunners and captured 450 rifles.

The Sarhad.

"Map 9"

During 1916 the centre of gravity shifted south again. Early in the year the Persian Baluch tribesmen of SARHAD under their chieftain Jiand Khan began attacking maintenance convoys between DALBANDIN and ROBAT, and Brigadier-General R. E. H. Dyer was sent out from India to take command in this area. Having failed in negotiation he characteristically at once took the offensive with the few troops at hand. These were one troop 28th Light Cavalry, one section of mountain guns, one machine gun section 12th Pioneers and 65 reinforcements of the XIX Punjabis then en route to KACHA. Starting from MIRJAWA on 7th April this little force marched straight on KHWASH FORT, the enemy centre. JIAND's lashkar of about 2000 which was encountered at the foot of KOH-I-TAFTAN on the second day was out-manoeuvred, bluffed into retreat, followed up during the next two days and driven into the hills east of KHWASH. The fort was then seized and garrisoned. A little later a temporary peace was made, and the force withdrew to KACHA.

No sooner had they arrived there than they hastened back to KHWASH, followed by the rest of the cavalry squadron and Captain Bennett's double-company. The Sarhadi chiefs had broken the pact, and were closing in on KHWASH with their forces. The troops got back just in time. Jiand and the other main leaders, on their showing treachery in Jirga, were dramatically arrested. The Sarhad blazed with fresh hostility. At the end of June these prisoners were sent away from KHWASH for safer custody. Their escort of one cavalry troop and a weak company of the XIX Punjabis were attacked in camp at the end of the first march, and in the dark and confusion all prisoners except JIAND and his son escaped. The situation at KHWASH then compelled the withdrawal of most of the company, leaving only a small party with the cavalry. The weakened escort were ambushed next midday in the LARIMHA PASS and pinned in the gorge until dusk. Those cavalrymen who were doing close escort to the prisoners were all shot down; the renowned Jiand and his heir got away.

The main campaign then began around KHWASH, and lasted throughout July and August. Three hundred of the 106th Hazara Pioneers, who had come out from QUETTA, formed the main part of the infantry, Captain Bennett's double-company in part accompanying them and for the rest garrisoning KHWASH. Regimental headquarters left BIRJAND for KACHA.

Action of GUSHT DEFILE, 20-21st July 1916.

Brigadier-General Dyer's column first drove on GUSHT at one entrance into the MORPEISH HILLS where the tribesmen's flocks and families had gone. On 19th July they entered the hills, the Hazaras and XIX Punjabis detachment piqueting the heights against some opposition. Next day in trying to force the narrowest part of the GUSHT DEFILE very heavy opposition was met, there were a number of casualties, and the column had to return to their last camp. Here they were heavily attacked that night, all next day and the night following by the ever-increasing and now fanatically elated tribesmen. By dawn on the 22nd almost every man in camp had reinforced the outer piquets to prevent their imminent capture. Then Halil Khan the tribal leader was shot. This, added to the enemy's other losses of 80 dead and further wounded, brought an end to a long and gallant action. A tribute to those who fought at GUSHT DEFILE in July 1916 is engraved on the Regimental War Memorial at FEROZEPORE.

The column advanced through the gorge next day, but were then forced back to KHWASH for lack of water. After two days' rest they again marched east to GUSHT and continued to JALK where, after one further brush, the tribesmen finally accepted defeat.

Reorganization, 1917.

1917 opened with the reorganiztion of companies in the Regiment; and "platoons" were introduced in September:—

No. 1 Company	three platoons	..	Punjabi Musalmans.
	one platoon	..	Yusafzais.
No. 2 Company	four platoons	..	Jat Sikhs.
No. 3 Company	three platoons	..	Jat Sikhs
	one platoon	..	Punjabi Musalmans.
No. 4 Company	four platoons	..	Punjabi Musalmans.

The second machine gun section of the 12th Pioneers which had been fighting in the Sarhad was incorporated into the Battalion. The officer strength was augmented by the arrival of Captain Drummond and 2nd-Lieutenants N.V. Hart, J.G. Miller, J.H. Davies, F.W. Stewart, R.F.G. Adams, L.S. Ingle and W.F. Gipps.

Isar Singh acted as Subadar-Major until Fateh Khan arrived from the Depot in the following year. Two drafts, one of 1 Indian Officer, 99 other ranks and the other of 2 Indian Officers, 99 other ranks, came out from HYDERABAD (SIND) during October and November. Just before the end of the year Major D.E. Knollys arrived to assume command with the temporary rank of Lieutenant-Colonel. He was replaced at the Depot by Captain Bennett.

Although the Ismailzai and other Sarhadi tribes had been subdued and the L of C secured by the end of the year, one company was still required at KHWASH. The other flank of the Regiment was 500 miles away at BIRJAND. In between were detachments at KACHA, DEHAN-I-BAGHI, NASRATABAD and NEH. As more cars and some lorries became available a great deal of regimental labour was expended on roadmaking. This not only made Cordon patrol work swifter but paved the way for the great development in communications which was to come in 1918.

Already it was probable that there would be a northwards extension of British activities. The Russian Revolution had opened the Caucasus and Western Persia to the Germans and Turks, who now redoubled their efforts to make contact with Afghanistan. The Russian portion of the East Persia Cordon seemed likely to collapse.

CHAPTER XIII

FIRST WORLD WAR, 1918.

PERSIA—TRANSCASPIA to the actions of KAAKHA.

(See maps 8 and 10, sketch K and photographs in Regimental Albums.)

The Russian Revolution.

In East Persia the Russians had held their 350-mile sector of the Cordon from QAIN to their own frontier with detachments from two Semeorichenski Cossack Regiments of Russian-speaking Christians from around VYERNI in Turkestan. Although they had done their work well and were friendly with British and Indian ranks, the Revolution of October 1917, particularly its impact on their homes, proved too much for these men. They decided to leave Persia. This they did in an orderly way, riding away quietly from post after post to concentrate in MESHED and leave their officers there. The gap they left had to be filled. The XIX Punjabis, relieved of some detachments, were further stretched northwards, while the two squadrons of 28th Light Cavalry which had returned to India in March 1917 were hurried back to Khorasan. In February 1918 Battalion Headquarters returned to BIRJAND. Next month a company under Lieutenant Adams reached MESHED through deep snow, and a detachment went to TURBAT-I-HAIDARI. Much work on improving roads was necessary in the area, and this the troops now undertook.

"Map 9"

The new German threat.

In these early months of 1918 when in the supreme crisis of the war in France the British Armies were fighting desperately to stem the last German offensive there arose a new danger in the East which could not be ignored. The capture with BAGHDAD in 1917 of the main Turkish route into Persia had removed much of the danger which the East Persia Cordon was designed to counter. But the end of 1917 had also brought the Russian Revolution. This led at once to the collapse of the Russian Army of the Caucasus, to a northern gap in the defences of India

"Map 8"

into which the Central Powers were quick to thrust, and to a Russian government acting more or less in concert with our enemies.

The campaign which was to destroy the Turks in Palestine had not yet begun, and the Salonika front was still inactive. The Germans now landed at BATUM, opened Corps Headquarters at TIFLIS and prepared for an advance along the Central Asian Railway towards MESHED and KANDAHAR. The Turks moved on BAKU.

British counter-action was first the despatch from BAGHDAD in February 1918 of "Dunsterforce", a mission woefully weak in fighting strength but carried along by the enterprise of Major-General Dunsterville, once Commandant of the 2nd Battalion. This force fought across Persia to ENZELI on the Caspian Sea, sailed to BAKU, failed to rally the White Russians to the defence of that city against the Turks and had to withdraw in September. But by seizing the Caspian fleet it prevented the enemy from crossing to KRASNOVODSK and thus imposed the essential delay. In East Persia steps were taken to mount a counter-attack of some size, and meanwhile to supply with arms and money any moderate Russian elements across the frontier such as the "Provincial Government of Transcaspia" at ASKHABAD. It was intended when necessary to destroy port facilities at KRASNOVODSK, to damage the Central Asian Railway extensively and by cutting off its water and other supplies to reduce the western part of Transcaspia to the desert it formerly was. The Mission with this task was under Major-General Malleson, a former officer of the Regiment, who established his headquarters at MESHED. As nucleus of the fighting force the 28th Light Cavalry and XIX Punjabis were now concentrated at MESHED as rapidly as possible. Battalion Headquarters moved up from BIRJAND. Captain Shute's No. 2 Company ceased road building between TURBAT-I-HAIDARI and MESHED. Captain Pigot's No. 3 Company marched up from NEH and NASRATABAD, followed by the detachment at DEHAN-I-BAGHI and eventually by the company at KHWASH. The 98th Infantry, 107th Pioneers and Indian Labour Corps took their places on the L of C. The latter was now reorganised into seven sections from NUSHKI to MESHED, and later extended 170 miles further to ASKHABAD.

The railway was to be extended to NEH. From the existing railhead at JUZAKH (100 miles south-east of ROBAT) light motor convoys of supplies could now reach MESHED in eight days by a new route west of the Seistan Hamun. Major-General Dickson was Inspector-General, and Major-General Dale became GOC L of C Defence Troops with headquarters at BIRJAND. Finally the

L of C was under the GOC Quetta Division, but the Mission and its troops were directly under Army Headquarters, India.

By July Headquarters and three companies had assembled at MESHED. After three years in barren regions both officers and men much enjoyed this brief respite in well-watered Khorasan, and found MESHED of absorbing interest with its 120,000 inhabitants, extensive bazars and the beautiful Mosque of Imam Reza. Officers greatly appreciated the hospitality of Lieutenant-Colonel and Mrs. Grey at the British Consulate-General. At the same time there was much cause for anxiety. The province was in a very disturbed state owing partly to famine, partly to inept government and for the rest to the influence of the Russian Revolution. There was much banditry. In the city, which sheltered 6,000 hostile Caucasian Turks, a rising was feared and night-firing affrays were frequent.

Transcaspia.

The former Russian province of Transcaspia (now the Soviet Republic of Turkmenistan) comprised the great desert tract between the Caspian Sea and the RIVER OXUS (AMU DARYA). Its southernmost strip along the Persian frontier was the only part capable of development. There streams from the 3,000 foot Persian plateau and rivers from the Afghan mountains descend to form oases at intervals along the Central Asian Railway, itself the connecting lifeline. This railway, strategic in conception and a standing menace to India, started from the Aden-like port of KRASNOVODSK and after a desert 200 miles closed in on the border mountains at KIZIL ARVAT. Here were the railway workshops, a point of importance in the swaying fortunes of what inevitably became a railway war. Skirting the Persian hills for another 150 miles the line reached the provincial capital of ASKHABAD, a well-built and electrified town with public buildings, hospitals, churches and parks and which was normally the headquarters of a division. After following the foothills for another 100 miles to DUSHAK the railway changed its direction from south-east to east-north-east and entered the wilderness of the KARAKUM (Black Sands). At another 30 miles was the town and oasis of TEJEND where the river of that name (the HARI RUD of Afghanistan) entered the desert. Twenty miles further on the MURGHAB RIVER was MERV, an ancient capital in ruins close by the modern garrison town. Running south from here up the re-entrant between Persia and Afghanistan was the 192-mile branch line to KUSHK. This was the hush-hush frontier post and arsenal, the point of the dagger so long directed towards India. Even in those days of the Revolution KUSHK was still the pride of Russian Army officers, so much so that it was only with great

"Maps 8 & 10,"

difficulty that Lieutenant-Colonel Knollys, as commander of the British force, succeeded in visiting the place when it again came into Menshevik hands. It was found to have a triple system of wired strong-points and excellent store sheds previously filled with weapons and stores of every sort. Twenty miles beyond MERV the main line passed through BAIRAM ALI, a small settlement with a large cotton factory and a well-kept Imperial Park containing a shooting lodge, a noble church, fine buildings and good roads. From this point the railway, running north-east, traversed the worst 130 miles of the KARA KUM to the OXUS RIVER, a region of large sand dunes. At CHARDJUI a fine girder bridge crossed the OXUS, and from there the line continued via BOKHARA and SAMARKAND to join the main railway system at TASHKENT.

The Central Asian Railway, broad gauge and single, was the main line of communication on which both belligerents were to depend solely for supplies, troop movement and often for water. The railway service, administered on the Menshevik side from ASKHABAD, was efficient. Permanent way repairs were effected more quickly than the enemy could destroy the line by shelling. Culverts were replaced with incredible rapidity by piers of sleepers or even compressed cotton bales. Engines were oil-fired. Oil came from BAKU, and at times supplies of it were very low on both sides. Rolling stock consisted of large corridor cars with a bunk for every passenger, smaller observation cars which were suitable for headquarters, hospital coaches, restaurant cars and the excellent standard covered wagon which was fitted with ramps for the entrainment of animals and planks for forming either stalls for horses or bunks for men.

A carriage road followed the railway along most of its length; but it was unmetalled, unbridged except over the main rivers, and was used mainly by camel transport. The road MESHED—KUCHAN—ASKHABAD, the L of C from India, had been well aligned by Russian engineers; but, except for the short stretch in Russian territory, it was unmetalled. It was used by fourgons (4-horsed wagons) and camels; there were no motor vehicles in any case to spare for it. There was a branch of this route, fit only for pack animals, which reached the frontier and railway near MUHAMMADABAD, 60 miles south-east of ASKHABAD. It was by this road that the Regiment was supplied while at KAAKHA during the summer of 1918 until the easier though longer route to ASKHABAD was adopted.

Of the desert routes those leaving the railway west of MERV all ran north to KHIVA; but east of the MURGHAB RIVER there were several tracks from one well to another which led from the

OXUS and provided possible enemy lines of advance when MERV was held by the Mensheviks. The OXUS was a lateral communication for the Bolsheviks, and the Mensheviks were often uneasy lest they move a force to KHIVA and thence cross the desert to KRASNOVODSK by the route following the river's ancient bed. Actually this was never practicable owing to the deterioration of the OXUS Flotilla, the Bolsheviks' lack of road transport, the enormous undertaking of carrying water for the desert march and the enmity of the BOKHARA and KHIVA Khanates.

The true natives of Transcaspia were the Tekke and Tejend Turkomans, the tall, robust Turki-speaking Muhammadans of Central Asia. They wore long, deep-sleeved, black-and-red-striped Kurtas above mocassins or Russian boots, and on their heads large white or brown sheepskins. The greater part were nomad, tending flocks and camels in the foothill oases and living in portable domed huts called "kibitkas", which were made of felt over a cane framework. Others clung to the fringe of the Russian settlements, growing grain or cotton and driving camels. The towns were mainly inhabited by Russians, Caucasians, Armenians and Persians.

Bolsheviks and Mensheviks.

The Russian Revolution of the Bolsheviks spread to Turkestan via the ORENBURG railway, and Soviet rule was established in TASHKENT early in 1918. The province of Transcaspia was thus by-passed. The predominately railway and military colonies at KRASNOVODSK, KISL ARVAT, ASKHABAD and MERV remained conservative and constituted the local Mensheviks (moderates) in opposition to the Bolsheviks (extremists). In June 1918, just as the Malleson Mission came into being, the Bolsheviks of TASHKENT, who had been infiltrating westwards, tried to establish their extremism in TRANSCASPIA, and to link up with the commissars of BAKU. Whereupon the Mensheviks of KIZIL ARVAT and ASKHABAD rose against their oppressors, drove them back across the OXUS and appealed to the British to add troops to their other assistance. The Turkomans; who in later years were to accept Bolshevism for its material advantages, had recently so suffered from it in Turkestan that they were ready to discriminate in their usual dislike of all Russians. The Tejend Turkomans in particular were implacably opposed to the Bolsheviks and formed a very useful Menshevik "fifth column".

Although the collapse of the Turks after defeat in Palestine and Mesopotamia had by now much lessened the threat of enemy operations east of the Caspian Sea, it was clear that unless more practical assistance was given to the ASKHABAD government the whole province of Transcaspia adjoining Persia and Afghanistan would be overrun by unfriendly Bolsheviks. They had already recrossed the OXUS and forced the Mensheviks back by stages to the BAIRAM ALI position covering MERV. In July therefore British Military assistance was sanctioned. Troops lent would be under Russian command, but would reserve the right to differ from this authority in case of unreasonable tasks.

The rival Russian forces.

At this date the Bolshevik troops in contact with the Mensheviks comprised about 200 cavalry, 15 field guns and howitzers, two armoured trains mounting 4.5 howitzers as well as field guns, and a mixed lot of Austrian, Hungarian and Russian infantry totalling 4,000. In addition there was a large number of men guarding the railway in rear against the attacks of Bokharans and Tejend Turkomans. The mainstay of the army were the thousands of Austrian and Hungarian soldiers who after being prisoners of war in Turkestan for the past two years were now promised repatriation if they would but cut their way to KRASNOVODSK through the Menshevik "bourgeois" and their "Hindu" supporters. Ignorant of the defeat of the Central Powers when it occurred, these unfortunate men fought bravely in the van of every Bolshevik attack. The Bolsheviks of Turkestan did not at this period receive much material help from Central Russia. The connecting railway through SAMARRA was constantly being cut by the ORENBURG Cossacks, while the White Russian leaders General Denekin and Admiral Koltchak were engaging the main energies of the Red Army elsewhere. But they had in TASHKENT a reasonably good base, and could utilise the resources of KUSHK. On the whole the discipline of the Bolsheviks was strict. They rarely gave quarter to either prisoners or wounded.

The Menshevik force was inferior in both numbers and armament. There were few real Russians, merely some 50 cavalry plus some troopers employed as orderlies, about 300 infantry and the outstanding gunners. These, ex-regular artillery officers to a man, served their field guns skilfully and dauntlessly, their armoured trains with dash and ingenuity. The guns at first consisted only of four modern 16-pounders and four muzzle-loaders which were useful for their sound effects. The remainder of the infantry were 700 faint-hearted Armenians distributed among the Russians and armed with the "3-line" rifle. Discipline and leadership were poor. The Turkomans produced about 100 infantry and 800 horsemen wearing the native costume already mentioned and armed some with the "3-line" and some with Lee-Enfields. Though they were actually indifferent horsemen, on their wiry mounts they could cover great distances and should have given the Mensheviks a great advantage in mobility. But these Turkomans proved reliable only in mopping-up or marauding ; their lax discipline made them disinclined for any major task in either attack or defence, while they were both slow and uncertain in reconnaissance. In fact, though personally attractive in many respects, they were, militarily speaking, as poor friends as they were unpleasant enemies.

The most important operational factor was the armoured trains. Their earliest edition comprised merely an engine with a 16-pounder field gun and machine guns in trucks, the whole protected by compressed cotton bales between sleepers. Railway workshops later evolved steel-armoured trains with improved armament and proper intercommunication.

The whole Menshevik force was for political reasons under the command of a charming but ineffectual Turkoman chief, Oraz Sirdar. His staff, mostly Russians with little real claim to be officers, hardly knew the rudiments of tactics and organization. The Turkomans had a striking personality in their own commander and chieftain, Obesbaief, a former Russian cavalry officer. Directing policy, and interfering with command, were the bureaucrats of the ASKHABAD government under one Drushkin.

Facing each other as they did in the uninhabited and waterless KARA KUM both sides inevitably clung to the railway line. In fact there was no alternative route. There was practically no water except that supplied by train. The troops had no other wheeled or pack transport. Summer heat in the desert was severe, and winter temperature often 8 degrees below zero Farenheit. So virtually both armies lived in railway trains, long strings of as many as twentyfive carrying also water, supplies, cookhouses, hospitals, nurses and even artillery with their horses. Armoured trains protected front and rear. A governing factor was that the 4.5 inch guns of the Bolshevik trains outranged the Mensheviks, whose leading armoured train could therefore only make a stand where a bend round sand dunes or foothills provided a covered position.

At night both sides would be almost entirely train-borne and ready for withdrawal. At dawn infantry and artillery, preceded by cavalry patrols, would detrain to hold a narrow and shallow position astride the railway as local protection for the leading armoured trains. The force bent on offensive would accumulate a number of extra trains with reinforcements. If this manoeuvre itself did not cause the enemy to retire, troops would march by night along the line to within 1,000 yards and deliver frontal and flank attacks as soon after dawn as the leading armoured train had closed the range, and perhaps extra rails had been laid. Any sign of firm opposition usually halted such an attack, which would then melt away as the heat haze rose. If it effected surprise the defenders would precipitately retire in their trains to the next armoured train position. The usual role of the cavalry was to cut the railway behind the enemy trains in order to prevent such withdrawal. After the fourth enemy attack on KAAKHA the staunch crew of the Menshevik rear armoured train used to cut the railway in rear of themselves during alarms so as to render impracticable any sudden retirement by their own side !

The arrival of the Austro-Hungarian prisoners on one side and of British units on the other somewhat modified this procedure; but the force with the more effective armoured trains continued in general to call the tune.

There was usually one aircraft in use on each side ; but except for the counting of trains they gave little advantage.

Intervention at BAIRAM ALI.

"Map 10."

On 19th July 1918 No 2 Company under Captain Shute and Lieutenant Gipps together with one machine gun section left MESHED for MUHAMMADABAD where they would be well placed for quick intervention. The last section of the 144 mile march, the branch track over the ALLAHU AKBAR PASS beyond KUCHAN, was found very difficult for the camel transport suplied, and destination was not reached until the last day of July. The detachment's arrival on the frontier, which was expressly notipfied to the Belsheviks, had the undesired effect of making them accelerate their offensive preparations. Their trains increased until in hestitating response to a fresh Menshevik appeal for help "Malmiss" allowed the machine gun section under Lieutenant Gipps, with a Major Bingham as liaison officer, to go up to the front at BAIRAM ALI.

A week later, on 15th August, the Bolsheviks attacked on both flanks and the day was lost in a few hours. Abandoning their trenches the Armenian rabble entrained and went 70 miles back to DUSHAK. No. 1 armoured train, supported only by the machine guns under havildars Ilam Din and Nand Singh, hung on till dusk when this combination went back together to TEJEND. Thereby demolition and fire they held up the enemy pursuit all next day. They then fell back on DUSHAK just as the Menshevik main body pulled out on a change of plan to stand at KAAKHA instead. The men of the section, already worn out with lack of proper food and sleep, now succumbed en masse to fever. They were withdrawn by rail to MUHAMMADABAD. Havildar Nand Singh and one other rank had been wounded. Their three-day stand had been gallant if unfortunate. They had made history in Central Asia.

It was now clear that British support must be in greater strength to be of any avail. Accordingly Captain Shute's company was entrained for KAAKHA on 24th August, and the rest of the XIX Punjabis in MESHED, who had marched from there on the 16th, reached the railway station of ARTIK near MUHAMMADABAD on the morning of 26th August. Accompanying was one section of Combined Field Ambulance under Captain J.A. Sinton, VC, IMS.

There was a tremendous welcome from Russians and Turkomans alike. It was in truth a great occasion. The British were assured of complete commissariat and medical arrangements, and of signal and transport services, if they would only remain independent as regards weapons, ammunition and peculiar foodstuffs such as ghi. From this moment indeed the Regiment—and this applied to subsequent units—became dependent on the Mensheviks for their very existence. If results were not always as hoped for; if it was often a choice of Russian black bread or no chapatties; if dhalls and turmeric did not materialize, and if medical equipment proved inadequate it must be owned that the Russians gave loyally and generously of the little they had, and in their hospitals treated the Indian, sick and wounded without discrimination.

The British Officers now with the Battalion were:—

Lieutenant-Colonel D.E. Knollys,	Commanding, and OC British Troops.
Captain G.E.F. Shute	2nd-in-Command, and OC No. 2 Company.
Captain G. Pigot	OC No. 3 Company.
Captain R.F.G. Adams	Adjutant.
Lieutenant W.F. Gipps	Officer No. 2 Company.
Lieutenant F.W. Stewart	Quartermaster.
Lieutenant J.E. Stephen	OC No. 1 Company.

No. 4 Company was still moving up the L of C. Subadar Isar Singh continued to act for Subadar-Major Fateh Khan. Certain Russian-speaking officers were attached. These were Major Bingham and Captain Teague-Jones of the Indian Army, Lieutenant Ward, KRRC and Captain Lamkirk, a Russian. There were also interpreters—one for Headquarters and one per company—outstanding being an elderly Russian named Gnieson and naval cadet Patsevich.

First action at KAAKHA

The entente at ARTIK was cut short by an urgent request from Menshevik headquarters that the British move to KAAKHA at once since the enemy was then attacking! The Battalion moved off by tactical train, but on arrival it was found that the Bolsheviks had not pressed their attack and No. 2 Company in reserve had not been engaged. The night passed quietly in an orchard bivouac, and next day, the 27th August, was available for appreciating the situation and position.

Sketch K.

KAAKHA was a large village which had grown up around the well-built railway station at a point where small streams from the adjacent foothills formed a little oasis. The village houses were of Persian type enclosed by high garden walls, separated by winding alleys and surrounded by vineyards and melon beds. A mile east of the station the railway crossed a stream by steel girder bridge and then bent round the bluff end of a spur rising up to the foothills to the south. This high ground, entrenched and with guns in rear, constituted the Menshevik position. It was only a couple of hundred yards in depth and half a mile in extent. But the outstanding weakness in this first example of Menshevik skill was that apart from a half-ruined OLD FORT 2,000 yards away into which some hundreds of Turkoman cavalry had been crowded there were no troops or defences north of the railway with which to stop an enemy attack on that flank. To make matters worse, there was 1,000 yards east of the RAILWAY BRIDGE and, immediately north of the railway a wide and commanding PLATEAU which the Mensheviks had not felt strong enough to occupy and which they scarcely attempted to patrol. Yet this feature dominated the low ground around KAAKHA and overlooked the entrenched spur across the railway to the south. From it the enemy could obtain the necessary artillery observation. Behind it they could mass, and round its northern edge launch an attack under cover from view. The leading Menshevik armoured train, with local protection, was by day about 1,000 yards forward of the RAILWAY BRIDGE position. Administrative trains were massed in the sidings of KAAKHA station, where Menshevik headquarters was. The Bolshevik force on this day was concentrated somewhere behind the PLATEAU, with their trains strung together at ARMAN SAGAD a minor station 9 miles from KAAKHA, and their armoured train somewhat nearer.

Lieutenant-Colonel Knollys' recommendations on the afternoon of the 27th were that one of his companies should extend the entrenched position to the north side of the railway well back from the PLATEAU and that the rest of his regiment, including No. 2 Company which the Menshevik Command had all this time kept forward at the RAILWAY BRIDGE, should be further back so as to deal better with a left flank attack. This same evening, however, the Bolsheviks were reported to have doubled the number of their trains and to be preparing to attack. The Battalion was at once ordered up to the RAILWAY BRIDGE position near the WHITE

HOUSE. On arrival it was found that No. 2 Company with its (No. 2) machine gun section had been moved by the Mensheviks to strengthen the extreme right flank where they expected the blow to fall. Lieutenant-Colonel Knollys insisted that the remainder of the Battalion should not be expended similarly, but that the other flank be extended. So No. 3 Company moved out in the dark to dig in 400 yards north of the WHITEHOUSE, and was joined at dawn next day by No. 2 Machine Gun Section.

Second action at KAAKHA, 28th August 1918.

Nothing happened during the night, but at about 0730 hours on 28th August the Bolsheviks, having marched to positions on and north of the PLATEAU, opened with an artillery bombardment of KAAKHA and the position south of the railway which was intended to cloak their movement on the opposite flank. Shortly afterwards weak infantry attacks with the same object were made on No. 1 Armoured train near HUT 647, but these were repulsed by the Russians there. Later two more serious attacks down the slopes of the PLATEAU towards the VILLAGE immediately north of the RAILWAY BRIDGE were driven back by the fire of No. 3 Company and Russian artillery supporting them. This was the first occasion that Lewis Guns were fired in action by the Battalion. Sepoy Natha Singh was conspicuous in serving his gun from the roof of a hut until at last located by enemy machine guns and wounded. As the Russians had been adamant that they remain there, Battalion Headquarters and No. 1 Company were still near the WHITEHOUSE. From there Lieutenant-Colonel Knollys was able to watch the development of the Bolshevik main attack, which seemed to be undisturbed by the Turkoman Cavalry which had been sent out on the left flank. Enemy infantry left the distant cover of the PLATEAU at about 0830 hours and moved in several lines and short columns across the plain to the north. Wheeled machine guns could be distinguished, and horsed artillery seen stepping up in rear. As this attack approached the OLD FORT at about 0930 hours enemy shelling, which had not been very effective, was switched to that flank. The Turkomans offered little resistance and then cleared off. A little later the enemy could be seen advancing between the OLD FORT and the gardens of KAAKHA. Knowing that there was now nothing to stop them reaching the RAILWAY STATION area Lieutenant-Colonel Knollys obeyed his restrictive orders no longer. He launched No. 1 Company diagonally back across the railway so as to strike the enemy attack in flank north of the STATION, and shortly followed himself with Headquarters. Meanwhile Lieutenant Stewart, the Quartermaster, mobilized all ranks and followers available in the regimental bivouac a couple of hundred yards north-west of the railway station and delayed the enemy considerably with his stout resistance. Just as the Bolsheviks

Sketch K.

were enveloping this party on both flanks the Punjabi Musalmans and Pathans of No. 1 Company fell upon them with the bayonet. With Lieutenant-Colonel Knollys in command, two hours of confused fighting followed among buildings and gardens until the enemy were driven back to the OLD FORT. At one time there was a lull when friend and foe became indistinguishable. For a crowd of Russians and Turkomans under two British liaison officers had also lent a hand, and many Bolsheviks deliberately mingled with these Russians and shot their opponents in the back. There was further trickery and mistaken identity at the OLD FORT before the enemy were driven out of it. The Bolsheviks then withdrew rapidly to the east across the plain, abandoning four machine guns. An advance by No. 3 Company at 1400 hours to cut them off was too late, and Turkoman cavalry sent out to harry the retreat accomplished nothing. This was the end of the action. The Mensheviks' leading armoured train had gradually been forced back by fire to the WHITE HOUSE, but there had held its own. British casualties were four IORs killed, Lieutenant Ward (liaison officer) died of wounds, Captain Teague-Jones (liaison officer), Lieutenant Stewart and fourteen IORs wounded. Lieutenant Stewart was awarded the Military Cross for his gallant leadership. General Malleson signalled "I congratulate and thank you for your victory".

Third action at KAKHA, 11th September 1918.

Sketch K.

The enemy attacked twice more, but in the intervals the Menshevik situation was improved. On 29th August one company 4th Battalion The Hampshire Regiment of Dunsterforce joined from KRASNOVODSK. From ENZELI on 5th September came one 18-pounder section 44th (British) Field Battery, which at once went into a position of observation to support the left flank. On 21st September two squadrons 28th Light Cavalry arrived from MESHED. Lieutenant-Colonel Knollys as commander of what was now called "British Forces in Turkestan" at last induced the Russian staff to desist from issuing orders direct to his units and sub-units. Battalion Headquarters and reserve were now back near the regimental camp, though one company was still maintained forward as local reserve to the right flank sectors. A company position was dug at the north-east corner of KAAKHA so as to extend the defences up to the OLD FORT. The whole front was wired with single-apron and divided into seven sectors of which the Battalion always held at least one. Russian engineers built a high observation tower near the RAILWAY STATION. A British Main Dressing Station was opened.

Between genuine attacks there were frequent alarms, particularly whenever the tempting target of massed Menshevik trains was shelled by the enemy. Until the Indian cavalry had arrived to put distant reconnaissance on a proper basis wild Turkoman stories accounted for many a scare. By day No. 1 armoured train was forward near HUT 647, duelling with its opponent morning and evening when the heat haze was absent. By night it would be back at the WHITEHOUSE protected by an infantry piquet and by mines laid on the track ahead. Another armoured train protected the rear of KAAKHA. Mines played an important part in the battle of wits between the opposing train crews. Delay-action and selective types were countered by increasing the number of shock-absorbing flat trucks in front of vital vehicles and loading them appropriately with rails. Funnel smoke was carefully controlled when creeping into position, or was belched as a decoy. When a third armoured train became available two would work together forward. With No. 1 in concealment in order to catch any enemy follow-up, No. 2 would often retreat rapidly and show signs of having been hit. Shelling the line behind the opposing armoured train and closing the range was a manoeuvre only adopted when the Bolsheviks were believed to be out of ammunition! Menshevik gunnery was the better, and a Bolshevik hit on an armoured train was, fortunately, a very rare occurrence. An enemy ruse which once succeeded was the gradual widening of the track gauge during the night so that next morning the forward gun truck of No. 1 train followed the leading flats in falling between the rails.

On 10th September when the enemy trains at ARMAN SAGAD had increased to twenty-six the British guns went out under escort to engage them. However, the Russian cavalry clumsily disclosed this movement north of railway, and the Bolshevik trains were already on the move back when the guns opened. Nevertheless the Bolsheviks adhered to their plan, closed the gap in the line during the night and at 0600 hours next day started searching the RAILWAY STATION, regimental camp and certain sectors of the position with about ten guns. At 1000 hours two or three hundred infantry attacked towards the VILLAGE, but were driven back onto the PLATEAU by Russian gunfire alone. A platoon of the Hampshires had reinforced this sector when the enemy attacked it again an hour later with the same result. There was lively armoured train duelling. A little later a movement against the OLD FORT by one squadron and two companies with artillery support was stopped by fine British gunnery before it came within range of No. 3 Company. No. 2 Company was moved over to the extreme left sector, but the enemy now withdrew altogether. The Turkoman horsemen could not be induced to follow them up! One mountain and two field guns were abandoned by the Bolsheviks north of the railway, and this third failure against KAAKHA was for them a serious set-back.

Fourth action at KAAKHA, 18th September 1918.

Sketch K.

On the evening before their final attack on this position the Bolsheviks had again concentrated 26 train-loads of troops. At 0615 hours on 18th September it was reported that cavalry were making a wide detour round the north flank. The rearguard armoured train was called in from the next station to the west; No. 2 Company from general reserve was moved out north-west of KAAKHA; and. too late, Russian infantry were railed westwards to meet this threat to communications. The enemy cavalry who succeeded in reaching the railway unopposed three miles west of KAAKHA ripped up a length of rail, cut telegraph wires and burnt a small wooden bridge. They then retired north to a village where they remained till afternoon. From 0800 hours onwards KAAKHA position sustained its heaviest shelling from fifteen guns on the PLATEAU. Towards noon the Bolsheviks mounted an attack from a nullah 2000 yards north of the OLD FORT towards that bastion, but each of three attempts to advance was driven back by Menshevik and British shrapnel. At 1500 hours No. 3 Company from 5 Sector and some dismounted Turkomans from the OLD FORT followed up the enemy retreat into the haze, but no contact was made.

Although armoured train activity continued daily the Bolsheviks now seemed depressed by repeated failure. Simultaneously the arrival of the 28th Light Cavalry allowed offensive reconnaissance to be started against them. The Menshevik aeroplane, a 80 horse-power Henri-Farman biplane, now rose to the peak of its usefulness. It bombed DUSHAK several times, and established regular communication with Sirdar Aziz Khan of the Tejend Turkomans who were then preparing to rise against the Reds. Unfortunately it crashed on 8th October, and for long was written-off. The Bolsheviks had a faster Morane-Saulnier monoplane as well as a Farman, but operated only one aircraft at a time. This bombed KAAKHA ineffectually a couple of times, and even machine-gunned trains in the STATION, but never challenged the Menshevik machine. Another innovation was the issue of Russian respirators to British and Indian troops following a report that the enemy intended to use gas shell. The health of the men remained good through the heat of this summer notwithstanding the unusual food and the insanitary condition of the trenches and dug-outs as they found them on taking their turn in the various sectors of the front.

CHAPTER XIV

FIRST WORLD WAR, 1918-19.

TRANSCASPIA, the Actions of DUSHAK and ANENNKOVO.

(See Map 10, Sketches L, M and photographs in Regimental Albums).

Offensive, 1918.

With October came the decision to attack at DUSHAK, 24 miles away. The exasperating "Soviet" in ASKHABAD were now pressing for a counter-offensive. But that depended on British agreement, since it was clear, and indeed admitted, that without "Britforce" in the leading role nothing would be done. It was however a weighty decision in view of the enemy's general superiority, the lack of British reserves, the rottenness of the Menshevik command and the duplicity of their government. It was known, for instance, that they were planning the removal of all Turkoman influence, and the liquidation of the ex-officers now serving them so well, as soon as Transcaspia had been cleared of their rivals. It was the probability that unless the TEJEND oasis was occupied the force could not be supplied during the winter that turned the scale. Certain improvements in command were, however, insisted on—the principal being the removal of the chief of staff, Colonel Sikolaef.

"Map 10"

The object was to cripple the Bolshevik force—which could be as elusive as quicksilver—or at least to capture TEJEND. DUSHAK would not suffice, since its position was not tenable by armoured trains facing towards the OXUS. The plan finally adopted was a two-night left-flank march by a main column of artillery and infantry, who would remain concealed by day, and a right flank movement by the 28th Light Cavalry through the foothills south and east of the railway. At dawn on the second day these pincers were to close on DUSHAK from west and east. The two columns, helped by an attack down the railway, were to destroy the enemy in the STATION and in their trains to the south-west of it. The TEJEND Turkomans were to cut the line behind DUSHAK so as to stop the Bolsheviks withdrawing or obtaining reinforcements. A strong stop was to be left in front of KAAKHA to prevent the enemy counter-attacking into that position, which their armoured train superiority made possible.

The Advance on DUSHAK.

Sketch L.

After dark on 9th October the left column assembled outside the wire of No. 5 Sector. Captain Harrison's field guns were included. The Battalion supplied Nos. 2 and 3 companies and both machine gun sections. No. 1 Company was to help defend KAAKHA. The Russian contingent of all arms was three hours late! The Turkomans while waiting lit large warming fires! Nevertheless the 9 miles over the PLATEAU to the deserted village of KARAKHAN were covered before dawn on the 10th and the troops successfully concealed there.

Daylight showed ARMAN SAGAD and locality to be entirely clear of enemy trains. Captain Fardell's company of Hampshires advanced along the railway to the station. The gap in the line was closed and No. 1 Armoured train steamed in, followed by the Russian and British headquarters and many hangers-on. But anxiety over the whereabouts of the enemy's armoured trains coupled with a breakdown in their ration-supply now caused the Russians to make changes in the plan. The two squadrons of 28th Light Cavalry who had got as far as 6 miles to the south of DUSHAK were recalled to ARMAN SAGAD! The left column also was brought in to that desert station and spent a cold night around it.

At dawn on the 11th October the Bolshevik armoured trains opened up and their aircraft bombed ARMAN SAGAD just as the troops were dispersing for day concealment. Yet the left column appears to have been unobserved as it trailed away to the north-north-east into the empty village of NAUROZ CHASHMEH—artillery, Russians, Armenians, Turkomans and Punjabis now reinforced by No. 1 Company. There they remained for the next two days while the column commander, the same Colonel Sikolaef, evolved local enterprises and the cavalry on the opposite flank counter-marched and set off again! This cautious Russian officer had persuaded his headquarters that until the enemy's leading armoured trains had been neutralized nothing further should be done. Accordingly before dawn on the 12th and 13th, Russian guns on the first day and the British on the second, artillery went out from NAUROZ CHASHMEH to ambush the armoured trains. Both attempts failed: there was no backing from ARMAN SAGAD; but particularly the range was too long and the withdrawal of the Russian infantry escorts too immediate! The timidity and procrastination of this commander with the unfortunate name moved the Hampshires at ARMAN SAGAD to signal the Punjabis as follows:—

"Read to tune of 'The Church's one Foundation'

We are Transcaspia's Army;

No bloody use are we.
We're sick of life and Sikolaef
Attacking his A. T.
We started out from KAAKHA
to make a grand attack ;
ARMAN SAGAD was not too bad,
now WHAT about DUSHAK !"

Eventually it was decided to risk the enemy armoured trains and push on with the attack. But the Russians were adamant that the Hampshires should remain in general reserve at ARMAN SAGAD.

Battle of DUSHAK, 14th October 1918.

Sketch L.

The left column restarted from NAUROZ CHASHMEH at dusk on 13th October and marched straight on KARTUS CHASHMEH, a small village just north of DUSHAK. Guides and the Battalion led. Then came the artillery escorted by a party of Hazaras of the Seistan Levy Corps who had arrived with the Indian cavalry. Next were Russian machine guns carried in carts; after them the Field Ambulance Section (Captain Sinton and Lieutenant Nawas, IMS); finally the Russo-Armenian infantry. Turkoman cavalry were said to be wide out on the left flank. The going was good throughout most of a cold starlit night. This time Menshevik march-discipline was much better, and it fell to the Regiment to cause the only interruption. During a halt shortly before dawn when only 3½ miles from DUSHAK two patrols from the advanced and flank guards respectively came into conflict with each other only 150 yards from the column. A few sharp shots from one of these and almost every Lewis gun and machine gun mule burst from the grasp of their sleepy holders and went galloping north-westwards : The astonished Punjabis remained where they sat ! the Russians rose as one man and followed the mules! Only the British gun teams seemed completely unmoved. Dawn broke as the column resumed its march minus nearly one quarter of the Lewis Guns and several machine gun ammunition packs, all of which however were recovered later. As KARTUS CHASHMEH was approached the Turkoman cavalry arrived from somewhere, but instead of pushing on to help cut the railway north-east of DUSHAK they fell to sacking this village, which appeared to be an abandoned enemy outpost.

The left column now deployed for attack on a start-line to the north-west of KARTUS CHASHMEH and one mile from DUSHAK RAILWAY STATION, which was the first objective. The Russians and Armenians were on the right. In the centre was No. 2 Company with No. 1 Machine gun section on its right. Then came No. 3 Company, while the Turkomans were on the extreme left in KARTUS CHASHMEH. No. 1 Company followed

No. 3 as local reserve with No. 2 machine gun section under havildars Jagat Singh and Imam Din protecting the left. The two British and four Russian guns came into action in the open. Needless to say, the R F A were ready the sooner; in fact only their guns supported the approach phase of the attack. There was no waiting for artillery preparation. Success was dependent on surprise. Noise, disorganization and delay had already occurred and it was now just daylight. So an immediate advance was made, the Russians on the right even setting a leading pace.

The advance lay over a flat plain devoid of cover except for bushes about two feet high, a few shallow irrigation channels within 600 yards of the station buildings and three nullahs. The nullah from the east of KARTUS CHASHMEH provided a covered approach to the STATION, but as there were no maps its existence was not known in time. One of the western nullahs sheltered the Advanced Dressing Station, and in the other many of the Russians soon found an easier alternative to advancing.

Without doubt this flank attack came as something of a surprise to the Bolsheviks. Their rear armoured train was absent. Troop trains and headquarters were still forward in their previous position in the railway CUTTING where their tail was now visible. Had they been certain that such a comparatively large force was encircling their flank it is probable that their rolling stock would have been north-east of DUSHAK STATION with the rear armoured train protecting it, No. 2 at the RAILWAY TRIANGLE immediately west of the STATION whence it could fire to the north and No. 1 in the CUTTING further west. As it was, the enemy's forward force seems to have been paralysed for quite an hour. This however was not so with their troops detailed to defend KAAKHA STATION, who may have heard the patrol shots before dawn or been apprised from KARTUS CHASHMEH. The infantry, apart from some forward groups who were quickly driven in, held a line of cultivation channels 400 yards in front of their artillery. The guns were in action immediately east of the railway on higher ground and partially concealed by the trees surrounding the station buildings. In between was an extended line of machine gun posts.

The Bolshevik batteries opened fire at about 3,000 yards and their fire, though at first ineffective, sufficed to echelon back the Russians on the right. But soon, firing at 1,000 yards despite the British gunners counter-battery fire, the Bolshevik guns were tearing gaps in the advancing line and in the reserve company following in rear. They were using open sights and both percussion shrapnel and grape. The Menshevik battery now came into action against the railway STATION. The Russian infantry on the right had gone to ground. The Turkomans on the left had characteristicly disappeared. Both regimental machine gun sections were now busy dealing with the flanks, especially on the left where their fire defeated several enemy attempts to counterattack from a group of houses and trees on the bank of the nullah leading to KARTUS CHASHMEH.

The station sidings were full of locomotives, store and repair trains, ammunition and oil wagons, etc. These and the tracks and station buildings were now being shelled to pieces and were enveloped in smoke and flames. One train, well alight, got away towards TEJEND only to fall in with the merciless Turkomans on the way. No. 2 armoured train, steaming back fast from the CUTTING to protect the rear was hit by a lucky round and went alight as it passed through the wrecked station. Thereafter the only store train capable of movement steamed out westwards towards the CUTTING.

Nos. 2 and 3 Companies were now advancing by short section rushes, the Lewis guns and supporting rifle sections concentrating on the enemy machine guns. The nearer infantry hardly troubled them. A few more Punjabi rushes and they started scuttling back. Then, after a pause in the vacated ditches and more fire preparation, the two companies leapt with the bayonet at the machine gunners beyond. But few of them waited for cold steel. The wave swept on to the guns, but the gunners too were on the bolt to the cover of buildings and vehicles. At this period the Regiment captured six field guns and sixteen medium machine guns, a number of which were afterwards got away.

As these two companies entered the STATION and began mopping up among the wreckage No. 1 Company passed through to clear the village of DUSHAK, which lay on the south side of the railway. Just before this they had lost their commander, Lieutenant Stephen. He was later buried where he fell; and when the Regiment left Transcaspia at the end of March next year the cross on his grave just north of the railway line still stood in memory of a good friend and gallant officer.

In the station area confused close-quarter fighting continued for some time, the remaining enemy sniping from or hiding in all sorts of places. Subadar Bal Singh of No. 2 Company was seen to pursue one quarry into the cab of an idle locomotive and thence into the empty firebox, where he was lucky to escape his own revolver shots! No. 2 lost both their British officers from wounds, Captain Shute in the shoulder and Lieutenant Gipps in the leg. No. 3 Company too was virtually under Indian officer leadership as Captain Pigot had been hit in the throat and could not speak. One of the last shells fired by the 44th Field Battery before it lengthened the range detonated three wagons of explosives in a siding. After that there were few trees and walls left standing, nor indeed troops! A train full of horses was also set ablaze, and the shrieks of the poor animals rose above the din. The Turkomans had now arrived from the east flank and fell first to looting and then to disappearing with their booty. The few Russians who now turned up on other flank gave valuable assistance, but their numbers were insignificant.

The two squadrons of 28th Light Cavalry under Major Kreyer had been ready at their rendezvous south of DUSHAK from 0300 hours, and the opening of firing was the signal for them to advance on the STATION. They were fired on *en route* and before they dismounted to enter the in-fighting zone they had killed sixty enemy with the lance.

The Bolshevik main body to the west, realizing that DUSHAK station and village had been captured, now began to shell them from the vicinity of their trains, and launched a strong infantry counter attack along the line. To face this No. 2 Company platoons swung right. The remnants of No. 3 Company and No. 2 Machine gun section also had to change position to meet a counter-attack by fresh troops coming up the railway from the north-east. These had come from TEJEND to detrain a mile away, and were the first evidence that the TEJEND Turkomans had failed in their task. The 28th Light Cavalry—numbering only 100 effectives when dismounted—now faced east on the left of No. 1 Company as these two attacks pressed inwards and the British and Russian guns engaged them. Captain Pigot had now been evacuated and the command of the Battalion in action devolved on acting Subadar-Major Isar Singh, himself wounded.

Withdrawal from DUSHAK.

These enemy counter-attacks showed real determination, the one in trying to cut their way back to base, the other to rescue what constituted the main Bolshevik force of Turkestan—in material if not necessarily in personnel. By 1600 hours the British troops were hard pressed. Ammunition was running short and automatics were choked with sand. The enemy had reached the outskirts of the station and village area. Major Kreyer accordingly got into touch with Colonel Sikolaef and obtained his agreement to withdrawal while a way was still open to the west. If only the Menshevik armoured trains and the small force of all arms which were still at ARMAN SAGAD had attacked the Bolsheviks opposing them, at least one of the enemy counter-attacks should well have collapsed, and at the best their whole force might have surrendered. But lack of initiative and boldness at Menshevik GHQ resulted in nothing being done, and so a bitter change in the fortunes of the day was inevitable.

Subadar-Major Isar Singh, faithfully representing the feelings of his men in the elation of success, refused to obey the message to retire, and Major Kreyer had to contact him personally. Thereafter he cooly arranged and conducted a staged withdrawal of the three companies to NAUROZ CHASHMEH. This was magnificently covered by the British and Russian guns and finally by the Indian cavalry. There was very little cover of any depth, and in this phase the 28th lost no less than thirty led horses killed. But once the troops were clear of the Station area enemy pressure ceased. There was no follow-up, and shelling was inaccurate. Not a wounded man nor a gun was left behind. The wounded as soon as possible went on by horsed transport to ARMAN SAGAD railhead, but the Regiment with the artillery and certain Russian troops halted for the night at NAUROZ CHASHMEH. Next day they went on to entrain at ARMAN SAGAD. The 28th Light Cavalry, marching direct, reached KAAKHA at 0500 hours on 15th October after being almost continually on the move and covering sixty miles since early on the 13th.

The Regiment's casualties at DUSHAK were :—killed—1 British officer (Lieutenant Stephen), 1 Indian officer (Subadar Mehdi Khan), 45 other ranks: wounded—3 British officers, 1 Indian officer and 135 other ranks. The 28th Light Cavalry had 8 killed and missing, with 11 wounded. All the wounded went to the Railway Hospital ASKHABAD where they were on the whole well and expertly treated. Many were evacuated further by various routes—via East Persia to India, via ENZELI to Mesopotamia, via BAKU to Egypt. The Bolsheviks' casualties at DUSHAK were estimated to be over 500.

The following congratulatory telegrams were received:— From C-in-C India to Malleson Mission—"Please convey to troops H.E. the C-in-C's warm appreciation of their very gallant conduct during the recent operation". From Malleson Mission to Commander British Troops in Turkestan - "The G.O.C. wishes you to convey to all the troops under your command his congratulations on their splendid success in the operations round DUSHAK. But for causes which there is no need to particularize but are well known to all there is no doubt the enemy would have been driven back to MERV or even further. He regrets to hear of the heavy casualties and wishes to be kept informed of the condition of the wounded".

Captains G.E.F. Shute and G. Pigot were awarded the Military Cross, Subadar Bal Singh the Indian Order of Merit and several ranks the Indian Distinguished Service Medal.

TEJEND TO MERV.

"Map 10."

When the British troops withdrew to KAAKHA to refit the Russian command left two armoured trains, the Hampshires, the British guns and a small force of their own to hold ARMAN SAGAD as an outpost position. They were convinced that the Bolsheviks had been hit so hard at DUSHAK that they were incapable of offensive action, and further, could not maintain themselves there. In this they proved right. On the 15th and 16th October the enemy were observed working feverishly to clear a single line through the wreckage of DUSHAK, and on the 17th they retired with all movable rolling stock to TEJEND. The Menshevik armoured trains followed up aggressively. This bold action was largely due to the initiative of that remarkable artillery cadet, Videnski, who now assumed armoured train command. As a result the enemy evacuated TEJEND on 23rd October, retiring to MERV. The Russians, reinforcing the armoured trains with the bulk of their force in an assembly of trains, established a new front at GOEK SIUR. "DUSHAK" could now be viewed in proper perspective. Though not destroyed, the Bolshevik force had been very severely mauled and its morale lowered. The resources of TEJEND had been secured by the Mensheviks, and the enemy thrown back to the last oasis.

BAIRAM ALI.

While organizing the GEOK SIUR position the Russian Command advocated immediate offensive by all forces so as to keep the enemy on the run and profit by the temporary height of Menshevik morale. In this they were right, but Lieutenant-Colonel Knollys had to resist their pressure as far as the XIX Punjabis were concerned. The Regiment was feverishly refitting at KAAKHA lest they miss the next operation, but there was much to be done. After the heavy casualties there were many new leaders, gun numbers and understudies to be appointed and tested. Certain training and the overhaul of weapons and equipment were essentials too. Some reinforcements had arrived, and another draft was on the way. But No. 4 Company was still on the L. of C. The three senior Indian Officers were given command of the remaining companies; for apart from Lieutenant-Colonel Knollys and Captain Adams the Adjutant there were no British Officers available. Lieutenant Stewart had been evacuated. The wounds of Captain Shute and Lieutenant Gipps were to have the same result. Major J.G.P. Drummond and Lieutenant L.S. Ingle were *en route* but did not join until December. It should be mentioned that the enemy's complete evacuation of DUSHAK on 17th October enabled the

Regiment to bury or cremate next day all of the dead that had been left on the field.

With other units, however, it was possible to give the Mensheviks enough backing for them to obtain their immedate aim. The 44th field Battery, the Hampshire Company and the 28th Light Cavalry were at once railed up to TEJEND. On 27th October one Squadron of the 28th, from GEOK SIUR, took part with 400 Turkoman cavalry in a movement to the enemy's rear, which included a complete day spent in conference near BAIRAM ALI! As a result, anyway, the Bolsheviks abandoned MERV and withdrew to the PESKI armoured train position in the desert. Next day the Indian cavalry occupied MERV—to be followed by all other troops in TEJEND and GEOK SIUR—while the Turkomans seized BAIRAM ALI 18 miles further on. The Menshevik armoured and advanced guard trains contacted the enemy north of UCHAJI. KUSHK was freed.

On 2nd November the Battalion moved from KAAKHA to BAIRAM ALI and began work on a defensive position, 6 miles further east, covering the MERV oasis. These were the same defences from which the Mensheviks and Lieutenant Gipps' machine gun section had retired 2½ months previously. In general they followed the eastern edge of plantations in the Imperial Estate, but were concealed by having scattered trees in front and were provided by an irrigation canal with a good obstacle. The position was not permanently occupied, and for most of the time the Battalion was quartered in BAIRAM ALI, enjoying the luxuries of fly-proofed and electrically-lit barracks. Headquarters, the cavalry and British gunners also moved up, leaving only the Hampshires at MERV.

On 6th November high policy orders were received that although they might be employed defensively no British troops were in future to take part in offensive operations without special sanction. The armistice now reigned in Europe and elsewhere in Asia. World War I was over. It seemed wrong for the British to be fighting in Central Asia against a German threat which no longer existed. Unaided the Bolsheviks would constitute no threat to India. Let Denekin and Koltchak alone conduct Menshevik operations in what had changed from an international war to an internal revolution. Those were the decisive arguments. On the other side it was argued that it was leaving allies in the lurch for the British to discontinue their help at this stage. The Mensheviks' morale was now as high as their munitions were low. The Bolsheviks were on the run. Now was the time to capture CHARDJUI on the far bank of the OXUS, establish a bridgehead there, seize all river craft and hold the line of the river. Then fairly and squarely might the Mensheviks be left to defend their recovered Transcaspia.

Whether it was that the Bolsheviks learnt of this decision or it was merely the outcome of their efforts to tighten discipline, subdue the Bokharans and establish their communications through ORENBURG, but from about now onwards the morale of the Bolsheviks was in the ascendant. A ruling which disheartened even the indomitable Videnski at a time when the Menshevik shell position was serious was that a British 18-pounder might not be mounted in one of the armoured trains.

The ANNENKOVO position.

On 15th November, Videnski being absent on one of his personal security leaves, panic arose at UCHAJI from a premature burst in No. 1 armoured train and the whole advanced force withdrew 30 miles to ANNENKOVO STATION. The BAIRAM ALI position was manned. In response to appeals for a stiffening, half of a 28th Light Cavalry squadron was sent forward with Captain Gowans as liaison officer. Two days later there was heavy artillery duelling and the Menshevik armoured train position and front became stabilized at the bend in the railway between the stations of RAVNINA and ANNENKOVO. On 2nd and 3rd December the Bolshevik nearly captured this position with infantry attacks. The Russian infantry—now mainly Armenians with some nondescripts from General Bicharakof in Caucasia—were proving very unreliable; so one company of the Battalion was sent to join the cavalry detachment at the front, and this arrangement was continued.

Sketch M.

By day the company remained concentrated about 1,500 yards behind No. 1 Armoured train while the cavalry patrolled towards RAVNINA. The 28th Light Cavalry more than maintained the reputation they had acquired among the Bolsheviks even before DUSHAK and there were many enterprising encounters. At night the XIX Punjabis manned three piquets astride the railway just ahead of the leading armoured trains. This required two platoons. The other two were in reserve in the I.T. CAMP about a mile back, while Company headquarters was in No. 1 armoured train in telephonic communication with the piquets and reserve. At intervals during the night patrols went out to front and flanks and particularly along the railway. A Turkoman "Cossack post" was in position about two miles out on the right flank, and another was found by the Russian cavalry, mainly Daghistani Cossacks, some three miles to the north where there was a little-used desert track from RAVINA to MERV direct. After the dawn "all clear" at the end of an icy "stand-to" the Russians assumed responsibility for holding the armoured train position. The forward platoons withdrew to the I.T. CAMP. The Indian cavalry patrols would start out to watch RAVNINA, their example followed by the

Turkomans galloping out by "sotnias" and "polsotnias" (squadrons and fifties) without regard for concealment or deception.

At this time the night piquets were mere scrapes on a bush-covered sandy ridge with Lewis Guns on fixed lines in cut-away SAA boxes. Later these posts were properly sandbagged, wired and provided with stove-warmed dug-outs. These cold nights "on piquet" had their many alarms and episodes. Occasionally the enemy armoured train would fire a few rounds. Sometimes— but never with Videnski in command—the Menshevik trains would do the same without the slightest warning. Whenever this fell to the turn of No. 2 armoured train it would fire from as close as possible to the rear coach of No. 1 train wherein the infantry company commander snatched his repose! Whenever the juggler in explosives and detonators was back late, morning or evening, from adjusting the "home-signal" mines on the line the Russians would stage an alarm of imminent attack. Sometimes this old man and his companions would take out a hand-trolley which would be fired on by some Turkoman patrol in mistake for the enemy's armoured train! A common pastime of No. 1 armoured train was to shunt at night, there being a small lay-by siding in the cutting where it could, for example, shed its fuel-tank wagon. This movement would invariably be without warning, and therefore much to the detriment of attached signal cables! At dawn enemy cavalry might be encountered or infantry reported to be massing. Many faint columns of engine smoke would tell of a Bolshevik concentration or relief. Or the enemy's leading armoured train might be found to have crept up close and be accompanied by field guns. But when this period had passed and day reconnaissances had gone out, there used to settle down a deep peace, to break which was the prerogative of the armoured trains alone.

Sketch L.

The Menshevik armoured trains lay in or behind the cutting. Their OP was in No. 3 piquet, with an alternative at No. 1. This view and the double bend gave the position the reputation of being the best for the Mensheviks between KAAKHA and the OXUS. About 2,000 yards ahead and half the distance to the enemy post at RAVNINA was small railway building known as the WHITE HOUSE. Sandbagged and entrenched around, it was used by the enemy as an OP and machine gun post by day. The Turkomans would draw fire from it daily, and once to the great relief of all gunners they failed in a dawn attempt to burn this most valuable reference point. Behind the Menshevik armoured trains was left a manoeuvre gap of about 600 yards, and then followed the long succession of administrative rakes. First came the trains for the Russian artillery and cavalry, abreast of which were Colonel Masevitch's wild Turkoman. These men lived in "kibitkas" with their headquarters in a gang cabin. Behind stretched the trains of Turkoman infantry, Russian and Armenian infantry, staff and hospital, stores and workshops, and lastly water butts—each train with its engine under partial steam. The INDIAN TROOPS CAMP was opposite the centre of this long line, concealed under the banks of a deep dry watercourse some 200 yards south of the railway. Accommodation was in felt "kibitkas", each twice the size of an Army bell-tent and warmed by stove or fire. A few hundred yards further south was a long ridge parallel to the railway which had to be considered as an enemy tactical objective. To the north of the line the ground rose more gently in a series of low sandy ridges. ANNENKOVO STATION was 6 "versts" in rear. Here were a few troops, and supply point. After dark train after train would slip quietly back for replenishment until the armoured trains, Indian troops and Turkoman cavalry alone remained. By dawn they would all be back again.

The cold during this winter was often intense. Snow lay deep on the sand, and the thermometer registered down to forty degrees of frost. Stoves roared in carriages and kibitkas, and uniform assumed a very furry appearance. The Russian staff train was kept as a hot-house-cum-public-house, and to the British officer the evening conference there was a severe trial of endurance for all his senses!

The Indian detachments at ANNENKOVO were relieved from BAIRAM ALI about every eight days. Although the days were varied the Bolsheviks undoubtedly were quickly informed of them. They also knew of a weakness in that for railway administrative reasons the infantry reliefs had to be carried out at BAIRAM ALI, and thus the front was denuded to that extent for the greater part of a day.

In December there was danger of a Bolshevik rising in ASKHABAD, which then had to be garrisoned by three companies of the Royal Warwickshire Regiment from KRASNOVODSK and by the 28th Light Cavalry's remaining squadron from MESHED. "Malmis" redoubled their propaganda to inform the Austro-Hungarians with the Bolsheviks of the defeat of the Central Powers, and assure them of safe-conduct on desertion to the Mensheviks. The Bolsheviks countered by broadcasting the British policy of "no further intervention in Russia" and declaring that all deserters to the Mensheviks were being killed by the Turkomans—which unfortunately was true in many cases where Turkoman patrols killed for the sake of acquiring warm clothes. Captain Pigot returned from hospital in ASKHABAD to resume command of No. 3 Company on Christmas Day. A few days earlier Lieutenant Ingle had joined as his company officer, while Major Drummond with

Lieutenant Cuvelier arrived to officer No. 1. These officer reinforcements came hardly a day too soon. In December too "Britforce Turkestan" was transferred to the "Army of the Black Sea", and before long the improved flow of supplies and casualties along the new L of C via CONSTANTINOPLE became agreeably apparent. On 9th Janaury 1919 Brigadier-General G. A. H. Beatty arrived to assume command of the force from Lieutenant-Colonel Knollys, and set up his brigade headquarters in the Tsar's shooting lodge at BAIRAM ALI.

Battle of ANNENKOVO, 16th January 1919.

On 16th January 1919 the Bolsheviks achieved complete surprise in an attack on a grand scale. Under their plan a main force was to advance direct on MERV from RAVNINA along the track avoiding BAIRAM ALI, and for this wheeled and camel transport was collected. The first preliminary operation was to be the capture of the ANNENKOVO force between a main attack on its north flank and a subsidiary advance along the railway. The next preliminary was to be a "holding" attack on the BAIRAM ALI position while the main force was passing round its north flank.

Sketch M.

In their flank attack at ANNENKOVO the enemy used 400 cavalry, 9 field guns, a large number of machine guns and 2,500 infantry. The "railway line attack" was initially made with 1,000 infantry and some machine guns. Secrecy was so good that no hint of an offensive had reached the Mensheviks. No more than seven trains were reported on the previous evening. No fires were seen during the night. The date was that on which the Indian infantry relief was due. Only the hour for the railway demolition was miscalculated; had it been half an hour later No. 3 Company would have been *en route* back to BAIRAM ALI.

At 0845 hours after a very cold night with a thick mist still lying No. 3 Company were waiting to entrain when four detonations were heard to the west, clearly indicating a raid on the railway line. Simultaneously all signal communication failed. Two troops of Daghistani Cossacks were quickly sent back, one to drive off the enemy and the other to contact ANNENKOVO STATION. 28th Light Cavalry patrols were also sent out to north-west and south-east. By 1,000 hours the latter had reported "all clear" up to two miles, telephone communication had been restored and the breakdown train from ANNENKOVO was at work. The Cossacks though they failed to intercept the enemy captured one of that demolition party, a German, while the other Indian patrol reported having had a brush in the mist to the north-east with what appeared to be a whole regiment of cavalry. British headquarters at BAIRAM ALI on being informed of what was happening arranged an emergency train for the relieving company, No. 1, and ordered the remaining British troops there to man the BAIRAM ALI position.

Fortunately the Bolsheviks had made some mistakes with their demolition. It was made before the attacks were ready. Though well chosen in a cutting and on a slight bend, the site was close to a small siding two versts from ANNENKOVO from which repair rails were quickly available. Thirdly the large body of raiders made no attempt to prevent repair work.

The German prisoner stated that the enemy was about to attack with infantry on the south flank and cavalry on the north. Though such action seemed unlikely the Russian command at once became permeated with a right flank complex. Captain Pigot agreed to one troop of 28th Light Cavalry under Lieutenant Gatehouse being sent out due east; but he declined to take over the armoured train piquets at once, considering that for the present No. 3 Company was best concentrated in the water-course by their CAMP.

Although further reconnaissances had been sent out by the Russians it was not till 1200 hours that a delayed report was received from the Cossack patrol supposed to be watching the track RAVNINA—MERV on the left flank that the enemy was concentrated in great strength no more than 4 versts (2¾ miles) north-north-west of the Menshevik trains. The Armenian and Turkoman infantry were sent north to attack them; but at 1230 hours they were reported to be retiring before the Bolsheviks, who had already deployed and outflanked them to the west. Simultaneously the enemy armoured trains began shelling the position and trains out of the mist, while small-arms fire broke out along the railway line to RAVNINA. Whereupon the Russian commander lost his head, sent all his Turkoman cavalry to the defence of the armoured trains, went personally to No. 3 Company Commander and, saying that "all was finished but for what the Indians might be able to do", surrendered control of operations!

Actually there was little else but the Indian troops left in hand—a squadron of Daghistanis, a crowd of train loungers already seeking cover, the armoured trains and the Russian gunners. The armoured trains might be relied on to fight under their Captain Shuvalof, a leader second only to Videnski, who again was not present. Captain Pigot now sent two platoons of No. 3 Company under Lieutenant Ingle to extend the left of the Armenians. They met the enemy infantry in the mist about 700 yards north of the railway, drove them back by fire and checked the retirement of their allies just visible on the right. But there was a considerable gap between the two, and by their machine gunners infiltrating here through the mist the enemy again enfiladed the Armenians' left and restarted their withdrawal. Although himself outflanked on his left Lieutenant Ingle transferred his left platoon to the right, which thus again was steadied. Company headquarters sent him up a third platoon for his left flank, but in spite of this it became obvious that the Bolshevik deployment far overlapped the Mensheviks in that direction and there seemed nothing to prevent the enemy wing reaching the railway. Two Lewis guns were choked with sand. Another was sent forward from the fourth platoon. Ammunition supply depended entirely on man-handling. The enemy's flank attack field guns were now firing, but the mist prevented observation, and most of the shells fell on the sandy ridge south of the watercourse. Their machine gun fire, however, was heavy and the administrative trains were being swept from end to end.

At this critical hour, 1500 hours, when it appeared that the last reserves must be put into the fight on the left flank, and that they must be insufficient to prevent envelopment, No. 1 Company's train rattled in amid a storm of bullets ! Never was a train emptied more quckly as the men found cover under the low embankment ! There were a hurried few words between the company commanders and then Major Drummond led his men north, less one platoon, to retrieve the situation. The three Pathan platoons deployed at the double and after a few hundred yards made contact with the enemy's right wing, which though thus checked continued to advance still further on the west. No. 1 Company Commander then sent Lieutenant Cuvelier and his remaining platoon out wide to deal with that. Captain Pigot sent two troops of Daghistani Cossacks on the same task, but it was primarily No. 4 platoon which by establishing a commanding Lewis Gun post on that flank prevented the enemy from reaching the railway.

No. 1 Company had not yet even sighted No. 3, but its right continued to press the enemy back—from sandhill to sandhill, rush by rush—until by 1700 hours the Bolshevik retirement bacame general in front of the two companies. Pursuit was maintained for about two miles and when darkness fell both companies returned to the I.T. CAMP without having seen each other.

Meanwhile Masevitch's dismounted Turkomans with the 28th Light Cavalry troop on their right, and well supported by two armoured trains and artillery, had held up the Bolsheviks attack along the railway line since noon. But one hour before dark, approximately when his retirement began in the north-west, the enemy redoubled his efforts in the railway sector with fresh infantry and artillery. At 1730 hours the Indian cavalry reported that their troop had been driven back on to the right of the piquet line, that the Turkomans were back at the cutting, and that the armoured trains were threatened from the north where the enemy was attacking No. 3 piquet from two directions. The last card had now to be played on the Bolshevik's final stake. Captain Pigot with the headquarters and last platoon of No. 3 Company doubled forward along the line. The remaining troop of 28th Light Cavalry galloped ahead to persuade the Turkomans to stand. The platoon reached the armoured train position at the critical moment. The Turkomans were streaming back mounted over the piquet line, firing from the saddle as they did so. The Russian field guns were being manhandled back. Both armoured trains were spitting fire through the gathering darkness, the turntable gun of No. 2 train firing north. The gun of No. 1 train was firing point blank down the cutting, while the machine gun on its roof was streaming lead against No. 3 piquet. The enemy had just captured No. 2 piquet within 60 yards of the leading armoured train when seven men, led by a private, leaped from its armoured door and went straight for the enemy party with the bayonet. The Bolsheviks did not wait. The Punjabi-Musalman platoon swept in the wake of these brave gunners and having crossed the cutting drove the enemy northwards on the east side of No. 3 piquet. These counter-attacks turned the scale. The Bolsheviks retreated rapidly from this sector too, and soon were being followed up in the dark by the rallying Turkomans. Darkness and fatigue ruled out further action by the Indian troops, who returned, some to outpost duty and some to rest.

Casualties were not heavy—the two companies lost:—killed—Subadar Hukam Singh of No. 3 Company and 7 Indian other ranks: died of wounds—2: wounded 36. Yet this was probably the most critical action of the campaign. Had the enemy's flank attack not been delayed by the mist but synchronized with the railway demolition there is little doubt that the whole Menshevik force would have been overwhelmed. Or even if at later period the enemy had been able to obtain artillery observation of the long line of trains, or to have prevented the arrival of No. 1 Company, or to have captured the armoured trains with his final effort, the result would have been much the same. With their armoured trains lost the Mensheviks would undoubtedly have left the defence of BAIRAM ALI and MERV to the British and Turkomans alone.

A reconnaissance next morning of the area of the left flank attack disclosed 176 enemy dead in that sector alone. All had already been stripped by the Tnrkomans.

The following congratulatory message was received from General Malleson:-"The G.O.C. offers his heartiest congratulations to the two companies under Major Drummond and Captain Pigot for their gallant conduct during the extremely critical action of the 16th at ANNENKOVO, and regrets most deeply the loss of Subedar

Hukam Singh and the men of the two companies who so gallantly gave up their lives". A few days later General Milne, commanding the Army of the Black Sea, added his own appreciation when he paid a visit to the front at ANNENKOVO. Immediate awards of the Military Cross were made to Major Drummond and Lieutenant Ingle. Captain Pigot was granted a bar to the Military Cross. Subedar Nihal Singh and several other ranks received the Indian Distinguished Service Medal.

Last Weeks.

General Milne's inspection resulted in a decision for British troops to withdraw finally at the end of March. The Hampshire Company left at once, being replaced in MERV by a detachment from the Battalion. One and a half companies, together with a cavalry squadron and a half, were maintained at ANNENKOVO at first, but later were reduced. Depth was given to the position there by the construction of additional strong points; counter-action by the cavalry was rehearsed, and the defence was based on action by the armoured trains, gunners and Indian troops alone. Troops from Denekin's Army of the Caucasus began to arrive—Daghistanis, 30 field guns, 5 aircraft etc.

The Mensheviks resolved to make a bid for the OXUS line before the British withdrawal, so as to have defensive assistance in case of a reverse, and perhaps with the hope of upsetting the decision. Their very modest plan was for a dawn attack on the enemy at RAVNINA. In spite of a bitter night the approach march started with enthusiasm and apparently was well conducted. Watching from the forward defences, No. 3 Company saw none of those fires which usually marked the night movements of the Turkomans. The first phase was an advance down the railway to the WHITE HOUSE, which was found deserted. Thence one column was to make a detour south of the railway, outflank the enemy's trenches and strike the line again between the rear of the position and RAVNINA STATION. The other column, followed by the armoured trains, was to advance frontally against the enemy defences. Turkoman cavalry worked on both flanks but were given no role worthy of their numbers and mobility. Yet next morning they alone found themselves at RAVNINA and well placed to appreciate the humour of the situation! The enemy had been completely surprised by the frontal attack and had bolted back to RAVNINA STATION, armoured trains and all, without firing a shot. Their attackers had occupied the vacated trenches and paused. Almost at once the other column reached the selected area and opened fire on their comrades! In the ensuing fire-fight each column considered the other to be the enemy. Next, each Menshevik party came to the conclusion that the other column had failed in its task, and decided to go home!

"Map 10."

Sunrise revealed two Menshevik columns trudging back on opposite sides of the railway while the fleeing Bolshevik trains had reached UCH AJI! The combined recoil measured 25 miles!

Evacuation of Transcaspla, 1919.

On the following morning, 15th March, the squadron and company handed over as usual after night duty to the Russians, said a very sincere goodbye to the crews of the armoured trains and left the front by road and rail for BAIRAM ALI. The secret of the actual date of withdrawal had only just leaked out and some of the hostility of disappointment now showed itself. At ANNENKOVO STATION and again at KURBAN KALA sullen Russian officials and engine drivers blocked the movement on a variety of pretexts, and the company had to take control of their own engine.

Then followed a fortnight in BAIRAM ALI, a period of regrets and the growth of Menshevik despair. On 27th March the 44th Battery RFA departed to BAKU, where also went the remaining sick and wounded. On the 30th and 31st the XIX Punjabis moved by train to ASKHABAD, where No. 4 Company had now arrived, and complete at last began the march to MESHED. The 28th Light Cavalry followed the direct route from DUSHAK.

For his outstanding leadership in the campaign in Transcaspia Lieutenant-Colonel D.E. Knollys was awarded the Distinguished Service Order. In due course the Battalion was granted the battle honour of "PERSIA 1915-19" to be borne on the Colours and the additional honour of "MERV" to commemorate the operations in Transcaspia.

The fate of the Mensheviks was not very long delayed, though commendable persistence was displayed. In May the enemy captured the ANNENKOVO position and gained MERV. Defeated again at TEJEND in June, and at KAAKHA in July, the Mensheviks were forced to surrender ASKHABAD. For some months they maintained a defence near KIZIL ARVAT. In the autumn they were driven from their last position east of KRASNOVODSK.

3rd AFGHAN WAR.

"Map 8."

This war broke out on 6th May 1919 shortly after the Battalion had reached MESHED and, along with the 28th Light Cavalry, Kashmir Battery and the 98th Infantry, were enjoying rest in garden camps around the city. It ended on 8th August. The large garrison of HERAT was a potential threat to the L of C through East Persia; but it was soon evident that the commander and troops there were not at all enthusiastic about the war which their country had declared ! The frontier was very closely watched by the L of C troops, whose strength was exaggerated to the Afghans by every means, and there was no fighting. For its nominal services in this campaign the Battalion earned the battle honour "AFGHANISTAN 1919".

Indeed the hostile Bolsheviks soon to be established in MERV and ASKHABAD caused more anxiety than the Afghans did. When the Battalion withdrew from ASKHABAD No. 4 Company had been left at KUCHAN. In June it was relieved by the two 28th Light Cavalry squadrons located on the frontier itself near BAJGIRAN.

"Map 10."

In September the Battalion was ordered to move to KARACHI. The march to DUZDAB and onward train movement were by companies, the last of which reached its destination on 18th November. There were still many ranks who 4½ years previously had marched all the way out from NUSHKI and who now could appreciate in full the blessings of the railway extension. From MESHED marched Lieutenant-Colonel Knollys, Majors Bennett and Drummond, Captains Adams and Ingle, Lieutenant Cuvelier. Others who joined *en route* were Lieutenants N. V. Hart, K. L. Bodenham, V. C. Tweedy and V. D. W. Anderson. Captain Pigot had gone on leave to England. Subadar-Major Fateh Khan once more headed the Indian Officers.

Great War Statistics.

At the end of these three chapters on the First World War it will be appropriate to give the following records :—

1. *Recruits enlisted by 1st Battalion* :—

   (From August '15 to November '19) . . . . 3015.

2. *Drafts to other regiments:-*

Theatre and actions	Regiment.	Strength
France	35th Divisional Signal Company	11
France, Neuve Chapelle *Egypt*, Senussi	2nd Bn., The Sikh Regt.	200
France *Mesopotamia* (Relief of KUT)	5th Bn., FF Rifles	200
Mesopotamia (Siege of KUT)	4th Bn. of the Regiment	70
Mesopotamia	8th Indian General Hospital	19
Mesopotamia	3rd Bn. of the Regiment	109
Mesopotamia	4th Bn. of the Regiment	148
Mesopotamia	4th Bn., 15th Punjab Regiment	100
		857

3. *Casualties in the 1st Battalion on Service:—*

    Killed ... 120: Died of wounds ... 14: Died of disease ... 65.

                                         Total ... 199.

    Wounded .... 323.

4. *Casualties in the 1st Battalion and 2nd XIX Punjabis on the North West Frontier of India:—*

    Killed, died of wounds, died of disease .... 77.

    (These casualties are named on the India War Memorial Arch in NEW DELHI.)

5. *Individual decorations and honours in the 1st Battalion:—*

    CMG 1   IOM ... 7   Brevet of Lt. Col. 1

    CIE 1   IDSM ...26   Mentions in Despatches 27

    DSO. 2   IMSM ... 7   Foreign Decorations ... 41

CHAPTER XV

1919—1923.

KARACHI—PESHAWAR—KHYBER—PALESTINE.

(Maps 1 and 6)

Post-War Reorganization.

The years 1919 to 1923 in India were that difficult period of demobilization, resettlement, economic distress and political unrest during which none-the-less the Indian Army had to be reorganized. If stirring events were few, it was however a period prolific in changes made after much discussion, experiment and hard work. There were also the difficulties of retrenchment.

The World War and the North-West Frontier operations which followed revealed grave defects in the make-up of the Indian Army. The organization for higher command was inadequate; ancillary services were lacking; for modern warfare the equipment was obsolete. Further, establishments were too low, pay was too meagre; administration was somewhat makeshift; and there was that weakness in the reinforcement system already mentioned in Chapter XII. The recommendations of the Esher Committee which were put into effect by General Lord Rawlinson after he became Commander-in-Chief in 1920 transformed the situation. The feeding, housing and clothing of the sepoy became the obligation of the state. His pay and pension were made more attractive. Artillery was increased. Mechanical transport was included as part of an Indian Army Service Corps. The Indian Signal Corps and Indian Army Ordnance Corps were formed. Air co-operation was introduced. Other important steps will be mentioned later. In fact the Indian Army was reorganised to take its place adequately among the Empire's forces.

KARACHI, 1919.

From November 1919, when they arrived from MESHED and the Depot from HYDERABAD, SIND, the XIX Punjabis resumed a peace-station life under the command of Major D.E Knollys. But at first there was only a skeleton. Indian ranks went on 3½ months' end-of-war furlough, and many officers on privilege leave. Streams

"Map 9"

of new young officers came, were attached and departed. Demobilization, discharge and transfers were the inevitable order of the day. Among others, good-byes were said to Captain R.F.G. Adams, Captain F.W. Stewart M.C. of the ICS and Lieutenant J.G. Davies of the same service. Immediate arrivals from the British Army were Captain C.H. Goldsland MC and Captain F.V. Smeeton, the latter soon to be appointed Quartermaster. From the Unattached list a little later came 2nd-Lieutenant F. Adams. Major Heath, who had won the Military Cross and been wounded in Mesopotamia, was now Commandant of the Seistan Levy Corps. Lieutenant-Colonel Pennefather Evans, Commandant on paper since November 1918, was now on leave pending retirement. On 20th December 1919 Lieutenant-Colonel Churchill DSO was killed in Waziristan in command of the 2nd Battalion XIX Punjabis, and next day Major Jarrett died at Army Headquarters DELHI. Major Ross was in staff employ. Major E.C. Barnes retired. Major Pemberton was transferred, and other pre-war officers were on home leave.

It should be mentioned that notwithstanding its very reduced state the Battalion created something of a sensation by winning every event for which it entered in the Karachi Brigade Athletic Tournament, viz. inter-company sports, inter-company cross-country race, and the physical training competition. This was capped by winning the Quetta Division Hockey Tournament. Now began, indeed, a good hockey era not equalled again until 1934. Havildars Banta Singh and Sunder Singh (both from the Band), Havildar Attar Singh (the signaller) and Sepoy Bhola Singh were prominent. Outstanding among officers were Hart, Bennett and Subadar Maula Bakhsh.

In March the Battalion was complete enough for inspection by the Brigade Commander, Major-General Fowler, and received a good report.

PESHAWAR, 1920.

"Map 6." KARACHI with its attractive sea and cool breezes proved to be but a transit station. On 9th April 1920 the XIX Punjabis left by train, and on arrival in PESHAWAR relieved the 1st Battalion The Sikh Regiment in Edwardes Lines. There was an immediate inspection by General Sir George Barrow, the District Commander. Then training and reorganization were begun in earnest. Captain Pigot was appointed Adjutant. Captain H.Y. Huthwaite MC joned a little later. Ghulam Muhàmmad IDSM became Subadar-Major.

Night guard duties were heavy in PESHAWAR as a result of tribal raids and 'badmash' activity. There had been outrage and kidnapping in KOHAT. Following the practice there, PESHAWAR Cantonment was now wired in completely and the perimeter flood-lit at night. This period also saw the beginnings of the "Royal Air Force Station, PESHAWAR". The Brigade Parade Ground was at this time shared between Edwardes Lines, the rest of the garrison and the aircraft which came in low over the rifle ranges and landed more or less where they could!

The brass band was reformed, and surnais and dhols introduced for companies. Unfortunately the Band had been discontinued on the outbreak of the war in 1914 and its members allowed to scatter. By 1922 its performance was again creditable; but up to its final abolition in 1930 it never quite attained to the excellence of pre-war days. Like a plant, a Band must not be disturbed by uprooting.

Re-equipment sould be mentioned. The Battalion had begun the war with just rifle and bayonet, plus two Maxim machine guns on pack mules. The Lewis light machine gun was received in 1917, the Vickers in replacement of the Maxim in 1918. Also introduced during the war were the Mills grenade with discharger cup and the Stokes 3-inch infantry mortar. All these were included in the successive peace establishments now tried out. The resultant scale included 8 Vickers and 2 Stokes, and one Lewis Gun per platoon. Throughout the war the Battalion had had leather bandoliers and waistbelts. Now at long last they received web-equipment, "pattern "08". In the cold weather before the war British officers had worn with corduroy breeches and leggings a jacket of light green serge with white collar and black tie. Instead, the service drab uniform of the British Army was now adopted.

In October 1920 the first company and battalion training took the Battalion for a month to JALOZAI on the road to CHERAT. Having been warned for a move to THE KHYBER gave extra impetus to training, and the General's second inspection in March 1921 produced the following report. "The Battalion is well commanded. All ranks show commendable interest and keenness in their work and games. Lieutenant-Colonel Knollys has worked hard to infuse the right spirit into his men and officers, and the results are highly satisfactory. The Battalion has made steady progress in training and musketry, and is in all respect fit for service".

THE KHYBER, 1921.

The march up the KHYBER PASS in April 1921 was uneventful. The destination was LANDI KOTAL, where the 2nd Battalion 54th Sikhs FF were relieved. Then came a change in composition and organization. A complete company under

Subadars Gurdas Singh and Lachhman was transferred from the 38th Dogras. There was natural regret at again losing some of the friendly, manly Afridis. But the new class—there had been no Dogras in the Regiment since 1861—were given a warm welcome; and steadily they have endeared themselves ever since.

The other change was the introduction into the establishment of a Headquarters Company (later called "Wing") to comprise the support and administrative sub-units. Thus its No. 1 group contained the Signallers and the Band: No. 2 was the Machine Gun platoon: No. 3 included mess, provost and sanitary personnel: in No. 4 Group were the transport personnel, tradesmen and the followers. This wing was commanded by the 2nd-in-command. The numbering of companies 1 to 4 had already given place to lettering A to D.

In May the Regiment extended its athletic reputation by winning, against ten other units and by a margin of 100 points, the Peshawar District Championship for the best all-round Indian infantry battalion. Out of thirteen events seven first places were obtained.

It was cool at LANDI KOTAL and life was pleasant. When not on an outer piquet tour there were few duties. Sports grounds were available and there was competition with the British battalion as well as with the 1st/1st and 2nd/2nd Gurkha Rifles. But in July 1921 came a three months' turn in the heat of LANDI KHANA down at the Afghan frontier. Conditions there were reversed, and detachment duty in the coolth of BAGH SPRINGS was much sought after. Lieutenant-Colonel Tancred was in officiating command. Major Knollys was on home leave.

JULLUNDUR, 1921-22.

On 15th November 1921, a month after return to LANDI KOTAL, the Regiment marched down THE KHYBER again for overseas duty in the mandated territory of Palestine. Entrainment was at JAMRUD; for in those days the Khyber Railway was still under construction. JULLUNDUR, which was to be the jumping-off station, was reached on the 18th. From then until the end of January 1922 the Indian ranks as a whole were on embarkation leave, and for the rest there was much administrative preparation.

Brevet-Colonel C. J. B. Hay, CMG, CBE, DSO, of the Guides Infantry now became Commandant, and Major Heath rejoined. Colonel Hay had indeed been appointed from 1st March 1921, but could not be spared from staff employ overseas. The men were back in time to win the Brigade Sports Tournament early in February with four "firsts" out of six events.

On the 25th February 1922 H.R.H. the Prince of Wales visited JULLUNDUR to lay the foundation stone of King George's Royal Indian Military School for the sons of Indian soldiers. The Regiment with Band and Colours helped to line the processional route, and at the ceremony was represented by a company.

The Battalion were eager to leave when at length they entrained on 27th February. The great majority of the men were seeing the sea, ships and land beyond India for the first time. It was indeed the first move overseas in the Regiment's history. All could see that India was politically disturbed; and in particular there was a "kirpan" (Akali) agitation among Sikhs which it was good to leave behind.

PALESTINE, 1922.

After a pause at DEOLALI the XIX Punjabis embarked at BOMBAY on 5th March 1922 in the ex-German S.S. "Franz Ferdinand" which sailed on the 9th. At ADEN on the 15th there was a happy ship-side meeting with the 20th Punjabis, old friends who soon were to be closely linked. Disembarkation at SUEZ on 21st March was followed by a train journey to KANTARA the same day. After spending the night in the rest camp on the east bank of the SUEZ CANAL the Regiment travelled by train all next day and early on the 23rd detrained at LUDD. This place, now called LYDDA and best known as an airfield, was then a mere village. Close by were the equally historic village of RAMLEH on the JERUSALEM to JAFFA road and, on its edge, the war camp of SARAFAND. Here the Regiment relieved the 2nd Battalion The Highland Light Infantry, sending one company at once to JAFFA.

PALESTINE had hitherto been garrisoned by a considerable number of British and Indian units organised into "North" and "South" Brigades, all under Major-General Wardrop the General Officer Commanding. But reductions were now taking place. For military police duties a British Gendarmerie was being formed, and as units were withdrawn the remainder were grouped into a single "Palestine Brigade" under Colonel-Commandant Costello, VC (late of 22nd Punjabis) with Headquarters at SARAFAND.

The operational role of the Battalion was internal security. With the passing of war political consciousness had come to Palestine. The hostility born of conflicting promises to Jew and Arab was in the making. One storm centre was JAFFA, where the spreading suburb of TEL AVIV exemplified Jewish ambitions. Another was JERUSALEM, always the scene of heated religious competition during Easter, and now the natural focus of rival political manoeuvres.

The following officers were now present :—

Colonel Hay, CMG, CBE, DSO, Commandant.
Major Tancred, 2nd-in-Command.
Major Knollys, DSO.
Major Heath, MC.
Major Bennett, MC.
Captain Godsland, MC.
Captain Pigot, MC, Adjutant.
Captain Hart.
Captain Ingle, MC.
Lieutenant Bodenham, Quartermaster.
Lieutenant Tweedy.
Lieutenant Anderson.
Lieutenant Adams.

Subadar-Major.

Ghulam Muhammad, IDSM.

Subadars.

Maula Bakhsh.
Bal Singh, IOM.
Gurdas Singh.
Bak Khan.
Nihal Singh, IDSM.
Lachhman.
Mir Dast, IDSM.
Zarullah Khan.

Jemadars.

Ram Ditta.
Sher Ahmad, IDSM.
Massa Singh, IDSM, Jemadar Adjutant.
Hazara Singh.
Said Akbar.
Ilam Din.
Daulat Ram, Quartermaster Jemadar.
Ganga Singh.
Jiwand Singh, Head Clerk.
Manohar.

On 1st February 1923 2nd-Lieutenant C.A. Cornell joined. He was to be the last British officer posted from the Unattached List. Officers were permitted to have their families in Palestine; accordingly Mrs. Hay had accompanied the Regiment from India as well as the wife and children of Major Heath, the only other married officer.

The XIX Punjabis soon settled down to a happy, interesting and profitable tour which was to last 1½ years. The JAFFA detachment was found by companies in turn until withdrawn altogether at the end of September. The ancient port of JAFFA was always popular for its bathing, shops and bazars. TELAVIV, adjoining, was then just arising from the coastal sand. Headquarters and the remainder of the Battalion were in SARAFAND CAMP, which was shared with the 31st D.C.O. Lancers. Two companies went to JERUSALEM in March 1923 when the 5th Mahratta Light Infantry left for India. After the anxieties always attendant on Easter in the Holy City this detachment was halved. But long before this EL KUDS (JERUSALEM) had become popular with all ranks, but particularly of course with the Muhammadans. Duty or leave took officers and parties of other ranks to almost every part of this fascinating land—to HAIFA and MOUNT CARMEL, to GAZA and BEERSHEBA, to NAZARETH and the SEA OF GALLILEE, to JERICHO and the DEAD SEA. Certain officers were able to go further afield—to DAMASCUS, to BEIRUT and LEBANON, to TRANSJORDAN and even to mysterious PETRA. The local training area was dotted with Jewish colonies such as RISHON and NES ZIONA, where the men were able to learn much from these pioneers about orange farming, vineyards and modern agriculture. In short this land of three religions, of countless sects and many races, of contrasts in sloth and energy, of backwardness and education, proved a valuable eyeopener and example to the visitors from India.

Having completed the basic reorganization begun in PESHAWAR Colonel Hay was now able to elaborate all branches of administration. Everything was closely overhauled, improvements were made, novel ideas implemented and new Standing Orders issued. Historical records were brought up to date. Particular attention as never before was paid to dress, turn-out, paint and polish.

There were, it so happened, a succession of Guards of Honour to be found as Emir Abdullah of Trans-Jordan and High Commissioners came and went, and when a new General Officer Commanding, Major-General Tudor, arrived.

Training facilities were good. There were the rocky hills of Judea close at hand, the rolling downs of the Shepelah outside barracks, and the sandy plain by the sea. The lessons of the Palestine Campaign of 1918 could be studied on the original ground.

While in Palestine the majority of British officers visited the United Kingdom on privilege or combined leave. Some went every year!

The Regimental System.

The 2nd Battalion XIX Punjabis was disbanded in India rom 1st July 1922. From 2nd December 1922 there was introduced a regimental system of training, reinforcement and record-keeping which was of vast importance to Indian infantry. Further, it involved a change in the designation which had been borne unaltered for 20 years—"XIX Punjabis (Sherdil-ki-Paltan)". At the end of the World War there were 115 different infantry depots in India each serving a battalion overseas, each isolated from the others yet competing for personnel and equipment, and all struggling on an improvised basis to keep the records of the enormous numbers which had passed through. Now certain of the post-war infantry units were to become static "Training Battalions" and be located at permanent Regimental Centres to enlist and train recruits, in peace as in war, for the remaining "active" battalions which would make up each "Regiment". In war the Regimental Centres would also operate the personnel records and accounts of the mobilized battalions. Each Training Battalion was to have a permanent "headquarters"; but for the rest it would consist of "training companies" staffed and turned over by active battalions, who would thus have a distinct share in the instruction of their own personnel. Terms of service were later fixed at 7 years with the Colours and 8 in the Reserve. If necessary transfer from one battalion to another was obligatory. Gurkha Regiments apart, there were to be thus twenty new Regiments each of from three to six existing battalions and all given new designations. The 21st Punjabis were selected to be the 10th (Training) Battalion of the 14th Punjab Regiment, and the rest of the Regiment were :—

XIX Punjabis, as 1st Battalion.
20th Punjabis, as 2nd Battalion.
22nd Punjabis, as 3rd Battalion.
24th Punjabis, as 4th Battalion.
40th Pathans, as 5th Battalion.

The Regimental Centre was to be at FEROZEPORE.

This reorganization was introduced with effect from 1st January 1923, but of course took some time. Apart from the problems of procedure, posting and common promotion rolls, there were innumerable matters which could only be settled gradually—eg, uniform dress, the regimental badge, subscriptions and standing orders. Above all there had to be created that wider esprit-de-Regiment, which was a new idea inevitably involving some self-sacrifice in each battalion. In this spirit, wisely led by their Commandant and proud of their premier place, the 1st Battalion set off down the new road.

Reorganization of command.

The divisional system of command introduced for India by

Lord Kitchener in 1904 was now changed. It was found that divisions and headquarter staffs designed for operational and training functions could not at the same time cope with internal security duties and be burdened with much local administration. Accordingly "Commands" were created—Northern, Southern, Eastern and Western—each subdivided into military "Districts" closely corresponding with the civil boundaries. In each District units were specifically employed as "Frontier Covering Troops", "Field Army" or "Internal Security Troops", and were trained accordingly. Staffs were increased. Local authority was raised by decentralization and the delegation of powers. The Field Army was reduced to the maximum which India could sustain at the start of mobilization, namely, four cavalry brigades and four infantry divisions.

Indianization.

On 16th January 1923 the Battalion was inspected by Major-General Tudor and included in the following report :—"I am directed by the General Officer Commanding to refer to his recent inspection of the troops under your command (Palestine Brigade) and to say that he is quite satisfied with the general efficiency of all units. Discipline is well maintained, and the good behaviour of the troops is very pleasing to note. Commanding Officers are to be congratulated on the high standard of interior economy reached, which is reflected in the health, comfort and happiness of the men".

February 1923 was momentous for the introduction of what henceforward was called Indianization. At the end of the World War Indians had been declared eligible for King's Commissions in the Indian Army. This was in recognition of their loyalty and valour, but also was a natural consequence of the high appointments already held by them in the Civil Services. Ten vacancies were offered annually at Sandhurst, and after one year's attachment to a British unit the "King's Commissioned Indian Officer" was posted to the battalion as a company officer. It was in October 1923 that the first new entrant, 2nd-Lieutenant S. M. Khurshid, joined the Battalion. This supply continued until 1933 when it was supplanted entirely by the Indian Commissioned Officer now to be mentioned.

In February 1923 the Commander-in-Chief, General Lord Rawlinson, announced that in recognition of the proved efficiency of commissioned Indians a start was to be made with officering units entirely with them—a vision of the ultimate Indian Army. Two Indian cavalry regiments and six infantry battalions were to be built up with the KCIO and a new type of officer, the "Indian

Commissioned Officer" trained at an Indian Military Academy to be established at DEHRA DUN. The supply of junior British officers would cease. Among the units selected for this conversion was the 1st Battalion 14th Punjab Regiment.

A corollary was the gradual elimination of the Indian Officer promoted from the ranks, henceforth called Viceroy's Commissioned Officer. ICOs would be posted as platoon commanders. They would work their way up to become specialist officers, company officers, and company commanders as in a British battalion. One after another the VCOs would go. The special advisory function of the Subadar-Major would be filled by the Regimental Warrant Officer, that of the senior company subadar by a Company Warrant Officer. Indian Warrant Officers were also to replace the Jemadar Adjutant, Jemadar Quartermaster and Jemadar Clerk.

This prospect was rather startling. From sepoy to officer the Indian Army tends to be conservative. There are also personal feelings. The policy of thus concentrating Indianization in a few units rather than spreading it evenly over more might prove unattractive to both KCIO and ICO. VCOs must view their eclipse with disappointment. NCOs would find in the lower status of Warrant Officer a lesser incentive to promotion. So let it be remembered to the credit of Officers, VCOs and NCOs that they accepted the Commander-in-Chief's decision with loyalty and cheerfulness, determining to plough this long furrow both deep and straight.

Conversion went on year after year. Difficulties were many. Disappointments were not a few. Weaknesses were evident. But there was the will to work the new order, and on the whole it worked well. By the outbreak of the 2nd World War in 1939 the last stages had been reached. Of British officers only the Commandant and four company commanders remained. All other officer appointments were filled by KCIOs and ICOs. The last VCO, the Subadar-Major, had been replaced.

Last days in Palestine, 1923.

On 1st July 1923 Colonel Hay relinquished command on appointment as Colonel-on-the-Staff, General Staff, Headquarters Southern Command, and amid general regret left for India. Of the dead* it is permissible to give full credit while speaking no ill. "C. J. B. H." was at once respected and admired for his great driving force, attention to detail, love of smartness: yet withal for

---
* NOTE—General and Mrs. Hay were killed together during the German bombing of LONDON in the Second World War.

a kindly nature. Under him progress attained twice its ordinary speed. His mark on the administration of the Battalion, as his generosity, was still in evidence many years later. Under him The Sherdils further straightened their backs for the tasks ahead; held heads higher in confidence and pride. Since she too has passed, every officer who knew her will support this exceptional mention of a Commandant's wife. To the restless energy of "C. J. B. H." Mrs. Hay was the ideal foil. Her interest in the Battalion's welfare was no less. Her personal kindness was magnetic.

Then followed last weeks in Palestine; for the mandatory garrison was to be further reduced, and the Battalion had been warned for return to India. Early in August 1923 the JERUSALEM detachment was withdrawn. This was occasion for the following letter from the Governor of the Jerusalem-Jaffa District.

> "I shall be much obliged if you will accept yourself, and convey to the officers and men under your command, my very sincere thanks, coupled with those of the CITY OF JERUSALEM, for the prompt and never-failing courtesy and efficiency with which you have throughout your sojourn here assisted the authorities in the preservation of the public peace. The departure of the 1/14th Punjab Regiment will be greatly regretted by all sections of the population".

On 9th September the Battalion entrained for KANTARA under the command of Major Knollys, and sailing on the 11th reached BOMBAY eleven days later. Again there was a reunion at ADEN. This was with the 22nd Punjabis, now drawn closer still as the 3rd Battalion of the new Regiment.

CHAPTER XVI

1923—34.

SAUGOR—MANZAI—AURANGABAD—KHYBER.

(Maps 1 and 6)

SAUGOR, 1923-27.

"Map 1." On disembarking at BOMBAY on 22nd September 1923 the Battalion at once entrained for SAUGOR in the Central Provinces. A tragedy occurred in the troop train en route. During a hot night the sentry in one of the corridor military coaches in which some sixty men were sleeping lost his reason and started shooting indiscriminately. He killed two of his comrades and wounded three before he could be overpowered. The casualties were left at BHOPAL, where in due course the wounded recovered.

Lieutenant-Colonel C.C.R. Murphy, the new Commandant from the Madras Regiment, was awaiting the Battalion at SAUGOR. Within a few days Brevet Lieutenant-Colonel J. C. Macrae rejoined from staff employ as 2nd-in-Command. He succeeded to the command on 2nd March 1924 when Lieutenant-Colonel Murphy retired. Major Heath soon went as Commandant of the Indian Army School of Education, BELGAUM. Major Knollys, a brevet lieutenant-colonel from January 1925, was appointed 2nd-in-Command of the 10th (Training) Battalion, which he eventually commanded. Captain Godsland had transferred to the Indian Army Service Corps, and Lieutenant-Colonel Tancred to command the 4th Battalion in CHITRAL, before the Battalion left Palestine. Lieutenant Ingle was seconded to the Royal Air Force in Egypt.

A 1924 list of officers was:—

Lieutenant-Colonel C.C.R. Murphy .... Commandant,
Brevet Lieutenant-Colonel J.C. Macrae, 2nd-in-Command.
  DSO.
Major A.D. Bennett, MC.
Captain C.P.F. Williamson .... From Hyderabad
                                                   Regiment vice
                                                   Major Heath.

Captain G. Pigot, MC. . . . . Adjutant.
Captain H.Y. Huthwaite, MC.
Captain L.V. Fitzpatrick. . . . . with 10th Battalion.
Captain E.C. Spencer, MC.
Captain N.V. Hart.
Lieutenant K.L. Bodenham . . . . Quartermaster.
Lieutenant V.C. Tweedy . . . . Adjutant from May 1924.
Lieutenant V.D.W. Anderson. . . . . . Later Quartermaster.
Lieutenant F. Adams . . . . Signal officer and later Quartermaster.
2nd-Lieutenant S. M. Khurshid.

With the coming of November 1923 almost all Indian ranks went on 3½ months overseas service leave. There were thus no troops for a parade when General Lord Rawlinson, the Commander-in-Chief, visited the Battalion in the same month.

The 3rd December 1923 was notable for the unveiling of Regimental War Memorials at FEROZEPORE, and next day for the first all-battalions conference on regimental matters at the now flourishing 10th (Training) Battalion. This occasion was taken to assemble as many pensioners as possible, and these Regimental Reunions at FEROZEPORE have been repeated periodically ever since. The 1st Battalion was represented by Brevet Lieutenant-Colonel Macrae, Major Ross and Captain Pigot. The two obelisks stand opposite to each other on THE MALL. The one commemorates on its face those who were killed in the First World War from among the "linked" XIX, 22nd and 24th Punjabis. The crests and action honours of these battalions are engraved on the other three sides of the stones. Below the crest of "Crown, XIX and Scroll" there are shown:—

"LERADIK.
GUSHT DEFILE.
KAAKHA.
DUSHAK.
ANNENKOVO.
———

British officers   4.
Indian officers   2.
Indian other ranks 114".

The other monument unveiled simultaneously by the General Officer Commanding-in-Chief Northern Command in an imposing ceremony was to the fallen of the 20th Punjabis. The war memorial of the 40th Pathans already stood above the INDUS RIVER at ATTOCK.

The Battle Honours now awarded to the 14th Punjab Regiment were as follows. They are shared by all battalions of the Regiment, those *underlined* being borne on the Colours.

<u>YPRES 1915</u> : ST JULIEN : AUBERS : <u>*FRANCE AND FLANDERS 1915*</u>.

MACEDONIA 1918.

SUEZ CANAL : EGYPT 1915.

MEGIDDO : SHARON : NABLUS : <u>*PALESTINE 1918*</u>.

BASRA : SHAIBA : KUT EL AMARA 1915, 1917 :

<u>*CTESIPHON*</u>—DEFENCE OF KUT EL AMARA :

BAGHDAD : KHAN BAGHDADI : <u>*MESOPOTAMIA 1916-18*</u>.

<u>*PERSIA 1915-1919*</u> : MERV.

<u>*NW FRONTIER OF INDIA 1915-17*</u>.

NARUNGOMBE : <u>*EAST AFRICA 1916-1918*</u>

AFGHANISTAN 1919.

The battalion was destined to spend 3½ years in SAUGOR, the longest period passed in one spot since well before the First World War. It was an attractive little place where the Equitation School was the centre of station activities. The climate was mild, training areas good, and the shooting excellent. Disadvantages were the absence of other infantry, and separation from the rest of the 20th Brigade 100 miles away at JHANSI. There was also a two-company detachment at PACHMARI during the first half of the period.

Nevertheless a great deal of training was done every year. The Battalion joined either the JHANSI or the JUBBULPORE Brigade in collective training in 1925, 1926 and 1927, establishing a high reputation. With the Commander-in-Chief's concurrence of "very satisfactory", the final report of the General Officer Commanding-in-Chief Southern Command ran—"A first class battalion in every respect; every item of administration and detail is very thorough; it is thoroughly well trained. This battalion stands out in general excellence". It is important to note that there was during this period great concentration on the centralized instruction of NCOs. What was now called the Battalion Training Cadre was but an extension of the pre-war Drill Staff, and like that was under the

Adjutant. But much of the thought and drive behind training and smartness came from the pre-war Adjutant, Brevet Lieutenant-Colonel Ross, who rejoined from the staff in August 1925 and officiated in command from November. He became Commandant from 1st February 1926 when Lieutenant Colonel Macrae, on his return from leave, took over the Training Battalion at FEROZEPORE. Further, the post-war spirit of order, spit and polish first inculcated by Colonel Hay was watched over by him from Southern Command Headquarters. To his many gifts to the Battalion he soon added a magnificent set of Hay (Erroll) tartans for the Pipes; and be made numerous visits.

One of these was on an occasion which of itself merits record. On 30th October 1926 the Colour was trooped for the second time in the history of the Battalion. British and Indian officers were 'at home' to a considerable gathering which included Lieutenant-General Sir Harold Walker, Major-General Sir Herbert Holman, Colonel Hay, Major Heath, Captain (Flight Lieutenant) Ingle and Lieutenant Isar Singh, Bahadur, the late Subadar-Major. The great distances from their homes prevented other pensioners from attending. The parade was commanded by Lieutenant-Colonel Ross; Jemadar Muhammad Akram carried the Colour. A pleasant setting, good weather and remarkable drill all made for its success. In the Order of the day congratulating all ranks on the admirable display the Army Commander was kind enough to say that he had "rarely, if ever, seen Indian troops better turned out, or drill with such precision and steadiness".

This ceremonial event was fixed as close as possible to the anniversary of the action of DUSHAK described in Chapter XIV. Before the war the anniversay of the battle of AHMED KHEL on 19th April 1880 was marked by a holiday. Now the 14th October was introduced as a second Battalion holiday to commemorate that day in 1918 when so many gallant men fell around a far-off Russian railway station.

The Pipes have just been mentioned. Although The Band at this date meant the brass band under the direction of Mr. Curtis, it had became clear that the very factor of expense could not long justify its continuance in an Indianizing battalion. An embryo pipe band was therefore started, and formally adopted in 1927.

The years in SAUGOR saw numerous change in organization. In the pre-war days of double-companies the two companies of each pair were usually of different classes. The idea was traditional, and had always worked well. Because of this, when the four-company organization was introduced while on service in 1917 no change in company class composition was made; and the mixing of classes in

A and C companies was continued after the war, even after the coming of the Dogras. But in October 1925, on Army Headquarters order, all companies became "class" as follows:—

    A Company .... Yusafzai Pathans and (one platoon) Afridis.
    B Company .... Jat Sikhs.
    C Company .... Punjabi Musalmans.
    D Company .... Dogras.

In July 1928, following a decision to concentrate the Afridis of the Regiment in the 2nd Battalion and the Yusafzais in the 4th, the 1st Battalion lost its last Afridis and for a while had no other Pathans. Two of the Yusafzai platoon were transferred to the Baluch Regiment, the third and the Afridi platoon as indicated above. The Punjabi - Musalman company of the 2nd Battalion came in to take the Pathans' place in 'A' Company.

This happened when the Battalion was at MANZAI. Only a year later, when in AURANGABAD, there was another change in policy which disturbed all developments since 1925. It was decided to organize the platoon of six medium machine guns as "D(MG)" Company, for tactical reasons to give each rifle company four platoons instead of three and to compensate by reducing the number of rifle companies to three. Simultaneously Indian other ranks strength was reduced by 32 to 708. Cis-Frontier Pathans were restored. Back came the Muhammadzai platoon from the Baluch Regiment. Two platoons of Yusafazais were transferred from the 3rd Battalion, and two of those Punjabi Musalman platoons received from the 2nd Battalion in 1928 now went to the 3rd Battalion. The Pathans were very welcome; but this "general post" was somewhat upsetting, particularly as it was accompanied by a reversal of class policy.

Henceforward the Battalion was organized thus:—

HQ Wing.

    Groups)   Punjabi Musalmans.
       1)   Yusafazais.
       2)   Sikhs.
       3)   Dogras.

Platoon.	A Company.	Platoon.	B Company.
1.	Punjabi Musalmans.	5	Punjabi Musalmans.
2.	Yusafzais*	6	Yusafzais.
3.	Sikhs.	7	Sikhs.
4.	Dogras.	8	Dogras.

NOTE—These were Muhammadzais until the elimination of this sub-class was ordered in 1932.

Platoon.	C Company.	Sub-Section.	D(MG) Company.
9.	Punjabi Musalmans.	1.	Punjabi Musalmans.
10.	Punjabi Musalmans.	2.	Sikhs.
11.	Sikhs.	3.	Punjabi Musalmans.
12.	Dogras.	4.	Sikhs.
		5.	Yusafzais.
		6.	Dogras.

This arrangement caused over-distribution of classes, was administratively inconvenient and did not last long. Soon too the need for a fourth rifle company came to be recognized as greater than the necessity for the fourth platoon per company.

The Viceroy's Commissioned Officers at the time of this reorganization in 1929 were:—

Subadar-Major..	Maula Bakhsh.
Subadar	.. Godar Khan.
Subadar	.. Massa Singh, IDSM.
Subadar	.. Hukmat Khan (Muhammadzai).
Subadar	.. Khushal Khan—with 10th Battalion.
Subadar	.. Allah Ditta.
Subadar	.. Ram Ditta.
Subadar	.. Sher Muhammad.
Subadar	.. Kehr Singh (Dogra).
Jemadar	.. Sheikh Muhammad Abdullah—with 10th Battalion.
Jemadar	.. Karam Khan.
Jemadar	.. Banta Singh—with 10th Battalion.
Jemadar	.. Kishen Singh.
Jemadar	.. Fateh Muhammad—with 10th Battalion.
Jemadar	.. Muhammad Akram—Jemadar Adjutant.
Jemadar	.. Painda Khan, Education officer.
Jemadar	.. Muzaffar Hussain—with 10th Battalion.
Jemadar	.. Dharam Singh, Jemadar Clerk.
Jemadar	.. Nasib Singh (Dogra).
Jemadar	.. Abdul Shakur (Yusafzai).
Jemadar	.. Bahadur Singh (Dogra).
Jemadar	Sultaj—with 11th (Territorial) Battalion.
Jemadar	.. Attar Singh.
Jemadar	Ram Ditta, Jemadar Quartermaster.

Subadar Zarullah (Pathan) had died at MANZAI in May 1927 following a motor accident. Quartermaster-Jemadar Kehr Singh had retired in the same year.

Regimental conferences at FEROZEPORE followed one another yearly and sometimes oftener in the necessary but delicate task of forming a Regiment that should be one throughout in spirit and in those material matters where uniformity is essential, yet with the several battalions retaining their individuality. This co-ordinating duty was laid on the officer commanding the Training Battalion; and thus with Lieutenant-Colonels Dyke, Macrae and Knollys began a line of 10th Battalion Commandants whose central leadership grew and grew until during the Second World War the position reached was that of Regimental Commander. Among the many matters standardized were the Regimental Crest (a Kandahar star with scroll), certain Standing Orders, and dress in many directions. But cherished distinctions were still retained, such as the black pagri fringes of the 2nd Battalion, the Khaki fringe of the 1st, the black putties of the 4th. An all-India arrangement was simultaneously introduced of differently coloured strips worn by the various battalions under the regimental shoulder title.

The outcome in dress was that 1st Battalion men now wore a thin red strip across the headdress fringe and a red strip under the shoulder title. Officers lost the red pag triangle from their helmets. Officers and VCOs used regimental crest buttons. The Wolseley helmet was replaced by the Cawnpore. Short-length pagris were introduced for field service and training. Short putties were adopted. Chapplis came in as alternative footwear. From 1920 the buttoned khaki drill tunic had replaced the men's blouse.

An admirable sequel to the World War was the facilities granted to Viceroy's Commissioned Officers for having their own mess. The 1920 beginnings of a "Club" were put on a proper subscription basis in 1924, and by a later development became the VCOs' Mess. As usual the Army was leading India in making class prejudices vanish.

Another innovation accompanying the march of progress was the appointmeut of an Education Jemadar in subordinate charge of this now extensive training. Not only was there now a natural urge to learn, but educational tests had become essential steps to promotion.

In 1924 was born the Regimental Dinner Club and Regimental Year Book, the one designed to bring past and present officers of the six battalions together in LONDON once a year, the other to provide in light and handy form a battalion-by-battalion history of the Regiment. Well started by General Dunsterville and devotedly managed throughout by Lieutenant-Colonel Murray (retired), both these enterprises have prospered and have survived the impact of another World War.

Sports and games prospered at SAUGOR. C Company won

the Brigade Hockey Tournament in 1924, while the Battalion side gained the Sassoon trophy. Both wins were repeated next year. In 1926 the District Wrestling Championship was won for the third year in succession, and the Sassoon Cup again annexed.

Keenness in markmanship was raised to a new level during these unruffled days which allowed of steady practice. The Inter-Company Trophy was reserved for rifle shooting, as it always had been. But the principal prize was now The Inter-Platoon Shooting Trophy, a cup presented by the 2nd Battalion XIX Punjabis for the best performance with all platoon weapons. With this went The Shooting Flag to be flown on a flagstaff outside the quarters of the platoon commander.

MANZAI, 1927-29.

In November 1926 the Battalion was pleased to receive warning for a move to Waziristan in the following year. There was a feeling of having had indeed a good long period of peace and training, and of being fit and ready for a change.

There had been considerable changes among officers. When Lieutenant-Colonel Ross became Commandant in 1926 Major T. B. Minnikin, from the 8th Punjab Regiment, filled his place as 2nd-in-command. Major Drummond came back from the Burma Military Police in January 1926, but shortly afterwards went as Adjutant to the Territorial (11th) Battalion, a unit of the recently formed Indian Territorial Force and affiliated to the Regiment. Captain Pigot was at home on leave and at the Staff College CAMBERLEY during 1925, 1926 and 1927.

Captain Fitzpatrick, the first commander of No. 1 Training Company in the 10th Battalion, was relieved in March 1925. He was followed there by, successively, Captains Spencer, Huthwaite and Hart. Captain Huthwaite was then transferred to the 4th Battalion.

Captain Bodenham went to the 11th (Territorial) Battalion, and later retired from the service.

Newly-joined from Sandhurst and British regiments came Lieutenant A.S.B. Shah, Lieutenant Gurdip Singh Dhillon and 2nd Lieutenant Sant Singh. Lieutenant-Colonel Ross went on home leave just before the move.

The following entrained with the Battalion on 1st March 1927 :—

Major T.B. Minniken.
Major A.D. Bennett, M.C.
Captain L.V. Fitzpatrick.
Captain V.C. Tweedy, Adjutant. For 12 months' leave home.
Captain F. Adams, Quartermaster. Adjutant from 21 June 1927.
Lieutenant A.S.B. Shah. Later Quartermaster.
2nd-Lieutenant S. Sant Singh.

Captain L.S. Ingle, MC, rejoined from the Royal Air Force later in the year, and Captain Williamson from furlough towards its end. 2nd-Lieutenant S.P. Thorat was posted in October.

Reaching MANZAI by train on 5th March the Battalion found itself quartered partly in barracks and partly in tents in the 10th Indian Infantry Brigade under Colonel-Commandant R.C. Wilson. After taking over from the 2nd Battalion The Sikh Regiment (relieved so many times before as the 15th Sikhs) there followed a very opportune sortie for training at the outpost camp of KHIRGI, and then a most complimentary inspection by H.E. the Commander-in-Chief. In those days MANZAI as a place was but small improvement on TANK, which it had just replaced. It was half-built, trees had only just been planted, hockey grounds were still in the making, perimeter duties were rather heavy. What made the tour pleasantly memorable was the friendly spirit within the Brigade and the many excursions of the Manzai Mobile Column.

The first extensive "Column" was from October to December 1927, WANA being visited and a protracted stay made at SAR-WEKAI. In those days WANA was not garrisoned, nor were the South Waziristan Militia securely established in their area. The passage of the SHAHUR TANGI and certain other ill-reputed sectors of the route was therefore a matter for high vigilance and training. In 1923 the Column went twice to camp and train at DARGAI OBA, two marches short of WANA, and had some lively brushes with the unrelenting Wazir. Captain Hart commanded 'A' Company: Captain Williamson 'B' : Captain Pigot 'C' ; Captain Ingle 'D' : Captain Anderson was Machine gun officer : Lieutenant Thorat Signal Officer. It was on these columns that oil cooking was first introduced.

Thus the two years passed busily and surprisingly rapidly. The 2nd and 5th Battalions were at this period in Waziristan at BANNU and IDAK, respectively; but lack of time and of good communications prevented any but rare contacts. Just before Christmas 1927 news came that the next station would be KARACHI: but the prophet proved false.

AURANGABAD, 1929-34.

On relief by the 1st Battalion The Baluch Regiment the Battalion left MANZAI by train on 6th February 1929 and arrived at AURANGABAD in the Deccan on 1st March. During recent years a railway bridge had been under construction between MARI INDUS and KALABAGH on the opposite bank, and this was the last occasion that the Battalion had to cross the RIVER INDUS by ferry. There was a welcome break in the journey at RAWALPINDI from 9th to 23rd February, so as to allow short leave to the greatest possible number of men while close to their homes. There was also quite a reunion of pensioners. Later there was a stop of some hours at FEROZEPORE for a most enjoyable welcome from the 10th Battalion. Further on there was a glimpse of officers and VCOs of the 5th and 11th Battalions as the train halted at DELHI.

"Map 1."

"Map 6."

This was the Battalion's first tour in AURANGABAD. The one-time queen of the Hyderabad Contingent stations was now something of a backwater. It was served only by the metre gauge railway leading to distant SECUNDERABAD. Roads were indifferent, and the lack of river bridges particularly restricted access to the nearest big station, AHMEDNAGAR. But there were compensations. By treaty two battalions had to be maintained, so that there were at least some competitions and outside friendships, first with the 5th Battalion The Rajputana Rifles and later with the 4th Battalion The Sikh Regiment. There was only one small detachment, a platoon at AHMEDNAGAR. The Hyderabad Contingent officers' mess was a fine one. Duties were light, games grounds ample and the country very fair for training. There were even American and other exciting visitors to this sleepy little town; for it was the starting point for visits to the ELLORA and AJANTA CAVES. Looking back, the main criticism was the protracted stay of four years, which is really too long in one place under any circumstances.

AURANGABAD was an ideal opportunity for still further improving individual training methods and perfecting interior economy. A popular Loan Fund had recently been started. The presence of families enabled Child and Family welfare to be put on a permanent basis.

An importnnt milestone which may here be mentioned was the introduction of new terms of service for the men, a combination of colour and reserve service totalling a minimum of 15 years. Seven years was to be the normal colours period for infantry. Reserve service was compulsory.

Major-General Ruggles, the first Colonel of the XIX Punjabis, had died. Now, to everybody's great satisfaction, Major-General Hay was appointed to succeed him from 7th July 1928. Every year while the Battalion was in AURANGABAD General Hay was able to pay a welcome visit, first from the Sind Independent Brigade Area and then from Lucknow District, which were his successive commands.

One such visit was for the 1929 anniversary of DUSHAK on 14th October when the Colour was again trooped. Lieutenant-Colonel Ross once again commanded the parade, the salute in the march past being taken by the Colonel. Jemadar Painda Khan carried the Regimental Colour. Lieutenant-Colonel Minniken and Captain Huthwaite, now with the 4th Battalion, came up from SECUNDERABAD. Captain Fateh Khan, a famous ex-Subadar-Major, journeyed all the way from PESHAWAR. The Pipes and Drums, by now well trained, rigged in full dress with green facings and with their handsome green tartan, made their first ceremonial appearance on this parade. Next year, as had been foreseen, it was decided to abolish the brass band.

Each year in AURANGABAD the isolation was overcome for a period by brigade training and manoeuvres, first at IMAMPUR, then near AHMEDNAGAR 70 miles away, again at CHAS in the same direction and finally at SANGAMNER towards DEOLALI. In all this the reputation of the Battalion stood high, as records show.

There were numerous changes among officers. Joining as almost the last King's Commissioned Indian Officers came successively 2nd-Lieutenants Misri Chand, Muhammad Ayub Khan (destined later to become Commandant), Jamal Dar, Khan Ata Muhammad Khan and Rajinder Singh Kalha. Lieutenant-Colonel Minniken returned from the 4th Battalion to become Commandant when, on 1st January 1930, Lieutenant-Colonel Ross completed his four years' tenure. Lieutenant-Colonel Minniken in his turn retired from 1st July 1933, and was followed by Lieutenant-Colonel Bennett. Major Drummond rejoined, but almost at once proceeded on leave and then returned to the Burma Military Police. Captain Pigot was back with the Battalion in MANZAI, but in 1929 went to staff employment. He reappeared in AURANGABAD in 1933 as a Brevet Major, but was off again in March of next year to train Indian Commissioned Officers at the Indian Military Academy. Captain Hart, back from the Training Battalion, died tragically of pneumonia on 22nd February 1934. His loss was keenly felt by all ranks. Captain Doherty, long with the 11th and 10th Battalions, served in AURANGABAD before being transferred to the 5th Battalion (40th Pathans). Captain Lee was welcomed on attachment from the 4th Battalion. Captain Tweedy transferred to the 1st Battalion The Sikh Regiment shortly after Lieutenant-Colonel Heath became its Commandant. Captain Anderson had followed Captain Adams as Adjutant from 16th June 1931. Subadar Massa Singh, IDSM, succeeded Subadar-Major Maula Bakhsh, OBI, in August 1931, and next year was appointed an Honorary Lieutenant.

To the great regret of the 1st and 10th Battalions Lieutenant-Colonel Knollys retired in March 1931.

THE KHYBER, 1934.

Much that happened at AURANGABAD has been left untold: the comings and goings on courses and leave: the annual and General's inspections: successes in sports and games: competitions for regimental and Indian Army shooting trophies: visitors: epidemics, etc. All this quietly ordered life in a secluded green station was changed to the daily uncertainties of the barren frontier when on 20th March 1934 the Battalion moved to SHAGAI in the KHYBER PASS.

The road protection duties and hill training now undertaken were opportune experience for the Mohmand Operations which were to come next year. But after less than three months at SHAGAI there was a move to JAMRUD in the chain of local reliefs. Here duties were less exacting and life rather dull. But it soon became known that there was to be a move of permanent posting to JHELUM early next year, and time passed rapidly in anticipation of being in a Punjab station at long last.

CHAPTER XVII

1935-39.

JHELUM—MOHMAND OPERATIONS—WAZIRISTAN OPERATIONS—BANNU.

(Map 6, Sketches N and O)

JHELUM 1935-36.

The 1st/14th moved from JAMRUD to JHELUM on 27th February 1935, and quickly settled down to work and play in this 3rd Indian Infantry Brigade station. The other battalions were the 4th/16th Punjab and 3rd Jat. The Regiment had never before been stationed here. Indeed, except for a transit pause at JULLUNDUR in 1922, the 1st/14th had not served in the Punjab since celebrating their Jubilee there 27 years previously!

The two years which ensued saw great progress in the process of Indianization last mentioned in Chapter XV. Commissioned Indian Officers soon outnumbered the British. 2nd Lieutenant R.N. Nehra, who joined in March 1935, was the last to be trained at Sandhurst. Next year saw the first products of the Indian Military Academy at DEHRA DUN, namely, 2nd Lieutenants Muhammad Zaman Khan and Mohan Singh. Thereafter I. C. Os. come at the rate of three or four each year; they were Muhammad Zaman Kiani, Hardial Singh Randhawa, Shahnawaz Khan, Kanwar Gajinder Singh, Habib ur Rehman Khan and others to be mentioned later. As these platoon commanders arrived, so the V. C. Os. whom they replaced were pensioned; and in that respect the process was a sad one. A further sign of the times was the selection during this period of several N. C. Os. out of the Battalion for training as officers at Dehra Dun. Another peculiarity of an Indianizing battalion was that whenever additional British officers were required they were attached for a tour from other battalions of the Regiment. In this way, after Major Lee had been posted to the Special Unemployed List in October 1935, there came successively Major Sheehan from the 2nd Battalion, Major Dawes from the 5th and Major Pouncey from the 3rd.

The following officers were on the books during early days in

JHELUM :—

Lieutenant-Colonel	A. D. Bennett, MC	Commandant.
Major	A. B. Craddock, OBE, psc	DAAG, Meerut District. Later on home leave.
Major	G. Pigot, MC, psc	GSO II Indian Military Academy.
Major	L.V. Fitzpatrick	On home leave.
Major	T.R. Lee	Officiating 2nd-in-Command.
Major	L.S. Ingle, MC	
Captain	V.D.W. Anderson	No. 1 Company Commander. Later Adjutant at the Training Battalion.
Captain	F. Adams	On home leave.
Captain	Muhammad Akbar Khan, MBE	From Probyns Horse. Later to RIASC.
Captain	Gurdip Singh Dhillon	Adjutant since August 1934. Later to RIASC.
Captain	Sant Singh	Later to 11th (Territorial) Battalion.
Lieutenant	S.P.P. Thorat	Quartermaster. Later with the Training Battalion.
Lieutenant	Misri Chand.	
Lieutenant	Muhammad Ayab Khan	Company officer at the Training Battalion. Later officiating Adjutant.
Lieutenant	Jamal Dar	With RIASC
Lieutenant	Vir Singh	Later officiating Adjutant.
Lieutenant	Khan Ata Muhammad Khan	Leave ex-India.
Lieutenant	Rajinder Singh Kalha	Leave ex-India. Later Quartermaster.
2nd Lieutenant	Mahabir Singh Dhillon	Later to RIASC
2nd Lieutenant	R.N. Nehra.	

Subadars, 1935

Godar Khan, Subadar-Major vice Hony Lieut Massa Singh, OBI, IDSM, from April 34.

Hukmat Khan, son of ex S.M. Capt. Fateh Khan, OBI. Retired 1937.

Jemadars, 1935

Muzaffar Hussain, Education Jemadar. Retired as a Subadar 1939.

Bahadur Singh. Retired as a Subadar 1938.

Nand Lal. Retired 1936.

Subadars, 1935	Jemadars, 1935
Kehr Singh, SM from January 1937. Retired 1938.	Kartara Singh, Head Clerk. Retired 1938.
Banta Singh. Retired 1936.	Gurdit Singh. With 10th Bn. Retired as a Subadar 1939.
Karam Khan. Later the last SM.	Ghulam Haidar, Jemadar Adjutant. Retired as a Subadar 1938.
Kishan Singh. Retired 1936.	
Muhammad Akram. Later lent to RAF as SM.	Shah Muhammad. Later to 10th Bn.
Ram Ditta. Retired 1938.	Laurasib Khan. Retired as a Subadar 1939.
Painda Khan. Retired 1938.	Munshi Ram. 11th Bn. Retired 1937.
	Muhammad Akbar.
	Bainta, Jemadar Quartermaster. Retired 1937.
	Harbhajan Singh. Retired 1936.
	Mangat Ram. Retired 1938.
	Abdulla Khan. Later to 10th Bn. as Subadar.
	Rajah Khan. Retired as a Subadar 1939.

The great number of VCO retirements shown above is a measure of the pace of mustering-out to make room for Indian Commissioned Officers.

The 1st/14th had scarcely settled down at JHELUM when there intervened those Mohmand operations which will now be described. After they were over there followed a busy medley of training, competition shooting, athletics and hockey throughout the undisturbed year of 1936. The Brigade Athletic Cup was annexed. In the Punjab Native Army Hockey Tournament of 1936, played as usual at JHELUM, the Battalion team did not survive the 2nd round. But two hockey wizards were discovered, Lance Naik Dara, who played for India at the Olympic Games of this year, and 2nd Lieutenant M.Z. Kiani. Battalion training took place one year at DINA, and the next at SHEKHUPUR. The Lewis Gun was replaced by the Light Machine Gun (Vickers Berthier and later Bren).

MOHMAND OPERATIONS, 1935.

"Map 6."   The Mohmand trouble was a recrudescence of that incompletely settled in 1933. In that year dissensions between the Upper and Lower Mohmands over the latter's loyalty to Government led to the former under the Haji of Turangzai invading the GANDAB VALLEY. The Nowshera Brigade had had to intervene and the Gandab Valley MT Road had been built up to just short of the NAHAKKI PASS. Failure to insist on its extension over that historic high ground was interpreted by the Upper Mohmands as weakness, and led them to truculence. They refused to hand over certain outlaws; they quarrelled with the Lower Mohmands over the distribution of the road contract money; finally in mid-August they started to demolish the road. Their lashkar at first numbered 1,400 Burhan Khel and Isa Khel, but was soon greatly increased from the Safis and other tribes.

While the Peshawar and Nowshera Brigade Columns including light tanks concentrated near SHABKADR as "Mohforce", air bombing was undertaken, but without sufficient effect, against the hostiles' villages. Advancing on 23rd August the two brigades reached GHALANAI next day against appreciable opposition, and during the next few days cleared the locality and established the L of C. Before extending the MT road over the NAHAKKI PASS, as was now decided, it was necessary to increase the force.

Sketch N.

The 3rd Brigade was warned on 23rd August. All officers and men on leave in India were recalled, and a depot under Lieutenant Vir Singh was left behind in JHELUM. After a train move to PESHAWAR during the night of 5th/6th September, the Battalion marched up via MICHNI (first night) and SIKANDER POST (2nd night). The 3rd Brigade first took over the L of C sector from KILAGAI to KARAPPA KANDAO, and then, on the 13th, concentrated at GHALANAI. Several officers were still away; Lieutenant-Colonel Bennett officiated in command of the Brigade, Captain Sant Singh was first Brigade Intelligence Officer and later officiating GSOI of Mohforce; Captain Muhammad Akbar Khan commanded the Battalion until Major Lee arrived; Captain Misri Chand acted as Adjutant. The other battalions in the Brigade were the 2nd Battalion The Argyll and Sutherland Highlanders and the 4th/16th Punjab.

The first operation of significance was the passage of the NAHAKKI PASS. Advancing by night the other two brigades secured the crest of the pass without opposition by 0600 hours on 18th September while the 3rd Brigade secured the left flank by blocking the upper GANDAB KHWAR. The Battalion left GHALANAI at midnight and was in position near BADISIAH by 0550 hours. The evening withdrawal to GHALANAI CAMP was equally without incident. Then followed some days spent in building the MT road over to NAHAKKI while the enemy harassed all they could. On 21st September the Battalion helped to build a camel track from GHALANAI to the KHAIRUDDIN KANDAO leading into the PINDIALI VALLEY, and on the 25th reconnoitred SARUNE SAR on the opposite flank.

As a subsidiary to the main Mohforce operation next day, on the night of the 28th/29th the 1st/14th laid a successful ambush for the enemy parties now actively sniping WUCHA JAWAR CAMP. The venue was the upper GANDAB VALLEY near the villages of TORATIGGA whence many of the hostiles came. Lieutenant-Colonel Bennett, who was now back in command, personally staged this operation, which was to be carried out by five selected platoons and officered by VCOs only. They included Subadar Hukmat Khan, in command, and Subadar Karam Khan. On the 28th, while their men were marching up from GHALANAI, the platoon and section commanders went ahead in lorries to KATSAI CAMP to reconnoitre. This they did by looking up the valley from the slopes of a hill south of BADISIAH, having moved up in the guise of a platoon of the company of the 3rd Battalion the Sikh Regiment which was patrolling as usual in the area. The ambush platoons left KATSAI at 2000 hours carrying their LMGs and with their boots silenced by sacking. Though the night was very dark they reached their pre-determined positions within two hours. These dispositions covered a frontage of 900 yards on the north slopes of the valley with four platoons facing northeast towards the crest, and the fifth facing the other way in rear to deal with possible interference from the TORA TIGGA Villages. The platoon positions straddled tracks commonly used by the hostiles.

Sketch N.

The sniping of WUCHA JAWAR CAMP could be plainly heard over the ridge, and soon became very heavy. It ceased at about 0030 hours on the 29th, and a little later a whistle call and the sound of voices close in front of the ambush line indicated that the snipers were on their way back towards TORA TIGGA. First fourteen of them bumped into No. 4 platoon, who opened fire at twenty yards. While some fell the remainder of the enemy ran left until ambushed at very close range by No. 2 platoon and suffered further casualties. Five minutes later much the same was repeated by another batch of tribesmen. Both parties now moved further west until they were almost shot off the muzzles of Nos. 1 and 5 platoons. Thence they doubled back on their tracks only to be again engaged by No. 4 platoon. The men were enjoying themselves hugely. It is not often that tribesmen are driven from pillar to post. The Mohmands too were conscious of this, for they started hurling abuse until sprayed by LMGs. But their blood was up ; further they had now been reinforced to a strength of about 150, and they were soon to be helped from TORA TIGGA. Moving wider to that flank they concentrated attacks aga nst

No. 5 platoon, coming down hill several times in knife charges under covering fire from close by. All these attacks were halted by fire, as well as a separate one made against No. 3 platoon from the southwest.

This virtually ended the operation. There could be no firing after 0245 hours owing to the advance of the Nowshera Brigade. Strong parties of the enemy remained in position, but the wailing of women from TORA TIGGA showed that the majority had gone home. The 1st/14th platoons slipped away at 0530 hours, having killed eight hostiles and wounded fourteen without loss to themselves. For their bravery and leadership in this action the Indian Distinguished Service Medal was awarded to Sepoy Nawab Khan, Subadar Karam Khan and Subadar Hukmat Khan.

The Battalion had meanwhile moved up to the south-east corner of BADISIAH HILL, and were soon disposed in that locality as part of the screen which the 3rd Brigade maintained throughout the 29th astride the GANDAB KHWAR. This was to protect the left of the Nowshera Brigade on the heights at the head of the WUCHA JAWAR VALLEY. They in their turn were securing the left of the Peshawar Brigade operating about MUZI KOR. By 1000 hours the latter brigade had completed its task and was ready to withdraw to NAHAKKI CAMP. But in the Nowshera Brigade the Guides Infantry had early become involved in very heavy fighting on difficult ground against great odds, and this delayed the movement. In the 3rd Brigade the 1st/14th had a quiet day. There was merely artillery firing against large numbers of tribesmen at the head of the GANDAB KHWAR where they were seen climbing the heights towards the Guides. The Battalion got back to GHALANAI CAMP at 1730 hours with the distinction of having carried out a most successful and model night ambush.

The tribes submitted on 3rd October, the final jirga being held twelve days later. In the meantime the road was completed over the pass to NAHAKKI. The Jhelum Brigade was the first to be withdrawn, and the 1st/14th left GHALANAI on 18th October. They staged at MICHNI, reached PESHAWAR next day, and on the 21st arrived in JHELUM. Majors Craddock and Fitzpatrick were already back there from home leave. It had been a hot but interesting little war, and not marred as so often happens by being long drawn out. Lieutenant-Colonel Bennett was awarded the OBE and mentioned in despatches. Others "mentioned" were Subadar Ram Ditta, Naik Hunar Khan, Lance-Naik Sadhu Singh, Lance-Naik Saidullah and Sepoy Bhal Singh.

WAZIRISTAN OPERATIONS, 1937-38.

The remainder of 1935 and the whole of 1936 were spent in JHELUM as already outlined. In March 1936 Lieutenant-Colonel Bennett took leave pending retirement. Except for a short period with "censorship" at the beginning of World War I he had spent the whole of his service actually with the XIX Punjabis and 1st Battalion. He was indeed the embodiment of all the best in the "fanatically-regimental" type. Lieutenant-Colonel Craddock officiated and was later appointed in his stead. But ill-health intervened. Affected originally by anti-rabic treatment just before the Battalion went to Waziristan he was absent from those operations and had to go home on sick leave. Continued unfitness prevented his return, and he retired in April 1939.

"Map 6."

The 1937 operations in which the 1st/14th now took part along with the 3rd (Jhelum) Infantry Brigade were to punish the Tori Khel Wazirs in the KHAISORA VALLEY and to occupy the SHAM PLAIN. There had been comparative peace in Waziristan for some years. Government control had been extended; and early in 1936 the Razmak and Bannu Brigades had uneventfully visited the little-known KHAISORA VALLEY. But during the previous year an implacable enemy had arisen in Mirza Ali Khan, the Faqir of Ipi, whose increasing influence throughout Waziristan now stirred the Tori Khel into revolt. It was decided therefore to send troops into their country again, and at the same time to evict the malevolent Faqir. Columns from RAZMAK and BANNU entered the KHAISORA from opposite ends late in November 1936, but met surprisingly strong opposition and had to withdraw to MIR ALI.

Sketch O.

Air action was at once started; a MT road from MIR ALI to the KHAISORA was begun; and in December the two brigades, now increased by the 2nd Brigade, returned to the area of operations. By mid-January 1937 opposition had been overcome, demolitions carried out, new roads started and Ipi bombed at ARSAL KOT whither he had retreated. Everything seemed over. But in the next three months of 1937 there were outrages and incidents all over Waziristan, and the Faqir felt strong enough to declare a jehad. A more extensive campaign was obviously necessary.

The Battalion left JHELUM on 11th March, the eve of another Reunion at the Training Battalion, and crossed the INDUS next day. Gone now was the process of ferrying; it was merely necessary to change to narrow gauge stock at MARI INDUS before crossing by the railway bridge. After a day's halt at BANNU the 1st/14th marched up the TOCHI VALLEY to MIR ALI along with other troops of the 1st Division.

Major Fitzpatrick was in command, with first Major Sheehan and then Major Dawes as 2nd-in-Command. Captain Dhillon was Adjutant.

The 3rd Brigade's first task was the security of the TOCHI VALLEY east and west of MIR ALI. Accordingly March and most of April were spent in garrisoning KHAJURI POST and piquets in the SHINKI DEFILE, as well as in working mechanized columns in the Khassadar-protected sector as far as ISHA CORNER to the west. Twice for a while the Battalion was based on IDAK CAMP. Night-sniping was frequent; and sometimes day-piqueting met opposition, as on 27th March when one sepoy was wounded.

Sketch O.

By mid-April the 2nd Brigade was back again in Waziristan, and on 23rd April led an advance from MIR ALI to the KHAISORA with the 3rd Brigade in support. The latter still included the 2nd Battalion The Argyll and Sutherland Highlanders; but comparatively new to the 1st/14th were the 3rd Battalion the Jat Regiment and the 1st Battalion of the Dogras. Among the attached units were the 81st Field Battery RA, 2nd Light Battery RA, one armoured car section of the 7th Light Tank Company RTC and the 4th Indian Field Company.

On the first day the Battalion helped to secure the crossing of the TOCHI RIVER south of MIR ALI, and the 2nd Brigade passed through. Lance Naik Azam Khan was wounded in a brush with the enemy which ensued. That evening the 1st/14th reached "TOCHI CAMP (SOUTH)" on the KHATIRA RIVER. During the next six days, while the 2nd Brigade moved on to BICHHE KASHKAI, they were on road protection and camp piquet duty. On 3rd May, after once again opening the road for the advance of the 2nd Brigade, the Battalion withdrew to IDAK with the rest of the Brigade. Two days later they moved up to DAMDIL, and for the next fortnight were engaged on road protection near ASAD KHEL. Aims had been achieved in the KHAISORA, and it was now General Coleridge's intention to strike at Ipi's headquarters from DOSALI. And so there the 3rd Brigade concentrated on 12th May. It was early on this day of King George VI's crowning that the famous night advance by the Bannu Brigade took place. Climbing the steep and trackless IBLANKE SPUR from DOSALI they forestalled the Wazir lashkar in the elevated SHAM PLAIN, established themselves there in "CORONATION CAMP" and facilitated the arrival of the 1st Brigade by the nala route.

The Battalion left the 3rd Brigade at DOSALI on 17th May and marched up to CORONATION CAMP. It was indeed a pleasant change from the heat of the UPPER KHAISORA VALLEY. Next morning they piqueted the first mile and a half of the advance of the Bannu Brigade and Tochi scouts to GHARIOM. C and D Companies had to establish six piquets astride the route, and it was only when putting up the last two on the right that serious opposition was met. When the fire of the machine gun platoon and the 13th Mountain Battery failed to silence the enemy, A Company under Lieutenant Muhammad Zaman was ordered to capture the scrub-covered hills dominating the approach to the piquet sites. As the two leading platoons, Nos. 2 and 4, neared this objective very heavy firing was opened on them, particularly from two knolls on a spur to the left front. Lieutenant Muhammad Zaman had already directed No. 3 platoon to seize these. When nearing the crest through dense scrub where vision was limited to ten yards this platoon came under point-blank fire from three sides and lost one man killed and four wounded. The Company Commander now went to their aid with his remaining platoon and was just in time to prevent them from being overwhelmed from both flanks. In this fighting, none-the-less, No. 1 Platoon had four killed and two wounded. A little later a combined advance by both platoons, using hand grenades, drove these determined hostiles back, captured the knolls and recovered four dead along with their rifles. The piquets were established, and later in the day when all traffic had ceased the Battalion withdrew to CORONATION CAMP. By outstanding bravery on this occasion Naik Bela Singh and Sepoy Makhmad won immediate awards of the Indian Distinguished Service Medal. For his leadership Lieutenant Muhammad Zaman, together with Major Fitzpatrick and Sepoy Amar Singh of A Company, was later mentioned in despatches.

After further road-protection duty in the same area the 1st/14th moved back to "KACH CAMP" on 23rd May. But on 13th June they marched up again to GHARIOM and took over twelve camp piquets, including STIRLING CASTLE. The Battalion was once more in the 3rd Brigade. Captain Ayub Khan was now officiating Adjutant, Captain Dhillon having returned to JHELUM to join the Royal Indian Army Service Corps. From now until December the 1st/14th were at GHARIOM or in one or other of the adjacent camps of "BAHADUR", "BROMHEAD" and "SHAWALI" in the UPPER SHAKTU VALLEY. When not on camp-piquet duty there was daily road protection to be done, or reconnaissances in force, or road-making, or permanent piquet construction, etc. There were several tribes to reckon with at this junction of their boundaries. They were still hostile, and sniping was frequent. Meanwhile the 1st, 2nd and Bannu Brigades had destroyed ARSAL KOT, without however capturing the Faqir of Ipi, and had overrun most of the surrounding country. Roads were made in all directions and Tochi Scouts were installed at GHARIOM. In September the Tori Khel as well as some other tribes accepted settlement terms. But elsewhere, particularly in South Waziristan, there was sufficient outrage and defiance to necessitate continued punishment and action by all brigades. The 2nd Battalion of the Regiment took part in these operations in the 9th and Bannu Brigades.

The 3rd was the last of the extra brigades to withdraw. Before December snow lay on the ground at GHARIOM and cold ousted flies as the greatest enemy. In November 1937 Brevet Lieutenant-Colonel Pigot returned from home leave and assumed command of the Battalion. Other officers present at this time were Majors Fitzpatrick, Dawes and Pouncey, Captains Ayub Khan and Vir Singh (now Adjutant), Lieutenants Ata Muhammad, Nehra (Quartermaster), Muhammad Zaman, Mohan Singh, Kiani, Randhawa, Shahnawaz, Gajindar Singh and Habib. Captain Adams was trying the RIASC, from which corps however he rejoined in January 1938. Captain Misri Chand went to the Depot.

At last on 12th December the 1st/14th left GHARIOM CAMP with the Brigade, and three days later went into a tented camp at MIR ALI. Road protection duty up and down the TOCHI was resumed, and thus passed January and February of 1938. A cross-country team sent off to the Rawalpindi District Tournament had no difficulty after the recent physical training in winning their event.

Apart from occasional sniping there was only one exciting incident in these months. Gagu, the outlaw, and his Kabul Khel gang suddenly besieged the Scouts in SPINWAM POST, and during the night of 17th/18th January the 3rd Brigade hurried out to deal with this. The difficult portion of the route, as the 9th Brigade had experienced three months previously, was the TABAI NARAI. While the 1st Baluch seized the greater part of this defile with but little opposition from an enemy who had boasted that it would be held, the 1st/14th cleared the lower slopes of the high TARAKAI feature to the west and then swung in again to piquet the northern end of the NARAI. They reached SPINWAM in the evening with no more fighting than an engagement with 15 hostiles on TARAKAI. Next day, after a night of some sniping, the Battalion was back again at the TABAI NARAI to pass a supply convoy through. All of A, B and C companies had a few targets. On 21st January there was a brigade drive over the slopes of the DARWESHTA massif north-west of SPINWAM, and again B Company had a brush. Next day the Brigade marched back to MIR ALI, B Company drawing the only fire that was encountered.

Sketch O.

By taking part in these Waziristan operations the Battalion earned another clasp to the Indian General Service Medal.

BANNU, 1938-39.

BANNU had been nominated as the next station as long before as September 1936. And so the 1st/14th marched the 25 miles there on 7th March after relief in MIR ALI by the 1st Battalion the Dogra Regiment. For a while BANNU was very welcome for its comparative comfort, its amenities and the presence of families. But the Lines in The Fort were thoroughly bad, the summer heat intense and the night protection duties a heavier strain than the operations just over. The countryside became progressively more unsettled, and except when under arms the whole garrison were prisoners within the perimeter wire. Heavy duties and this insecurity limited training, athletics and games. Even by May 1938 when the 3rd Battalion of the Regiment passed through the 1st/14th would gladly have accompanied them to RAZANI !

At first there was only one detachment to be provided, namely two platoons at MARI INDUS. But later for varying reasons and periods platoons or companies relieved the Frontier Constabulary posts at KURRAM GARHI, DREGHUNDARI, JANI KHEL, GUMATTI, GAMBILA, PEZU, and regular troops at SAIDGI. Probyn's Horse, and later Skinner's Horse, shared these duties and excursions. But BANNU's second battalion, for short periods represented first by the 2nd Battalion The Rajputana Rifles and later by the 2nd/6th Gurkha Rifles, was generally away in some other role. The effect on nights-in-bed can be imagined !

As the Battalion reached BANNU Major Ingle and the Depot joined from JHELUM. Captain Thorat returned from the Training Battalion and became Adjutant. Major Fitzpatrick, Anderson and Adams all took home leave at various times. New arrivals were 2nd Lieutenants Rajendra Singh, Abdul Jabbar, Stracey and Muhammad Sadiq. This raised the number of Indian Commissioned Officers alone to eleven. Fortunately the officers' mess building was a large one ! Not only were all but the last few VCOs now transferred or mustered out in quick succession as the list earlier in the chapter shows, but the new cadre of Warrant officers began to be built up. In October 1938 Subadar-Major Kehr Singh (Dogra) generously retired so as to allow one VCO more to have the honour of his position; this was Subadar Major Karam Khan, IDSM. Old friends in Captain Fateh Khan, OBI, of BUBAK and Subadar Fateh Khan of DULMIAL paid visits to see for themselves the old "Unis Namber" in its new set-up.

Mehar Dil, outlaw from the adjacent AHMEDZAI SALIENT, was the prime instigator of all the local trouble : but Bannuchis collaborated with him. His lashkar threatened the KOHAT road for months, and the Battalion shared with many other units—including the 2nd/14th from KOHAT—the pleasure of patrolling it. On 23 July 1938 a lashkar actually attacked BANNU CITY and for the next two days the City Disturbance Column had to fight panic. Major Adams was commanding the Battalion in this novel frontier task. After this the pastime of sniping the cantonment became a daytime one. Bomb traps were planted here and there. Raiders even entered the Punjab across the INDUS. The railway to MARI INDUS was damaged and the bridge there threatened. The famous "heat stroke express" on that line had to be escorted, and travelled the more slowly for the shock-absorbing flats which it pushed in front.

From 1st January there was introduced that further change in organization anticipated in the previous chapter. Rifle companies were increased again to four, while each had now only three platoons. The Support "(S)" Company, a development of the machine gun company, was abolished and the various fire, signal and administrative sub-units were organized as platoons of a Headquarters Company. At the same time there was a swing back, as far as possible, to the class company idea of 1925. Thus:—

```
Battalion Headquarters   )
Headquarter Company      )   All  classes.
    (Platoons 1,4,6      )
"A" Company (Platoons 7,8)      .. Yusafzai.
            (Platoon 9)         .. Punjabi Musalman.
"B" Company (Platoons 10,11,12) .. Sikh.
"C" Company (Platoons 13,14,15) .. Punjabi Musalman.
"D" Company (Platoons 16,17,18) .. Dogra.
```

The new class arrangement was both popular and administratively convenient. With these changes came the new parade formation of three ranks and the greatly simplified manoeuvre and arms drills. Parade and field movements at last became as one.

Except for the later issue of armoured carriers for medium machine guns and the substitution of trucks and lorries for pack mule 1st-line transport, the Battalion was now organized and equipped as during the early years of the coming World War. Each platoon had its quota of light machine guns, the basic tactical weapon. The same weapon had been introduced for anti-aircraft defence. Radio telephony was no longer a novelty. The anti-tank rifle had arrived. The 2-inch mortar took its place alongside the modernized Stokes. The Tommy Gun was the latest toy. All this made for administrative as well as training complexity such as would have startled those retired officers whose last view-point was the end of the first World War. Appendix D, which gives headings from the Battalion Standing Orders brought up to date this year, points to elaboration in regimental life. One new title will be noticed at once, viz. "The Battalion Warrant Officer". This was the Subadar-Major's successor. Warrant Officer Baboo Ram was already earmarked to succeed Subadar Major Karam Khan, IDSM, which he did at the end of January 1940. Another innovation which may catch the eye is "The Warrant Officers' Mess".

About "Dress" it may be mentioned that by now the XIX Punjabis khaki fringe on the officers' helmet had been discarded for a regimental flash, i.e. a dark green square of cloth bearing the crest in gold embroidery. From the earliest days of history the sepoy's kurta, blouse, jacket or shirt had been devoid of any form of collar. But now that he was conscious of the better appearance of a garment which does not stop short at the neck band, there was introduced as a battalion innovation a low roll collar for the light grey "mazri" shirt which served for most purposes during the hot weather. This collar idea came in officially with the bush shirt and battle dress blouse which were adopted during World War II.

To paint the picture for those who would otherwise pass lightly over "safe custody of arms—of ammunition" in Appendix D it may be pointed out that there was now much more to it than just rows of rifles in company kotes, a little pouch ammunition with them and a number of boxes in the Magazine. Bren guns, mortars and pistols with connected equipment and ammunition filled a considerable part of each company armoury, and presented special problems of safe custody and individual responsibility. The Headquarter Company armouries were veritable arsenals. The Magazine had to cater for explosives, detonants, combustibles and propellants as well as for small-arm ammunition of some seven different types, calibres or packings.

Such then was life on the epoch-making date of 3rd September 1939 during the second hot weather in BANNU. Operations against the Ahmedzai Wazirs were being mounted. The Battalion was fit and experienced after a recent campaign, though weary of very heavy protective duties. Unit organization and administrative efficiency were perhaps at a peak. A new band of keen young officers had assumed responsibility, found their feet and acquired the regimental spirit. "Indianization" up to the limit set twenty-seven years before was virtually complete. Now again came War, the tester, the scatterer, the dictator of destiny.

CHAPTER XVIII.

WORLD WAR II, 1939-45.

BANNU—LAHORE—SECUNDERABAD—MALAYA.

(Maps 1 and 11. Sketches P, R and S)

BANNU, 1939-40.

Although the war which began on 3rd September 1939 changed the form and fortunes of the Battalion far more than did the upheaval of 1914-19, its effect was more gradual and the first shock less. For a year England had been arming; an overreaching act of aggression by Germany was indeed widely expected; and when the rupture came German strategy produced only " phoney war " in Western Europe for the first six months. Thus, lacking the fighting and the crisis of 1914, and without any embarassing belligerency as there had then been with Turkey, India took the coming of war without great excitement. Much as happened in 1914, protective forces were sent to EGYPT and elsewhere; but now there was no immediate drain of manpower; this time there was no Indian Army in Europe. With a proper system of reserves and reinforcement in existence there was now little chance for man or officer of being fortuitously drafted overseas. For these reasons the start of the war in India was even more " phoney " than in the West, and there was no " DUNKIRK " to bring suddenly-transforming reality. Cantonment and frontier life continued virtually unchanged, and not for nine months was it decided to expand the Regiment.

All absent ranks were recalled—this included the Commandant, Major Fitzpatrick and Major Ingle from short leave in ENGLAND—and for a while all leave was stopped. Blue patrol indeed replaced mess kit, and the change of station to MULTAN was cancelled! But otherwise life in Bannu went on just the same. The perimeter was sniped frequently and ambushes were commonplace. Insecurity developed to such a pitch that womenfolk had to be escorted when playing golf on the course within the perimeter wire, and those living near the edge of the cantonment were moved to more central residences. The Battalion took part in one short round-up drive into SORANI country, but otherwise were tied to local defence and escort duty. They took no active part in the AHMEDZAI SALIENT operations which now began near BANNU, but being within the area qualified for the medal, i.e. the 1939-45 Star. In December the 1st Battalion Frontier Force Regiment and 1st/9th Gurkha Rifles arrived to complete the Bannu Brigade and afford some relief in the burden of duties. An athletic meeting could then be held, and this was followed by ten days battalion training in camp at DREGHUNDARI. Many young officers went on numerons courses of instruction.

In January 1940 Lieutenant-Colonel Pigot ended his regimental service on reappointment to the staff. He claimed to be unique among commandants in that whether by good luck or ill-management he had never held a Summary Court Martial! Subadar-Major Karam Khan, IDSM, was mustered out on pension only a few weeks later. He was the last of the VCOs, and his passing marked the completion of that substitution by ICOs which had been going on in the 1st/14th over the course of four years. His going was regretted the more when six months later this policy was reversed. There is in the mess albums an interesting photograph of 1939 which shows Subadar-Major Karam Khan and Subadar Muhammad Akbar carrying the Colours. They were then the only VCOs that remained, and therefore enjoyed the honour which usually goes to the two senior Jemadars.

LAHORE, 1940.

Honoured by a warm send-off from the 1st Battalion Frontier Force Regiment and a congratulatory telegram from the District Commander, the Battalion left BANNU on 17 April. Lahore, the station of the relieving battalion, the 2nd/1st Punjab, was reached two days later, the anniversary of "Ahmed Khel". Lieutenant-Colonel Fitzpatrick became Commandant.

Only five months were spent here while the war allotment was being decided. It was immediately clear from the receipt of instructional MT vehicles that the 1st/14th were to have an overseas role. The training of drivers and preparations for going onto an all-vehicle establishment became the major tasks. The activity in instruction under Captain Mohan Singh, the MT Officer, was tremendous. There was less profitable training in Passive Air Defence, and much time was spent in digging slit trenches, and blacking out against the air arm of our future ally Russia! There was also occasional "KHAKSAR" trouble in the city, and a letter from the Deputy Commissioner records his appreciation of the assistance so cheerfully and patiently given to him.

Now came orders for the formation of the 6th and 7th Battalions of the Regiment, and soon drafts were sent to both. Simultaneously No. 1 (1st Battalion) Training Company in the 10th Battalion was expanded to share the load of the extra war-time battalions. The first two were followed by the 8th, 9th, 14th and 15th Battalions, all of which served with distinction in various roles throughout the war.

Restriction of Indianization to the selected battalions had built up so strong a cadre of Indian officers in the 1st/14th that it now became the obvious subject of " milking " wherewith to officer newly-raised units. To the new battalions of the Regiment, as to others and to special appointments, there went in the course of a few months all British officers save two, every KCIO and numerous ICOs! Some of these changes will be mentioned later. Unexpected responsibility was thus rapidly thrust upon the remaining youngsters. A few emergency-commissioned officers were posted, but naturally they lacked any experience. With the restoration of the position of VCO, Subadars and Jemadars were appointed from the Warrant officers; and others came back from wherever recently transferred. All this meant an inevitable weakening of the battalion at a time when, as it turned out, operational service against the Japanese lay only 12 months ahead. The great turn-over of officers is strikingly shown by comparing the list of those who went to Malaya with that given in the preceding chapter.

The first VCOs to rejoin their old friends were Jemadars Santa Singh and Muhammad Hayat from the 3rd Battalion, Jemadar Ghulam Hussain from the 2nd Battalion. Warrant Officer Baboo Ram became Subadar Major.

SECUNDERABAD, 1940-41.

On 21st September sad news was received that Major-General Hay, Colonel of the Battalion, had been killed with his wife during an air raid on LONDON. On the same day the 1st/14th moved to SECUNDERABAD into the newly-formed 15th Indian Infantry Brigade commanded by Brigadier Garrett. Had the original destination of CAMPBELLPORE been adhered to the fortunes of war in another formation and in another theatre would undoubtedly have been different!

Here the posting away of experienced officers became serious. Major Sant Singh had already gone as 2nd-in-Command to the 11th Battalion the Dogra Regiment, Lieutenant Rajendra Singh as Adjutant to the 11th/14th (Territorials) at JHANSI, and Lieutenant Abdul Jabbar to the 12th (Territorial) Battalion, which was newly raised. Captain Vir Singh was in staff employ. Captain Zaman Khan was posted as Instructor to the Signal School. Lieutenant Gajinder Singh also went to the 11th Battalion. Lieutenant Kamta Prasad sailed for the 2nd Battalion in HONG KONG. In December Major Ingle was posted to the 7th Battalion at MARDAN, and later became Commandant of the 6th. Major Anderson succeeded him as 2nd-in-Command of the 1st Battalion. Major Thorat on promotion to that acting rank gave over the adjutantcy to Captain Kiani. Lieutenant Stracey replaced Captain Nehra as Quartermaster. Captain Ata Muhammad Khan was relieved by Lieutenant Shahnawaz Khan in command of No. 1 (Training) Company, and himself became Adjutant at FEROZEPORE. In January 1941 Major Thorat and Captain Misri Chand were lost to the Battalion by going to the Staff College, QUETTA. There was now a shortage of seven, and only the two senior officers had more than six years' service; which in the innocence of this early stage of the war seemed a dreadful situation!

Duties in SECUNDERABAD were extremely light, and training conditions excellent. Companies were out in camp at KOMPALLI two at a time. Service vehicles including motor cycles were received. There was much field firing and mechanized movement training. It was a very happy brigade.

The long-expected orders to mobilize which came in January were accompanied by unusual complications, viz., the issue of a new War Establishment which incidentally increased VCOs and NCOs, and a modification in class composition. Recent milking of NCOs and men to form the new Battalions necessitated a specially large draft from the Regimental Centre at FEROZEPORE. Headquarter Company now comprised No. 1 Platoon (Signallers), No. 2 (Anti-aircraft) Platoon, No. 3 (Mortar) Platoon, No. 4 (Carrier) Platoon, No. 5 (Pioneer) Platoon and No. 6 (Administrative) Platoon. Weapons and tradesman for these were not available, and Nos. 2, 3, 4 and 5 now had to be created from nothing. Lacking service carriers for LMGs, the Vickers machine guns were to be retained temporarily. "A" Company became all Yusafzai for the loss of the one Punjabi Musalman platoon. Ten per cent. reinforcements with an extra fifteen per cent. for "time lag" were collected. There were some hectically busy weeks. The exact reason for the withdrawal of greatcoats and the substitution of waterproof capes was not realized at the time. The 1937 pattern web equipment was not received until the night before entertainment. However, actual departure went smoothly on the 5th of March. There was no case of desertion, or of absence without leave. The GOC-in-C Southern Command, General Brind, was at BOLARUM station to see the Battalion off, also Major-General Barstow to whose 9th Indian Division the 15th Brigade had hitherto belonged.

On this date the cadre of officers was as follows:—

Commandant	Lieutenant-Colonel Fitzpatrick.
2nd-in-Command	Major Anderson.
Adjutant	Captain Kiani.
Quartermaster	Lieutenant Stracey.
Headquarter Company	Captain Mohan Singh.
No. 1 (Signal) Platoon	Lieutenant G.S. Dhillon.
No. 4 (Carrier) Platoon	Lieutenant H.G.V. Greer (Emergency commissioned officer now posted).
MT Officer	Lieutenant I. Hassan.
"A" Company (Yusafzai)	Captain Randhawa.
"B" Company (Sikh)	Lieutenant C.M. McCarthy. (The first ECO to be posted)
"C" Company (Punjabi (Musalman)	Lieutenant W.R. Longwill } ECOs posted from Regtl. Centre.
"D" Company (Dogra)	Lieutenant E.F. Morrey
1st Reinforcements	Lieutenant C.E. Corfield, Lieutenant Dickie, Lieutenant Newton } ECOs posted from schools.
Medical officer	Captain Abrahams, IMS.
With Brigade Headquarters	Lieutenant Habibur Rehman, Brigade Intelligence Officer. Lieutenant A.I.S. Dara, Motor Contact Officer.

Embarkation took place at BOMBAY on 7th March. The 1st/14th had their ship to themselves, and it was comfortable. She sailed in convoy on the 8th, and next day sealed orders were opened. MALAYA! Nobody had dreamed of that, notwithstanding the raincoats! There was intense disappointment at missing an active war role. So much training for the Western Desert appeared to have been wasted. Jungle training pamphlets were unsealed and studied. The 2nd Battalion in HONGKONG, and the 5th at PENANG, were suddenly remembered with new sympathy.

MALAYA, 1941.

The Battalion's arrival in MALAYA with the 15th Indian

"Map 11."

infantry brigade marked another step in the meagre build-up of the security forces in that country. Up to September 1940 the only mobile troops outside SINGAPORE were the 2nd Battalion The Dogra Regiment in TAIPING, and on PENANG ISLAND one British battalion along with the 5th/14th (Lieutenant-Colonel Stokes). At SINGAPORE there were the 12th Indian infantry brigade (Brigadier Paris) and, under the Fortress Commander, the 1st and 2nd Malayan Brigades of British, Indian and Malay infantry.

Early in October 1941 Major-General D.M. Murray-Lyon with part of his 11th Indian divisional staff, including Colonel Pigot, were flown out from INDIA and there was set up under him a command called "Northern Area" with headquarters at KUALA LUMPUR. He was responsible to the GOC Malaya Command (Lieutenant-General Bond) for the whole of the Malayan peninsula except the State of JOHORE.

Since war commitments elsewhere precluded the presence of either a fleet or land forces capable of defeating Japanese aggression at a distance, it had been decided that the long-range defence of Malaya and particularly of SINGAPORE should be undertaken principally by the Royal Air Force. First-line aircraft were to be increased to over 400. RAF stations already existed at KOTA BHARU in Kelantan State and at ALOR STAR in Kedah; now more aerodromes and strips were begun. Since all these required ground protection the Army was compelled to hold the whole of the peninsula so that SINGAPORE should be secure. Actually the RAF build-up was too slow; and when war came there were only three fighter squadrons and a total of 150 aircraft, mostly obsolete Buffaloes and Wirraways.

Major-General Murray-Lyon's tasks were:—

—to prevent an enemy landing on the Kelantan and Pahang coasts in the east so as to safeguard the aerodromes at KOTA BHARU and KUANTAN.

—in Kedah and Perlis to stop any invasion from Thailand (Siam), thus protecting the forward aerodrome at ALOR STAR and others behind it.

There followed therefore both before and after the arrival of the 11th Division a period of intensive reconnaissance, planning and administrative arrrangements with the RAF, the FMS Volunteer Forces, the Federal and State Civil Services and with the principal tin miners and rubber planters. New roads and telegraph lines were built; demolitions, beach defences and denial schemes were prepared; extensive hutted camps were constructed; hospitals were built; maintenance, installations and transport were arranged.

The first troops to arrive at the end of October were Divisional Headquarters, a number of Sappers & Miners companies, administrative units, and the 8th Indian Infantry Brigade (Brigadier Key) who at once moved to the east coast at KOTA BHARU and KUANTAN. There was also the 6th Indian Infantry Brigade who after temporary locations at IPOH and SUNGEI PATANI went into hutted camps at or near TANJONG PAU in North Kedah. In February 1941 the first brigade of the 8th Australian infantry division landed in Malaya and went to KUALA LUMPUR and PORT DICKSON. In March, as has been said, there came from India the 15th Indian Infantry brigade (Brigadier Garrett) as well as Divisional Signals from England.

Sketch P.

PERAK.

On arrival at GEORGETOWN (PENANG) on 18th March the Battalion ferried over to the mainland at PRAI and travelled in two trains to the tin-mining town of IPOH in Perak State. The vehicles followed along the 109 miles of excellent road. Accommodation was at the luxurious IPOH racecourse, partly in the grandstand and partly in the extensive stables which had been converted into billets. Officers lived at the Majestic Hotel.

Sketch S.

Training was begun immediately. Large numbers of reinforcements had been received on the eve of leaving India who had now to be instructed in the LMG and anti-tank rifle. Indeed some fired their rifles for the first time here on the Volunteers' rifle range. Other men were sent forward to the 6th Brigade for practical training on carriers and mortars, neither of which had yet been received. A start was made on jungle warfare, and the Battalion was acclimatized to prolonged rain and the moist atmosphere.

KEDAH.

During the next two months the Malaya Command began to approximate to the layout existing when war broke out with Japan. The uninspiring designation "Northern Area" was abolished, and "11 Ind div" was born. Its responsibility was restricted to Perlis, Kedah and Province Wellesley. The 22nd Indian infantry brigade came out to join the 8th on the east coast, and with it constituted the 9th Indian division (Major-General Barstow). These two divisions formed the 3rd Indian Corps under Lieutenant-General L.M. Heath. His headquarters was established at KUALA LUMPUR. Lieutenant-General Percival took over Malaya Command under the direction of Air-Marshal Brooke-Popham who was now in supreme control of both Army and Air Force. Both visited the Battalion at IPOH. In May headquarters of the 11th Division with most of the divisional troops and the 15th Brigade moved forward to SUNGEI PATANI, into the largest of the many rubber plantation hutted camps. The Dogras went to SINGAPORE. The 3rd/16th Punjab, under divisional control, were located at KROH on the extreme east flank so as to block the road from the Thailand port of PATANI. They were replaced in the 15th Brigade by the 1st Leicesters from PENANG. The Bahawalpur Infantry were divisional troops for aerodrome protection, and an "Independent Company" (under Major Fearon of the 5th/14th) was formed for "commando" activities.

Sketch P.

At SUNGEI PATANI service carriers, mortars and Tommy guns were received. The mortars and TSMGs were tested, but ammunition of all natures and facilities for firing were scarce. A particular regret was that the men could not adequately familiarize themselves before the war began with the Bren LMG which was here issued instead of the Vikers Berthier. Ammunition for the anti-tank rifle was not available until the day before hostilities started. The dense rubber plantation country of SUNGEI PATANI was excellent for jungle and coastal training, and a good deal of it was carried out from section work up to divisional deployment exercises. At the same time the Battalion were rehearsing their first war role, which will shortly be described.

From SUNGEI PATANI pleasant contact was established with the 5th/14th in PENANG, where they offered hospitality to men and officers whenever opportunity occurred to visit that enchanting island. Major Adams was with the 5th/14th until given command of a battalion in India. There was occasional reunion with Lieutenant-General "Piggy" Heath, and delight at being under his command.

"Map 11."

The peninsula of Malaya is largely occupied by a central mass of hills covered with almost impenetrable forest and almost completely devoid of communications. Flanking this on either side are coastal plains. That on the west is largely filled with rubber plantations and tin-mining fields. Through it runs the railway from SINGAPORE to BANGKOK in Thailand. Here the roads are excellent if narrow. The trunk road with many local feeders extends 585 miles from the JOHORE STRAIT to the Thai frontier, and then 52 miles further to the Siamese Gulf port of SINGORA. There are no comparable communications along the east coast. That coast indeed is served only by the laterals connecting it with the west, namely, the railway from KOTA BHARU, the road from MERSING (where the 12th Brigade was earmarked to operate), the road from KUANTAN and the aforementioned road from PATANI through KROH to SUNGEI

PATANI in Kedah.

Kedah State, which was to become a battleground, merits further description. The ALOR STAR airfield which had to be defended lies eight miles north of the town and alongside the trunk road. Four miles further north is JITRA village, and just short of it the estate of TANJONG PAU. Eighteen miles further is the frontier at BUKIT KAYU HITAM. A few miles west of this point the railway from BANGKOK crosses into Perlis at PADANG BESAR, and then runs south past BUKIT KETRI to ALOR STAR town. This railway, combined with the feeder road which starts at BUKIT KETRI and joins the trunk at JITRA, offered a western line of advance from Thailand. The main one was the aforementioned trunk road from SINGORA. Twelve miles north of JITRA the two roads are connected by the 11-mile lateral from KODIANG to CHANGLUN. A possible eastern approach was 40 miles by jungle track from the frontier at KUAN MET to KUALA NERANG. Thence it would be 40 miles to ALOR STAR by motor road.

Sketch P.

In Kedah north of ALOR STAR the trunk road is thickly bordered with rubber plantations. Approximately 2½ miles east of these lies a mass of jungle-covered hills. The plain between road and hills is covered with padi, jungle and plantation. To the west, towards the sea, the country is more open with extensive areas of padi and swamp. For nineteen miles south of ALOR STAR there is open padi country on a front of eighteen miles. The third belt starts at the 4000' KEDAH PEAK (GUNONG JERAI) and extends over the MUDA RIVER into Province Wellesley. This is a veritable forest of rubber plantations with a network of motorable estate roads.

Just north of GURUN at the junction of the last two belts lay the only suitable position for protracted defence. But that needed two divisions, and was equally dependent on not being turned by a Japanese advance through KROH. The ruling factor unfortunately was the defence of the ALOR STAR airfield, and this forced the Division to fight on the unfavourable ground first mentioned. The plan at first was to hold the enemy north of JITRA with the 6th Brigade, and to keep the 15th Brigade in reserve at GURUN ready either to occupy a position there, or to reinforce the other brigade, or to aid the detachment at KROH. The initial role of the Battalion in this plan was the defence of this nineteen miles of open country between ALOR STAR and KEDAH PEAK against landings from the sea and air. From their plantation hutments at SUNGEI PATANI the 1st/14th were prepared to move forward to BUKIT BESAR, which was a wooded hill in the centre of the great padi area and which formed a concealed base for their operations.

The JITRA position.

But in August this role was changed. As soon as the availability of another brigade from India (the 28th) had been assured, it was decided to employ both of the existing brigades to hold the JITRA defensive position. The front of this extended from BUKIT PENIA, a 500-foot jungle-clad foothill, across the trunk road at the 13½ milestone just north of JITRA, across the BUKIT KETRI road at milestone 13 3/4 and thence to the railway where it bridged the KUROK CANAL. This meant nearly 7 miles to be held by two brigades, with one of the battalions patrolling a further seven miles of canal to the sea. The position was chosen as having the fewest disadvantages as regards natural obstacles, observation, gun positions and communications. It was nevertheless weak in all these respects, and lacked proper depth. Nobody liked it in fact. But there was really no alternative if the enemy was to be stopped north of the aerodrome. Had the alternative been adopted of merely delaying the enemy and discounting the ALOR STAR airfield, the battle of JITRA in December might well have been a successful action lasting days longer than it did, and finishing with the Division still in fair fighting trim.

To help dig this position the Battalion now moved up to be attached to the 6th Brigade who were camped at TANJONG PAU. Then followed three laborious months in very rainy weather. At first the work lay in preparing the reserve defences of the left (15th) brigade sector. The ground there was semi-open and waterlogged. Breastworks predominated and material had to be carried long distances. Then the fighting positions of the two brigades were reversed, and the Battalion moved east of the main road to construct its own reserve defences in the wooded area of the right sector. The rest of the 15th Brigade had by now moved up to TANJONG PAU. There were training days in each week, and other plans too to think of as will now be mentioned; but in the main the labour went on unbrokenly in enervating weather and in the depressing dim light of rubber plantations. Although the 1st/14th were fated never to fight as a unit in the JITRA position they knew it only too well.

Offensive plans.

It must now be mentioned that there was a strategical alternative to this defensive outlook. On Air Marshal Brooke-Popham's arrival a forward policy was considered and this developed into a succession of plans which were to be put into operation if there were favourable circumstances at the outbreak of hostilities.

The general idea was to forestall the Japanese at SINGORA in Thailand, and defeat their landings there. As regards the other port of PATANI, the 8th Brigade could not seize it without exposing KOTA BHARU, and both distance and a shortage of troops precluded its occupation from KROH. Any enemy advance from PATANI was therefore to be stopped by demolitions and a defensive block on the precipitous portion of the road called THE LEDGE, 29 miles over the frontier from KROH.

The first edition of this plan was contemplated as early as the end of August. Relations with Japan were fast deteriorating; and so when the 1st/14th moved forward to TANJONG PAO as mentioned above their war role was to advance in the rear of the 6th Brigade and secure the Thailand L of C at HAADYAI. This plan was later merged in another, which was that current when hostilities broke out, but the connection of the Battalion remained. Their role lay in Thailand, in forward movement. So much the greater was the disappointment over the course which events actually took.

Calm before storm.

Midway through November the Battalion was refreshed by a return to the comparative comfort and dryness of the SUNGEI PATANI camp. The eighteen days there were mainly devoted to collective training and to refitting. There was a three-day continuous battalion exercise: river crossing training was carried out with newly-received equipment: the few new units were met, e.g. the 3rd Indian Cavalry (mechanized). Corps manoeuvres were impending when the international situation worsened and the 1st/14th hurried back to TANJONG PAO. There were now huts to live in there; but it was not to be for long, indeed for just a few days.

CHAPTER XIX.

WORLD WAR II, 1939-45.

MALAYA, 1941.

(Map 11, Sketches P, Q, R)

The Japanese Invasion.

The forward policy plan already outlined was only feasible if the 6th Brigade could reach SINGORA before the Japanese. Thus it was dependent on early and certain information of enemy designs. It was hoped that this would be obtainable, and so the plan was given priority—with the saddest consequences. From the first day of December the troops were keyed to a high state of tension, and were specially disposed for a rapid advance. Badly-needed work on the JITRA position was necessarily reduced.

Just after noon on 6th December the 11th Division was placed at thirty minutes' notice to advance. Air reconnaissance had revealed a large Japanese convoy off the southern tip of French Indo-China. It might be bound for BANGKOK, or it might be heading to reach the coast of Malaya about midnight on the 7th/8th.

"Map 11."

Sketch P.

The 6th Brigade group, to whom the Battalion had handed over most of their MT, were ready for a mechanized dash to SINGORA, mostly by road. The 1st/14th were to move by train to HAADYAI JUNCTION, and by holding a position astride the railway a little further north were to prevent Japanese or Thai counter-action along the line from BANGKOK. The Leicesters were to accompany. The third battalion of the 15th Brigade, the 2nd Jats, had one company at BUKIT KAYU HITAM blocking the main road at the frontier, and another as a stop at ARAU on the western approach from BUKIT KETRI.

On the 7th it was raining hard and aircraft failed to locate the enemy convoy until late in the afternoon. It was then heading towards Malaya! To those so informed it seemed certain that we must be forestalled at SINGORA, as indeed was the case. For early on the 8th December the Japanese were fighting on the beaches at KOTA BHARU. On the same morning they landed unopposed at SINGORA and PATANI. Yet not until 1330 hours on the 8th was the current plan cancelled and the JITRA scheme put into operation. This delay gave the enemy a start after their landing, and in particular won for them the race to THE LEDGE. Further, the switch-over from a quasi-offensive plan to another of static defence had a psychologically lowering effect. The change also led to dislocation and further delay. The extra movement in bad weather caused serious fatigue.

8th December '41.

Early on this morning the Battalion were at ANAK BUKIT STATION waiting to entrain for Thailand. At 0700 hours Japanese air-bombing started, first against KODIANG, then against the aerodromes at ALOR STAR and SUNGEI PATANI. The Royal Air Force were badly hit, and, so small were their resources, never recovered. Frequent bombing raids, almost unopposed, became the order of every day. *Sketch P.*

The officers now present with the Battalion were those who had arrived with it in Malaya (see Chapter XVIII) except that Captain Randhawa had been drafted back to India and Captain Muhammad Akram (one-time Subadar in "D" Company) had arrived.

The change of plan sent the 1st/14th marching back to TANJONG PAU past the wreck of the ALOR STAR airfield. This was from 1630 hours onwards. The Battalion's first task was now to delay the advance of the enemy from the frontier at BUKIT KAYU HITAM and then on the outpost position at ASUN, 2½ miles north of the main defences. Their further role was to act as brigade reserve in the JITRA position where the SUNGEI BATA crosses the trunk road. Looking back now it is clear that it would have been wiser for the 1st/14th under the offensive plan to have had the role actually allotted to the 2nd Jats. Thus when the counter-order came the Battalion would have been no further south than TANJONG PAU and with a company already at the frontier. Further, they could conveniently have sent the flying column into Thailand which was in fact found from the 1st/8th Punjab of the 6th Brigade. Consisting of two companies and a carrier platoon with anti-tank guns and some Sappers, this detachment went nine miles into Thailand to BAN SADAO and there drew first blood from the Japanese. They provided information that the enemy's advance was being led by tanks ! *Sketch R.*

As it was, C and D companies (Lieutenant Longwill and Captain Stracey) embossed at TANJONG PAU and raced up to the frontier. Along with them went the carrier platoon (Lieutenant *Sketch P.*

Greer), the 4th Mountain Battery and a detachment of the 23rd field company of engineers. The whole were under Major Anderson. This wing of the Battalion reached BUKIT KAYU HITAM at 2200 hours and relieved the Jats. The rest of the Battalion marched under Lieutenant-Colonel Fitzpatrick and arrived at ASUN about midnight. Except that the causeway over the marsh had been prepared for demolition no work had yet been done on any defences there. At KAMPONG INAM on the western approach road there was a similar outpost position where a detachment of the 6th Brigade was due to make a stand. After the flying column of the Jats had disengaged from their action in Thailand and recrossed the frontier at 0130 hours on 9th December the 1st/14th were the foremost troops in North Malaya. They were destined to parry the first blows, and to bear the brunt of the earliest armoured thrust.

Sketch R.   Meanwhile the rest of the Division were manning the JITRA defences. In the 15th Brigade the Jats struggled through rain and dark into their right flank sector. On their left were the Leicesters from 300 yards east of the trunk road to the BUKIT KETRI road, just beyond which they touched the 2nd East Surreys of the 6th Brigade. A field regiment of artillery and many other units hurried forward from SUNGEI PATANI. Advanced Divisional Headquarters was established at ALOR MERAH, the northern suburb of ALOR STAR. On this day the 28th Brigade began moving up from IPOH and TAIPING.

Sketch P.   On the KROH front the plan of seizing "THE LEDGE" was much the same under either plan. But surprise effect was not obtained; for on advancing at 1500 hours on the 8th the 3rd/16th Punjab at once met determined opposition from Thai troops. By dark they had only gained four miles and it took all next day to reach BETONG, a mile further. On the 10th the Japanese were found in possession of THE LEDGE; and they had tanks. There was nothing for it but to withdraw to the KROH position, where the 5th/14th from PENANG and a mountain battery had by then arrived.

Contact—9th and 10th December.

Sketch P.   After their check at BAN SADAO the enemy were more cautious in crossing the frontier. Contact was first made by the Battalion about midnight on 9th/10th December near the now demolished causeway at mile 26½. The "C" Company platoon covering the obstacle denied its passage for two hours until half encircled. Major Anderson's command then began a skilful fighting withdrawal over 6 miles of enclosed country. The enemy repeatedly made outflanking movements along the many tracks which lead to the lateral road through CHANGLUN. There was continuous enemy air reconnaissance without any sign of our own aircraft. It was pouring with rain.

The first delaying position was at milestone 28½ where "C" Company covered the second demolition, already blown. The enemy massed against it at 0500 hours on 10th December. After half an hour's fire-fight "C" Company withdrew through "D" Company's position to another at milestone 25. There had so far been seven or eight casualties, and one carrier had had to be abandoned after engine failure.

Shortly after 0600 hours "D" Company withdrew from its position at the 27th mile and leapfrogged "C". But an hour later, following a visit from Lieutenant-Colonel Fitzpatrick, "D" Company deliberately advanced again to its previous position. The enemy had not followed up; the obstacle at milestone 27 was the last before the CHANGLUN position, and the Japanese were now known to have landed tanks. Patrols reported the enemy to be feverishly repairing every demolition. To prevent the three prepared at CHANGLUN from being seized by an armoured drive Lieutenant-Colonel Fitzpatrick now had the pioneer platoon erect a road-block at the Immigration Road Barrier just north of the crossroads there. The Japanese made contact again at midday, and shortly after 1300 hours "D" Company were ordered back to the CHANGLUN line. At 1545 hours "C" Company in their turn withdrew to the same position behind the SUNGEI LAKA. The lateral road through CHANGLUN was already being patrolled by one platoon of "A" company and one carrier section of the Leicesters, both under command of Captain Muhammad Akram. There had been a few casualties more in "D" company, and another carrier had been lost.

Sketch Q.

This loss happened during "D" company's reoccupation of the 27th milestone position. A section of carriers went ¼ a mile further to regain contact. The leading carrier came under gunfire and swerved off the road into the rubber. The second had its engine demolished and the crew badly wounded. The third kept under cover till level with the derelict vehicle; then its crew dashed out under enemy fire, but supported from the leading carrier, and rescued the wounded men. It was a gallant little affair.

There now occurred a change of plan which was to have far-reaching consequences for the 1st/14th. In order to gain a few hours more for the completion of the JITRA position, at which task all ranks were now striving in the rain, the divisional commander decided that the enemy must be kept north of the ASUN outpost position until 12th December, that is for another 36 hours. This meant that the rest of the Battalion must join the forward wing and abandon work on the ASUN defences. Brigadier Garrett brought these orders to Battalion Headquarters there at 1715 hours. The 2nd/1st Gurkha Rifles less one company were to take over the outpost position at once. Leaving Captain Mohan Singh and a small party to hand over to the Gurkhas on their arrival Lieutenant-Colonel Fitzpatrick at once marched his half battalion forward. By now the Royal Air Force had withdrawn from ALOR STAR aerodrome and thereby the main justification for fighting on unfavourable ground had disappeared. But denial of this airfield to the Japanese still necessitated adherence to the JITRA plan.

The stand at CHANGLUN : 10th and 11th December.

Sketch Q.

The dispositions now taken up at CHANGLUN by the complete Battalion were as shown in Sketch Q. The Divisional Commander had actually required the enemy to be checked at mile 25, which was 1½ miles further forward and already vacated by Major Anderson's detachment. Lieutenant-Colonel Fitzpatrick however knew that no obstacle could be devised there to stop tanks, and he felt that disengagement would be difficult. He considered it sounder to utilize the SUNGEI LAKA obstacle from the beginning, and he reported that he was acting accordingly. The forward companies were still "C" and "D", both behind the stream and respectively east and west of the trunk road. The road was "C" Company's responsibility. The road bridge, which was not to be destroyed unnecessarily, was commanded by two Breda anti-tank guns of the 4th Mountain Battery. It was also obstructed with concrete blocks and wire. The two flank bridges carrying the right by-pass track and the KODIANG road had been blown. The 3.7s of the mountain battery supported the forward companies. The reserve companies behind "C" and "D" respectively were "B" on the right with the Leicesters carriers in their area, and "A" on the left extending west to the KODIANG road. Battalion Headquarters and carrier platoon were where the two by-pass tracks joined the main road. This night of the 10th/11th was a busy and tiring one of marching, patrolling, digging and sniping.

Late in the night an ambush party which had been established forward at the Immigration Post road block was driven in by the enemy with the loss of two men, and patrols reported MT accumulating in the vicinity. Before dawn on the 11th a Japanese party were driven off as they tried to force the road bridge, and at day-break our guns shelled enemy machine-guns which were firing from a small clump of trees to the south-east near KAMPONG BELUKAR. At first-light a fighting patrol of two platoons of "A" Company were sent out west of the trunk road to ascertain more about enemy concentrations near milestone 25. This party under Captain Muhammad Akram were cut off by the enemy attacks and unable to rejoin before the Battalion withdrew.

At about 0900 hours an attack on "C" Company was decisively stopped, and the enemy withdrew. But shelling of the whole position, and particularly of the Battalion Headquarters area, continued to increase. A Japanese in Malay dress was caught in "C" Company area signalling to aircraft with coloured strips. Shortly after 1130 hours enemy shelling further intensified, especially near the bridge. Telephone lines to all companies were cut. Brigadier Garrett was wounded while visiting Battalion Headquarters. With his approval the bridge was then blown, but only one span was effectively destroyed. About noon the machine gun fire from KAMPONG BELUKAR increased, and what appeared to be a battalion attack was launched against "C" Company. In general this was held, but one forward platoon was overrun and there was hand-to-hand fighting. "B" Company now counter-attacked with great eclat and restored the situation. Even though elsewhere the enemy managed to capture the bridge and the Breda guns there, this success by "B" Company caused a lull in the fighting, and the men were in great spirits.

It will be noticed that hereafter in this account no figures of casualties are given. Unfortunately they were only too numerous; but events moved too fast, and with too many changes in officers, for them to be memorized even approximately. All official records were later destroyed rather than be left to the Japanese.

The disaster at ASUN: 11th December.

Sketch P.

At 1500 hours the Divisional Commander arrived with Brigadier Garrett and OC 2nd/1st Gurkhas, and was informed of the situation. Both Lieutenant-Colonel Fitzpatrick and the Brigade Commander favoured withdrawing into the ASUN outpost position by dusk so as to have the protection of a tank obstacle. But Major-General Murray-Lyon, again with the object of imposing the maximum delay while the JITRA position was being made ready, required the 1st/14th to stand for the night in advance of the Gurkhas. Brigadier Garrett selected the only possible area, which was south of a belt of padi-land at the 12th milestone. Sappers were ordered to prepare the causeway there for demolition, but this task was not completed in time. Lieutenant-Colonel Fitzpatrick ordered the withdrawal to continue and then went back with Major Anderson to reconnoitre the new position and settle the plan for the 2nd-in-Command to communicate to company commanders when they arrived.

By 1630 hours these orders had been issued, forward company

commanders were beginning their own reconnaissances, platoon commanders were assembling for their instructions and the commanding officer had gone further back with his battery commander to fix Headquarters and gun areas. Battalion MT was struggling to get out of its sodden harbour at mile $17\frac{1}{2}$ and go back to about $15\frac{1}{2}$. One section of guns was at milestone 17; the other two were still right back at mile $14\frac{1}{2}$ in accordance with the earlier orders for supporting the ASUN position. A company of the Gurkhas were at milestone $18\frac{1}{2}$.

Forward all was fairly quiet. The Battalion had disengaged successfully, but it was raining a deluge which reduced visibility to 20 yards and deadened noise. The carriers were in two hidden positions near mile 19. The anti-tank guns and "C" company were at the 20th milestone, and "D" company were passing back through them. Subadar Muhammad Hayat, temporarily in command of "A" Company, had warned the OC anti-tank section that he would be moving shortly, and the guns were limbered up. "A" and "B" Companies were on the move to their rendezvous at mile 18.

Then, at about 1645 hours, came the first Japanese armoured "blitz" of the campaign. Amid a pandemonium of noise and fire sixteen medium tanks followed by twenty one-man tankettes or carriers rolled down the streaming road out of the storm and broke past the rear-party section of carriers. Firing right, left and centre they raced past the unprepared anti-tank guns and through "C" Company; they scattered "D", "A" and "B" companies who simultaneously were attacked out of the rubber from the east. They plunged into the 2nd/1st Gurkhas, knocking out both carrier sections and overwhelming the forward guns of the mountain battery. Swept along in the middle of this spearhead was one gallant carrier of Lieutenant Greer's platoon. It was on fire behind, but its No. 2 was heroically pumping lead against the enemy tanks immediately behind and in front of him. The rear of the enemy column was made up of a dozen infantry-carrying lorries and some staff cars.

Scattering the reconnaissance parties at the 18th milestone, the armoured vehicles swept on. Lieutenant-Colonel Fitzpatrick was wounded as one of their shells hit the battery car he was in. He improvised a momentary road-block with the battalion vehicles unharbouring at mile $17\frac{1}{4}$; and when the leading tank got through he tried to outdistance it to the ASUN causeway by driving through the rubber parallel to the road. The swamp at that causeway was the only obstacle before JITRA. In this race the Battalion Commander's truck came under heavy fire from the tank and was finally stopped by a wire fence. The leading tank raced on to the causeway, splashing it with shells and bullets. The Sapper VCO in charge of the demolition was hit. His company commander was killed as he took his place. The demolition failed from a faulty charge, but the situation was temporarily saved by the prowess of the Gurkha havildar behind one of his battalion's two anti-tank rifles. He stopped three tanks in quick succession and thereby blocked the road. But fire from other tanks and encirclement by debussed infantry who waded the "impassable" marsh soon overwhelmed the forward company. By 1900 hours the tanks were right through the 2nd/1st Gurkhas area and had liquidated their Headquarters.

This bold armoured drive by the "Saeki Unit" had scattered and half destroyed two battalions and brought the enemy to the JITRA position. The Japanese wrote in the "Nippon Times" - "He who took advantage of the storm was victorious, while he who was upset by the storm was defeated". But there were reasons other than the weather. The 1st/14th had been caught by this thrust at the most critical moment of their withdrawal. Anti-tank guns were sadly inadequate in numbers. In the presence of tanks it was an unwise decision to stand at milestone 18 where there was no tank obstacle and where no good demolition could be arranged. The risk of unsuccessful defence could hardly be justified by the twelve hours saving in time which the change of plan was designed to secure. Had the Battalion been permitted to withdraw direct to ASUN from CHANGLUN, they would probably not have been caught on the move. The 2nd/1st Gurkha Rifles too would have been properly in position at a tank obstacle.

With the enemy in possession of the road over a considerable distance there was no natural rallying place for the scattered 1st/14th. In the dark and the rain the remnants of platoons and companies, mostly without their officers, made wide detours in attempting to get back to the JITRA position, or got lost only to be rounded up by the enemy next day; or they immediately bumped the Japanese on the road and were captured.

Lieutenants Greer and McCarthy with about 100 men and others of the Gurkhas and Gunners reached the right of the JITRA position early next afternoon (12th). Lieutenant-Colonel Fitzpatrick after vainly trying to regain his men, fell in with Captains Mohan Singh and Muhammad Akram and some 30 men of the latter's fighting patrol. This party did not get to the Jat's sector till the 13th, when it had been abandoned. They went on to reach KUALA NERANG on 14th. Having learnt there that the Japanese held ALOR STAR, they were just starting next day for SUNGEI PATANI by a jungle route when they were captured by an enemy patrol.

Sketch R.

Early on the 12th Major Anderson with Brigadier Garrett and another 100 men of the Battalion reached the Leicesters. A further party comprising one platoon of 'A' company with part of 'C' and Battalion Headquarters, the whole under Subadar Major Baboo Ram, withdrew west of the trunk road through this night of continuous rain. Just before dawn on the 12th these 70 weary men struck the BUKIT KETRI road near where the JITRA defences crossed it and later contacted Major Anderson near JITRA. They were directed to the Leicesters for their first food for 36 hours. A composite company was now formed with Subedar Hazara Singh, Jemadar Abdul Hanan and Havildar Amar Nath as platoon commanders, and allotted a defended locality just west of the trunk road.

Other parties came in from both flanks during the next two days, and some even by sea to ALOR STAR. All were dropping with fatigue and lack of sleep, soaked and tattered. Other officers captured were Lieutenants Dhillon and Hassan and Captain Stracey.

The Battle of JITRA: 12th December '41.

Sketch R.

The first real battle of the campagin now began. The armoured blitz against the Battalion and the 2nd/1st Gurkhas had been the overture; this was Act I of the tragedy. The 1st/14th were for the most part scattered. However, they were to some extent represented in this day's hard fighting by two composite companies, one on each flank of the 15th Brigade.

The battle comprised three Japanese attacks on the foremost defences, a partial withdrawal to a reserve line and a fourth enemy attack during that movement. It took place exclusively on the fronts of the 2nd Jats and the Leicesters in the 15th Brigade sector. It was primarily a brigade battle, fought by Brigadier Carpendale who had taken over command of the 15th Brigade when Brigadier Garrett was temporarily missing. There was no attack on the front of the 6th Brigade, though parts of its Indian battalions were soon involved in the fighting east of the road. So were the 2nd/2nd Gurkhas of the 28th Brigade who took the place of 1st/14th, and also the remnants of the 2nd/1st Gurkhas.

The evening before the 12th was full of disquieting events. Following the report at about 1730 hours that the 1st/14th and Brigadier Garrett had been cut off at ASUN there came, two hours later, the realization that the 1st/2nd Gurkhas had also been shattered. In the 6th Brigade the KODIANG detachment of the 2nd/16th and an outpost company of the 1st/8th Punjab when withdrawing in conformity with the 1st/14th's movements were held up by the premature blowing of the MANGGOI bridge. The railway line track, the only alternative route for vehicles, had as part of the plan been cut at the JERLUN bridge. Carriers, trucks and some guns were thus isolated; and when strenuous efforts to bridge or fill the demolition gap showed that this could not be done before dawn they had all to be abandoned. On the other hand demolition failed at the vital KAMUNTING causeway on the trunk road when enemy tanks arrived there at 2030 hours from their check at ASUN. Anti-tank guns and an artillery concentration imposed a halt by knocking out sufficient tanks to block the road; but the causeway was now in Japanese hands. By midnight enemy infantry east of the road had made contact with the Jats and Leicesters all along their front from BUKIT TUNGGAL KECHIL on the right to the BUKIT KETRI road on the left. There was some penetration by snipers, and much unnecessary firing by battle-green troops. There was however some reason to think that the Japanese were passing round the mountainous right flank, and so companies of the 2nd/16th and 1st/8th were brought across from the other brigade to KAMPONG KELUBI and the SUNGEI BATA. These troops were already tired. One company had marched 17 miles, and by their move they missed their meal. The 6th Brigade's reserve was thus reduced to half of the 1st/8th.

Of the 28th Brigade, which was the divisional reserve, there remained only the 2nd/9th Gurkha Rifles. They were divided between guarding the KUALA NERANG road and anti-paratroop duties along the road to SUNGEI PATANI. Major-General Murray-Lyon had already this evening come to the conclusion that the Division should, if permissible, withdraw to the GURUN position during the next night.

In heavy rain at dawn on the 12th December the enemy attacked the junction of the Jats and Leicesters. Repulsed elsewhere, they made one serious penetration by capturing a pill-box OP on the extreme left of the Jats. Counterattack failed to eject them, and from this point of vantage the enemy pressed into the MARKET GARDEN behind the right company of the LEICESTERS which was just east of the trunk road. The CO reinforced that flank as best he could, while Subadar Major Baboo Ram's composite company was now inserted into the Leicesters' defences west of the road. A counter-attack by two companies of the 2nd/8th under their CO was launched at 0930 hours to clear the MARKET GARDEN. Reduced by casualties before its start, and with its carriers bogged, this heroic attack was a failure. Three officers and thirty-eight men lay dead before the unconquered pill-box.

The Japanese second attack came at noon, a whole battalion being launched at the left company of the Jats. An hour and a half later, after a splendid defence during which artillery support had to be reduced for lack of shells and small arms ammunition was completely exhausted, the remnants of gallant "D" Company were overwhelmed by a mass assault. The enemy pressed on into the hole thus enlarged, and by 1430 hours were up against the Battalion's one-time position on the SUNGEI BATA, now held by the 2nd/2nd Gurkhas. The right and centre of the Jats had meanwhile not been hard pressed. The hundred men of the 1st/14th under Lieutenants Greer and McCarthy had reached their right flank company at about 1330 hours and thereafter fought alongside them.

The enemy's third attack was in battalion strength against the centre company of the Leicesters between the two roads. Another critical situation resulted, but was restored by the East Surrey's carriers counter-attacking from the 6th Brigade sector. By 1500 hours all enemy attacks appeared to have ceased. Only the exposure of the Leicesters' right flank and extreme fatigue of all troops was at this moment really disturbing.

In any case all immediate idea of withdrawal from the JITRA position had ended with Malaya Command's ruling that it must be defended to the last. Brigadier Carpendale accordingly decided to adjust his line after dark by withdrawing to the SUNGEI BATA, and to concentrate the Leicesters just north of that stream and west of the road in readiness for a counter-attack towards the north-east at dawn. This adjustment was carried out; but the situation deteriorated too rapidly for the counterstroke to take place.

Just as the Leicesters were regretfully leaving the positions which they had defended so successfully the enemy launched the fourth attack of the day against this battalion. A running fight followed in the dark, and inevitably the unit reached its destination somewhat depleted and scattered. Major Anderson and Subadar Major Baboo Ram's Company had just previously been sent back to report to 28th Brigade Headquarters in TANJONG PAU camp. This little column got involved in the Japanese thrust and a part was temporarily scattered. The enemy eventually reached the IRON BRIDGE on the main road, thus denying to the Leicesters their only point of withdrawal over the SUNGEI BATA.

This river line was held below and above the bridge by the 2nd/2nd Gurkhas along with two Sapper and Miner companies and one of the 1st/8th Punjab. To the right of these troops there was a gap of 1000 yards, the original "tactical gap", before the readjusted line reached the Jats near the foothills. With them were the composite company of the 1st/14th and two of the 2nd/16th. On this flank there was some enemy penetration during the night, and intermittent sniping, infiltration and noise effects. Our men, though regulars, were young and green. They were opposed by

Withdrawal from JITRA : 13th December.

The plan was that the 15th Brigade were to withdraw over the SUNGEI BESAR near the aerodrome, and on by the East Road through PENDANG to a reserve area behind the GURUN position. On the way they were to return their Gurkha units to the 28th Brigade. The latter brigade, after holding a forward intermediate position on this road at LANGGAR and on the West Road at ALOR STAR town, were to occupy the eastern sector of the GURUN defences. The 6th Brigade were to withdraw by the West Road, hold a temporary intermediate position along the SIMPANG AMPAT canal six miles south of ALOR STAR, and then occupy the western sector at GURUN from inclusive the main road to the sea.

Sketch P.

Lieutenant Geer's company of the Battalion was to move with the Jats. Subadar Major Baboo Ram's accompanied Brigade Headquarters at about 2100 hours and reached GURUN village at 0500 hours on 13th December. Major Anderson moved there too with his skeleton Battalion Headquarters. 'B' echelon 1st line transport were already back in SUNGEI PATANI.

Orders reached 15th Brigade Headquarters at 2200 hours. The Leicesters who were to withdraw at once through the 2nd/2nd Gurkhas got into difficulties. Their left two companies had never received the order to withdraw during the earlier adjustment of the line and were still in their original defences near MANGGOI. They had been accounted lost, and were not sent the final order. At dawn they engaged the Japanese at the start of what the enemy intended to be a brigade attack on the 6th Brigade sector. Realizing at last that the Division had withdrawn during the night, these two companies managed to disengage and after considerable casualties to reach the coast and rejoin by sea some five days later. The main body of the Leicesters, unable to use or force the IRON BRIDGE which the Japanese commanded, were forced across country to the west. One party crossed the bridge at ANAK BUKIT and rejoined via ALOR STAR where they were ambushed by the Japanese. The other party joined up with the coastal company of the 2nd/16th and some men of the 1st/14th under Captain Dhillon. From the SUNGEI JERLUN these troops managed to get boats to PENANG.

The right company of the Jats together with the composite company of the 1st/14th were also believed lost and received no orders. Not till dusk on the 13th did they realize that they ought to go. En route in the dark and rain both companies were largely dispersed by a false-alarm ambush. Lieutenant McCarthy was among the many who lost direction and were captured. Lieutenant Greer with a very few men struck west across the flow of Japanese movement, and from the coast managed to reach SUMATRA. The rest of the Jats disengaged without difficulty, but they too were ambushed and greatly scattered while passing through TANJONG PAU camp. Thence, with the detachment of the 2nd/16th, they made their weary way through LANGGAR to PENDANG.

Sketch R.

At 0230 hours the 2nd/2nd Gurkhas blew the IRON BRIDGE and withdrew to LANGGAR through the 2nd/9th, who in their turn fought their way back to and across the river. The 90 men who now composed the 2nd/1st Gurkha Rifles were still in position in TANJONG PAU camp. Orders had not reached them but they were able, although they did not move till 0700 hours, to reach and ferry the river above the blown bridges.

The delaying position was now taken up and held throughout the day. At LANGGAR there were the 2nd/2nd and Headquarters 28th Brigade. The 2nd/1st arrived there at dusk. At ALOR STAR bridge there were many stragglers, also the 2nd/9th and what remained of the East Surreys. Headquarters 6th Brigade with the 1st/8th and 2nd/16th Punjab marched back to the SIMPANG AMPAT line. Divisional Headquarters was now as PENDANG on the East Road, which was in a bad state from rain and much congested with traffic and derelict vehicles.

After repulsing enemy attempts to gain the ALOR STAR railway bridge, the demolition of which had failed, the 2nd/9th and East Surreys disengaged after dusk, embussed and moved through one traffic block after another to the GURUN position. At 2030 hours the 2nd/2nd Gurkhas withdrew from LANGGAR.

The 6th Brigade were not out of the SIMPANG AMPAT position until 0500 hours on 14th December and did not reach their sector of the GURUN defences until 1000 hours. Divisional Headquarters moved back to the HARVARD ESTATE four miles south of GURUN.

Thus ended the withdrawal from JITRA. The 11th Division still existed, but only as a shadow of its former self; and it was fortunate that at the end the Japanese follow-up was not armoured or even forceful. The feeding arrangements of Indian units had broken down. The men were as weak from hunger as from strain. The artillery had lost two 25-pdrs, six 3.7 hows, thirteen anti-tank guns with fourteen Bredas and-18-pdrs; almost all because they could not be extricated from mud. The 28th Brigade were still in fighting trim, but the 2nd/1st Gurkhas were reduced to two rifle companies and were without carriers, 3-inch mortars and much important equipment. The 6th Brigade had been battered more by misfortune than battle. The East Surreys had lost two platoons. The 1st/8th were reduced to two companies, with a third made up of survivors from the MARKET GARDEN counter-attack. The 2nd/16th Punjab had only one company, but were almost unique in having their carrier platoon.

The 15th Brigade had been shattered, and now comprised only 500 very exhausted men. The Leicesters had merely their carrier platoon and 200 men. The Jats mustered 4 officers and 97 men. The 1st/14th at this moment had only Major Anderson, a skeleton Headquarters, a few carriers and two weak companies commanded by Subadar Major Babu Ram and Subadar Hazara Singh. These companies were survivors of the ASUN blitz, where, further, almost all unit equipment had been lost. Lieutenant Morrey, the Quartermaster, and 2nd Lieutenant Corfield were at SUNGEI PATANI. Captain Habib-ur-Rehman acted as Adjutant, since Captain Kiani had been evacuated sick. There were now only four officers, and none, apart from Major Anderson, of any appreciable experience.

GURUN : 14th-15th December '41.

Sketch 'P'.

The GURUN position where the 11th Division was now to delay the enemy as much as possible has already been described as a relatively good one. But now the troops beside being insufficient in numbers were very shaken and desperately tired. The position was held by the 28th Brigade on the right and the 6th on the left. The foremost localities of the 28th Brigade ran along the East Road, from where it crossed that to JENIANG two miles east of GURUN, up to CHEMPEDAK RAILWAY STATION. The railway was the boundary between the two brigades, being inclusive to the 6th. This brigade's line extended from the railway station across the trunk road at the 20th milestone to the hamlet of TITI TERAS under the steep slopes of KEDAH PEAK. It had originally been intended to align the left flank immediately north of the road to YEN, but for concealment against air attack and easier communication it was now brought back well south of that road. The consequent inability to control the important GUAR crossroads, and the limitation on observation and fire imposed by rubber plantations had an important effect on the battle.

The 6th Brigade had the 2nd/16th astride the railway, the East Surreys between railway and main road, and the 1st/8th holding that road with all ground to its west. Brigade Headquarters was at the southern edge of GURUN. A squadron of 3rd Cavalry were under command of the Brigade, but they were merely lorry-borne and had no fighting vehicles.

This time the battle was fought and lost on the front of the 6th Brigade. But the diminutive 15th Brigade, which was in a divisional reserve position astride the trunk road 3/4 mile south of GURUN, was also involved. The 28th Brigade had not the opportunity to play a full part.

At noon on 14th December Japanese patrols were in contact with a forward section of the East Surreys covering the anti-tank gun and demolition at the GUAR crossroads. At 1400 hours enemy tanks arrived there but were held. By 1500 hours, however, Japanese infantry had driven back this detachment and were heavily pressing the 1st/8th astride the trunk road, and infiltrating through them. After an abortive counter-attack by the weak squadron of 3rd Cavalry, another by the 2nd/16th's carriers and odd parties under the Brigade Commander's personal leadership restored the situation at milestone 20.

A further counter-attack by the East Surreys was planned to capture and retain the GUAR crossroads next morning; but during the night the road front collapsed. Night attacks were what, above all, the tired and outnumbered troops could not cope with. At about 0200 hours on 15th December the Japanese charged and obliterated the remnants of the main road company of the 1st/8th whom they had heavily mortared for five hours previously. Between 0400 and 0500 hours they broke through the adjoining company of the East Surreys. The East Surrey Headquarters on the road was wiped out; so was that of the 6th Brigade shortly after 0600 hours. The break-through reached the GURUN road junction, and soon enemy tanks were on the spot. A company of the Leicesters was brought up from the 15th Brigade; and Subadar Hazara Singh's company of the 1st/14th was sent to aid the 28th Brigade, whose headquarters and rear elements on the JENIANG road were now in action. Practically all line communications had by now been cut, and the whole of the 6th Brigade appeared to have been lost. Actually the 2nd/16th and the right company of the East Surreys were unaware of what had happened; but Headquarters and the remnants of the 1st/8th were definitely cut off and had to make their way west to the sea.

From 0700 hours onwards the troops of the 15th Brigade consisted merely of small parties of the Leicesters and Jats, the squadron of 3rd Cavalry, Battalion Headquarters 1st/14th and Subadar Major Baboo Ram's company. The whole were disposed to form a box near milestone 23. Many stragglers from further forward were coming into the area, and there was an air of alarm. Subadar Major Baboo Ram's company were actually sent up onto the lower slopes of KEDAH PEAK to deal with an enemy threat which never materialized. Subadar Hazara Singh's company returned from the 28th Brigade area somewhat disorganized and without having accomplished anything. Reaching Brigadier Carpendale's headquarters just as the Leicesters were being driven back from GURUN, the company had been swept back in the general confusion without carrying out the counter-attack assigned to it.

After 0930 hours when enemy artillery fire had become intense Brigadier Garrett withdrew the 15th Brigade seven miles to the SUNGEI LALANG, which was to be their next position. In this movement the 1st/14th under Major Anderson acted as rearguard.

The Japanese were now pressing eastwards from GURUN against the 28th Brigade. Brigadier Carpendale was for counter-attacking with the 2nd/2nd Gurkhas to recapture the village; but with the left of the GURUN position already broken Major General Murray-Lyon was unwilling to get a battalion of his only remaining brigade into a possibly inextricable position. Instead he ordered the Brigade to withdraw by stages along the East Road to the SUNGEI PATANI river line.

Withdraw from GURUN : 15th and 16th December '41.

The previous afternoon the Divisional Commander had had general instructions from Lieutenant-General Heath, who visited his headquarters. If forced to withdraw from GURUN he should retire first behind the SUNGEI MUDA and then across the KRIAN River. The situation elsewhere was that the PENANG garrison were preparing to evacuate the island. The Japanese while forcing the 5/14th and 3rd/16th out of the KROH position towards BALING had got access to the other road through GRIK. The 12th Indian Infantry Brigade had moved up the KROH road to BATU PEKAKA. The 8th Brigade in KELANTAN had withdrawn in good order to the railhead at KUALA KRAI. The Corps Commander now had no reserve. At KUANTAN and MERSING all was still quiet.

Sketch 'P'.

"Map 11."

Sketch P.

At 2300 hours on the 15th after one company of the East Surreys and two battalions of the 28th Brigade had passed through, the little 15th Brigade together with its field and anti-tank artilery and Independent Company withdraw successively from its positions on the BONGKOK, GETAH and LALANG streams. A demolition party was left on the LALANG bridge until at last the rearguard of the 9th Gurkhas and 2nd/16th crossed it early next morning. Thus on 16th December the 1st/14th, now increased by more stragglers from ASUN, JITRA and GURUN, went back in MT to near BUKIT MERTAJEM.

There is not the space properly to describe and keep on re-iterating the unceasing strain caused by lack of rest, by lack of proper meals and by continuous air attack. Added factors were the novel noise effects used by the enemy and their bold encircling movements. There were the feelings of being in retreat; of being without tanks, without effective aircraft and without adequate anti-tank weapons. Above all was lack of sleep and rest. The bridge at SUNGEI PATANI was blown at 0700 hours on the 16th; whereafter the 28th Brigade as rearguard to the 11th Division withdrew over the SUNGEI MUDA. The Japanese had won Kedah.

CHAPTER XX

WORLD WAR II, 1939-45

MALAYA, 1941-42

(Map 11. Sketches S,T,U,V,W,X,Y.)

River MUDA to KAMPAR: 17th to 31st December '41.

Sketch S.

The condition of the 11th Division precluded any stand on the River MUDA. Further, the 12th Brigade protecting the right of the Division near BALING was itself in danger of being enveloped. So PENANG was evacuated; the 11th Division was withdrawn behind the KRIAN River; and the 12th Brigade, onto which the 5th/14th and the remnants of the 2nd/16th had now closed, were moved back and round to the GRIK road. While the 28th Brigade held the KRIAN near NIBONG TEBAL on the 18th the other two brigades passed through to TAIPING under frequent air attack. The 1st/14th lorried straight back to IPOH to reorganize.

It was a sad return to the Battalion's first station in Malaya. But the few days rest, first in bivouac by the railway station and then in a rubber plantation hutted camp, effected a great change. "B echelon" under Lieutenants Morrey and Corfield with some reinforcements were found here. Many cut-off parties and individual stragglers rejoined. Arms, ammunition and clothing were completed. Lieutenant-General Heath visited and encouraged his old battalion. Reorganization produced the following result:—

Commanding Officer	Major (acting Lieutenant-Colonel) Anderson.
Adjutant	Captain Habib-ur-Rehman. (Later Lieutenant Dickie)
Quartermaster	Lieutenant Morrey.
Assistant Quartermaster	Lieutenant Corfield.
'A' Company (three platoon Yusafzais).	Subadar-Major Baboo Ram
'B' Company (two platoons' Dogras and one of Sikhs)	Subadar Hazara Singh.
'C' Company (three platoons PMs).	Lieutenant Dara (Later Captain Habib-ur-Rehman)

The strength was still only about five hundred.

After repulsing attacks at MAHANG, SELAMA and NIBONG TEBAL on 18th and 19th December the 28th Brigade acting as rearguard withdrew to the line ULU SAPETANG—BAGAN SERAI, and thence during the night of the 20th/21st right back to cover the pontoon bridge over the PERAK at BLANJA. Meanwhile the Independent Company had bumped the new Japanese advance on the GRIK road at SUMPITAN, delaying it there and again at LENGGONG in conjunction with a company of the Argylls of the 12th Brigade. The greater part of that Brigade on their arrival continued to impose this vital delay in the CHENDEROH LAKE area, while the 5th/14th crossed the PERAK River to SALAK NORTH for the defence of the main road and railway bridges there. Eventually, after the Japanese had by-passed them by rafting down the PERAK at night, the 12th Brigade withdrew across the river to first SUNGEI SIPUT and then CHEMOR. For with the Japanese in unexpected strength on the GRIK road as well as down the river at BLANJA, and with other enemy columns marching from TAIPING to embark at LUMUT, it was decided not to defend the line of the PERAK but to hold a position at KAMPAR.

The 15th Brigade had already moved there from IPOH on 23rd December and were at work digging and wiring. The 6th Brigade was now merged in the 15th. This was henceforward commanded by Brigadier Moorhead (of the 3rd/16th) and comprised:-

"The British Battalion" (1 Leicester with 2 East Surrey)
"Jat/Punjabi Battalion" (2 Jat with 1/8 Punjab)
1st/14th Punjab.
2nd/16th and 3rd/16th Punjab, attached from Corps reserve.

Brigadier Paris from the 12th Brigade assumed command of the Division.

Sketch T.

It had been proposed also to amalgamate the 1st and 5th Battalions; but as the 5th/14th were wanted elsewhere and had so far not lost heavily the idea was abandoned. Instead the 5th Battalion, who were withdrawn from the 12th Brigade to IPOH on the 24th December, were sent two days later to TELOK ANSON to support Major Fearon's Independent Company in opposing a threatened landing. This Commando Company, it should be noted, contained volunteers from both the 1st and 5th Battalions.

The men were by now somewhat rested, washed, reclothed and reshod. There were still only three rifles companies. Redistributed weapons allowed 2 LMGs per company (at 4 magazine each), 7 Tommy guns and 1 anti-tank rifle. Each Headquarter Company had 7 Vickers MMGs, 1 anti-tank rifle, 2 mortars and 4 carriers. There were no 2-inch mortars or Verey pistols, and but little signal cable.

The Battle of KAMPAR: 1st and 2nd January '42.

The defensive position now occupied by the 15th Brigade and their artillery was a semi-circular one of about 6 miles. It barred the main road at milestone 23 where there were small rubber plantations. The right flank was secure on the jungle-clad slopes of GUNONG BUJANG MELAKA. To the north-west and west lay open tin-dredge tailings which gave fields of fire up to 1200 yards. To the south-west was the CICELY RUBBUR ESTATE with tin-tailings between it and the trunk road. It was a good position for a division, but too extensive for a single weak brigade. The 28th Brigade were to hold a companion position north-west of KAMPONG SAHUM to block the eastern road round the mountain massif. There was virtually no reserve; for the 12th Brigade had to be employed elsewhere.

Sketch U.

Sketch S.

"The British Battalion" was on the right, holding the 800-yard "THOMPSON'S RIDGE" east of the road and up to a point about 600 yards west of it. From there the 1st/14th continued the defences across the railway with successively 'C', 'B' and 'A' Companies. 'A' Company denied the half-destroyed railway bridge across the SUNGEI KAMPAR, and until contact was made had a platoon forward at MALIM NAWAR. Next the 3rd/16th and then the 2nd/16th Punjab extended the position through SIMPANG LIMA. Its south face bending back to the road again was held by the "Jat/Punjabi Battalion." Brigade Headquarters was in KAMPAR itself.

On the night of 27th December the 28th Brigade withdrew from BALANJA to their SAHUM position. The Japanese simultaneously got across the PERAK River at KUALA KANGSAR. They heavily attacked the 12th Brigade south of GOPENG on 28th and 29th, making their second armoured blitz of the campaign. From there the badly-mauled 12th Brigade withdrew to BIDOR. No sooner there but they had to operate south-west towards TELOK ANSON where the enemy division from LUMUT landed on 1st January. The 5th/14th had previously been withdrawn from the coast to just south of KAMPAR to act as a reserve to the 15th Brigade.

Far from the north and from BLANJA two Japanese divisions were now closing in on the position. Air attack became almost continuous from Christmas Day onwards. 'A' Company's detachment was forced back from MALIM NAWAR, and large numbers of enemy infiltrated into CICELY ESTATE from across the KINTA River. For counter-attack in that area the 5th/14th were moved forward to milestone 27 on the CHANGKUT JONG road during the last night of the year. Actually the first attacks on the 30th and 31st came against the 28th Brigade. These were defeated.

On 1st January 1942 the Japanese concentrated all their resources against the 15th Brigade, particularly in the main road sector. All that day and next the battle swayed to and fro as the enemy strove to gain or retain "THOMPSON'S RIDGE". "The British Battalion" fought magnificently, and were as gallantly aided by Captain Graham's Gujar company (1st/8th) from the Jat/Punjabi Battalion. In the 14th's sector there was vigorous enemy patrolling as well as heavy shelling and air strikes. Several small attacks were repulsed. After dark, however, 'A' Company were strongly attacked by a battalion trying to force the railway bridge as to cross the stream by assault boat. The enemy were so effectively repulsed that later the same night a party of East Surrey men who had been cut off in Kedah and were following the railway line were able to enter the position over the broken girders of the bridge.

Confidence soared as a result of this first entirely satisfactory day's fighting in the campaign. 'A' Company and others were all smiles. Lieutenant-Colonel Anderson had the satisfaction of knowing that the Battalion had stood the first real test since their cruel losses at ASUN.

Next evening as the fight for THOMPSON'S RIDGE waned there came a sharp attack against 'C' Company. This was held, but continued right up to the time planned for withdrawal. For unfortunately enemy pressure against the 12th Brigade on the TELOK ANSON road now compelled the abandonment of the KAMPAR position just when the fighting ability of the Division was being reborn.

First the 28th Brigade withdrew through TEMOH to hold a covering position two miles south of KAMPAR; and here the 5th Battalion joined them. Between 2100 and 2230 hours on 2nd December units of the 15th Brigade slipped away from their sectors, first the "British Battalion", then the 3rd/16th, then the 1st/14th with 'C' Company still in contact. Finally went the 2nd/16th, likewise in action. The "Jat/Punjabi Battalion" had already been sent to deal with a new threat to the L of C further south.

By midnight the 1st Battalion had passed through the 5th.

How different the circumstances of their last meeting at PENANG, or of their only other association which was in Tibet! Moving back in MT the 15th Brigade took up another position at BIDOR, through which on the next night the 12th Brigade and Independent Company withdrew. From 0300 hours on 4th January the 15th Brigade were on the move again to SUNGKAI to cover another stage in the withdrawal.

By now Lieutenant Dara had been evacuated sick. Captain Habib-ur-Rehman took over command of 'C' Company in his stead, his own place as Adjutant being filled by Lieutenant Dickie who joined from Brigade Headquarters.

SLIM RIVER : 7th January '42.

The 1st/14th were spared this disastrous day when the 5th Battalion, along with the 12th and 28th Brigades, were half destroyed. The divisional plan was to construct and hold a main position at TANJONG MALIM, and with that purpose the 15th Brigade moved there during the night 4th/5th. The Brigade were now further weakened by the removal of the 2nd/16th Punjab for the ever-increasing commitment of rear L of C defence. The other two brigades held delaying positions in depth near the SLIM RIVER. The 12th, which again included the 5th Battalion, were at TROLAK. The 28th were 6½ miles further back near SLIM RIVER village. In this deep box the anti-tank mines were quite insufficient, the anti-tank guns too few and too far back. The concrete pillar obstacles of the 12th Brigade were to prove ineffective.

Early on 7th January twenty-four enemy tanks followed by a strong force of infantry penetrated into the 12th Brigade down the road and pressed on relentlessly for 19 miles until at last stopped by field artillery. It was the disaster of ASUN over again or a larger scale. First the 12th Brigade, then the 137th Field Regiment, RA, and then the 28th Brigade were filetted. The Japanese seized the SLIM RIVER road bridge intact and held it, together with other stretches of the road. The scattered brigades got back to TANJONG MALIM along the railway, but with considerable loss of men and transport. The 5th/14th were hit head-on by the tank column while marching forward to their action stations. There were heavy casualties, and for a while there remained only six officers with 135 VCOs and other ranks. Lieutenant-Colonel Stokes was wounded and later died.

SELANGOR RIVER : 7th to 9th January '42.

Even before the abovementioned disaster the threat of further enemy landings on the west coast had led to a change of plan.

Instead of at TANJONG MALIM a stand was now to be made in front of KUALA LUMPUR so as to enable the 9th Indian Division from the east coast, with the 8th Australian Division and part of the expected 18th Division, to prepare for a decisive battle on the line BATU ANAM—MOUNT OPHIR—MUAR. The weary, decimated 11th Indian Division were then to rest in Johore.

Sketch T.

Thus at 2100 hours on 5th January the 15th Brigade left TANJONG MALIM in MT for RAWANG. Arrived there the 1st 14th were at once drawn into the operations against those strong Japanese forces who had landed 8 miles north of the mouth of the SELANGOR River on 4th January. Detachments of the 3rd Cavalry, the Jat/Punjabi Battalion and the Independent Company were already in the coastal area; but they were unable to stop the enemy from advancing inland along the road up the north bank of this river. The 3rd Dogras of the 9th Division who were already at RAWANG failed in a night attack to gain control of this road opposite BATANG BERJUNTAI, and later the bridge there and those at RANTAU PANJANG two miles further upstream had to be destroyed. On the 6th January, the day of arrival at RAWANG, one company of the 1/14th relieved the platoon of the Independent Company at the higher bridges. Next day "The British Battalion" lorried forward to relieve the Dogras on the south bank at BATANG BERJUNTAI, while the remainder of the Sherdils with the 10th Mountain Battery and a detachment of the 15th Field Company Sappers and Miners moved out to RANTAU PANJANG. The 3rd/16th occupied a reserve position at BUKIT ROBINSON, while the 3rd Dogras went back to RAWANG and a little later joined the 28th Brigade.

Sketch V.

Meanwhile the battered remnants of the rest of the 11th Division withdrew from TANJONG MALIM to RASA, the 22nd Brigade of the 9th Division from KUANTAN joining them at KUALA KUBU. Together they were to stand about RAWANG to deny KUALA LUMPUR to the enemy for another 48 hours.

RANTAU PANJANG—9th January '42.

Sketch V.

As the 1st/14th reached its area the Japanese started concentrating in the rubber estates on the opposite bank. Nevertheless the first night and most of the next day passed quietly.

The SELANGOR River ran fast and deep, and in general through thick jungle. But just here was the connecting point of the estates on opposite banks, and the rubber trees reached almost to the water's edge over about 800 yards. The actual banks were very marshy except where the two bridges, now destroyed, had carried an estate road and a branch railway line. Elsewhere the river was a difficult one to ford or to bridge.

Accordingly 'B' Company were disposed in the south bank rubber to cover the road bridge and as far up stream as they could manage. while 'C' Company looked after the railway bridge and the loop of the river. 'A' Company were held in reserve at the edge of the jungle on the low hill of RANTAU PANJANG, where also was Battalion Headquarters. 'A' Company shared with 'C' the task of patrolling the long unguarded stretch of the south bank from the river loop to the right flank of the "British Battalion" near BATANG BERJUNTAI road bridge. The 10th Mountain Battery supporting both battalions was in position on the southern part of the RANTAU PANJANG ridge near the railway line.

At midday on 8th January Subadar Hazara Singh's 'B' Company were withdrawn for the local protection of Brigade Headquarters at RAWANG in place of the Dogras. Brigade Headquarters may have felt less uneasiness in thus weakening the Battalion from the fact that at the same time they sent forward a party of some thirty reinforcements just arrived from India. But these young Yusafzais were nearly all quite inexperienced.

Lieutenant-Colonel Anderson replaced 'B' Company with one platoon of 'A' plus twenty of the new Pathans under their own NCOs. He could do no more without unduly weakening 'A' Company's watch over the left flank. But the right flank had to be drawn in and was now doubly "in the air". The final dispositions are shewn on Sketch 'V'. The field of fire was much obscured by rubber trees on both banks. There were but few entrenching tools, and no wire.

In 'A' and 'C' Company sectors there was some sniping and firing on patrols at dusk; but the night eventually settled down quietly, and there was nothing to show that the Japanese had massed opposite the right of the Battalion. After midnight they threw a log bridge at a point well beyond the upstream flank of 'A' Company. Silently they passed over a whole battalion, which then moved to the RAWANG road in rear of the 1st/14th.

At 0515 hours on 9th January Subadar-Major Baboo Ram commanding the reserve portion of 'A' Company sent out one of his two platoons as a fighting patrol towards "The British Battalion", and one section to gain touch with the left of 'C' Company. A few minutes later some firing, grenade-throwing and other noise was heard in the transport area alongside the road behind Battalion Headquarters. At 0530 hours the Battalion Quartermaster Havildar arrived breathless to tell the CO that the Japanese had surrounded and rushed the transport lines. He had hardly finished speaking when there was a stirring at one point in the jungle bushes around the Command Post. Leaping from his slit trench Lieutenant-Colonel Anderson rushed forward and challenged with drawn revolver. He was met with a burst of automatic fire and died immediately. Then the enemy rushed Battalion Headquarters from three directions. In a moment the whole party were either scattered, captured, wounded or killed. Among the killed fell Lieutenant Dickie, the Adjutant.

Simultaneously the right flank party of 'A' Company were attacked in rear, pinned against the river and mostly liquidated. From Battalion Headquarters the enemy swept westwards across the loop of the river. Subadar-Major Baboo Ram with his two sections resisted in the dawning light, but were by-passed. Soon they were able to slip away to the Battalion Headquarters hill, and finding that deserted but cut off by Japanese parties from the forward troops they later made their way to Brigade Headquarters with the first authentic news of the reverse. The earliest report had reached RAWANG soon after dawn by a motor cycle despatch rider who had escaped from the transport area. He said that the Battalion had been "wiped out".

This was not so. 'C' Company under Captain Habib-ur-Rehman and Lieutenant Corfield held their position and repulsed several dawn attempts to cross the river. But the Japanese pressed inwards along the south bank where the forward platoon of 'A' Company had once been, and soon closed the net round the bend of the river. There was silence from Battalion Headquarters. Distant firing showed that the "The British Battalion" were heavily engaged too. Captain Habib-ur-Rehman determined to break out and occupy the only defensible high ground, the Battalion Headquarters site on RANTAU PANJANG. This counter-attack was carried out with only slight loss. The hill was found unoccupied save by dead and wounded friends. Here, greatly assisted by one Vickers machine gun and a 3-inch Stokes mortar, these 85 ranks of the 1st/14th resisted all attempts of the Japanese and their aircraft to oust them until afternoon. Then, when ammunition was almost exhausted and no Brigade counter action was apparent, Captain Habib-ur-Rehman withdrew his command from a field which was obviously lost. There was only one gap left, due south inside the edge of the jungle. Hardly had they cleared when heavy mortaring followed by yelling indicated an all-out assault on the vacated position.

The withdrawal was not followed up, and at first there was little difficulty except from snipers who were everywhere. Subadar Muhammad Hayat was killed by a sniper's bullet just when the Company had started to move down the railway line to BATU ARANG. When approaching the collieries just after dark there was a most unfortunate clash with what proved to be parties of "The

British Battalion, similarly withdrawing from the river. In the firing which took place between exhausted and shaken men at least six were killed and 'C' Company got badly split up. Captain Habib-ur-Rehman was among those who lost direction and were later taken prisoner. Others rejoined the Battalion later, but Lieutenant Corfield had only one VCO and forty-five other ranks with him when he reached RAWANG early next morning. It was the Battalion's second disaster. In an insecure position, and weakened by detachment, they had been set a task beyond the strength and capacity of any single battalion of the Division at this time.

RAWANG : 10th January '42.

Here the Sherdils reformed for the third time. The strength was now but 320; and only two rifle companies could be formed, 'A' (PMs and Yusafzais) under Subadar-Major Baboo Ram and 'B' (Sikhs and Dogras) under Subadar Hazara Singh. There were still a few carriers. 'B' echelon transport were fairly intact under Lieutenant Morrey, who was the senior of the only two officers left. Battalion Headquarters was practically non-existent for the moment, and this factor upon others caused the Battalion to be attached to the 2nd/9th Gurkhas in the 28th Brigade until amalgamation with the 5/14th should become feasible.

Sketch T.

The rest of the 15th Brigade had had to be withdrawn from the SELANGOR RIVER area and only the gallant defence of KLANG by L of C units now stood been the enemy's new coastal landings and KUALA LUMPUR. The federal capital was to be abandoned at midnight 10th/11th January. While the 15th Brigade went back later to LABU as a first bound the 28th, now holding off the frontal enemy at SERENDAH, were to withdraw to SEREMBAN thirty-five miles to the south. Thus until a late hour on the 10th 'B' Company and the carriers were engaged in covering back their future brigade through the RAWANG position. Having embussed at midnight, the 1st/14th passed through the 5th Battalion holding the MANTIN PASS in the 12th Brigade and caught up the 2nd/9th Gurkhas at SEREMBAN. They finally debussed in TAMPIN at dawn on 11th January. Heret here was a day's respite.

PONTIAN KECHIL—11th to 30th January '42.

The two brigades of the 9th Indian Division now joined the two of the 8th Australian Division in the main position BATU ANAM—MOUNT OPHIR—MUAR. This was "Westforce", which also included at MUAR the newly-landed 45th Brigade of the 18th Indian Division. Troops further east in Johore State formed "East force" under Lieutenant-General Heath. Under his direction

Map 11.

Sketch 'W'.

the 28th Brigade and 3rd Cavalry were sent to PONTIAN KECHIL to deal with coastal landings between BATU PAHAT and KUKUP. The 5th/14th went to aerodrome defence at KLUANG, while the rest of the 12th Brigade were withdrawn to SINGAPORE. The remainder of the 11th Division, now commanded by Major-General Key, halted at KLUANG and RENGAM.

The battle began again on the 14th January. Successful though heavy fighting took place around GEMAS up to the 19th; but a new landing near MUAR forced the 45th Brigade back on YONG PENG and threatened the whole position. The 15th Brigade was soon heavily engaged at BATU PAHAT. The Japanese established a road block in their rear at SENGGARANG, and this brigade for the most part had to be extricated by sea. A general withdrawal to the Island of SINGAPORE was now decided on, and for this operation Lieutenant-General Heath assumed command of all forces on the mainland.

Meanwhile the 28th Brigade (Brigadier Selby) were actively guarding the coast further south. They were also preparing to cover the rest of the 11th Division and the 53rd Brigade through PONTIAN KECHIL and thence inland over the 26 miles of narrow, marshy road past the GUNONG PULAI reservoirs. Fighting patrols of the Japanese had already infiltrated over the SUNGEI PONTIAN BESAR from the north. The Sherdils worked hard at preparing the "BOULDER POSITION" near the reservoirs. The 5th/14th arrived on 20th January to make the third battalion of the brigade, and were allotted to the seawards and river line defence of PONTIAN KECHIL. Major Fearon, whose gallant Independent Company had just been disbanded in SINGAPORE, took over command of the 1st/14th on 22nd January; but the battalion continued to be attached to the 2nd/9th Gurkhas.

Withdrawal from the mainland—31st January '42.

When the 53rd Brigade started passing through on the 24th the 1st/14th held part of the BOULDER POSITION, with first 'A' and then 'B' Company detached on GUNONG PULAI. There was considerable air bombing of the position and of the reservoirs; and there was a clash that night with a company of the "Johore Military Forces" who took upon themselves to patrol this road and were mistaken for Japanese. They were disbanded next day. On the 26th and until the 28th one company went to the assistance of the 5th/14th at PONTIAN KECHIL.

After waiting until the remnants of the 15th Brigade had been extricated by land and sea the 28th Brigade began withdrawing on the 29th in close rearguard contact. That night and next day the Battalion were in brigade reserve when the 2nd/2nd Gurkhas and the 5th/14th leapfrogged back from the two PONTIAN villages. There was also fighting in the BOULDER POSITION area when bodies of enemy crossed the PONTIAN river and tried to cut the road. However, the rear and flank were successfully guarded until all other troops of the Division had cleared SKUDAI and crossed over to SINGAPORE. Finally, very early on 1st February while the Navy were evacuating a 5th/14th platoon from KUKUP the two sister battalions passed over THE CAUSEWAY onto the Island. The long withdrawal of 585 miles in 55 days was at an end.

JOHORE STRAIT—1st to 8th February '42.

The Island of SINGAPORE was organized for defence into three areas. The JOHORE STRAIT front of the Northern Area under Headquarters 3rd Indian Corps extended from CHANGI to the SELETAR River (1900 yards held by two brigades of the 18th Division), and thence along the NAVAL BASE (defended by the 11th Indian Division) to the CAUSEWAY exclusive. The Western Area held by the 8th Australian Division and the 44th Indian Infantry Brigade had the tremendous extent of coastline onwards to the JURONG River. The rest of the Island's coast was in the Southern Area under the Commander Singapore Fortress troops. The 12th and 53rd Infantry Brigades were the general reserve. *Sketch 'W'.*

In the 11th Division the 15th Brigade (later relieved by the 53rd Brigade) were on the right. The 28th Brigade was on the left, holding 6000 yards of water front from west side of the DOCKYARD to the CAUSEWAY. Beyond that were successively the 27th and 22nd Australian Brigades. The 8th Indian Infantry Brigade, which was all that remained of the original 9th Indian Division, now joined the 11th Division and was at first in reserve south of the NAVAL BASE. *Sketch 'X'.*

Immediately on crossing the CAUSEWAY the 1st/14th went to defend the extreme right of the 2/9th Gurkhas' frontage along the JOHORE STRAIT. This was the inlet immediately west of the NAVAL DOCKYARD. On the extreme left of Brigade touching the Australians at the CAUSEWAY were the 2nd/2nd Gurkha Rifles. Next day, 2nd February, the 5th/14th from reserve changed place with the 2nd/9th Gurkhas. The sister battalions were at last side by side, and amalgamation was carried out simultaneously with the strenuous preparation of beach defences. *Sketch 'X'.*

On 5th February the united Battalion changed places with the 2nd/9th Gurkhas and prepared for counter-attack while continuing to develop the reserve position south of the DOCKYARD. Battalion Headquarters was in some coolie huts near the SEMBAWANG Gate. The Japanese were by now in strength on the opposite shore of the STRAIT; but the only contact with them was in reconnaissances by boat, and these failed to obtain any important information. Hitherto there had been constant air attack, but from the 5th began artillery action which swelled to the heaviest bombardment in Japanese records. At first this was mainly directed against the DOCKYARD and other targets in the NAVAL BASE area, but significantly concentrations began to fall later on the Australians' front. There was an unchallenged observation balloon over JOHORE BAHRU from which the enemy could detect almost every daytime movement in the comparatively open country of the Brigade sector. Fuel tanks in the NAVAL BASE were burning, and hot oil rained from the sky.

The condition in which the Brigade found this obviously important sector of the Island's defences came as a great disappointment to all ranks. Not a trench had been dug, not a yard wired. There were no coastal guns. The NAVAL BASE, precipitately evacuated, was entirely unguarded and in a state of great confusion. There was still no support from the air. The troops were not to know of or imagine the difficulties and shortages; they only knew of SINGAPORE Island as a "fortress" with formations reserved for its defence. They had quitted the mainland with high hopes of going to prepared positions in a powerful defence which would be as successful as TOBRUK. That apparently nothing had been done in the past weeks, and that there was haste and confusion, caused a shock to morale which did not easily pass.

Amalgamation, no more than a proposal before KAMPAR, was now an obvious necessity. The combined unit of headquarters and four rifle companies was designated "14 Punjab". Officers apart, the united strength was but that of a single battalion. Specialist personnel were so few that there was no headquarter company. Major Fearon was in command until he met with an accident on 4th February. Major Morton, who had arrived with Captain Shahnawaz Khan from FEROZEPORE on the 3rd, officiated until the joining on 8th February of Lieutenant-Colonel MacAdam of the 8th Punjab Regiment who had been flown out from India. Baboo Ram was Subadar-Major. 'A' Company were Pathans, 'B' Company Sikhs and 'C' Company Punjabi Musalmans. 'D' Company (Dogras) under Captain Dara were attached to the 53rd Brigade from the 5th as a machine gun unit. This left only three companies for the earlier fighting.

The officers, shown by battalions of origin, were as follows :—

1st Battalion

Lieutenant-Colonel D.L.D. MacAdam	Commandant.
Major M. Z. Kiani	Back from hospital.
Major B. Morton	A Company.
Captain Shahnawaz Khan	B Company.
Captain A. I. S. Dara	D Company.
Captain E. F. Morrey	Quartermaster.
Lieutenant C. E. Corfield	Assistant Quartermaster.
Lieutenant H. G. V. Greer	Back from escape to SUMATRA.
Lieutenant R. Ward-Close.	

5th Battalion

Major S. P. Fearon	In hospital.
Captain D. B. Juneja	In hospital.
Captain H. B. Harpham	
Captain P. N. L. Dickson	
Captain R. J. S. Franks	
Lieutenant F. L. E. Davin	In hospital. Later HQ Malaya Command.
Lieutenant E. A. J. MacLaren	C Company. From the Independent Company.
Lieutenant E. J. Ellis.	
Lieutenant C. E. N. Hopkins Hussan.	
Lieutenant Johnson.	
Lieutenant C. C. Cavill	From the Federated Malaya States Volunteers.
Lieutenant B. F. Welsh	
Lieutenant P. Paxton-Harding	

The Invasion—9th February '42.

At midnight 8th/9th February Japanese forces who had embarked at JOHORE and up the SKUDAI River forced a landing on the front of the 22nd Australian Brigade and a little later near WOODLANDS, built up their strength and pressed inland. By the afternoon of the 9th they had captured TENGAH airfield. After dark the 44th Indian Infantry Brigade, including the 6th/14th under Lieutenant-Colonel Ingle, had to be withdrawn from the western coast to the JURONG River. During the same night the 27th Australian Brigade were forced back along the BUKIT TIMAH Road, surrendering their hold on the broken CAUSEWAY and WOODLANDS. Very soon afterwards the Japanese had the CAUSEWAY in use again. Till then there had been no contact with the enemy by the 11th Division.

Sketch 'X'.

Sketch 'W'.

Counterattack—10th and 11th February '42.

Sketch 'X'.

Now came counterattack. Early on 10th February 'C' Company of the Battalion in conjunction with the left of the 2nd 2nd Gurkhas were launched to oust the Japanese from hills "125" and "95" in the rubber estate country overlooking WOODLANDS and the road. For a long time there was no news of their progress. 'D' Company became available again, and Lieutenant Colonel MacAdam led them forward to assist 'C'. The latter company, it proved, had been seriously checked and had had Lieutenant MacLaren wounded. A renewed attack by the two companies during the afternoon gained hill "125"; but the Japanese still held "95" which was the vital one for commanding the road. After 'B' Company had come up to take over "125" the two companies tried again in the evening, but were finally held up by fire at an unclimbable steel fence enclosing this part of the NAVAL BASE area. A passage was forced after dark, and the enemy were found to have vacated their position. But meanwhile the 8th Brigade had been ordered to capture the hill from the south, and a dawn attack by the 1st Frontier Force Rifles had been staged. This was allowed to go in; whereafter the 14th took over and consolidated their old objective. By now the rest of the Battalion had moved west to this area.

Withdrawal to SINGAPORE—11th and 12th February '42.

Sketch 'W'.

But all this was in vain towards stopping the Japanese thrust into the island, because further south along the main road things had gone badly. During the night the Japanese had got tanks across the CAUSEWAY and launched them towards BUKIT TIMAH. Australian counterattacks there on the 11th were unsuccessful. The 15th Brigade in the same area were nearly decimated for the fifth time. Their remnants withdrew to join the 44th Brigade on the line of the road BUKIT TIMAH - PASIR PANJANG. The 11th Division must now finally destroy the DOCKYARD and leave the NAVAL BASE area, or else be cut off.

Sketch 'X'.

After being heavily sniped and mortared in their unenviable position throughout the 11th the Battalion successfully disengaged during that night, and with the rest of the 28th Brigade moved to cover in estates about NEE SOON. There, soon after dawn on the 12th, the Battalion received orders to transfer to the 8th Brigade (Brigadier Trott) and to move further back towards the City.

The last stand at BIDADARI — 12th-15th February '42.

A shortened perimeter was now to be manned through the residential areas and park land around the City of SINGAPORE.

Bombing and shell fire were intense. The Japanese were spreading over the island, but still exerted their principal strength along the main road. The last water reservoirs were falling into their hands, and the large, bewildered population of the city were threatened with thirst and pestilence on top of everything else.

The 8th Brigade were on the right of the 11th Division, holding from PAYA LEBAR airstrip to near WOODLEIGH, whence the 28th Brigade extended the line to the WIRELESS STATION. From there the 18th Division (now including the 53rd Brigade) held the most vital sector along ADAM ROAD up to the main road inclusive. Then the Australian Division took on as far as TANGLIN HALT, while the 44th and 1st Malayan Brigade completed the perimeter to the sea. On the other flank the 2nd Malayan Brigade filled the gap between the 8th Brigade and the sea at ST. PATRICK'S SCHOOL. *Sketch 'Y'.*

The Battalion faced north-east along the foremost crest of a low ridge just north of the PAYA LEBAR airstrip. Foreward, right to left, were 'D' Company at the airstrip, 'B' on the ridge at BIDADARI and 'A' on the left in the CEMETERY area. Company frontages were extremely wide for the enclosed country. 'C' Company in reserve were just south of the airstrip, and Battalion Headquarters in the one time REINFORCEMENT CAMP at BIDADARI. To the north west were the other forward battalions of the brigade, first the 2nd Baluch and then the 1st Frontier Force Rifles. Remnants of the 1st/8th Punjab, the Garhwalis and the Bahawalpur Infantry were in brigade reserve. The Manchesters of the 2nd Malayan Brigade were on the right of the 14th, but were very weak and widely dispersed.

On the 13th there was heavy bombing and shelling all along the line with the enemy concentrated against the 18th Division, who stood firm. Next day pressure spread to the 11th Division front, and at noon the Japanese attacked from the east. Heavy fighting followed, particularly at the point of junction with the 2nd Malayan Brigade. At 1400 hours the right forward locality of D Company was overrun, but was recaptured in an immediate counterattack led by Lieutenant Paxton-Harding. There was, however, serious penetration through the Manchesters, and all available reserves of the 8th Brigade, a squadron of the 3rd Cavalry and fifty men of the 3rd/16th Punjab were used to restore the situation. Tanks appeared, but were gallantly held at the Battalion's road block where MACPHERSON ROAD crossed the airstrip until anti-tank guns arrived. The attack died away at dusk, but the progress achieved by the enemy necessitated the brigade's line of resistance being brought back after dark to the MACPHERSON ROAD. Later during the night 'B' Company under Captain

Shahnawaz Khan repulsed a strong attack in which there was close quarter fighting with grenades. Lieutenant Paxton-Harding and his standing patrol who were forward during this attack were wiped out. Battalion Headquarters for the modified position was in ALAKAFF GARDENS.

Sketch Y.

On the 15th February the Japanese attacked the 2nd Baluch defences, but again failed. In the Battalion sector PETROL HILL was lost, but regained by the 3rd/16th detachment under Major BROWN. An afternoon attack on the 1st Frontier Force Rifles was defeated before it ever came to close quarters. The Battalion, the Brigade, the Division were full of spirit and restored confidence. They were less tired and more concentrated than in any previous action. They were not to know, even from the noise of furious battle, how much heavier was the fighting and critical the situation on the 18th Division front, or that the 1st Malayan Brigade had been pressed back from PASIR PANJANG to east of BUONA VISTA. They never imagined that consideration for the fate of helpless civilians was at this time leading the British Commander, Lieutenant-General Percival, to decide on terminating an ultimately hopeless situation. The ceasefire order at 1600 hours and capitulation at 2030 hours the same evening left everybody stupefied, from sepoy to Commandant. Realization of the inevitability of this came only later; for the regimental soldier's duty on the battlefield is bounded by his immediate surroundings. If there was any solace it came from knowledge of duty done and of capacity for more. The end as it came thus found all ranks of the 1st and 5th Battalions, and equally of the 6th Battalion close by, crouching obediently at their posts.

Interlude : 1942-46.

With this passing into captivity under the Japanese occurred the first break in the active life of the 1st Battalion 14th Punjab Regiment. Along with the 2nd Battalion at HONG KONG and the remnants of the 5th and 6th here at SINGAPORE the Sherdils now ceased to be on the effective strength of the Indian Army. It is therefore fitting that here shall end the firsty twenty chapters of their history. Later narrators with more sifted information and maturer reflection should tell of the transition into internment : of the three and a half years in captivity : of ill-treatment and slavery at the hands of the Japanese : of the torture of loyalty : of eventual recovery and repatriation to India after the collapse of Japan : and of the reconstitution of the 1st Battalion on the 16th May 1946 with previous titles and precedence.

Until a balanced account of the captivity comes to be written let it be generously remembered of those officers and men whose loyalty then failed or quailed under Japanese pressure, as happened more or less in many Indian units, that what they did or did not had no connection with their fine record of duty all through the trying days and nights of the Malayan operations. Be it also remembered that by the end of this tragic campaign the 1st/14th (apart from the 5th Battalion) had had 1738 ranks on their strength, and had lost 3 officers, 9 VCOs and 138 other ranks killed or presumed dead. Thereafter 120 men died in captivity.

APPENDIX A.

COLONELS, COMMANDANTS AND ADJUTANTS.

1st BATTALION, 14th PUNJAB REGIMENT.

(LATE XIX PUNJABIS.)

COLONELS.

Major-General J. RUGGLES, CB.
 13 May 1904 to 15 November 1920.

Major-General C. J. B. HAY, CB, GMG, CBE, DSO,
 p. s. c. 7 July 1929 to 1940.

COMMANDANTS.

Captain J. F. STAFFORD. (Later Hony Major-General).
 1 Aug 1857 to 1 Sep '75.

Lieutenant-Colonel J. RUGGLES, CB. (Later Hony Major-General).
 17 Sep 1875 to 1 Sep '76.

Brevet-Colonel E. B. CLAY. (Later Hony Major-General).
 15 Sep 1876 to 31 Dec '79.

Lieutenant-Colonel A. COPLAND, CB.
 1 Aug 1880 to 23 Jan '94.

Lieutenant-Colonel A. J. BRANDER. (Later Brevet-Colonel).
 24 Jan 1894 to 17 Nov 1900.

Lieutenant-Colonel A. H. WILMER.
 18 Nov 1900 to 3 Apr '05.

Lieutenant-Colonel L. N. HERBERT, CB. (Later Brigadier-General), 4 Apr 1905 to 3 Apr '12.

Lieutenant-Colonel T. Y. SEDDON. (Later Colonel).
 4 Apr 1912 to 22 Nov '16.

Lieutenant-Colonel G. A. DALE, CMG. (Later Brigadier-General).
 23 Nov 1916 to 18 Nov '18.

Major D. E. KNOLLYS, DSO. (Later Lieutenant-Colonel).
 Officiating from Dec 1917 to Apr '21.

Lieutenant-Colonel G. PENNEFATHER-EVANS, CBE.
> 19 Nov 1918 to 8 Nov '20.

Lieutenant-Colonel J. Y. TANCRED,
> Officiating from Apr 1921 to 18 Nov '21.

Brevet-Colonel C. J. B. HAY, CB, CMG, CBE, DSO, psc. (Later Major-General). 1 Mar 1921 to 30 Jun '23.

Lieutenant-Colonel C. C. R. MURPHY.
> 1 Jul 1923 to 1 Mar '24.

Lieutenant-Colonel J. C. MACRAE, DSO, psc. (Later Brigadier).
> 2 Mar 1924 to 31 Jan '26.

Lieutenant-Colonel D. B. ROSS, CSI, OBE, psc. (Later Brigadier).
> 1 Feb 1926 to 31 Jan '30.

Lieutenant-Colonel T. B. MINNIKEN.
> 1 Feb 1930 to 30 Jun '33.

Lieutenant-Colonel A. D. BENNETT, OBE, MC.
> 1 Jul 1933 to 25 Mar '37.

Lieutenant-Colonel A. B. CRADDOCK, CIE, OBE, psc.
> 26 Mar 1937 to 2 Apr '39.

Major L. V. FITZPATRICK,
> Officiating from 18 Mar 1937 to 15 Nov '37.

Brevet-Lieutenant-Colonel G. PIGOT, MC. (Later Brigadier).
> Officiating from 16 Nov 1937 to 2 Apr '39
>
> Commandant from 3 Apr 1939 to 2 Jan '40.

Lieutenant-Colonel L. V. FITZPATRICK.
> 3 Jan 1940 to 15 Feb '42.

Major V. D. W. ANDERSON. (Later Lieutenant-Colonel),
> Officiating from 12 Dec 1941 to 9 Jan '42.

Major S. P. FEARON,
> Officiating from 22 Jan 1942 to 7 Feb '42.

Lieutenant-Colonel D. L. D. MAC ADAM, Officiating from 8 Feb 1942 to 15 Feb '42.

ADJUTANTS.

Lieutenant A. GODBY,
> Officiating from raising in 1857.

Lieutenant T. E. VANDER GUCHT,
> Officiating in 1857.

Lieutenant J. C. P. BAILLIE (Later General).
   1857 to 1859.

Lieutenant A. COPLAND (Later Commandant).
   1859 to 1866.

Lieutenant C. H. BERGMAN (Later Major-General).
   1866 to 1871.

Sub-Lieutenant H. A. SAWYER (Later Colonel).
   1872 to 1874.

Lieutenant D. E. GOULDSBURY (Later Colonel).
   1874 to 1878.

Captain H. T. FAITHFUL (Later Colonel).
   1878 to 1885.

Lieutenant A. H. WILMER (Later Commandant).
   1885 to 1888.

Lieutenant G. J. FITZ. M. SOADY, CB. (Later Brigadier-General).
   1889 to 1895.

Lieutenant R. G. McPHERSON (Later Lieutenant-Colonel).
   1895 to 1899.

Lieutenant G. R. D. CHURCHILL, DSO. (Later Commandant, 2/XIX Punjabis). 1899 to 1903.

Lieutenant H. C. D. JARRETT (Later Lieutenant-Colonel).
   1903 to 1907.

Lieutenant J. Y. TANCRED (Later Lieutenant-Colonel).
   1907 to 1910.

Captain D. B. ROSS, CSI, OBE, psc. (Later Commandant).
   1910 to 1914.

Captain L. M. HEATH, KBE, CIE, DSO, MC. (Later Lieutenant-General). 1914 to 1918.

Captain R. F. G. ADAMS. Officiating from
   1917 to 1920.

Captain G. PIGOT, MC, psc. (Later Commandant).
   1920 to 1924.

Captain V. C. TWEEDY (Later Lieutenant-Colonel).
   1924 to 1927.

Captain F. ADAMS (Later Lieutenant-Colonel).
   1927 to 1931.

Captain V. D. W. ANDERSON. (Later Offg Comdt).
　　1931 to 1934.

Captain G. S. DHILLON (Later Colonel).
　　1934 to 1937.

Captain VIR SINGH (Later Major).
　　1937 to 1938.

Captain S. P. P. THORAT, DSO, sc. (Later Brigadier).
　　1938 to 1940.

Captain M. Z. KIANI.
　　1940 to 1941.

Captain HABIB-UR-REHMAN.
　　Dec 1941.

Lieutenant DICKIE.
　　Jan 1942.

APPENDIX 'B'

THE COLOURS.

1876 Colours.

These were presented nine years after the raising of the Regiment (1857), and are preserved in the Officers' Mess.

The King's Colour is the Union Jack with "XIX" in gold in the centre surmounted by the Imperial Crown.

The Regimental Colour is dark blue with a small Union Jack in the inner top corner. In the centre is "XIX" in gold encircled by "REGIMENT, PUNJAB NATIVE INFANTRY". These words are again encircled by a gold wreath of roses and thistles. Added later on a scroll at the foot are "AHMED KHEL" and "AFGHANISTAN 1878-80".

1896 Colours.

That the undermentioned Colours were in use in 1896 must be presumed from a clear painting of that date in the Officers' Mess. There is no actual record of their introduction or disposal.

The King's Colour was the Union Jack with "XIX" in gold in the centre, surmounted by the Imperial Crown and encircled by "PUNJAB INFANTRY".

The Regimental Colour was dark blue, quartered by a Crimson St. George's Cross. In the centre of the Cross was "XIX" in gold; encircled by "PUNJAB INFANTRY" and surmounted by the Imperial Crown. Outside these again was a gold wreath of roses and thistles which was flanked on the arms of the Cross by the Battle Honours "AHMED KHEL" and "AFGHANISTAN 1878'.

1908 Colours.

These are the present Colours, which were received on 24th January 1908 at JULLUNDUR from Major-General POLLOCK. The Battle Honours of the First World War were added in 1926.

The King's Colour is the Union Jack with "XIX" in gold centrally, encircled by "PUNJABIS" and surmounted by the Imperial Crown. The above are flanked by the First World War Battle Honours of the 14th Punjab Regiment :—"YPRES 1915". "FRANCE AND FLANDERS 1915", "CTESIPHON", "DEFENCE OF KUT-EL-AMARA", "NORTH-WEST FRONTIER 1915-17" "EGYPT 1915", "PALESTINE 1918", "MESOPOTAMIA 1914-18", "PERSIA 1915-1919", "EAST AFRICA 1916-18".

The Regimental Colour is dark mauve with "XIX" centrally and encircled by "PUNJABIS". Around these is a wreath of roses and thistles, and on top is the Imperial Crown. On the flanks are the Battle Honours of the 14th Punjab Regiment earned before and after the First World War, "TAKU FORTS", "PEKIN 1860", "ALI MASJID", "KANDAHAR 1880", "TEL-EL-KEBIR", "PUNJAB FRONTIER", "PEKIN 1900", "CHINA 1860-62", "ABYSSINIA", "AHMED KHEL", "AFGHANISTAN 1878-80", "EGYPT 1878-82", "MALAKAND", "CHINA 1900", "AFGHANISTAN 1919".

APPENDIX 'C'

MEDALS.

The following medals and clasps are in possession of the Officers' Mess: -

Medal	Clasp	Inscription
The Indian Mutiny, 1857-58.	Defence of LUCKNOW	Lieut. J. RUGGLES, 41st Regiment, N.I.
The Chinese War, 1860-62.	...	Capt. J. RUGGLES, 15th B.N.I.
The Burmese War, 1865.	BHOOTAN	Major J. RUGGLES, 19th N.I.
The Afghan War, 1878-80.	AHMED KHEL	Sep. WALI KHAN, 19th P.N.I.
The India Medal	BHOOTAN HAZARA 1891 SAMANA 1891 WAZIRISTAN, 1894-95.	Hav. ILAHI BAKSH, 19th Regiment, N.I.
Tibet, '03-'04.		234 Sep. ADAM KHAN, 19th Punjabis.
Indian General Service Medal	NWF 1908	2324 Spy. BUR SINGH.
Indian General Service Medal	AFGHANISTAN, NWF 1919.	2509 Spy. ZEARAT GUL, 1/19th Punjabis
The 1914-15 Star	...	1503 Spy. BHAGAT SINGH, 1/19th Punjabis.
The British War Medal, 1914-18.	...	Sepoy GANGA SINGH, 1/19th Punjabis.
The Victory Medal	...	...
Indian General Service Medal.	NWF 1935 NWF 1936-37	... ...

APPENDIX D.

HEADINGS FROM THE "CONTENTS" OF BATTALION STANDING ORDERS, 1940.

SECTION   B.S.O.

I.—OFFICERS AND WARRANT OFFICERS.

	B.S.O.
The Commanding Officer	1
The Second-in-Command (see also 434)	2
Company Commanders	3
The Adjutant	9
The Quartermaster	14
Platoon Commanders	16
Officers—General	18
The Transport Officer	29
The Treasure Chest Officer (see also 416)	30
The Battalion Sports Officer	31
The Captain-of-the-Week	33
The Orderly Officer	35
The Battallion Warrant Officer	37
Company Warrant Officers	42
The Quartermaster Warrant Officer	45
Warrant Officers—General	47

II.—NON-COMMISSIONED OFFICERS.

	B.S.O.
Quartermaster Havildars	51
Platoon Havildars	55
The Provost Havildar	58
Drum and Pipe Majors	60
Non-Commissioned Officers—General	64
The Battalion Orderly N.C.O.	71
Company Orderly N.C.Os.	74

III.—DISCIPLINE.

	B.S.O.
Turn Out	81
Bounds	87
Money and property	94
Personal Conduct	102

SECTION	B.S.O.
Private Arms	117
Complaints and Petitions	118
Investigation	126
Offences and punishments	131

IV.—GENERAL ADMINISTRATION.

	B.S.O.
Organisation	141
Employment—	
General	147
Battalion Police	148
Orderlies	149
Training Battalion	155
Followers	156
Promotion	161
Duties	168
Orders	180
Orderly Room and Durbar	186
Sick Parade	189
Roll-Call	191
Animal Transport	194
Mechanical Transport	199
The Drums and Pipes	202
The Warrant Officers' Mess	211
Messing—Other Ranks	217
Institutes	221
The Colours	226
Holidays	229
The Lines	231
The Family Lines	237
Visitors	239
Handing over	241

V.—DRESS AND CLOTHING.

	B.S.O.
General	251
Detail of Parade and Mufti articles	269
Detail of Officers' Mess Dress articles	303
Orders of Dress	

OFFICERS AND WARRANT OFFICERS—

	B.S.O.
Review Order	308
Drill Order	309

SECTION	B.S.O.
Marching Order	310
Mess Dress	311
Undress Order	312

N.C.Os. AND MEN—

Review Order	313
Drill Order	314
Duty Order	315
Marching Order	316
Fatigue Order	317
Physical Training dress	318
Walking-out Order	319

VI.—EQUIPMENT-ARMS-AMMUNITION.

EQUIPMENT AND GENERAL—

Accounting	321
Inspections	323
Locks and Keys	326
Storage	328
Loss and damage	332
M.T. STORES	335

ARMS—

Care of Arms	341
Safe custody by individuals	346
Sentries-over-Arms	348
Company armouries	350
Checking arms	361
Arms under repair	364
Arms in camps	366
Records	368

AMMUNITION—

Safety precautions	374
Safe custody of ammunition	375
Checking ammunition	389
Ammunition in camps	393
Accounting for ammunition	395
Collecting lead	399

| SECTION | B.S.O. |

VII.—ACCOUNTS.

Security	401
The Battalion Treasure Chest (see also 574)	413
The Treasure Chest Committee	415
The Treasure Chest Officer (see also 30)	416
Disbursement of Pay	418
Regimental deductions	420
Proficiency Pay	425
Accounting	427
The Accounts Officer (see also 2)	434
Regimental Funds	436
Co-operative and Thrift Society	439

VIII.—MISCELLANEOUS ADMINISTRATION.

Leave—
Officers	451
Warrant Officers and Other Ranks	462
Long Service—Reserve—Discharge	483
Recruiting	490
Child Welfare	496
Relief of Ex-Servicemen	498

IX.—OFFICE WORK.

General	501
Clerks	518
Records (see also 602)	526

X.—GUARDS—PIQUETS—PATROLS.

General—
Classification	541
Parading	542
Administration	548

Ceremonial Guards—
Guard Duties	553
Guard Orders	560
Guard Rooms	562
Inspecting Officers	570

SECTION	B.S.O.
The Quarterguard—	
General	573
Treasure Chests (see also 413)	574
The Keys Box	578
Protective Guards, Piquets and Patrols	583

XI.—TRAINING AND GAMES.

General—	
System	591
Records (see also 526)	602
Competition Trophies	605
Drill and Physical Training	607
Parades	616
Weapon Training—	
Precautions against accidents	626
Ammunition procedure	635
Firing-point procedure	637
General	639
Education	642
Games	650

XII.—MOVEMENTS

By Road—	
Marching	661
In Mechanical transport	673
By Rail	678
Camps	691

XIII.—ALARM DUTIES

General	701
Fire Alarm—	
Preparation	708
Warning	711
Action	716

SECTION					B.S.O.

General Alarm—

Preparation	..	..	..	726
Warning ..	..	..	..	729
Action ..	..	..	..	732

XIV.—THE OFFICERS' MESS

General	..	..	..	..	741
Management ..	..	..	..	742
Accounts	..	..	..	..	754
Discipline	..	..	..	..	764

APPENDIX B.S.O.

A.—Some Administrative Responsibilities of the Commanding Officer	1
B.—Duties of the Quartermaster	15
C.—Captain-of-the Week's Report	33
D.—Orderly Officer's Report	35
E.—Qualifications Necessary for Promotion and Appointments	66
F.—Organisation of the Battalion	141
G.—Periods of Non-Permanent Special Employment.	144
H.—Normal Distribution of W.Os. & N.C.Os.	162
I.—Duty Demand	168
J.—Guard Roll	168
K.—Standing Orders required to be read at Roll-Call from time to time	184
L.—Form and Rules for keeping the Platoon Messing Fund Accounts	218
M.—Handing-over Certificate "A"	241
N.—Handing-over Certificate "B"	241
O.—Clothing and necessaries for N.C.Os. and other ranks	253
P.—Clothing and necessaries for followers	253
Q.—Office records to be inspected by the commanding officer in the first month of each quarter	532
R.—Time-limits for the destruction of documents	535
S.—Guard mounting report	76
T.—Guard standing orders	560
U.—Personnel excused parades	623
V.—A brief history of the Battalion	644
W.—Colonels, Commandants and Adjutants ..	

APPENDIX 'E'

STATIONS

Also Campaign Areas and Foreign Countries.

Notes. (*a*) Locations for operations and training for less than two months are not shown, unless they are cantonments.

(*b*) The stations of the Depot and of major detachments are included.

Locations	1758-1880	1881-1900	1901-1921	1922-1942
Afghanistan	1841-42, 1878-80	..	1919	..
Agra	1863-64, 1857	..	..	..
Aligarh	1864-67	..	..	..
Ambala	1857	..	..	..
Amritsar	1845, 1848, 1850-57	1884-88	..	..
Annekovo (USSR)	..	..	1918-19	..
Attock Fort	1874	..	..	..
Aurangabad	..	..	..	1929-34
Bairam Ali (USSR)	..	..	1918-19	..
Bannu	1851-56	..	..	1938-40
Bhutan	1865-66	..	..	..
Birjand (Persia)	..	..	1915-18	..
Black Mountain	..	1891	..	..
Chakdara	..	1898-99	1912-14	..
Chittagong	1758	..	..	..
Chumbi (Tibet)	..	..	1904	..
Dargai	..	1898-99	1912-14	..
Dehan-i-Baghi (Persia)	..	..	1915-18	..
Delhi	1857	..	..	..

Locations	1758-1880	1881-1900	1901-1921	1922-1942
Dera Ismail Khan	..	1894-96	1909-11	..
Draband	..	1894-96	..	..
Fatehgarh	1858, 1864-67	..	..	..
Ferozepore	..	1864-67	1903-04	..
Fort Sandeman	..	1891-93	..	..
Gangetic Doab	1857	..	..	..
Ghariom	..	..	..	1937
Girni	..	1894-96	..	..
Gulistan	1878	..	..	..
Gurdaspur	1857	..	..	..
Gwalior	1862-63	..	..	..
Harnai	..	..	1914-15	..
Hirok	..	..	1914-15	..
Hyderabad (Sind)	..	..	1916-19	..
Jaffa (Palestine)	..	..	..	1922
Jamrud	..	..	..	1934-35
Jandola	..	1895-96	1909-11	..
Jatta	..	1894-95	..	..
Jerusalem (Palestine)	..	..	..	1923
Jhelum	..	..	..	1935-37
Jullundur	1859-61	..	1904-08	1921
Julpesh	1865	..	..	..
Kaakha (USSR)	..	..	1918	..
Kabul (Afghanistan)	1842, 1880	..	..	..
Kacha	..	..	1915-18	..
Khajuri Kach	..	1894-96	..	..

Locations	1758-1880	1881-1900	1901-1921	1922-1942
Kandahar (Afghanistan)	1879-80	..	..	..
Kangra	1857	..	..	..
Karachi	..	..	1919-20	..
Kashmir	1814, 1819	..	..	..
Khojak Pass	1879	..	..	..
Khushdil Khan	1878	..	..	..
Khwash (Persia)	..	..	1916-18	..
Kila Abdulla	1875	..	..	..
Kohat	..	1900	1901-02	..
Lahore Cantonment	..	1883, 1887-90	..	..
Landi Khana	..	..	1921	..
Landi Kotal	..	..	1921	..
Logar Valley (Afghanistan)	1880	..	..	..
Loralai	1878	..	..	..
Malakand	..	..	1912	..
Manjhi	..	1894-96	..	..
Malaya	..	..	..	1941-42
Manzai	..	..	..	1927-29
Mardan	..	1898	..	..
Mastung	..	..	1914-15	..
Meerut	1857, 1861-62	..	..	..
Merv (USSR)	..	..	1918-19	..
Meshed (Persia)	..	..	1918-19	..
Mian Meer (Lahore Cantonment)	..	1833, 1878-90	..	..
Mir Ali	..	..	..	1937-38

Locations	1758-1880	1881-1900	1901-1921	1922-1942
Miranzai	..	1891	..	..
Mohmand	..	..	1908	1935
Morar (Gwalior)	1862-63	..	..	..
Multan	1875	1887-90, 1893-94, 1896-91	..	..
Nasratabad (Persia)	..	..	1915-18	..
Neh (Persia)	..	..	1915-18	..
Nepal Tarai	1858	..	..	..
Nili Kach	..	1894-96	..	..
Oude	1858	..	..	..
Pachmarhi	..	..	..	1923-24
Palestine	..	..	..	1922-23
Parachinar	..	..	1901-02	..
Persia	..	..	1915-18	..
Peshawar	1868	..	1908, 1920-21	..
Phari Jong (Tibet)	..	..	1904	..
Phillaur	1875	..	..	..
Quetta	1872-79	..	1914-16	..
Rawalpindi	1868, 1873	1885, 1890-91	1905	..
Sadda	..	..	1901-02	..
Samana	..	1891	..	..
Sarafand (Palestine)	..	..	..	1922-23
Saugor	..	..	..	1923-27
Secunderabad	..	..	..	1940-41
Shagai	..	..	..	1934

Locations	1758-1880	1881-1900	1901-1921	1922-1942
Sialkot	1880	1881-83 1898-1900	..	..
Sungei Patani (Malaya)	..	..	..	1941
Tal (Baluchistan)	1879-80	..	..	..
Talagang	1871-75	..	..	..
Tanjong Pau (Malaya)	..	..	..	1941
Tank	..	1894-96	..	..
Thal	..	..	1901-02	..
Tibet	..	..	1904	..
Transcaspia (USSR)	..	..	1918-19	..
Waziristan	..	1894	..	1927-29 1937-38
Zam	..	1894-96	..	..

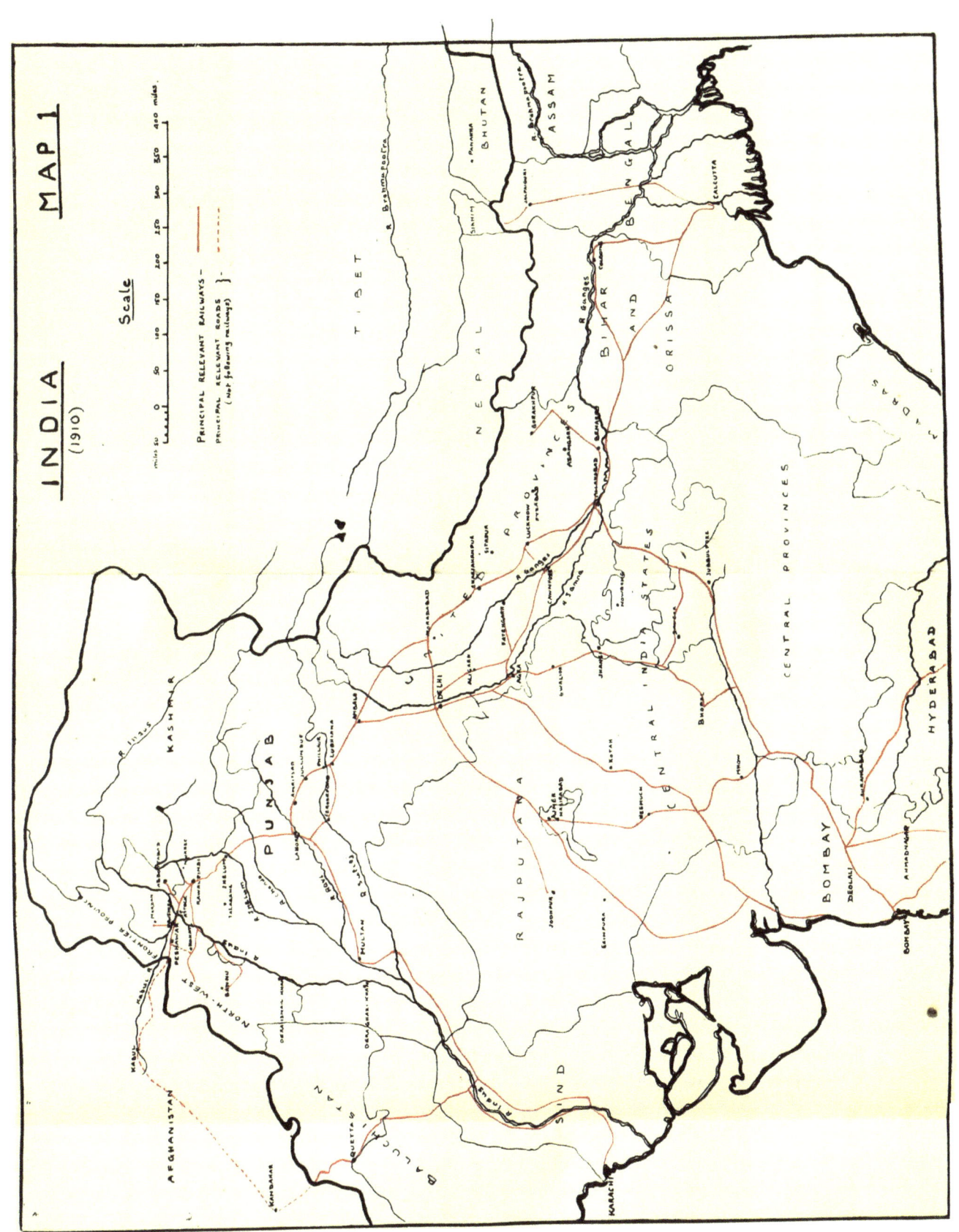

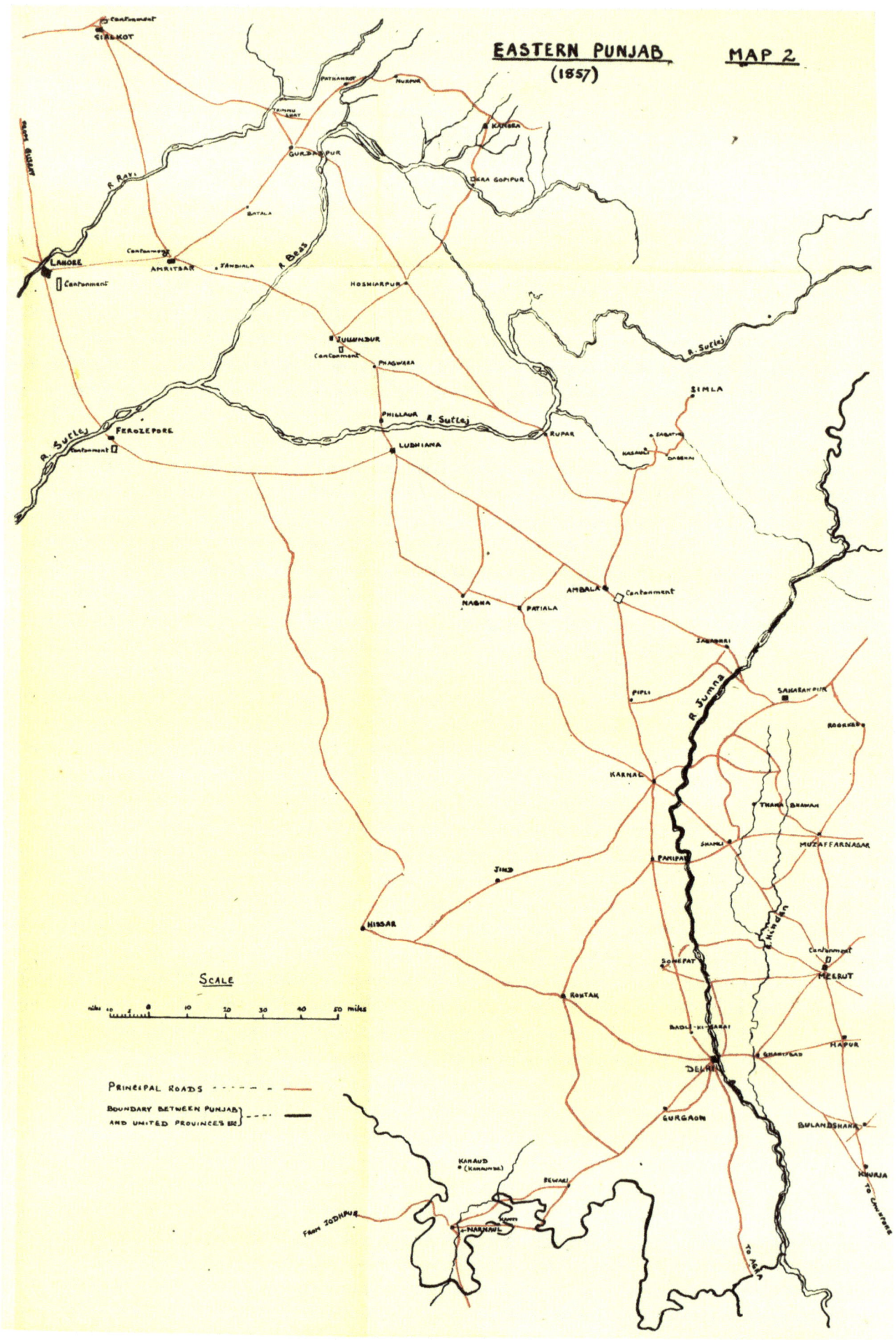

MAP 3

UNITED PROVINCES
(1857)

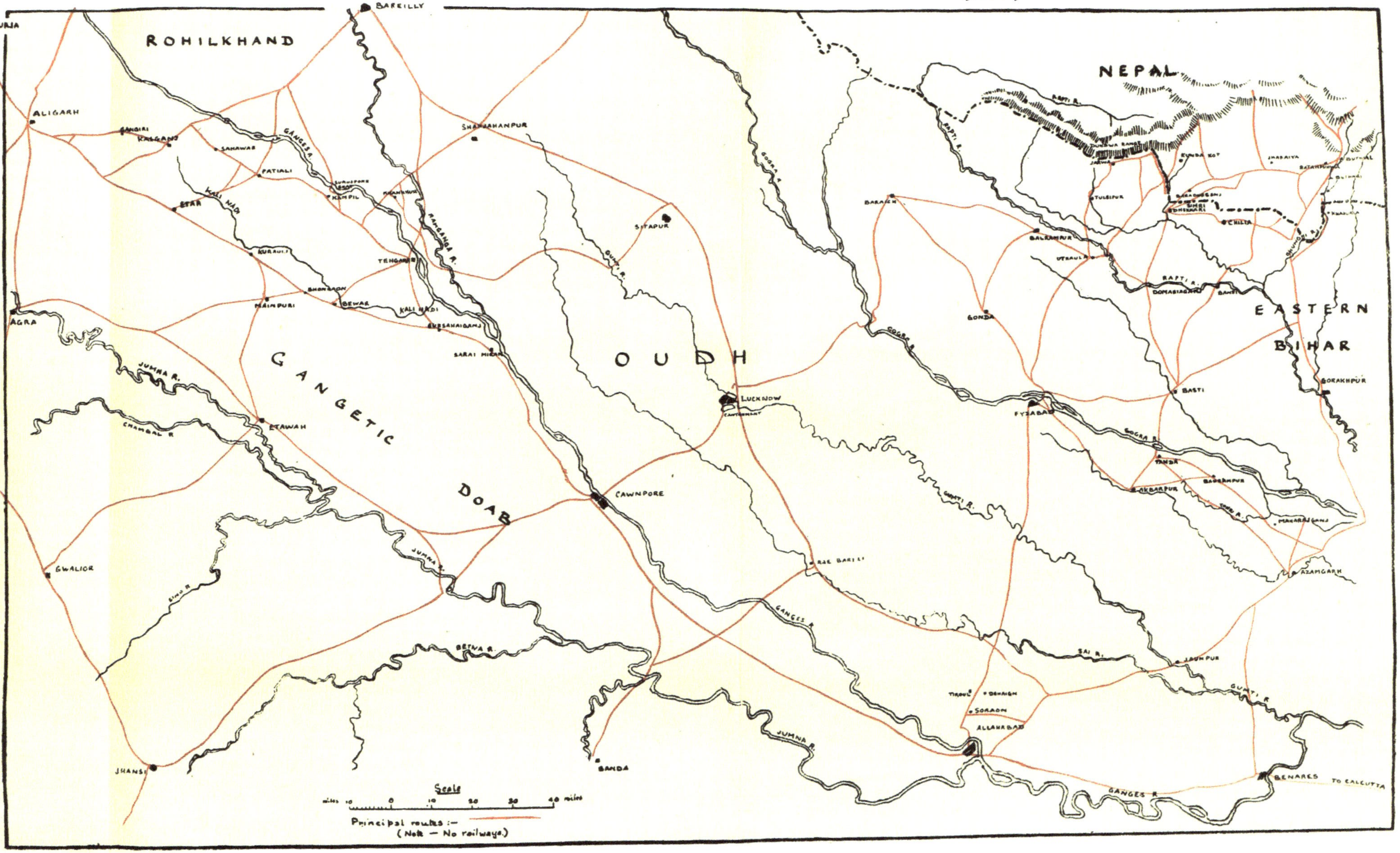

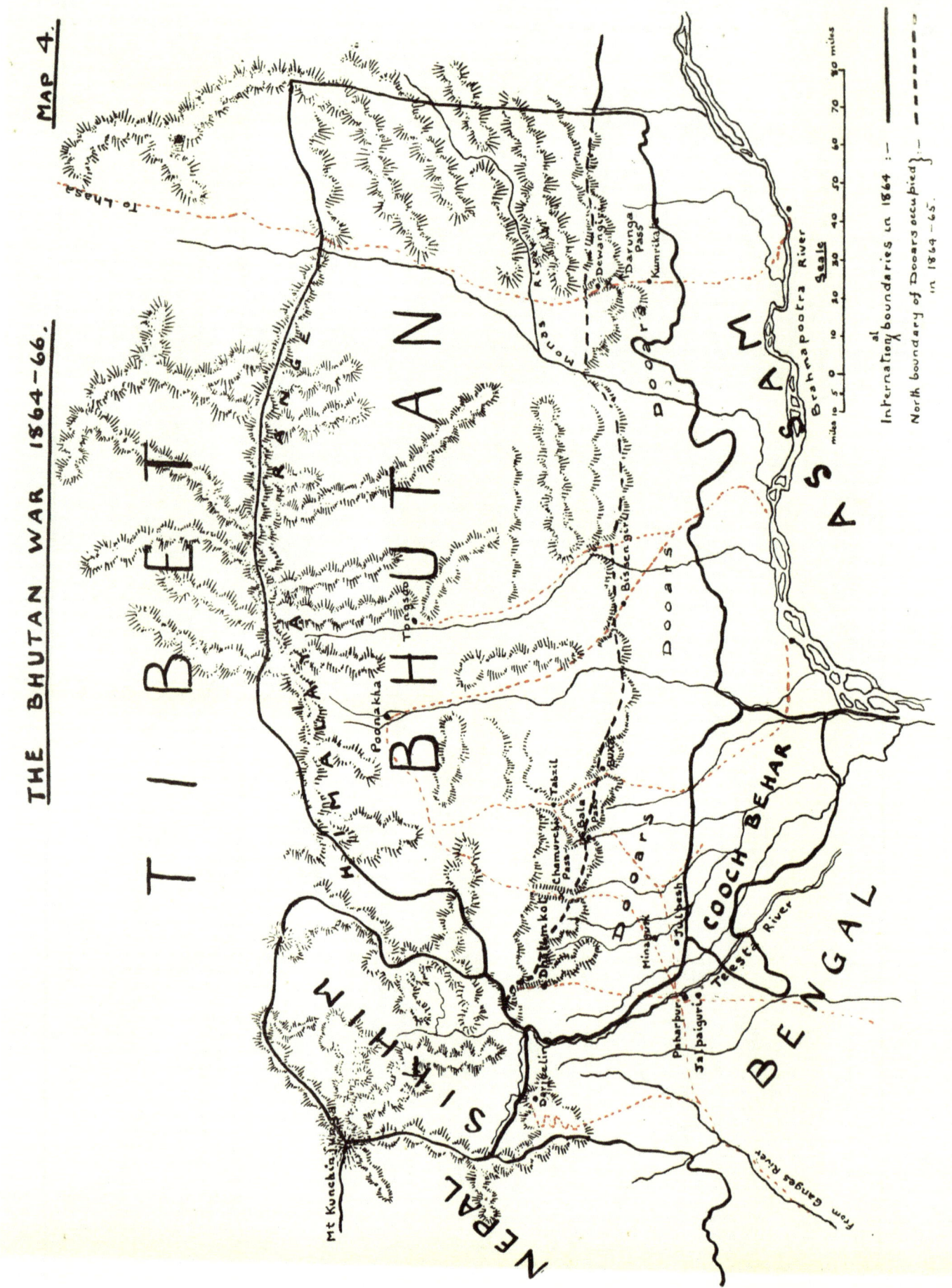

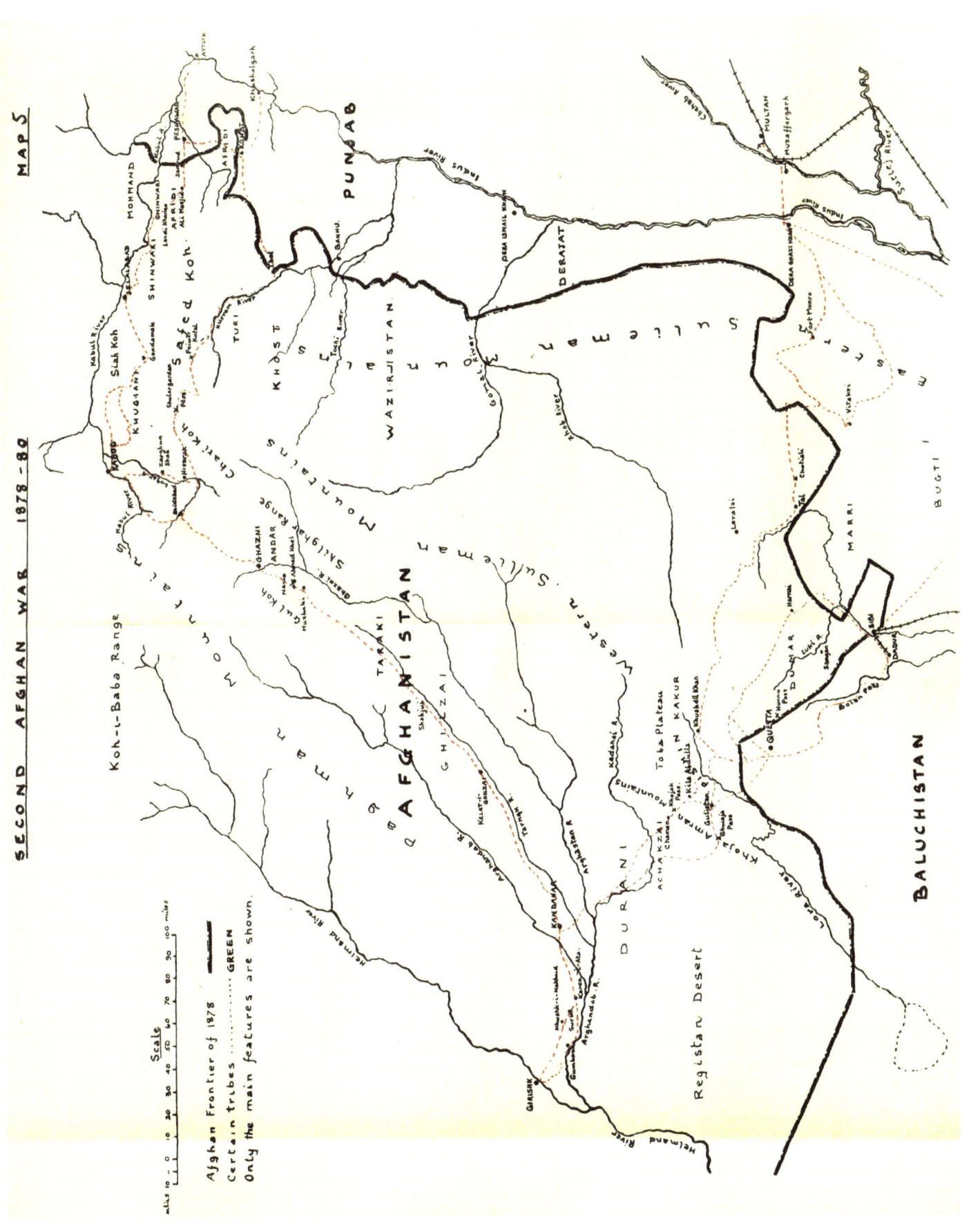

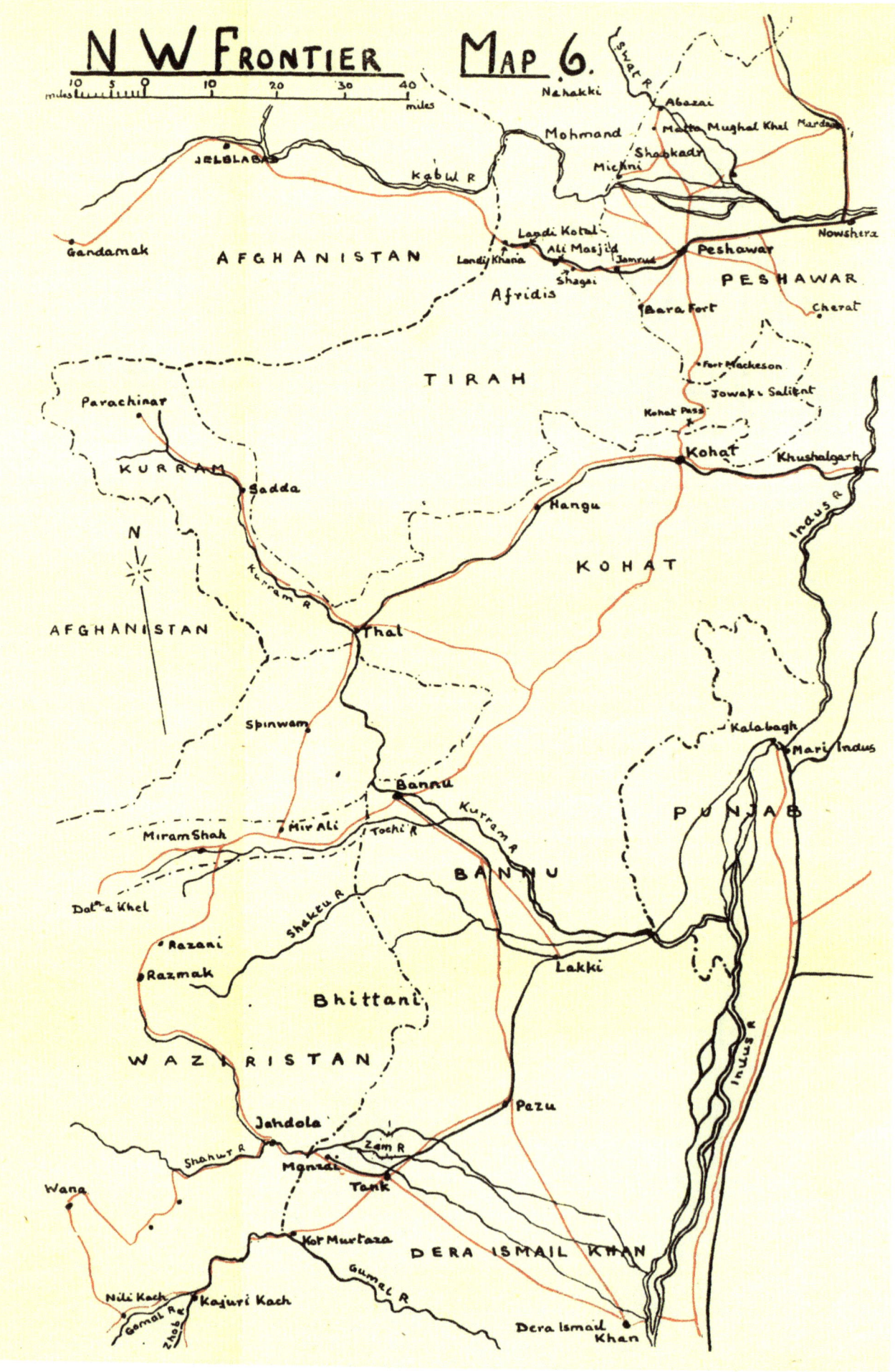

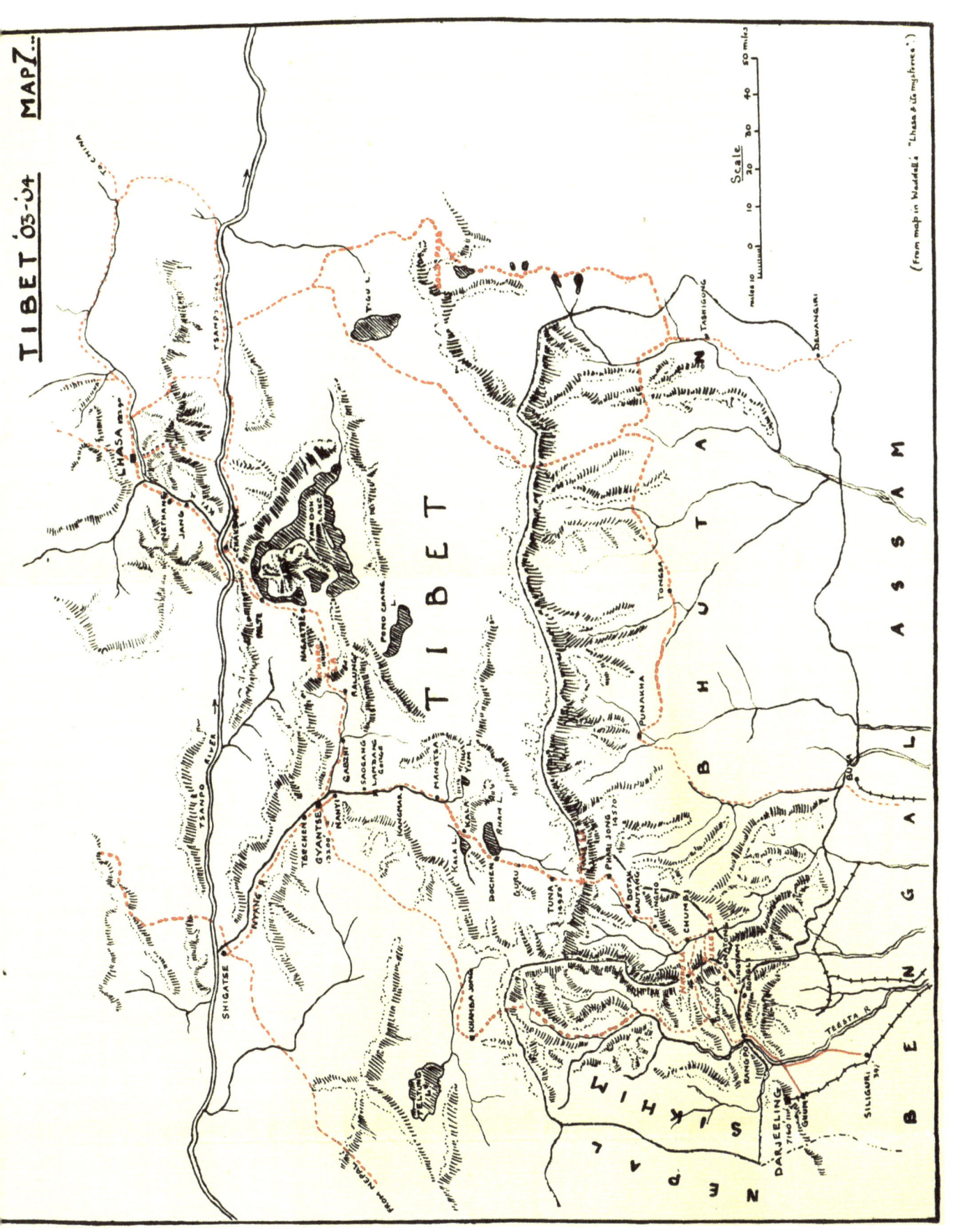

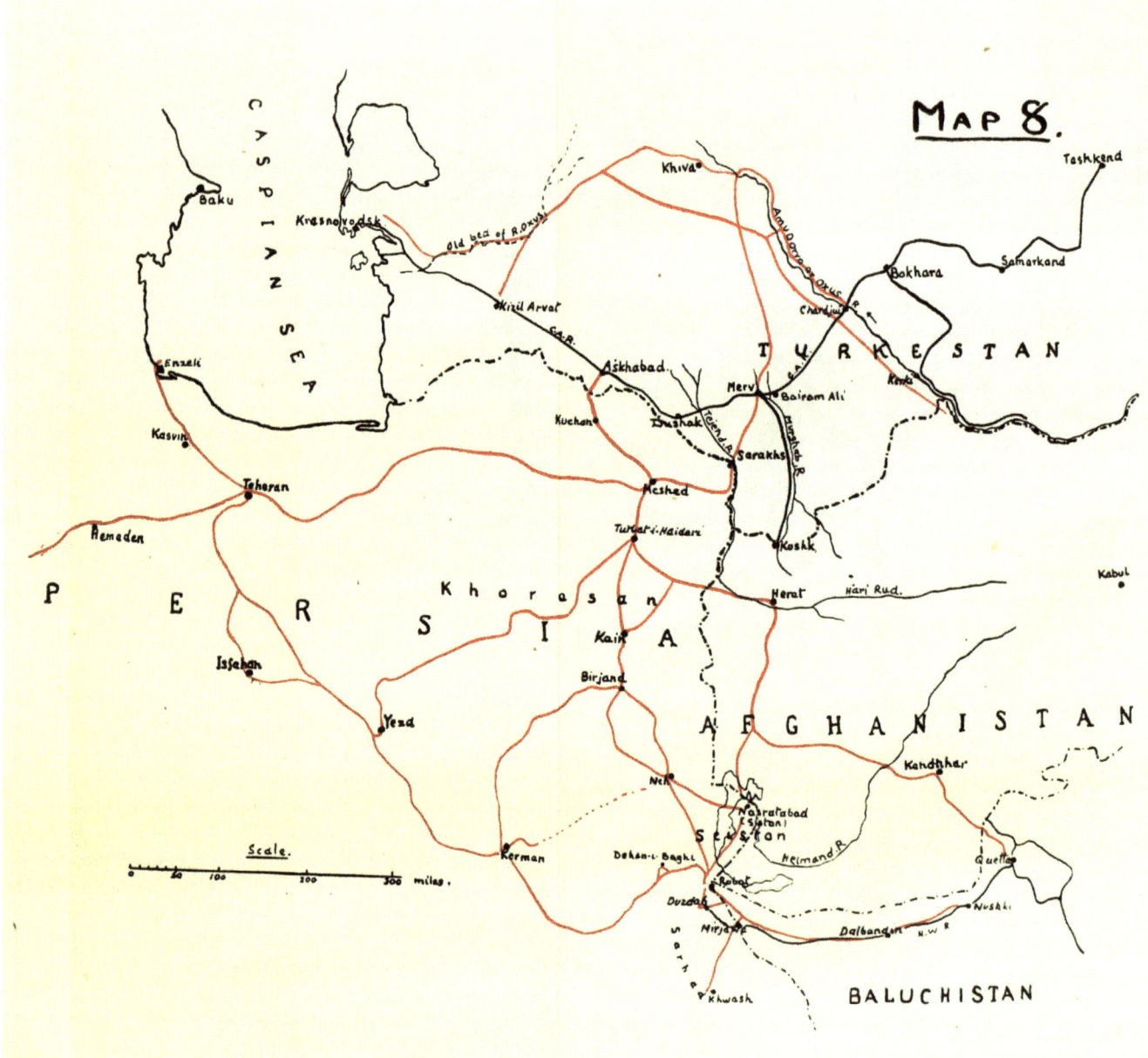

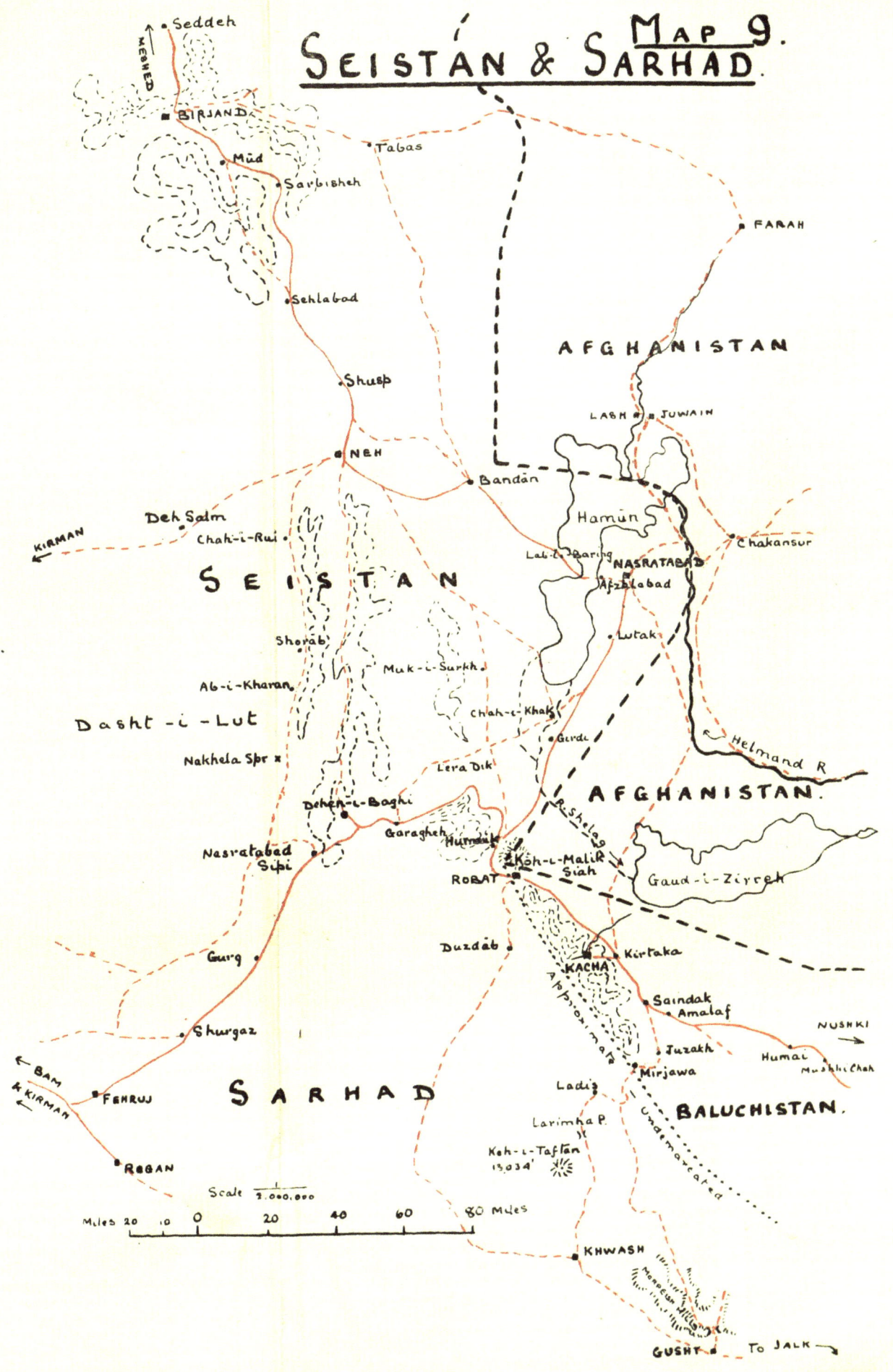

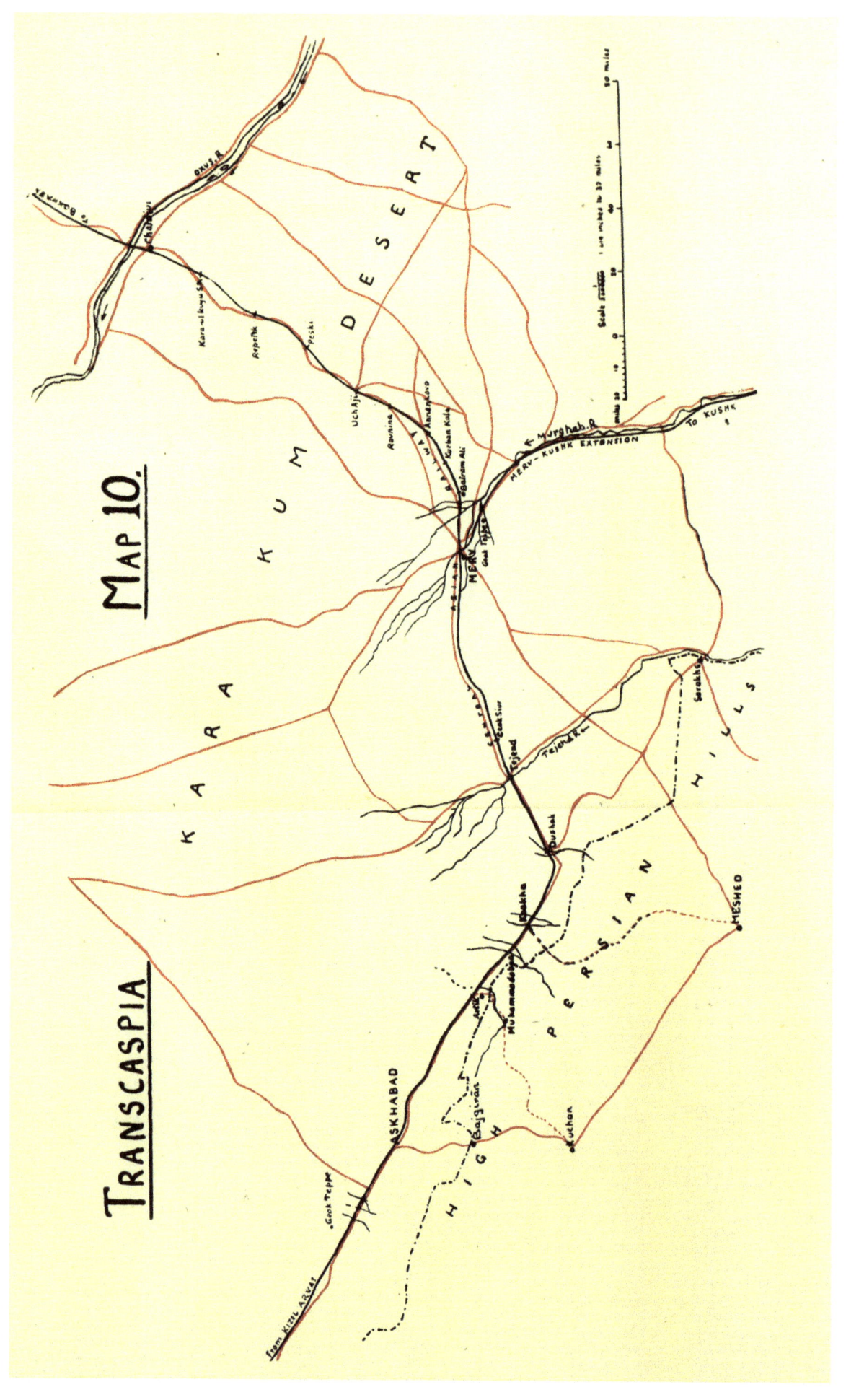

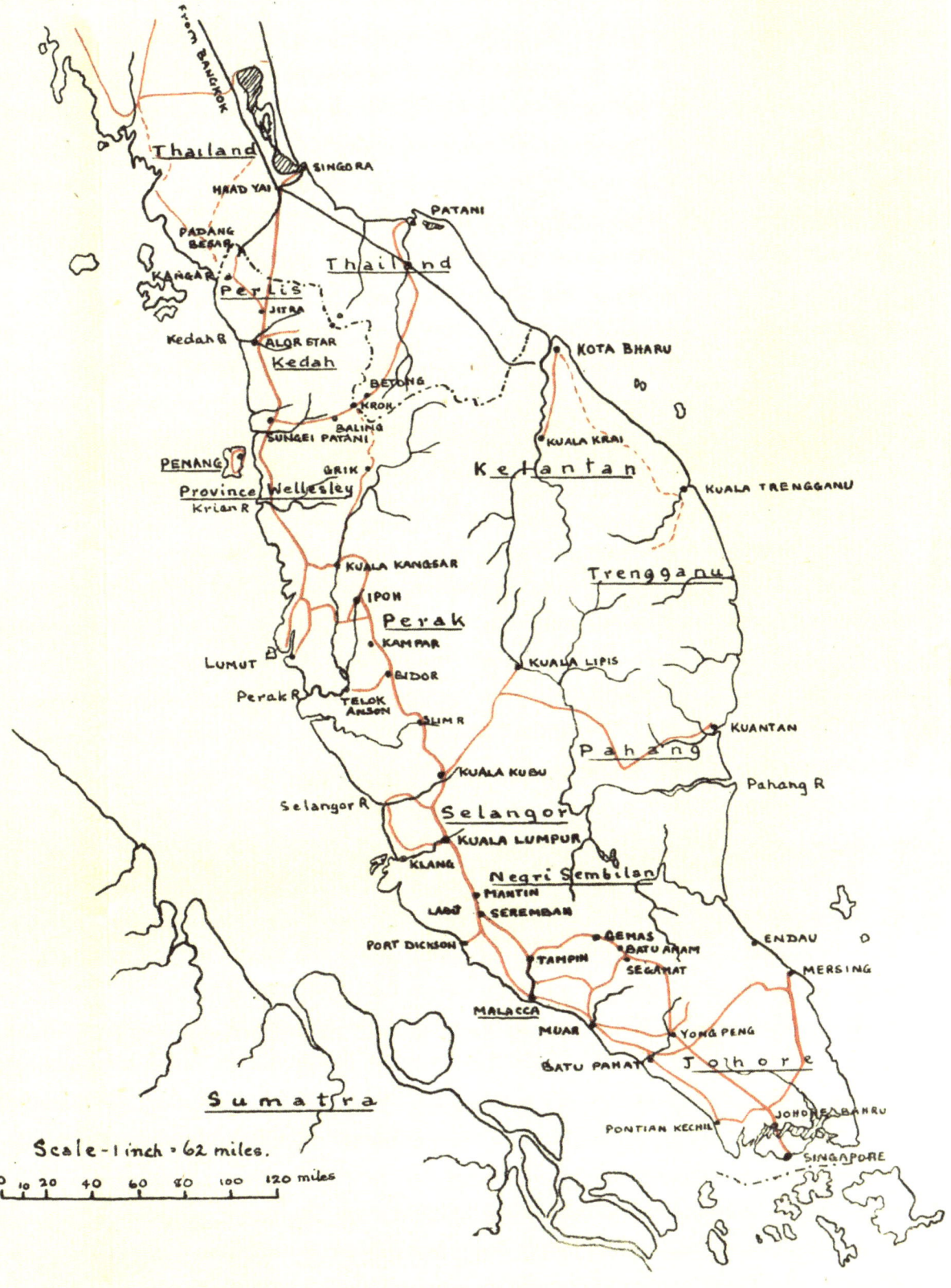

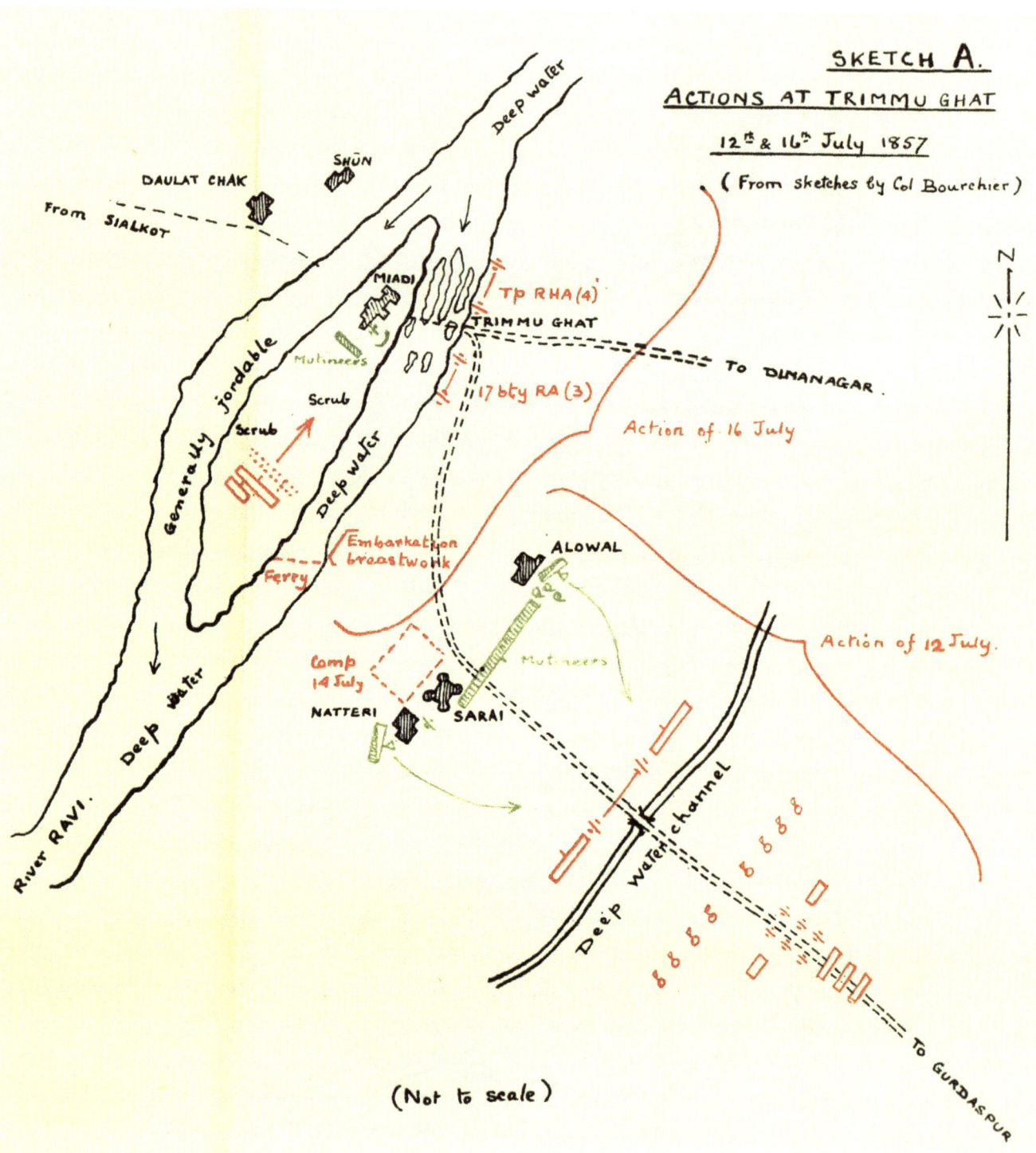

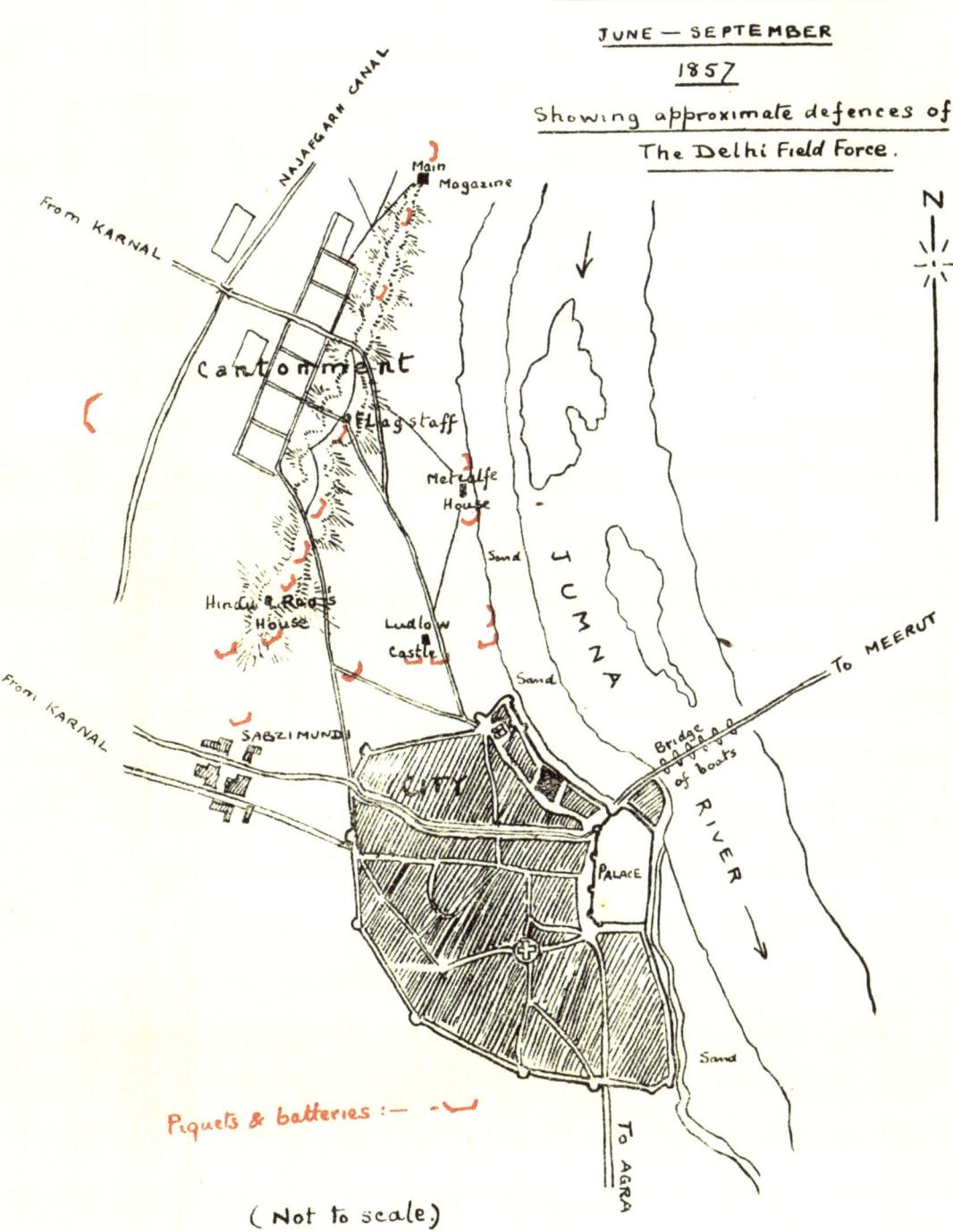

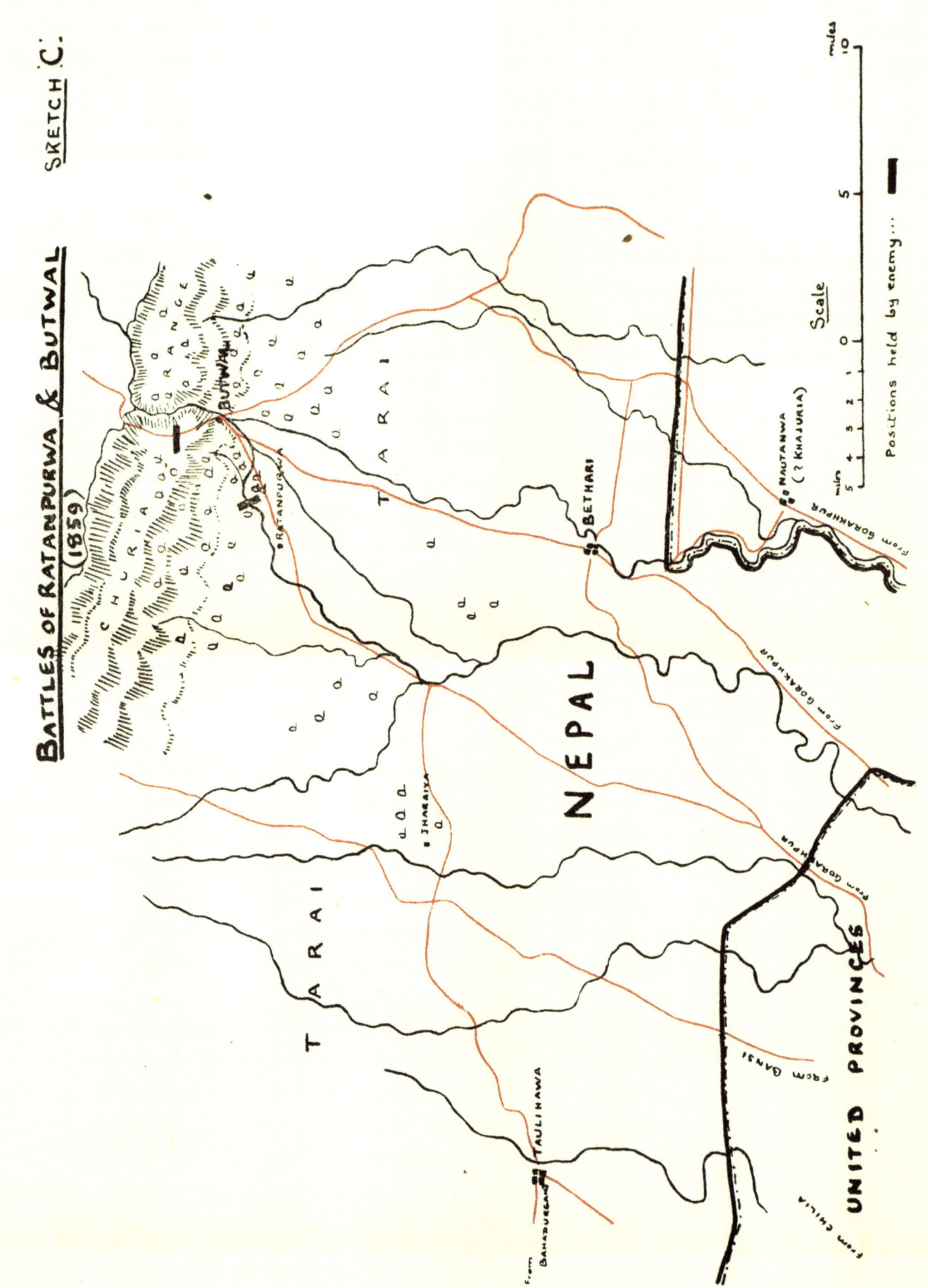

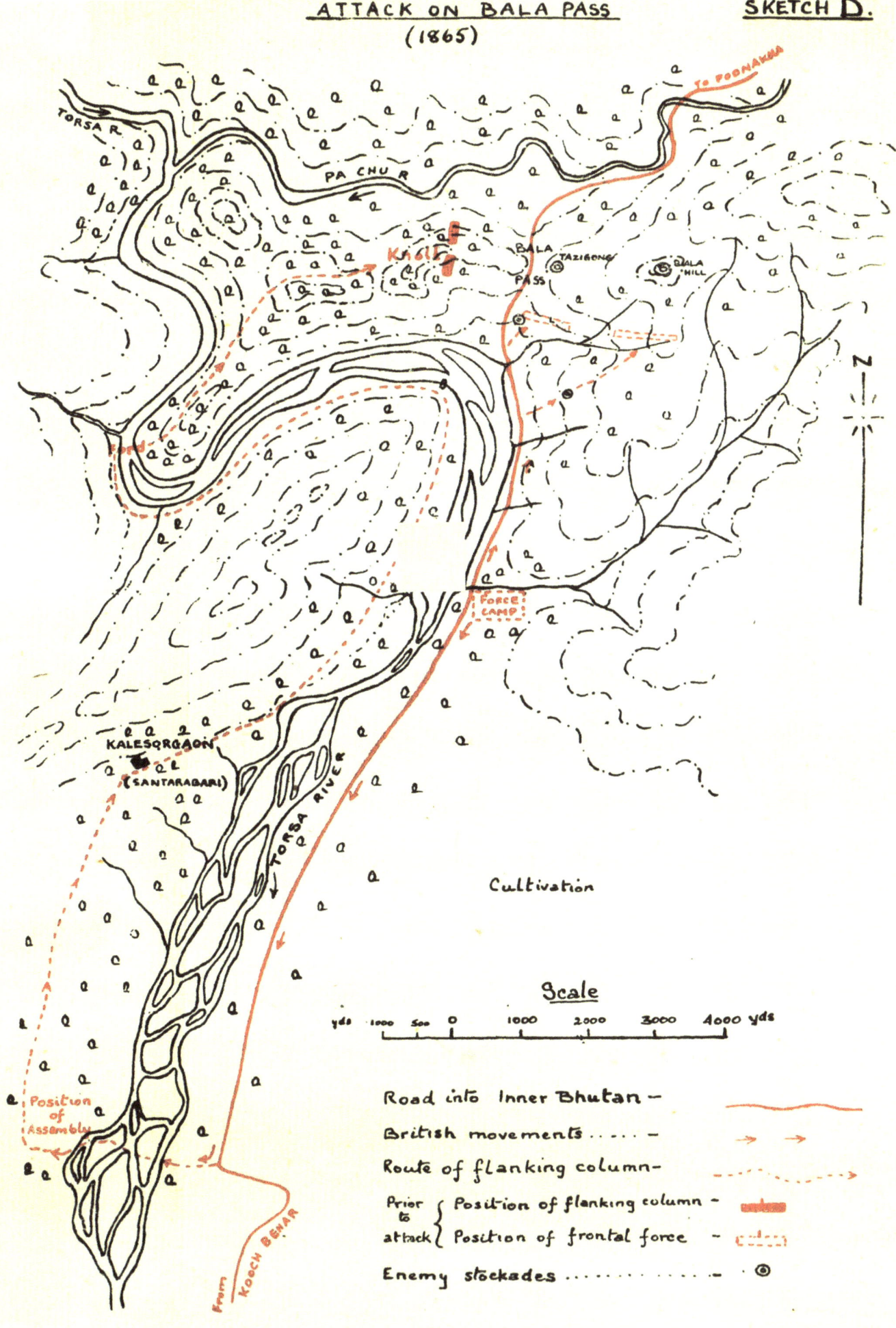

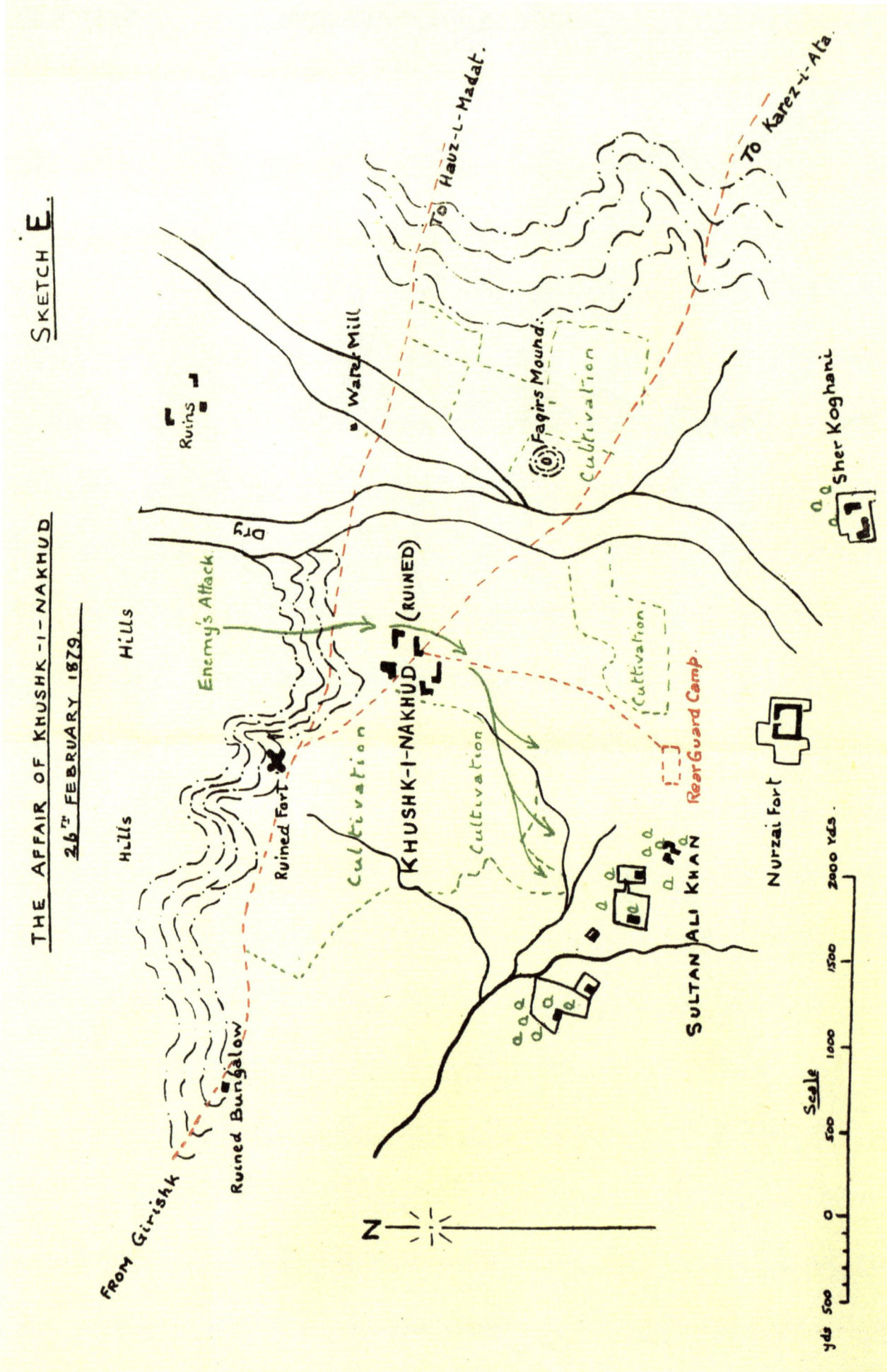

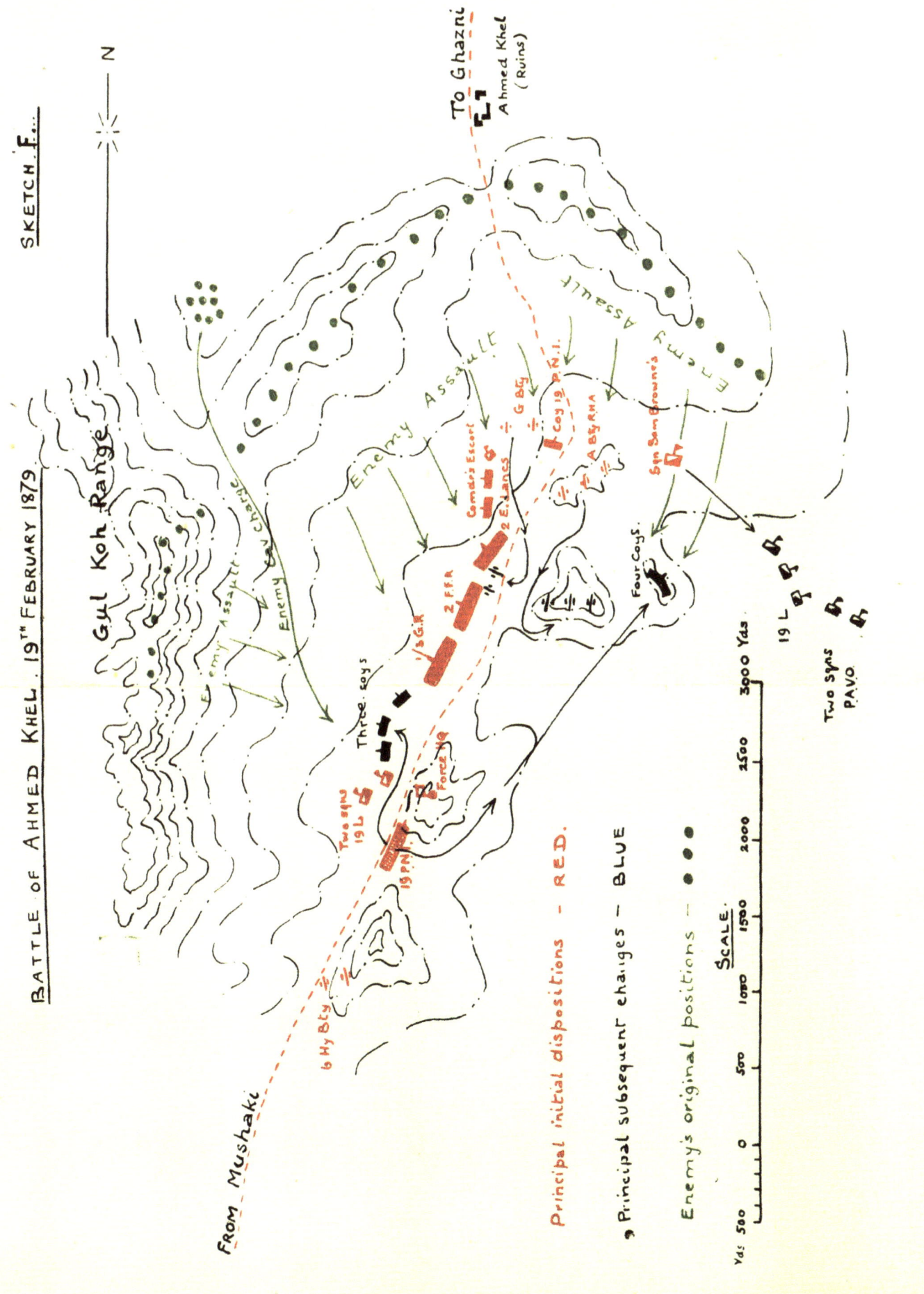

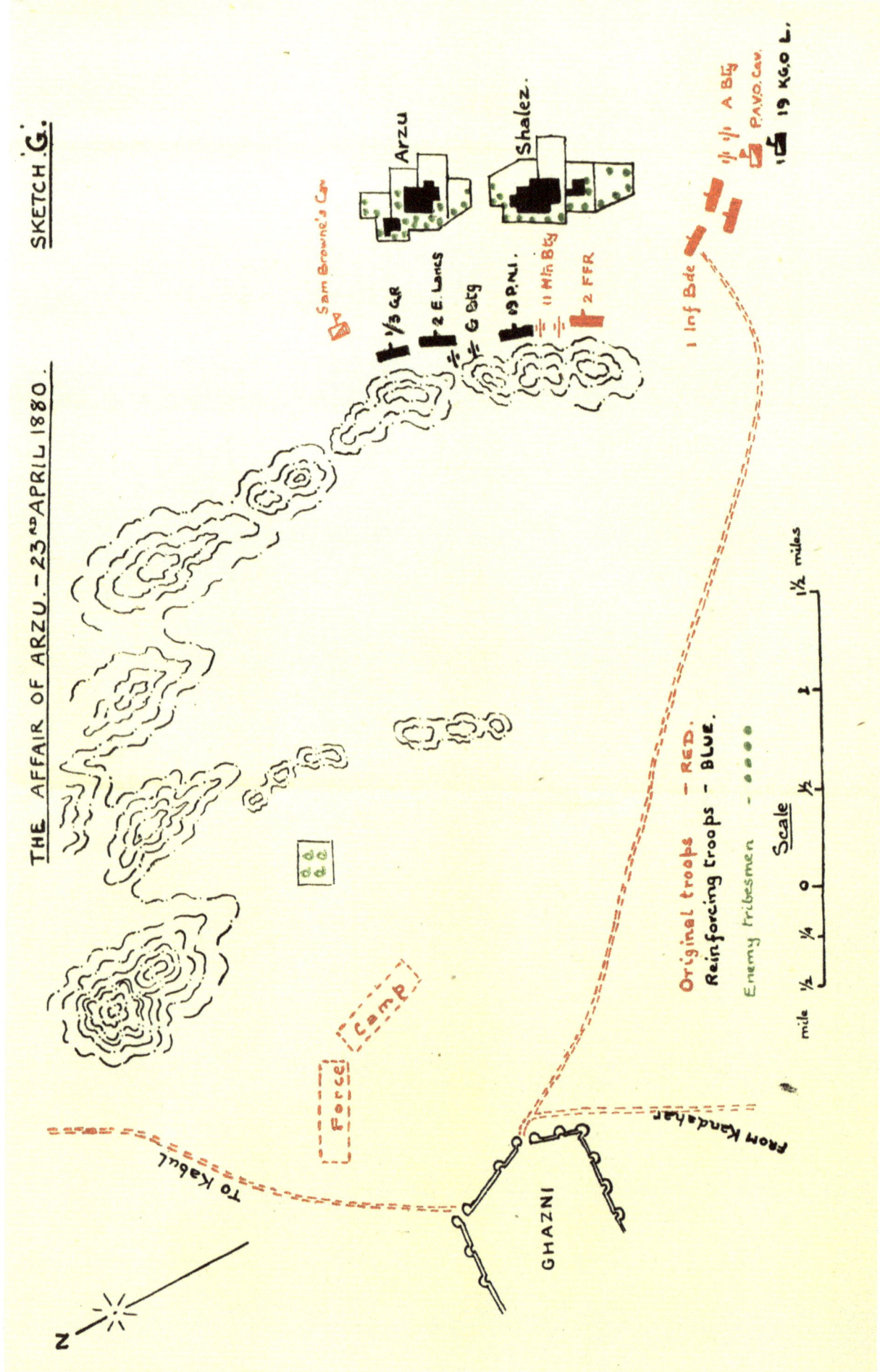

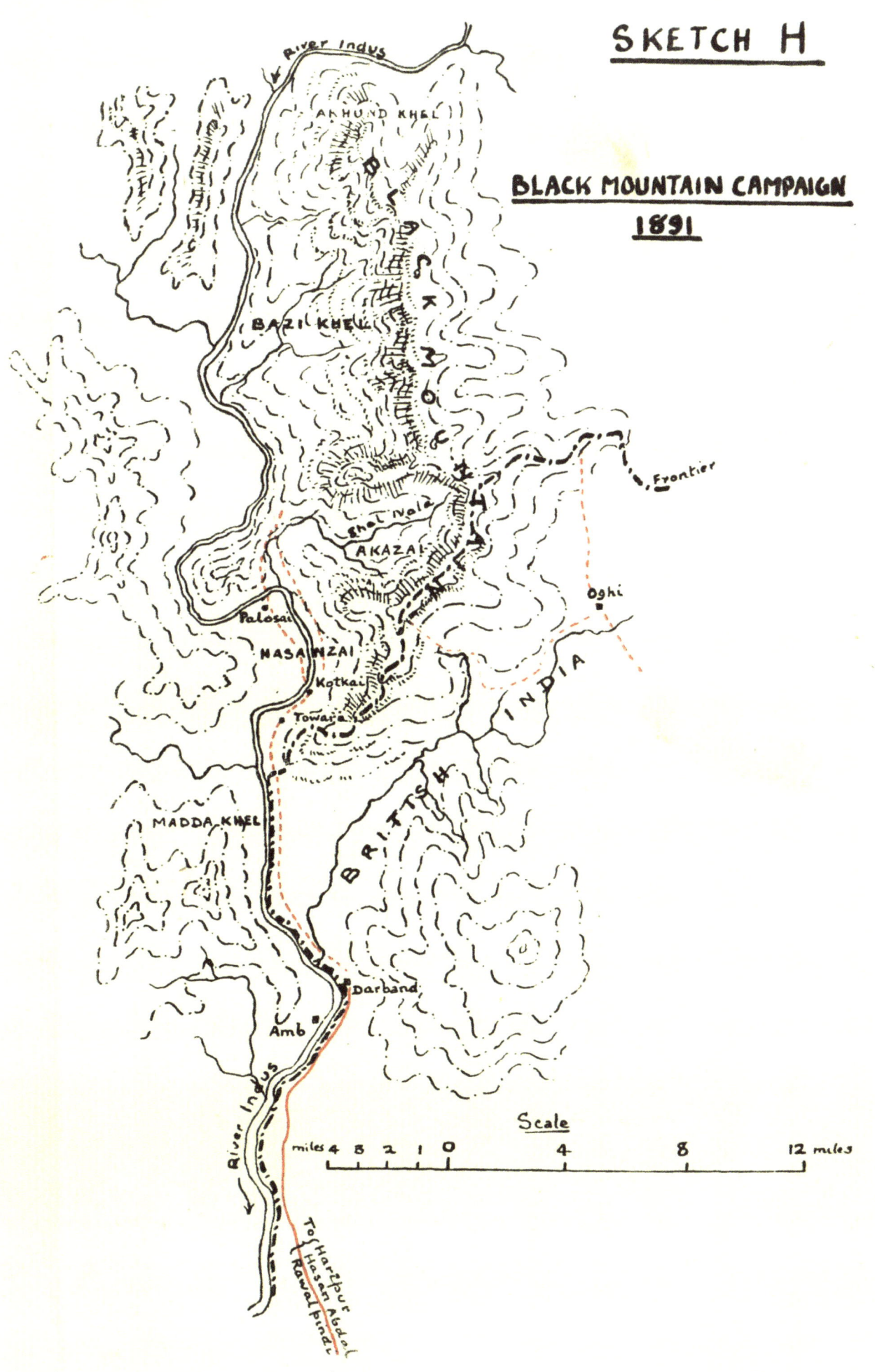

SKETCH J
SECOND MIRANZAI EXPEDITION 1891

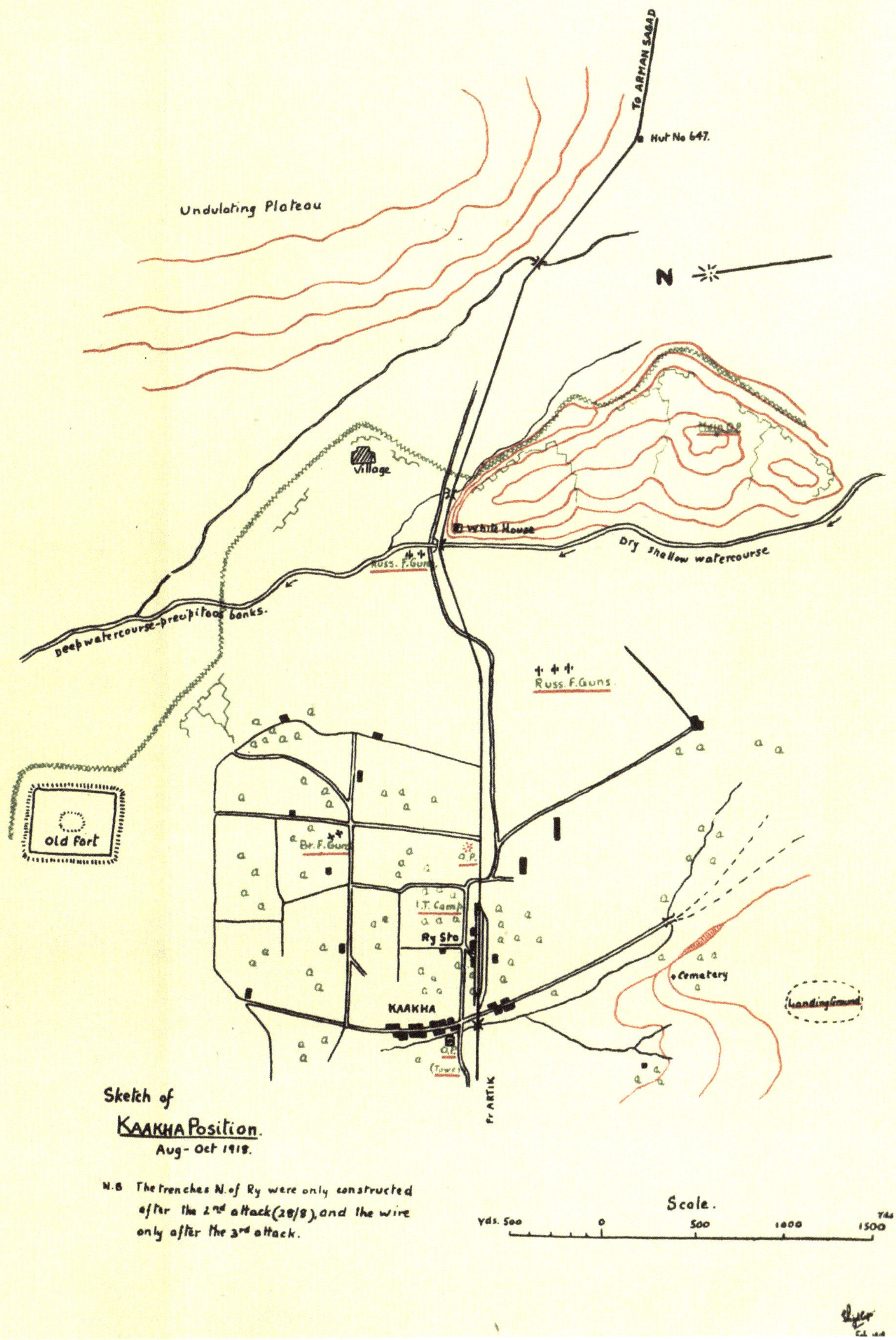

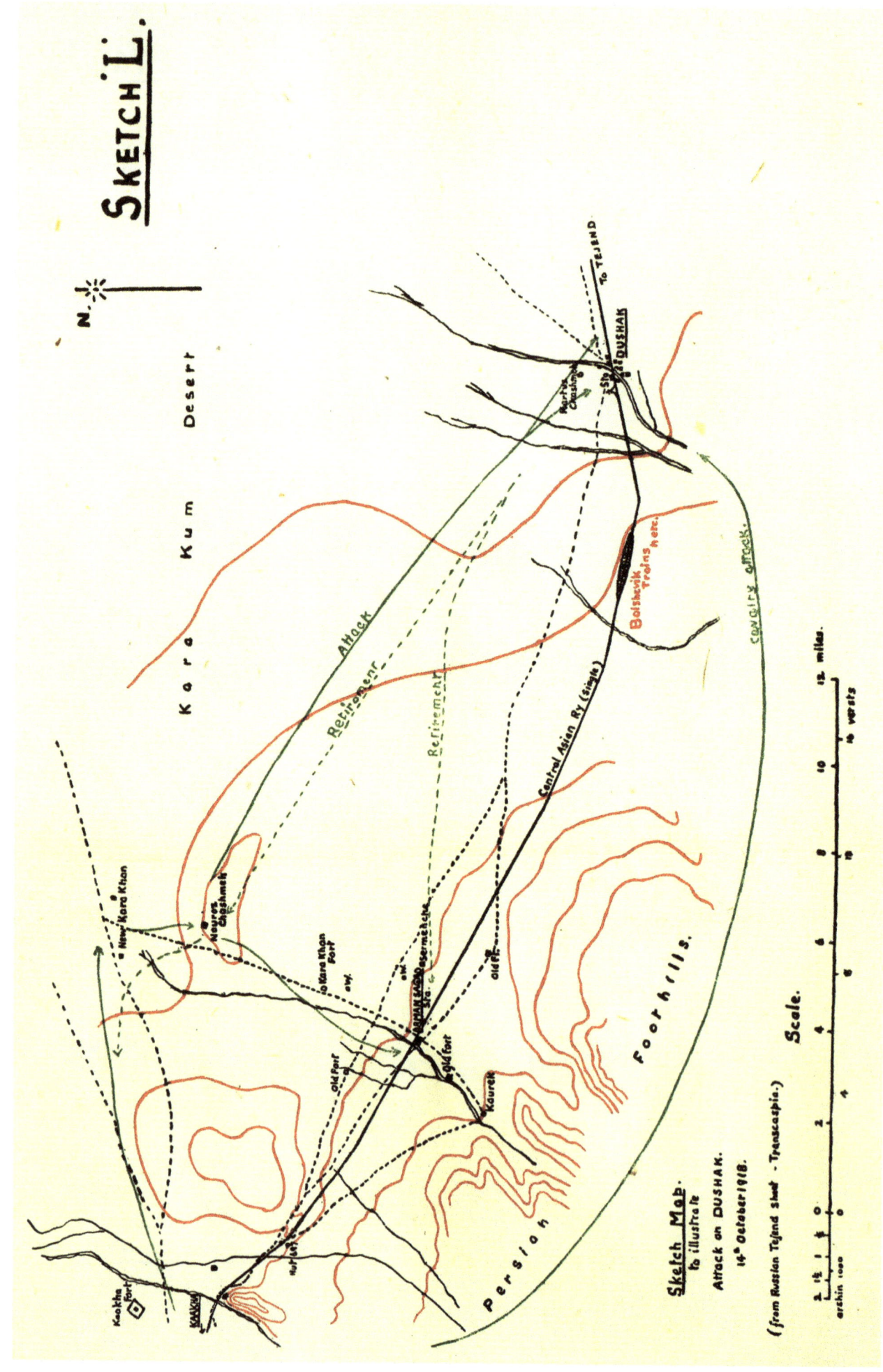

Sketch M.

Sketch Map.
to illustrate dispositions
during action on 16.1.1919
at ANNENKOVO position.

Approx Scale – 3 inches = 1 mile

Labels and annotations on map:

- Main attack of Bolsheviks
- Enemy's proposed advance on MERV.
- Kara Kum Desert.
- Direction of enemy holding attack and final strong evening attack.
- Succession of broken sandy ridges parallel to, and with a general fall towards, the railway.
- To RAVNINA
- 2 Sqdns Turkoman Cav. (Masevich)
- Troop 28Pb. Cav.
- No.1 Piquet
- No.2 Piquet
- No.3 Piquet
- Armoured Trains (Shuvaloff)
- 2 F. Guns.
- Turkoman / Armenian Infantry
- 2 Platoons No.3 Co.
- Succession of Menshevik Trains
- Russian Hospital
- O.T. watercourse.
- I.T. Camp
- I.T. Hospital
- I.T. Reserve & HQ.
- Sandy ridge bombarded by enemy.
- 4 Platoons No.1 Co.
- Detraining point No.1a.
- Route of Koshuliun Cossacks
- Railway cut by enemy
- Fr ANNENKOVO

N

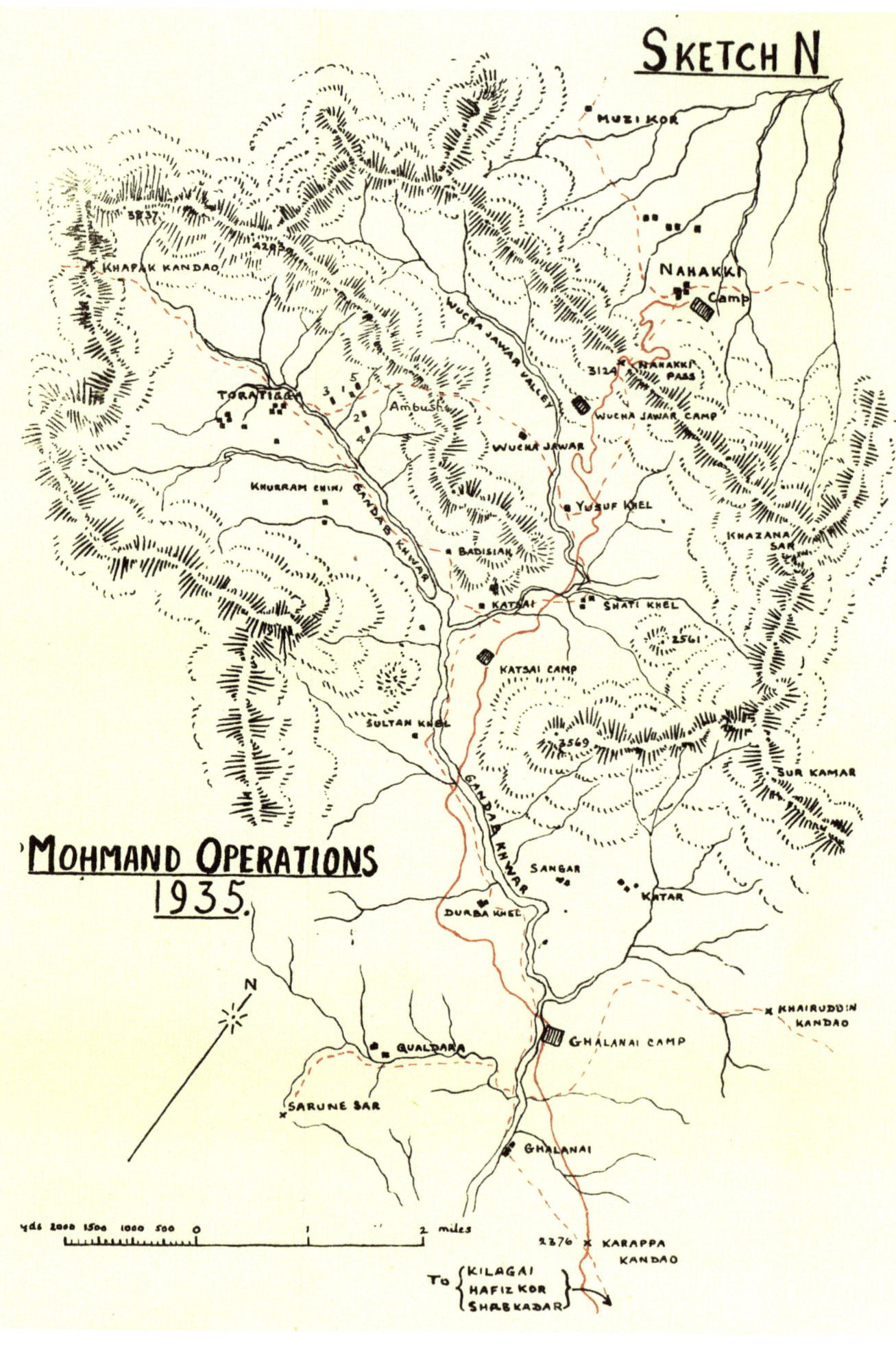

Sketch O.

Waziristan Operations 1937-38.

Scale: 0 1 2 3 4 5 10 miles

- Administrative border ·—··—··—
- Existing MT roads ————
- MT roads built during the operations ————

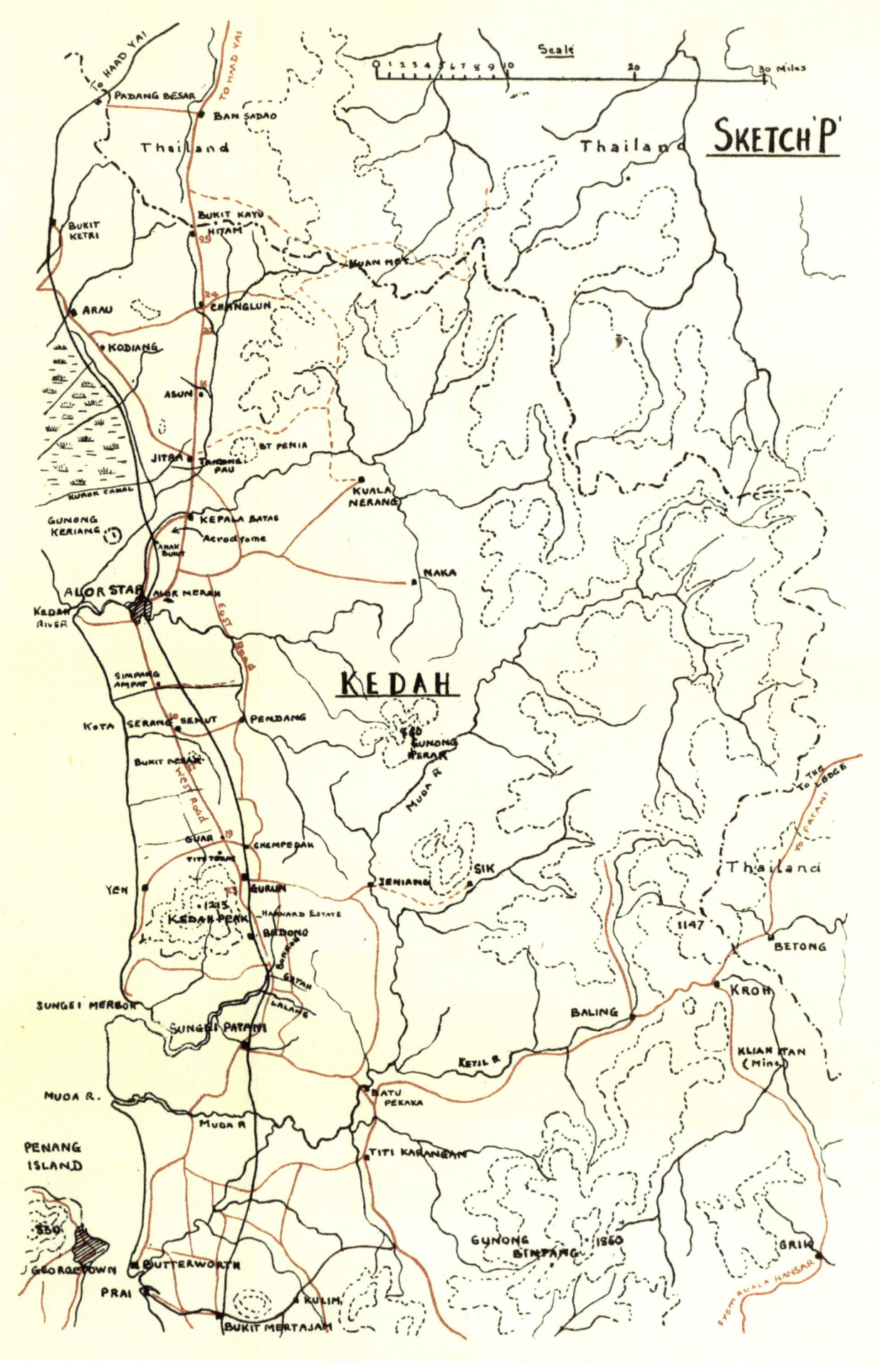

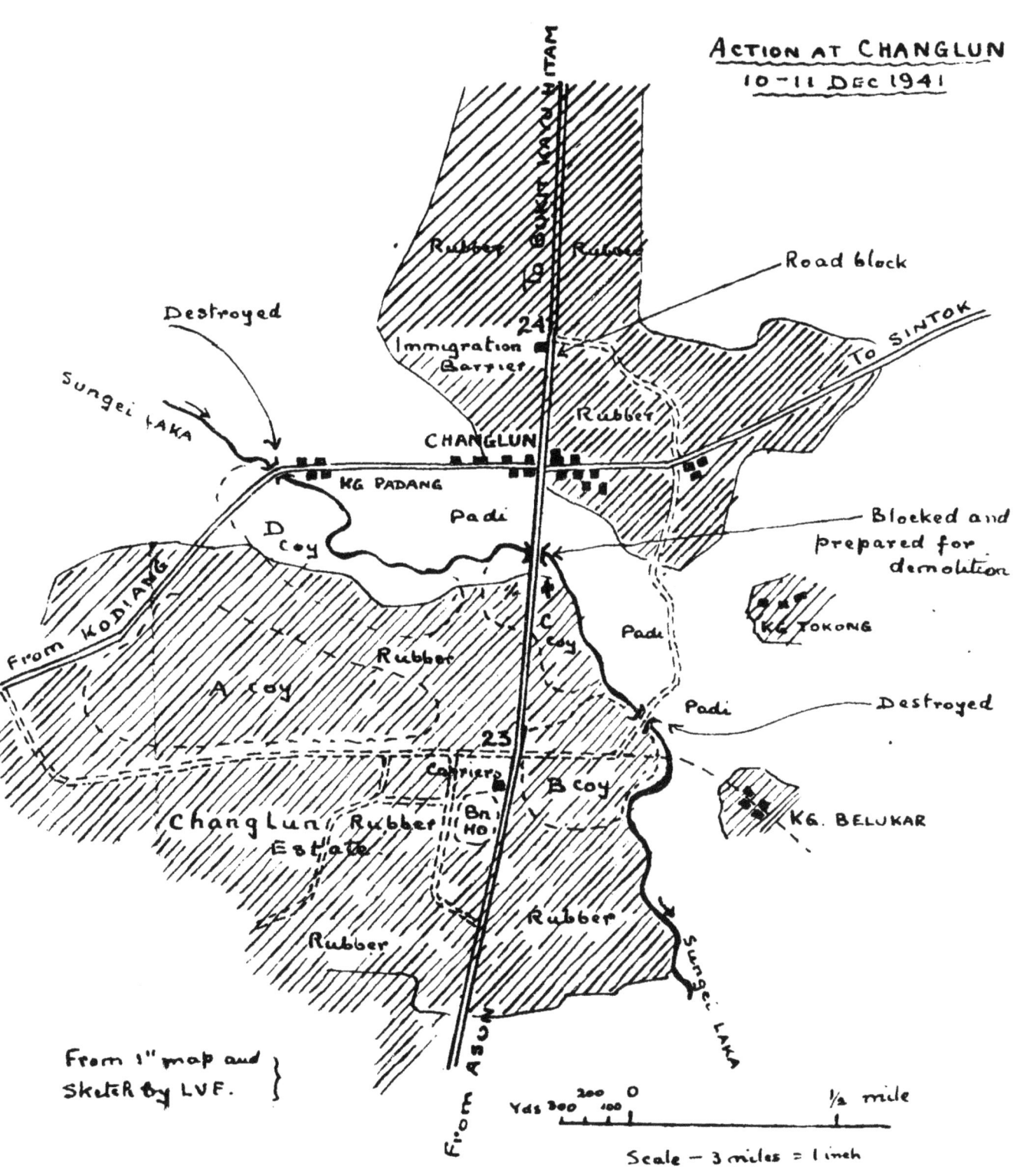

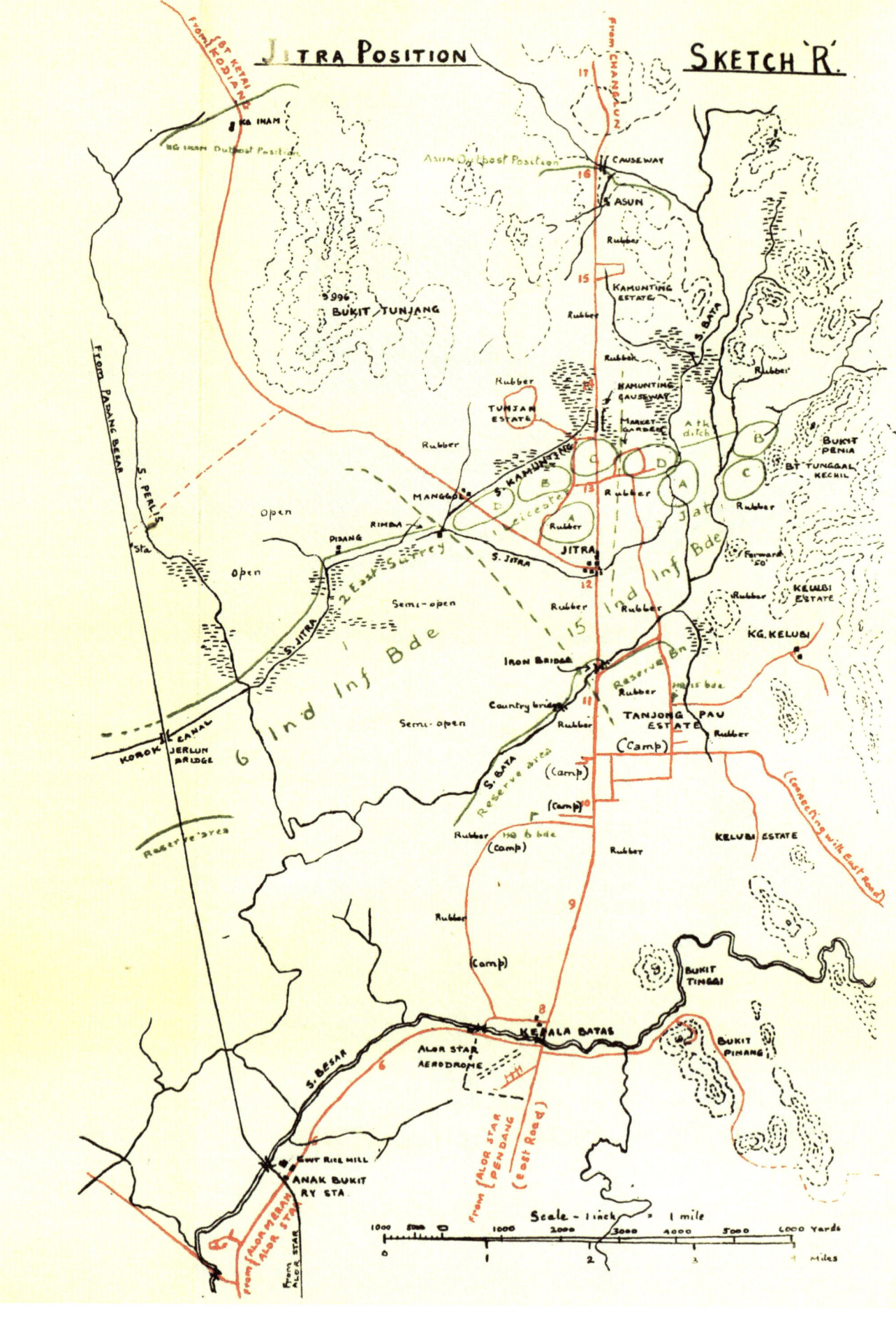

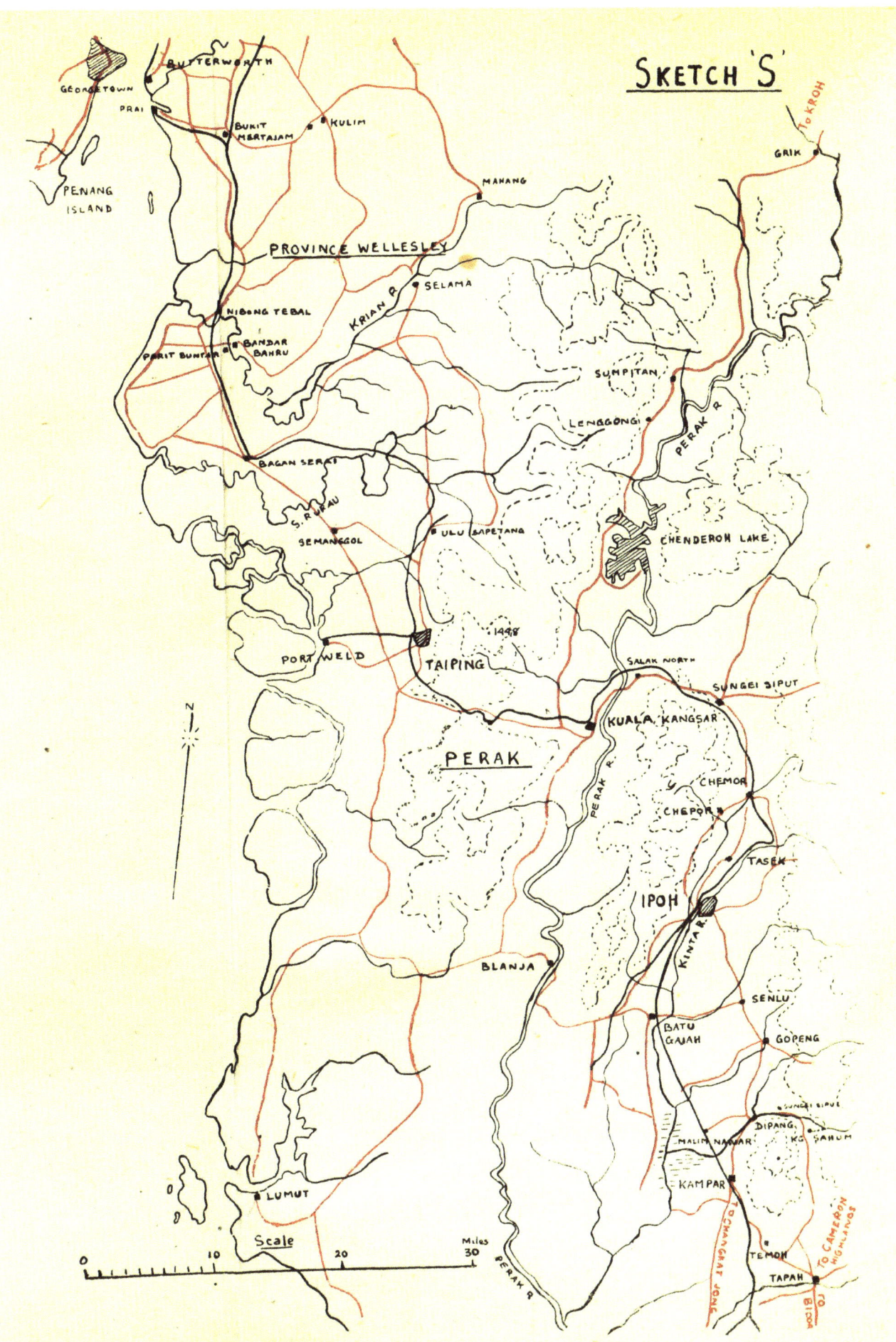

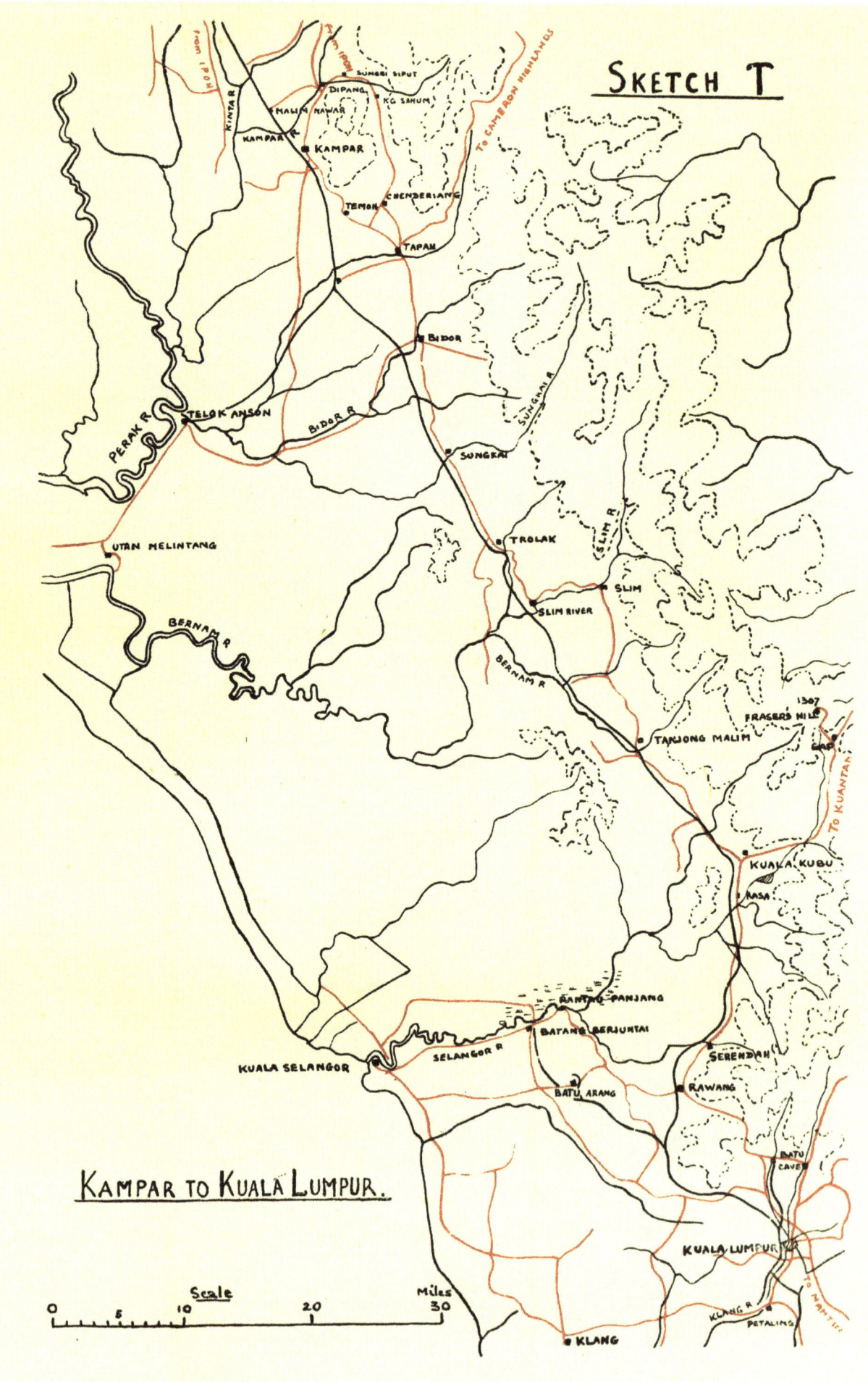

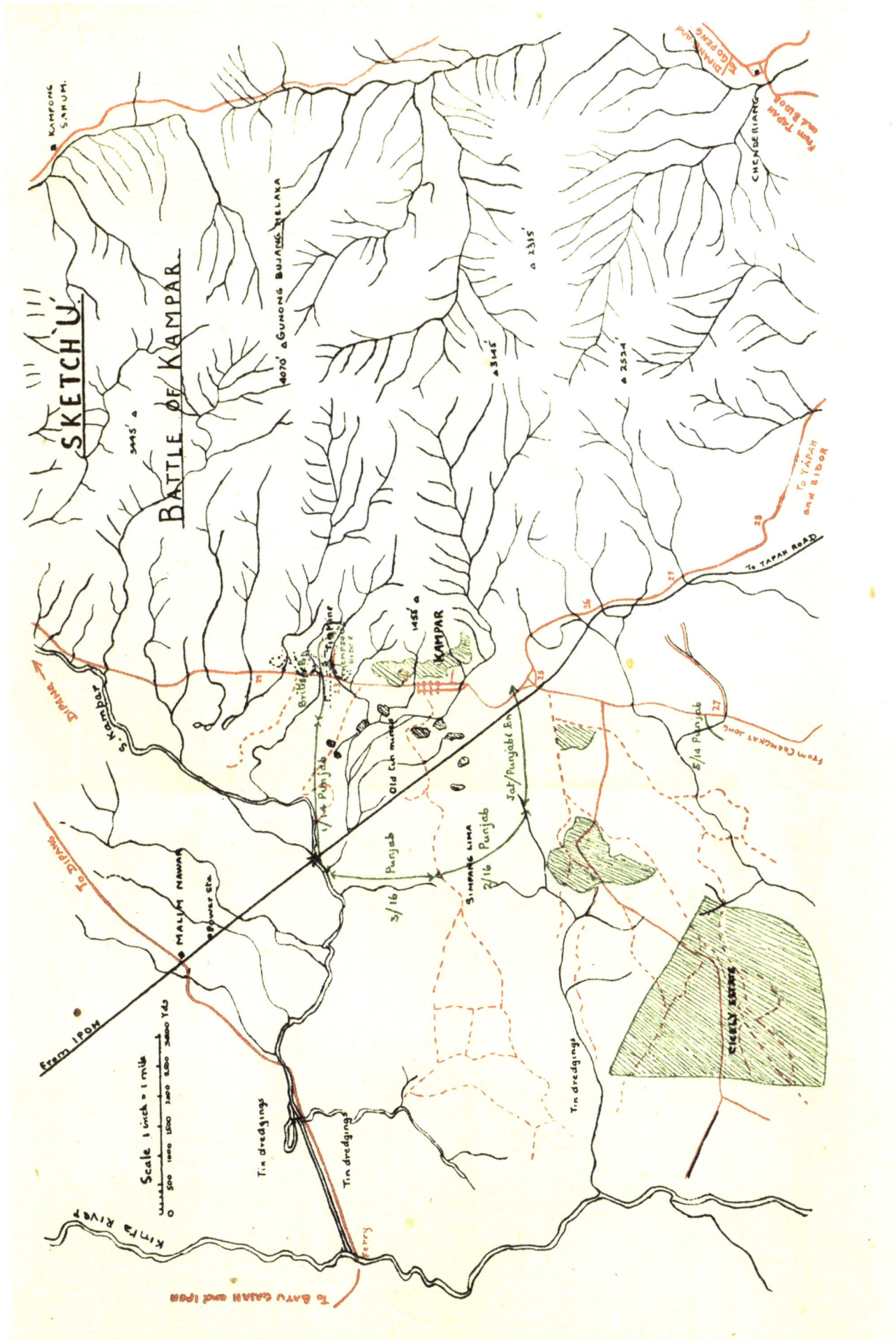

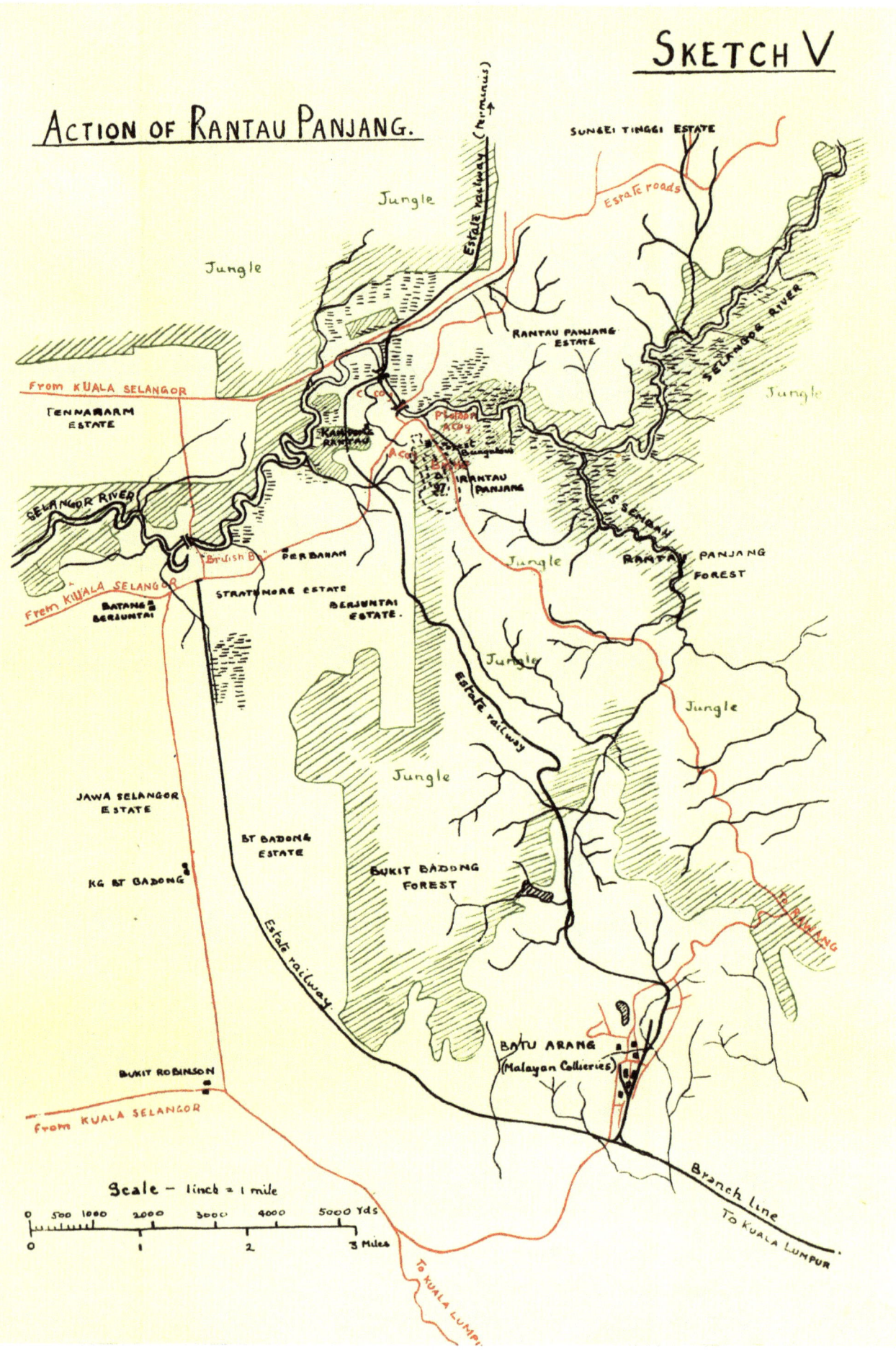

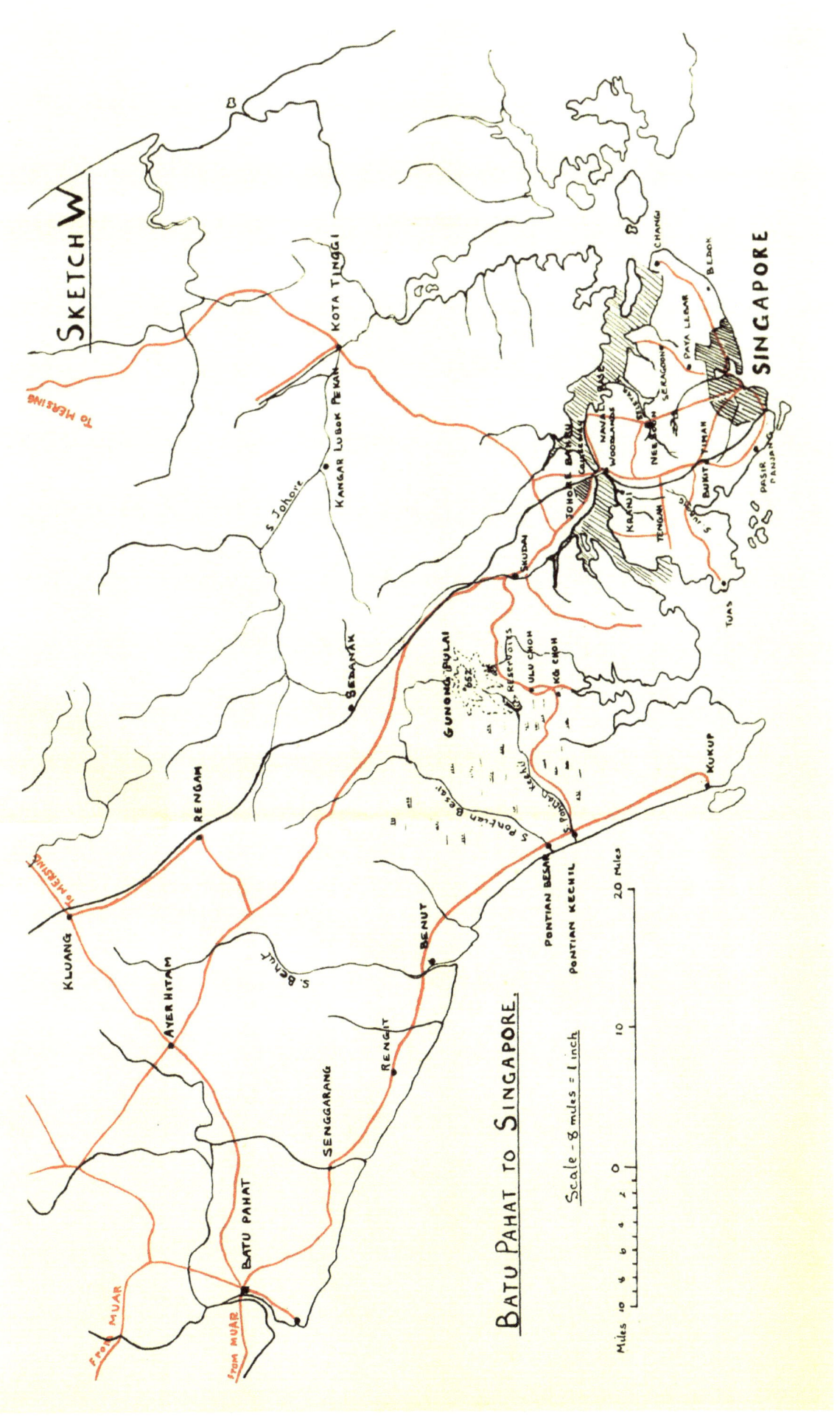

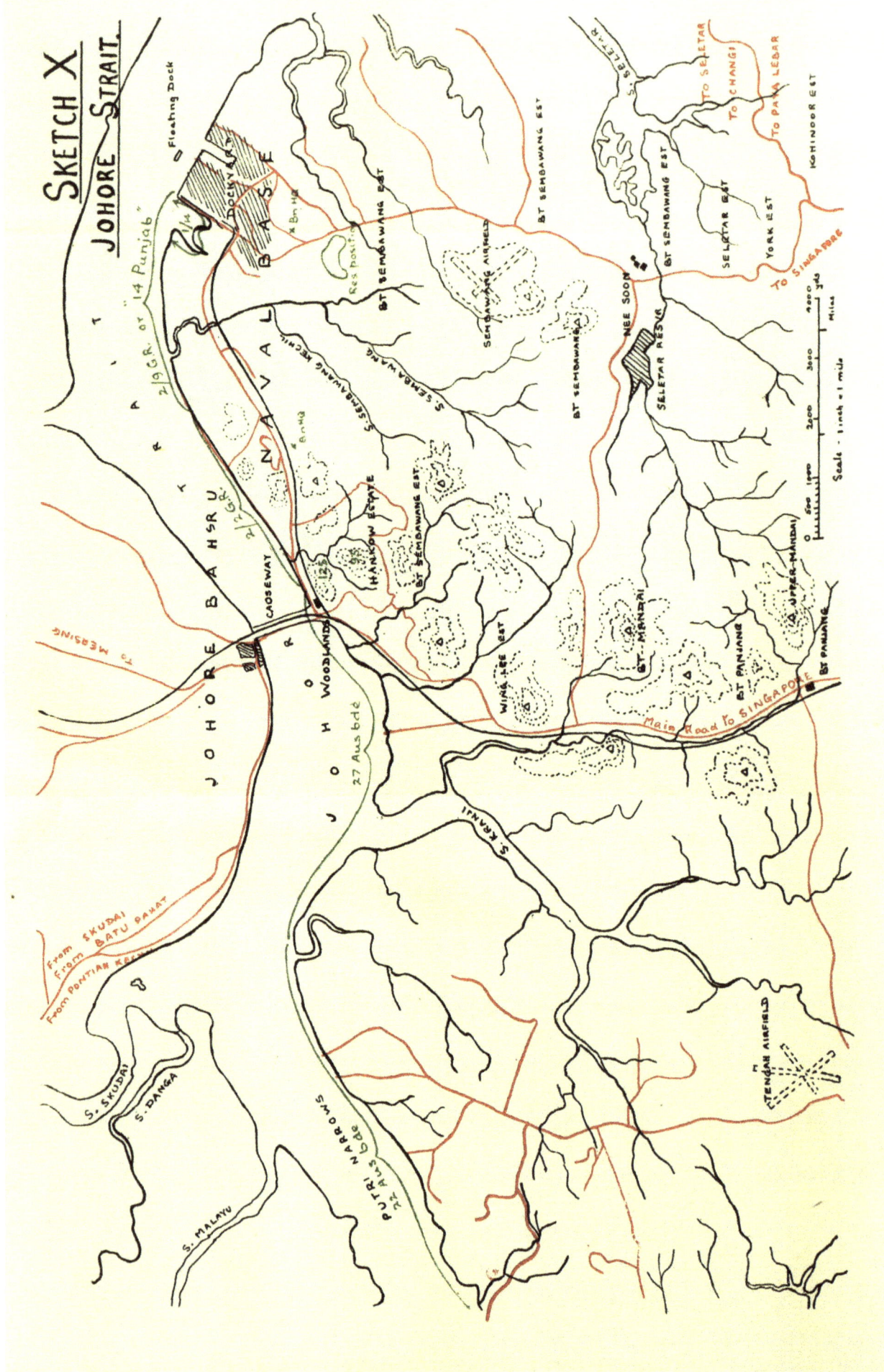

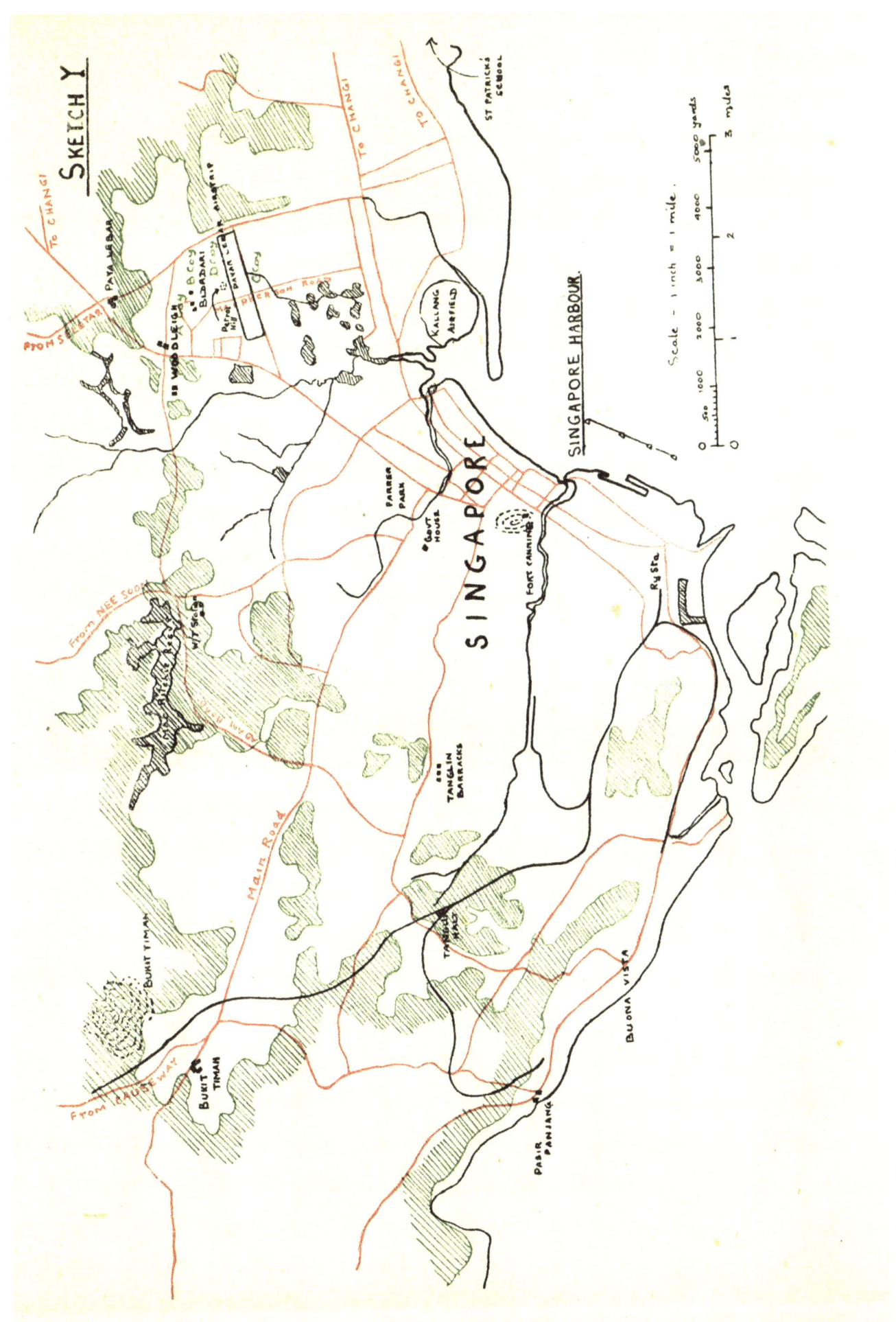

ERRATA

History of the 1st Battalion 14th Punjab Regiment—Sherdil ki paltan.

Page etc.		Correction.
2	last line	For "day" read "days".
3	last para	For "wafound" read "was found".
6	third line from bottom	For "then" read "them".
17	fourth para	For "Infantry Regiment" read "Infantry Regiments".
27	last para	In margin insert "Map 3".
28	second para	In margin insert "Map 3".
30	margin	For "Map 1" read "Map 3".
35	fourth para	In margin insert "Map 3".
60	third para	For "river RAJANPUR" read "river to RAJANPUR".
63	first para	For "corps" read "crops".
65	first para	For "deputed" read "deported".
76	margin	Below "Map 6" add "Sketch J".
84	first line	For "Seige" read "Siege".
90	third para	Add one "o" to "1600" and read "16,000".
91	first para	For "Dinsford" read "Dunsford".
97	first line	For "baunts" read "bounts".
99	second line	For "motly" read "motley".
115	third para	For "KISL" read "KISIL".
118	last para	For "Thereby" read "There by".
119	second para	Delete comma after "Indian" in last line.
145	margin	For "Map I" read "Map 1".
151	last line	For "rom" read "from".
166	fourth para	In seventh line for "1st January" read "31st January".
178	third para	In third line for "Major" read "Majors".
185	first para	Delete the bracket before "Musalman".
186	last para	In third line read "arrangements".
191	first para	In margin insert "Map 11".
191	second para	For "PAO" read "PAU".
193	last para	For "embossed" read "embussed".
197	fourth para	For "12th milestone" read "18th milestone".
198	last para	For "17¼" read "17½".
203	third para	For "Geer's" read "Greer's".
210	last line	For "magazine" read "magazines".
212	second para	For "as to cross" read "and to cross".

212	fourth para	In margin insert "Sketch T".
213	line two	After "association" insert "on service".
217	third para	In last sentence for "Heret here" read "Here there".
221	first para	For "Malaya States Volunteers" read "Malay States Volunteers".
223	second para	For "Malayan Brigade" read "Malayan Brigades".
224	first para	For "ALAKAFF" read "ALKAFF".
231	second para	For "EGYPT 1878-82" read "EGYPT 1882".
239	second column	Against "Agra" for "1857" read "1867".
239	fourth column	Insert against "Amritsar" "1904-08".
240	third column	Against "Ferozepore" for "1864-67" read "1884-87".
241	fifth column	Against "Lahore Cantonment" insert "1940".
241	third column	Against "Mian Meer" for "1833, 1878-90" read "1883, 1887-90".
241	fifth column	Against "Mian Meer" insert "1940".
242	third column	Against "Multan" for "1896-91" read "1896-98".
242	fourth column	Against "Multan" insert "1902-04".
242	second column	Against "Phillaur" for "1875" read "1857".
Map 3		Prefix "FA" so as to read "FATEHGARH" on river GANGES north-west of CAWNPORE.
Map 5		Add "R" to read "ZERGHUNSHAHR" in LOGAR VALLEY (Afghanistan).

www.ingramcontent.com/pod-product-compliance
Ingram Content Group UK Ltd.
Pitfield, Milton Keynes, MK11 3LW, UK
UKHW051351180426
11947UKWH00014B/877